BOOK REVIEWS

Entertaining and insightful. An enjoyable, practical read for aspiring hoteliers and those passionate about our beloved industry.

—Alan Fuerstman, President & CEO, Montage Hotels & Resorts

Larry Mogelonsky has been one of the leaders in observing and guiding the hospitality and tourism industry. Once again he has provided a detailed guideline to marketing and operations which could provide you with a competitive advantage. While observing a group of ostriches in Tanzania, I also learned that competitive advantage is everything. You don't want to not be in the back of the pack as you just might end up as a lion's (competitor's) dinner.

—Ed Fuller, President, Laguna Strategic Advisors

A great read for young and seasoned hotel management alike—definitely pulls your mind outside of the daily routine. The various sections of Larry's book make it easy to reference different concepts and ideas.

—Heather McCrory, Senior Vice President, Operations, Americas, Fairmont Hotels & Resorts

Larry Mogelonsky reminds us that the service experience is the key differentiator between a good brand experience and a great brand experience. A valuable, well-written book with important insights for anyone in the world of hospitality.

—Larry Light, Global Chief Brands Officer, InterContinental Hotels Group

Based on years of keen observation and analysis of hotel operations along with his marketing expertise, Larry provides poignant insights into the hospitality business. An engaging read, this comprehensive book should be read by all hoteliers and those planning a career in the industry.

—Klaus Tenter, Principal, G7 Hospitality

A great book to remind you how times are changing and how, as hoteliers, we aren't keeping up! Larry puts the market into perspective, focusing our minds to areas we need to reinvest some time. Just when I was running out of ideas on how to improve our hotel's operations, Larry gave me a whole new shopping basket! Well done, Larry. I would highly recommend this book to hotel operators everywhere who are looking for ways to improve their market share.

—*Anil Teneja, President, Palm Holdings*

Every hotel Sales & Marketing office should have a dog-eared copy of "Llama's Rule" handy. This book is chock full of step by step practical advice to help guide hospitality professionals through a wide realm of opportunities to maximize the financial success of their business. I was very excited to read this book and I plan to get several copies for my company.

—*Adele Gutman, Vice President, Sales & Marketing,*
Library Hotel Collection

Anyone associated with the hotel industry would benefit tremendously by reading "Llamas Rule". Larry brilliantly articulates why outstanding guest engagement and experiences translate to strong revenue streams and better margins. He is focused and logical, but also fun and entertaining. A must read for any hotelier!

—*Marco Selva, General Manager, St. Regis Bal Harbour*

This book unlocked my mind and made me reflect as a typical 'Homo Hotelus'. It is a must for anyone in the hospitality business who wants to keep a creative, innovative and out-of-the-box thinking style. It is fun to read and easily understandable regardless of age or years of experience. This book compels me to reevaluate how I engage guests, employees and owners to ensure that every one of them feels like a VIP.

—*Cornelia Kausch, President, CK Hospitality Advisors*

Larry Mogelonsky once again delivers the perfect cocktail: a generous shot of knowledge mixed with fresh perspective, a splash of humor and garnished with good sense—served straight up! Read "Llama's Rule" and become a better manager and leader; it's that simple.

—Keith Hill, General Manager, Timber Cove Inn

Larry may claim to be a true hotelier, but his spot on observations and insights come from his Procter and Gamble and Frito Lay marketing foundation. Hoteliers around the world should heed his warning that despite all of the technological advancements and application in our industry today, it is the face-to-face interaction between hotel staff and guests that humanize our brands, thereby creating the loyalty and long-term growth we all seek.

—David Brudney, Principal, David Brudney & Associates

With its bite size nuggets of brilliance, "Llamas Rule" offers practical and enjoyable insights in the ever-changing world of hotel management. The approachable language and flexible format allows for strategic and inspirational reading for all levels of management.

—David Mounteer, General Manager, Thompson Hotel Toronto

Larry has done it again! He calls his new book a collection of essays in hospitality marketing and management, but it's much more than that. It's a many-credit-hours course for these subjects. From the hilarious introduction detailing his first ever meeting to the purely excellent advice on how to manage a property's involvement with the OTA channels, "Llamas Rule" is another wonderful collection of sound advice for any hotelier, and definitely required reading!

—William J. Callnin, Chairman & Managing Director,
Cayuga Hospitality Advisors

LLAMAS RULE

ESSAYS IN HOSPITALITY MARKETING & MANAGEMENT

For Stephen

Always Think LLAMA

LARRY MOGELONSKY

authorHOUSE®

AuthorHouse™ LLC
1663 Liberty Drive
Bloomington, IN 47403
www.authorhouse.com
Phone: 1-800-839-8640

Published by AuthorHouse   09/04/2013

ISBN: 978-1-4918-1500-7 (sc)
ISBN: 978-1-4918-1499-4 (hc)

Library of Congress Control Number: 2013916116

CONTENTS

FORWARD

GUEST SERVICES

BRANDING

TRADITIONAL MARKETING

INTERNET MARKETING

OPERATIONS

FOOD & BEVERAGE

Technology

Social Media

ONLINE TRAVEL AGENCIES

EXAMPLES OF EXCELLENCE

CONCLUSION

For my daughter and son,
Samantha and Adam

FORWARD

Completed in 1929, the Fairmont Royal York is an icon for the Toronto skyline and for Canadian luxury, but this does not stop management from constantly refreshing their product.

INTRODUCTION PART I

When I first set out to write about the hospitality world and my knowledge of it, I never realized just how much I'd love it. It was this passion, this fervor, this need to instill my hotelier colleagues with wisdom which got me through innumerous late nights writing, rewriting and polishing op-ed articles outside of managing 20 some odd employees in addition to business trips and social engagements (my family!).

The impetus for my first book, "Are You an Ostrich or a Llama?" arose out of my desire to give hoteliers more than just links to a blog or an online publication. I wanted to deliver a holistic experience and get managers to think outside the box.

As for the titular animals, ostriches were a poetic choice to embody those businesspeople who are stubborn, parsimonious and otherwise afraid with their 'heads in the sand'. Judged purely by appearance, ostriches can be quite intimidating. I blame the sharp beaks atop long, slender necks. Llamas were born from both their own inherent characteristics as well as the English word's coincidentally similar lettering to my own marketing agency's acronymic naming—LMA. If you've ever met a llama face to face, what will strike you is their docile yet bold disposition. They'll approach you without trepidation; their coat soft to the touch. Comparing these two domesticated beasts, the metaphor for 'good manager, bad manager' is clear.

Additionally, there's something about staring at a computer screen all day that makes reading a hardcover just that much more meaningful. The feel of the paper. The smell of it. Even with the dawn of tablets, I still prefer a book to a PDF. But that's my preference, which may or may not have a direct correlation to my age that is pushing ever closer to that grand old threshold of 65. Retirement in and unto itself is a subject I discuss at great length in this book.

However much I liken myself as a managerial llama—open to the changes brought about by the digital revolution—but paperback is nonetheless a field for which I find myself resolutely on the losing side of the battle. Paper (hard cover, soft cover, newspapers, magazines) are going the way of the dinosaur, giving rise to new species of electronic publications and entertainment. We must embrace the sweeping changes that are occurring all around us.

And that gets at the point of this book—to give you a flavor of what is happening and how these evolutions can affect hotel operations and customer expectations. Through the writing of these articles, I hope to offer some anecdotal guidance to help you maintain your fleecy llama outlook on how you approach your management style in the hospitality industry.

MY FIRST MEETING:
A TALE OF TWO CITIES

Meeting planners. Automated RFPs. Meeting delivery. Ensuring the property delivers for the delegates. These are all terms hoteliers and their sales team are well familiar with. But 30 years ago (or thereabouts), I was tasked with the responsibility of being the sole meeting planner as part of my job assignment. This was my first big break and I thought you might enjoy this calamitous tale of two cities.

Before I was initiated into the hospitality industry, I worked in packaged goods as a product manager for Procter & Gamble (they called the position brand manager) and next as a category manager for Frito Lay. Business in those heady days of the early 1980s was all about hoopla and flash. Good employees were scarce, and to keep your staff motivated, new product launches were part Ziegfeld Follies, part Disney. It seemed that budgets for these activities were not in the least bit limited by austerity measures or corporate bean counters. Rather, the only limitations were the imaginations of the presenting marketing team.

As Frito Lay's category manager for potato chip products, I was tasked with the responsibility of launching a new brand, O'Grady's, a thicker cut potato chip. Being in Canada, two separate launch meetings were required: English language in Toronto and French language in Montreal. The goal of both meetings was the same: to introduce the product to the sales force and get them excited about selling the product to their customers.

Salty snacks share one key attribute with hotels: the product is fragile, meaning that if you do not sell it today, the purchasing opportunity will be lost forever. Thus, the role of the sales team is to get new product front and center in and off-shelf display units.

Our marketing department was no more than eight people split equally between potato chips and corn snacks. Compared to a sales force in the hundreds, it was silly to see the rivalry between these two teams. This all reached a climax in the marketing team's approach to sales meetings: aggressive, in-your-face and one-upmanship in everything that was done. With all this in the background, there was no one for me to delegate the responsibility of meeting planning.

First up was Toronto. Our selection of the Inn on the Park, back then a junior Four Seasons property and now a Lexus-Toyota dealership, was predicated mostly on our ability to actually drive a delivery van into the ballroom. A secondary reason was that a launch for a premium-priced product deserved a premium quality location. I recall little pecuniary interest in the double-occupancy room rate charged or the meals written off. There was, to my recollection, no price negotiation.

Perhaps not surprisingly, many of the sales delegates took their Frito Lay trucks to the event. Imagine yourself as a guest of the hotel that day, only to wake up and see a hundred such boxy vehicles in the parking lot!

The culmination of the sales launch was the new product portion of the meeting. This was not going to be just a PowerPoint-style presentation completed as a series of 35mm slides in a Kodak Carousel projector (remember that PowerPoint didn't exist yet). No, an event like this demanded action. And action is what they were going to get.

How best to demonstrate to an audience what is important to them? The solution we came up with was simple: take a delivery truck and turn it into an incredible delivery truck. At the time, the Mel Gibson movies "Mad Max" (1979) and "Mad Max 2: The Road Warrior" (1981) were still in their glory. Fittingly, we dressed our entire marketing team in the look of the Australian badlands, with leather, punk-rock hats, chains and all manner of post-apocalyptic doodads. Next, we modified the delivery truck by removing the muffler, adjusting the suspension to hold 20" mag wheels and adding racing slicks borrowed from the local drag strip. It was epic.

The plan was as straightforward as they come. The truck, with the new product and marketing team inside, would come onstage from behind the curtain at the point in time our president introduced us. This dramatic entry would sear into the minds of the awaiting audience as we drove one of their delivery trucks and proceed to distribute the new product samples for them to examine and taste. No question, this was going to be a sales launch for the ages; one they would remember for years to come.

We piled into the truck and awaited our cue. At the precise moment, my boss, the director of marketing, turned on the engine. The wild exhaust noise churned through the truck cabin. He shifted the truck into gear and once again gently put his foot on the accelerator. Nothing happened. He gave the accelerator a little more gas. Still nothing.

The audience was getting restless, or, in the very least, partially asphyxiated from the fumes. Still no movement forward.

My boss's foot was probably near the floorboards when I discovered what was wrong: the parking brake was still on! As I was in the passenger seat, rather than say anything, I simply released the brake.

Like a thoroughbred out of the starting gate, the modified panel van vaulted forward. The distance we had to travel was a mere 10-15 feet on the stage. Needless to say, we overshot. After the stage came a massive stack of unopened potato chip-corrugated boxes, followed by the double doors to the lobby!

We passed our center stage marker in what seemed like a nano-second. By the time my boss had figured out what had happened and jammed on the brakes, we had exploded through the product display and impaled the front end of the truck on the double doors, blasting them four feet into the lobby. Luckily no one was in range. A pregnant pause as all of us foreshadowed in our minds how this monstrous screw up would ripple through our professional careers.

The crowd had other ideas. In unison, they cheered as if this was the best thing they had ever witnessed in their entire lives. Perhaps it was. Few car accidents are ever staged indoors, fewer still on purpose! We looked at each other for a second, and then as they say on Broadway: the show must go on. It was a matter of taking the fame, even when the fame wasn't due. Without missing a beat, we jumped out of the truck and starting tossing away sample packs.

Needless to say, hotel management was none too pleased. The repair bill I received was turbocharged by the need to get the necessary refurbishments complete for a wedding that weekend some 72 hours later. With no one hurt and no structural damage, we nonetheless considered this a very successful event.

The following week, our team was off to Montreal for the French language launch equivalent. Management decided that, in the best interests of corporate accounts, driving a delivery truck onstage wasn't feasible. Accordingly, our plan was a little bit more conservative. Lessons well learned!

Montreal presented its own trials and tribulations. We were told that the Quebec sales group were even more 'rough and tumble' than their Ontario counterparts. My knowledge of the French language, being rather limited, precluded me from spending a lot of prior time in the field working with them. Ergo, I had no real benchmark from which to judge the merit of these comments. As a precaution, however, we agreed to remove the mini-bar fridge keys prior to their check-in, just to be safe.

Following the Toronto escapade, this launch was far more subdued. Without the truck, our team prancing around in Mad Max outfits might have seemed somewhat perplexing. We considered dropping them entirely, but a good costume is a horrible thing to waste. If the salesmen were confused, they certainly didn't show it. The round of applause was almost as boisterous as that following the aforementioned indoor MVA.

At the end of the Montreal meeting, I felt pretty good. No damages to report and everything went off without a hitch. Even a few new worthy business contacts to add to the rolodex. Then the bill arrived: damages.

Three mini-bar fridges were crow-barred open. And what's worse, three more were missing! To this day, I am not sure how they smuggled the fridges out of the building and onto a shuttle bus without anyone knowing (or any hotel staff catching them in the act).

I still don't know what the exact takeaway is from my Montreal experience. Maybe, never lock up the mini-bar when you are dealing with rowdy salesmen? Either way, it was a hell of a ride and a wild first encounter with the hospitality industry.

HOMO HOTELUS

For hobby reading, a popular crutch of mine is a light dabbling of pop economics books. They always have a few great observations on life, a few more interesting 'Did you know?' factoids and even a couple in-your-face 'Look at how stupid we are!' arguments. The point is to take each with a grain of salt, take what you can from each thesis then coalesce as you see fit into your own viewpoint on life's omnipresent ways.

One of the 'pop' trends that I've noticed amongst all these scholarly reads is the twisting of our Latin species name 'homo sapiens' towards whatever message the writer is trying to drive home. Three prominent examples that bubble up from the memory banks are 'homo economicus', 'homo rationalis' and 'homo politicus'. Each is used by their proscribed authors to elucidate and categorize human behavior to one set of patterns or another. Why not adapt this to our fair trade: 'homo hotelus'. A chic label, yes, but does it actually work? There are perhaps a few overarching characteristics shared by all of us passionately working in the hospitality industry. With this as a pretense, how would you define the typical hotelier?

Many of these quintessential traits I've evinced through the multitude of interviews conducted with senior managers and GMs across the globe. Really when we talk about a person who is 'passionate about hospitality'—someone with the homo hotelus gumption if you will—we are describing an individual possessing a fervor for helping others, an inquisitive nature about people and operations, and a steadfast duty to serve. I believe that the true difference comes from motivation. Is a hotelier motivated by a need to do what's best, or the comfort of following the rules and doing precisely as instructed?

Read over your property's or your brand's mission statement and see whether there is a place for this passionate individualism. If not, then inquire about drafting a revision or adopt your own mantra. In my mind, if you start with the passion, then you can teach everything else. But the 'yearn to learn' has to intrinsic to the person for this to happen, whether such an individual is a departmental director or a member of the line staff.

Now that you know the necessary traits, how does one go about finding the homo hotelus sorts and getting the right team together to produce results? That is something that begins with the interview process—ensuring that your candidates want to work for your organization as a career choice and not just a job—and extends all the way up to the top echelon of management. The owners, the GMs and the senior managers all have to lead and inspire all those around them to perform as best they can and to continuously learn how to do better on their own.

We are in the people business after all. I stress over and over again: you can use whatever marketing tactics or incorporate whatever new technology you so desire, but if your staff isn't doing their best to satisfy guests when they are on property, then all is for nothing. It all comes down to people interacting with people, and those of us who can be categorized under the 'homo hotelus' label must be especially adept at this skill.

INTRODUCTION PART II

Like with all of my customary readings in pop economics and pop science books, I don't expect 100% of the ideas put forward in this book to sink in on the first pass. The cognitive absorbency rate that I've heard tossed around on multiple occasions is that a maximum of 10% of what you see or hear latches onto the memory centers in your brain. Notes help, so do multicolored pens and recording devices. Rather than have you drill into this book like you were memorizing exact dates for a medical school final, I want you to keep certain themes on your mind while thinking of how each particular topic applies to your job or function in the hospitality industry.

What I consider to be the overarching principle of this book is that, yes, you must be flexible in the face of technological advancements turning the world upside-down, but you must also be assured of the fact that despite all this rapid change, human genetics is lagging behind. The psychological underpinnings of our nature were the same a century ago as they are today, even if everything else has gone pear-shaped.

We all still eat, our bodies waning and straining under various cultural shifts in nutrition. We all still eat, a good night's rest as important for the psyche today as it was a millennium ago. We all still communicate. Humans are social creatures. You need only examine the growth of social media to understand this maxim. But not all communication was created equal. I purport that face-to-face contact between hotel staff and guests is one of the most important aspects of success in this hotel that it is often overlooked because of its simplicity.

What face-to-face communication accomplishes is to humanize your brand. In an era of endless barrages of savvy advertisements through a breadth of mediums, people are not eager to talk to brands. They want to talk to people. In our case, they want to have a rapport with people who work for a hotel brand, not the brand itself.

If all of my writing could be deduced to a single principle, it would be that developing personal relationships between a brand and its customers is one of the best ways to ensure loyalty and long-term growth. This is why I place such prime importance on guest services—the first section in the book. But it's also a good paradigm to frame all the other article groupings.

For instance, what is it about various types of traditional and internet-based marketing techniques which promote a better, longer lasting, impression of your brand? Is it just the high commission rates which have driven me to scorn the growth of online travel agencies or is it that they are eroding guests' perceptions of various hotel brands? Will each new tech-laden vendor be a good investment for your property, or is merely something to think about in terms of motivating your consumers in a certain manner?

Not everything will apply to your hotel. You might not agree with all of it either (in fact, you shouldn't!). Take what you can and know that with continual learning, you are making yourself a better hospitality manager and a better all-round leader.

GUEST SERVICES

The St. Regis Bal Harbour epitomizes the resort of the 21st century: oversized with minimalist décor, exceptional contemporary art and strong guest services.

INTRODUCTION

There's a reason why guest services is featured as the first grouping of articles in this book (as well as in the previous book). I put great emphasis on this aspect of the hotel trade because it is the core of what makes for a good night's stay.

Look 'hospitality' up in the thesaurus and what words pop up? Generosity, kindness, friendliness, warmth—these are all characteristics that can never be properly replicated with an intelligent database system or state-of-the-art facilities. Warmth and kindness are bestowed from one person to another, all with good manners, a genuine smile and empathy. If you can deliver this with each and every staff-guest encounter, then your consumers will be singing your praises, on and off line.

I'd be remiss if I didn't share the credit with other essential facets of the hotel experience such as amenities, ambiance, F&B, facilities, location, attractions and so forth, but the core is nonetheless how well your staff treat your guests. At the front desk, in the lobby, at the spa—wherever guests have the potential to interact with property employees is an opportunity to gain their respect, admiration and advocacy.

As I blunderingly attempt to demonstrate through the articles in this section is that guest services is about establishing an emotional connection. Emotions, as you probably already know, can defy logic. By building a personal rapport with guests, you are in a sense defying logic.

Nowadays, logic would dictate that a guest should rationalize all aspects of a hotel with the proper weighting that each deserves. If this were the case, price, location and the comfort level of the room would often be the only three factors of any significance. The barebones function of a guestroom is for you to get a full night's rest. This is accomplished with a soft bed, freshly pressed linens and minimal noise disruptions. Once you wake up, logic would dictate that you should be situated in a place as close to your next scheduled appointment as possible. If a two star economy hotel can fulfill these basic needs as well as a five star property, why bother shelling out the extra few hundred dollars per night for the luxury accommodations?

It's a good thing our minds don't work like robots and we value other 'superfluous' attributes. We like decorative, inspirational lobby settings. We fancy exquisitely presented cuisine that excite our eyes as much as our palates. We appreciate high-end cosmetics available in the bathroom, even though most of us probably don't know how they differ from the stock cleansers. We value that extra 'Good day!' from a smiling bellhop as we exit, even though it doesn't add any rational value aside from uplifting our moods.

You'd be right if you think I'm describing the fundamentals of good branding. Guest services and branding are directly correlated when it comes to the hospitality industry because delivering great service is what builds your brand's reputation thereby instilling a long-term impression amongst consumers as well as allowing you to charge a premium for your guestrooms over what would be the 'logical' price.

I cannot stress this enough. Throughout this section, the message should be clear: always look for ways to heighten the quality of interactions between staff and guests.

WE ARE PLAYWRIGHTS

Most of us enjoy the theatre; sitting in the audience, in hushed darkness, waiting for the curtain to go up. As the play unfolds, actors and actresses follow their scripts and deliver remarkable performances. We come away a few hours later, happy or sad, depending upon the story, with fond memories. Several days later we may recall the performance of one or two of the cast members or a particular element of the staging, relishing and reliving such elements with friends.

I was giving this some thought and discovered that the main difference between a theatrical play and a hotel was the location of the audience along with the interactivity between the audience and the cast.

To force a comparison, think of your hotel as the theatre, your staff as the cast and the guest as the audience. The play opens as guests check in. They are quickly led through the first act—the 'getting acquainted' part of things—check in, reception, room presentation and unpacking. The hotel acts as the stage, amenities as the props and your line staff as the actors in this highly interactive play.

Other support staff act as stagehands (housekeepers, maintenance, kitchen staff, gardeners, engineering) and, of course, accountants manage the box office while your public relations and advertising agencies handle the outside buzz to draw the crowds in. As senior managers, your role is to write the play and produce a show of the highest quality your budget will afford.

In doing so, remind your cast that this is not an improv, and that there's an elaborate and time-honored script that must be followed. While a certain amount of improvisation is necessary, your team has to know their lines by heart to start with, then make necessary adjustments to reflect individual guest needs only once the sought-after experience has been properly attained.

A few other parallels are also quite obvious:
- The show must go on! So even if you have a low occupancy or a team member is a no-show, your cast still must deliver a perfect performance.

- There is no business like show business. Your team must be composed of enthusiastic performers and love the relationship with the guest. If not, they should not be in the biz!
- Reviews are important. Mind your TripAdvisor critiques and remember that future attendance is based on getting great reviews.
- The audience knows what they are getting. Be it a tragedy or a comedy, we know what a play will bring and we will be prepared to experience such emotions. Your hotel should be predictable in delivering these broad strokes, and then surprise or delight within the confines of the genre.
- Great actors take time to develop. You're not getting older, you're only getting better. Your staff will benefit from training and, given the right stage and directions, they'll surely improve with time.

MASLOW'S HIERARCHY OF HOTEL EXPECTATIONS

If you're looking for a good standard by which to evaluate your guest service priorities, or if you're simply looking for inspiration, you need only scroll through any basic management, human resources or motivation psychology textbook. For this particular article, allow yourself a cursory glance at Maslow's Hierarchy of Needs, a highly referenced and diagram-friendly developmental psychology theory.

Interestingly, we can use Maslow's principles to detail hotel guest behavior in terms of what their basic expectations will be and how they will act when certain expectations aren't met. From there we can distinguish what services or hotel features will be seen as fundamental rights versus which will be seen as value-added, loyalty-building drivers. This all makes for a fun, little exercise of transforming Abraham Maslow's 1943 groundbreaking research paper into Maslow's Hierarchy of Hotel Expectations applicable to the new millennium.

The hierarchy diagram has five generalized levels outlined in a pyramid—physiological, safety, social, esteem and self-actualization—with the base being the most important and hence the largest in terms of area. Next, evaluate your hotel's reviews from past customers (both from internal surveys and from third-party sites) to see how their points of criticism and praise line up with the five tiers of the Maslow pyramid. Take special care to note the emotional subtext of each review, particularly those that identify elementary faults in your operations.

My hypothesis is that any severe denigration you receive will be a direct result of errors made on the bottom end of the pyramid. As these mistakes pertain to more basic needs—those assumed to be immediate necessities—the criticism against such errors will be especially loud and harsh. This is in contrast to the upper layers of the pyramid where derision gradually morphs into praise. However, judging purely from the area given to each portion within the diagram, it's clear that such upper echelon exaltations will not be perceived with the same magnitude of importance as a lower level condemnation.

Therefore, this motivation theory model can be used as an excellent framing tool to understand consumer mindsets, to determine what aspects of your operations are most critical to improve and to develop a concrete order of priorities. Satisfy guest needs in accordance with the pyramid by building from the ground up. And so, we begin our analysis at the bottom and most critical layer for you to master.

Physiological Needs

At the base of the pyramid is the need for such rudimentary aspects of sustaining life such as food, breathing (air quality), water and sleep. Even at this primal and thoroughly understood level, there are still numerous questions by which to scrutinize your current operations.

Are your guests getting a good night's sleep? Do your lobby and guest rooms smell weird? How's the tap water that comes out of the bathroom faucet? Is it clean, clear and flowing properly? Do you overcharge for bottled water? And most importantly, is your food edible? Never underestimate just how crucial it is to master all aspects of this basal tier. You only stand to lose if you're not flawless here.

The quintessential function of a hotel is to give patrons a bed so they're chipper for the next day. If this can't be done, then it's a failed mission. Recall how you felt the last time you had a sleepless night. Irritable, bellicose, maybe even slightly delirious? In such a mood, a guest has a much greater propensity towards a negative evaluation. I'm not insinuating that every bed needs to have a triple-down comforter and thousand thread-count linens. Instead, stick to the basics. Is the room loud at night? How can you dampen the noise? Are the bed sheets and duvet perfectly clean? As you can see, any hint of bedbugs, or the risk of an infestation is a non-starter. This level is about being flawless, not necessarily perfect.

Next, very few people will comment on how fresh the air in the lobby was, but if the room smells—for example, of tobacco smoke— be ready for damage control. Bad smells are a primal, subconscious indicator associated with the fear centers of the brain and impending danger. Not exactly the feeling you want to evoke! The culprits here can range from spoiled food to rotten plumbing. If it's the latter, don't be stingy on maintenance. The stench of putrid pipes will render such a room unusable, or worse, worthy of scathing online critique. Furthermore, try adding a subtle but distinctive fragrance to instill positive feelings—fresh flowers, essence of vanilla or potpourri will do.

Overcharging for bottled water is another qualm I see fairly often in online reviews. When lensed through the hierarchy model, it's easy to see why this action enrages guests. Clean water is something of extreme importance to our body's survival. This is why it's available in nearly all stores that sell food or beverages, and it's also why the governments doll out billions of dollars to cleanse our aquifers. Clean water is expected to be readily available and nominally charged. To improperly leverage this necessity for corporate gain—that is, flagrantly overcharging for bottled water—is a wholly justifiable cause for scorn.

Cuisine, I believe, is a topic that bridges several layers of the pyramid, but for this instance, you have to look at it not as art but as meeting a patron's metabolic requirements. No doubt your food can be consumed for energy, but does it taste and 'look' edible? Red flag any reviews you come across where the word 'inedible' or any other similar vocabulary is used. Ensure that the fundamentals are maintained: meats are cooked but not overdone and all hot dishes are actually hot when served, to name two.

Also, be aware that people eat with their eyes as much as they do their mouths and noses; presentation matters just as much as taste. Bright primary colors look more appetizing than browns or charred blacks. It's like painting a picture: do you want to evoke feelings of dark, shadowy despair or bright, fruitful contentment? Note how one of the first markers of spoilage is a foodstuff losing its vibrant color and texture. One gray area to this color wheel pertains to blues and purples. Nature has had a propensity to marry these two hues onto poisonous species and over the epochs we've been coded to be subliminally wary. As a demonstrative example, name five naturally occurring blue foods aside from blueberries which can be eaten in their raw form.

Safety Needs

The second stratum involves more cognitive aspects of one's life dealing with personal health, shelter and security. Like the more intimate physiological needs, there are many questions to pose. How secure is your hotel? What about the neighborhood? How safe are the rooms? Are the elevators secured, or the floors secured with key card access? Does each room have a safe? Are there any safety hazards that should have proper signage or be removed entirely? Are there any apparent health risks? As it pertains to a guest's immediate family, are the grounds safe for children? Are your staff members trained to deal with kids and elderly guests?

As you can tell, security is a complex issue. Look at it through the pyramid and you'll understand that much like physiological needs, personal and familial safety is a matter that serves to do more harm than good. Safety is peace of mind. When it's infringed, it's an excuse for bad press, or even a lawsuit.

I have little doubt that you, as a manager, take this matter lightly. Most security systems work and are frequently reassessed. However, a lot of these features don't have any 'presence'. What I'm insinuating here is security theatre—the front-end rather than the back-end. For instance, a camera hangs from a blatant vantage point overlooking a parking garage. Is it in plain sight to warn and ward off potential criminals or to catch them in the act? If the camera's only purpose was the latter, then wouldn't it be more appropriate to hide the recording lens?

To satisfy guest concerns, analyze your safety measures from a pragmatic as well as a visual point of view. The camera is a blunt example, but security theatre can be much more subtle. The presence of a doorman, valet and exterior staff fit within this paradigm, instantly reassuring guests with a warm smile and helpful hands. This also goes for the attentive staff member whose domain is only the elevator. As well, team members who consistently ask passing guests if everything is alright are subconsciously imbuing a sense of protection. On the other end of the spectrum, loose wires running along a corridor's baseboards will likely never spark an electrical fire, and yet their mere presence is enough to set off the warning sirens in one's mind. Long, dimly lit corridors might also trigger ill feelings.

The need for quality cuisine rears its head again at this level. I address it twice for similar reasons because it's just that important! Aside from food being edible, does it pose a health risk? Do you offer a menu with a full array of healthy choices (as well as a few savory indulgences)? Are there any allergy concerns that should be made explicit on the menu? How well do you accommodate vegetarians, vegans, celiac disease sufferers or anyone else who might deem junk food as hazardous to the body? Is your food prepared in a clean, germ-free environment? How do you source your ingredients? Do you emphasize your quality control methods? Again, you only stand to lose by neglecting these worries.

The primary concern I see cropping up here is food poisoning. In the unlikely event that this does happen, steps must be taken immediately to placate the victim, or else you run the risk of creating an enemy. You may not actually be at fault, but if you are blamed, that's what other online shoppers will read about. What sort of crisis communications protocol do you have to handle these sorts of situations? How would you respond to someone who posts online, claiming that this happened to them at one of your restaurants? Even though you've likely lost the food-poisoned patron forever, what would you publicly say to reassure future guests?

Social Needs

As we cross the midway point, we begin to deal less with the bare necessities and more with true emotional fulfillment. People need to feel as though they belong. We're no longer meeting the expectation of not doing harm but satisfying a guest's need for an enriching environment. Errors at this level are far more subjective and highly dependent on each person's individual experience. The most suitable word for success at this level is warmth, although friendliness, attentiveness and acceptance also apply.

As you can tell, a hefty chunk of this stage pertains to the degree of compassion extended by your staff to your guests. Although this is paramount for quality guest services, it's also wholly apparent and part of any proper hotelier training. Guests expect professionalism.

Rather, think more about the physical presence of your hotel. When the guest arrives, what is the atmosphere of the exterior? Is it warm and inviting? Does the lobby match this feeling? Does the lighting provide for an intimate, relaxing atmosphere? From a meetings perspective, what social features does your space provide to enhance productivity?

Your F&B choices also bridge this territory, but reflect on your cuisine more in terms of the social experience. What's the atmosphere like in your restaurants? Do your staff members make people feel at home, or do they make patrons feel inferior? Is the setting festooned with several potential conversation starters? What's the standard procedure for when a mistake is made? Do you offer any deals or host events to incentivize patrons and encourage a more crowded, vivacious mood?

Esteem Needs

The fourth stratum is where we transition from expectations to value-added features, although the line between the two is blurred and exceedingly subjective. Instead of merely fulfilling a guest's need for belonging, esteem deals more with reputation and importance. We're moving away from satisfaction towards indulgence.

In terms of importance, how can you make your guests feel like VIPs? Do you attend to individual requests promptly and with care? How do you make people feel as though you value and appreciate them choosing you?

In terms of reputation, are your guests proud to stay at your hotel? Is it something to brag about? How do you reward your loyal customers to demonstrate that this is a mutual feeling and that there is an actual connection, not just a transaction?

Self-Actualization Needs

The expectations at the apex of the pyramid are the hardest to attain and also the most mercurial. Maslow delineated the summit from its supports via the motivators for someone to achieve his or her personal best. How can your hotel facilitate this? If you operate in a downtown area that caters to business clientele, what can you do to ensure that every guest is maximally productive and feels fulfilled? If you operate in a resort or retreat locale, what services do you offer and what minor touches do you add to ensure that each visitor is fully relaxed and entertained as well as endowed with a profound sense of wellness?

Self-actualization also comes from creating new experiences for the guest. An example: providing the guest with an opportunity to learn about the ecological environment of the property with complimentary guide books and binoculars, offering a guided hike of the local area or classes with the chef. Even a bar with several hundred different scotch whiskeys and a knowledgeable bartender could form the basis of a self-actualizing activity. A personable sommelier leading an afternoon wine tasting can satisfy the F&B quotient as well. It is these types of 'wow' activities that a guest recalls years later as they continue to re-actualize their previous experiences within their own mind.

Guests may not say outright that they are seeking enlightenment, but on a subconscious level, they want to be wowed and entranced.

Self-actualization is the charm, the love, the unbridled happiness, the sense of harmony and the unique touch that only an experience at your hotel can supply. And only when all levels of your operations are functioning at their personal best can you deliver as such. Maslow advised that only a small percentage of people ever reach self-actualization and the same applies to hotels. Humans are curious creatures and our demand for new experiences and knowledge is insatiable. Give your guests exactly that!

Summary

To draw upon a very personal experience, my father suffered from a bout of food poisoning in the early 1980s—salmonella in the chicken from a fast food restaurant. Not only did he ban us from visiting that chain ever again, but he never ate any poultry product again, right up until he passed away. Whenever my family would have chicken, he'd remind us of his horror story, making sure to note the name of those responsible. A tad extreme, yes, but nevertheless a stern lesson in human behavior.

Never forget that we are (regretfully) fear-based creatures. We tend to remember bad experiences more so than the good ones. This is ingrained into our genetic makeup, but has served us quite well in terms of survival and proliferation. We are designed to actively avoid potential dangers, devoting an enormous amount of energy to this task. Maslow's Hierarchy of Hotel Expectations is intrinsically linked to this principle and that's what makes it so important to understand. Satisfy all basic needs first to ensure that people aren't afraid to visit your hotel, and then, and only then, should you move towards exceeding expectations.

FIRST ASSURANCES

The front desk is the nexus of any hotel. They manage guest requests, coordinate incoming calls and help with reservations. Above all, they handle check-ins and, apart from bell staff, are thus the most likely point of first contact between guests and staff.

You know how they say first impressions are everything? Well, it's true. Guests will often make snap decisions about your property based on what might only amount to a five minute encounter upon arrival. This is your time to shine, and I would say you cannot underestimate just how important the check-in process is.

Think of the first impression you make on a guest at check-in as your first opportunity to assure them of your brand quality and the satisfying experience that awaits. And this 'first assurance' boils down to the caliber of your front desk team.

The front desk is not a position for untrained beginners. In order to make a comforting and impactful first impression, your staff must always bring their A-game. They have to be overtly warm, attentive, knowledgeable, quick and empathetic. A guest may arrive in the best of spirits and ready to answer a front desk clerk's barrage of questions and explore the hotel. Then again, your guests may have just driven for the past six hours in horrendous touch-and-go traffic, leaving them with sore backs and a dollop of unneeded stress. In this case, they are probably more than ready for a nap and might confront customary check-in questions with mild hostility.

In this latter case, you don't want to have a trainee greet them; you want someone who can read these abrasive social cues correctly and usher the fatigued guests to their rooms as fast as possible. An experienced staff member will be able to flawlessly execute the check-in request and answer questions matter-of-factly, all within a few minutes and without referring to another source. Even better would be a clerk who addresses concerns before they are asked!

Put yourself in this scenario. You just got off a four and a half hour flight from JFK to LAX. You woke up two hours early to make the flight. Traffic on the way there. A 40 minute wait through airport security. Flight delayed half an hour. Traveling economy, sandwiched between a sniffling sneezer and a blabbermouth. Long lineup for the car rental. More traffic on the freeway. Got lost finding the hotel. Now, how would you feel when you finally arrive on property and are greeted by a junior trainee who fumbles on the check-in process?

Even though you may feel relieved to have reached your final destination and you may still have the energy to be patient with the rookie, the point is that traveling can be a very draining experience. The last thing you'd probably want is another obstacle at the check-in counter. In this potentially irrational frame of mind, any problems at the front desk might subconsciously translate to other aspects of the hotel operations.

It's unfair, but that's how first impressions work; they are made from an emotional state of mind. Accept that you will be judged for things that are beyond your control. But are they really out of your control? Aside from putting the best team members at the front desk and continually reassessing their performance for ways to improve, here are a few subtle tricks I've picked up along the way.

First: sugar on the countertop. A more scientific way to classify fatigue is sugar deprivation. Your brain chews up sugar by the spoonful when it's stressed or when it has to make a series of difficult decisions. As such, it's best to leave out some snacks to replenish guests and thus make them more receptive to the check-in process. This can come in the form of chocolates, packaged candies, mints, juice, bottled water or fruit. Treat this as yet another way to demonstrate your brand differentiators and allegiances. If you promote healthy living, then there should definitely be a fruit bowl. If you are an avid supporter of regional produce, then what local bite-sized and sweetened goods can be offer at the front desk?

The next tip applies to high volume hotels. After waiting on the tarmac, in airport security and on the freeway, the last thing a weary traveler wants to encounter is a lineup at the check-in. But sometimes—especially during peak hours—this can be unavoidable. Rather than scrambling to assign an extra person or two to the front desk, consider placing a pre-front desk clerk. That is, someone at the start of the lineup to reassure guests that the wait time will be short and they needn't worry. Offer bottled water to people waiting in line. It costs little and is a nice touch. If it is exceptionally hot and humid, pre-moistened towelettes in foil packs are also worth your consideration.

Third: don't under-estimate the value of a human face to comfort first timers. When you get tired, your decision-making skills go out the window. Tasks that would otherwise be no-brainers like figuring out where the front desk is in the lobby and navigating your car to the parking garage are now riddled with anxiety. This is where your valet, bellmen and all other outside staff members come in. They must understand the mindset of the exhausted traveler and must be as personable as the front desk staff. Elevate them to your energy level through your charm and cheerfulness. Sorry to say, but Walmart does a better job with their 'Greeter' program than many of the properties I have experienced. On a tangent, to prevent stormy weather from damping a guest's mood, perhaps install a carport, if at all possible.

Fourth: Many properties now have electronic monitors at their check-in area. Usually these serve as interactive boards for groups, showing meeting room locations and directing traffic. Depending upon the number of monitors available in your lobby, consider changing some over to newsfeeds such as CNN, Bloomberg or coverage of major sporting events. These visual distractions will help comfort those waiting and improve the social atmosphere of the lobby.

Fifth, free WiFi in the lobby ensures that those waiting can quickly get caught up on emails through their smartphones. Make sure that if you do in fact offer free internet connectivity, you also add some signage so people are adequately informed about the feature.

A few suggestions, and with any luck, a few minor improvements will work wonders to turn first impressions into great first impressions. Just remember that as with nearly all guest service issues, it boils down to the genuine warmth and perceptive nature of your staff. Assure your guests from the start with a positive interaction at the front desk and set the tone for a spectacular experience.

BREAKING DOWN GUEST SATISFACTION INTO INDIVIDUAL INTERACTIONS

Guest service and our fair hospitality industry go hand-in-hand—a strong grasp of the former is critical for the any semblance of success in the latter. It would be foolhardy, however, to view great guest service as any sort of grandiose machination or elusive phenomenon. In practice, the concept of guest satisfaction boils down to the moments between the monumental; a little smile here, a helping hand there, all of it culminating into something ebullient, tepid or even appalling depending on each interaction.

In this day and age when even a minor, fickle grievance can precipitate into a far more damaging online torrent, there's simply no room for errors when it comes to guest services. Everyone now has the potential to broadcast a sob story and drive away future bookings. Moreover, consumers just don't follow the rigorous standards for stars and diamonds that were once the emblems of competence for our industry. Travelers must contend with their own varying and emotionally-driven agendas for satisfaction.

Add to that the near-universally heightened level of global competition and there's all the more reason to dissect your interactions as meticulously as a brain surgeon. Nowadays, anything adequate is simply mediocre and unworthy of the glory of laudable word of mouth or word of mouse. Achieving greatness requires superb guest services which also happen to be adaptable to a myriad of incoming personalities.

What I advocate is a return to the idea of guest satisfaction as an exercise in addition rather than division. The responsibility for delivering the highest quality of customer service should not be segmented and isolated within departments—for instance, F&B operating separately from housekeeping—but treated as the binding reagent for overall success. Compile all the small and seemingly insignificant encounters, and this forms the overall impression of your property.

One Interaction at a Time

Start by thinking of each member of your visible staff as a point of interaction with the chance to promote positive or negative changes in a customer's state of mind. I bring this up because, as humans, we are libel to make mistakes, whether owner, manager or line staff. As trite as it is to state, put yourself in a guest's shoes and look at all the instances where errors might arise.

Imagine yourself arriving from the airport. Who might you encounter?
- Doorman greeting and ceremonial door opening
- Valet offering to park car
- Bell staff unloading and carrying luggage
- Front desk clerk confirming reservation and credit card
- Concierge for additional assistance
- Manager with a personal introduction

Imagine yourself dining at the hotel's restaurant one evening. Who might you see then?
- Host to escort you to your table
- Server to take orders and offer recommendations
- Associates to fill water glasses, offer bread selection
- Bus staff to place orders and clear the table
- Sommelier with wine suggestions and tasting
- Manager or chef with a personal introduction

It's important to note that these are potential encounters; some may happen, some may not. But for each that does, the opportunity to alter a guest's mood abounds. There's always a chance for one staff member or another to induce a change, either subtle or drastic. And this only encompasses our fictitious customer arriving, relaxing in the room and heading down for a meal. No doubt there'd be dozens more over the course of a few days.

What should also be evident from these manifold points of contact is that we are discussing a cascade of events. If any one of the earlier interactions, like that with the valet or front desk, is found to be irksome by the guest, then it will set a challenging precedent for all subsequent communications.

This concept extends far beyond guest-staff encounters. There are so many factors beyond your control, making it all the more vital to have those in your control running immaculately. Guests have their own lives and their own stresses, and they may inadvertently redirect any glowering energy onto the hotel. Maybe they arrive as happy as a clam, but then bad news strikes and they turn caustic. Like a powder keg, one little wrong move could set them off.

Am I advocating that telepathy be mandatory teaching for hospitality students? Hardly, although that would solve a lot of problems. Rather, I subscribe to the belief that sheer, unwavering positivity can surmount all other dispositions. A smile trumps a frown. A sour guest should never embitter a chipper staff member—empathy, respect and attentiveness at all times no matter what.

In reality, this is a difficult credence to actualize as an effective means to sway guest satisfaction in your favor. Negative experiences have a way of entrenching themselves in the mind and outlasting their positive counterparts. Sometimes, no matter how hard you try to compensate for a supposed wrongdoing, a guest may never come around.

Psychology at Play

Why do negative emotions linger, even when we try to erase them? Basic, instinctual survival. When we fall as a child and hurt ourselves, we learn both consciously and subconsciously to take special caution on uneven surfaces and atop lofty perches. When a particular food causes illness, it takes great willpower to overcome the trepidation of taking that next first bite for precisely this reason. We hardwire our bad experiences into our memory circuits in order to avoid similar circumstances in the future; this is the same as any other evolved vertebrate.

Our brains have programmed us to ardently avoid dangerous environments. As it pertains to guest services, if a stimulus causes a traveler to feel this way, their own mental conditioning will act out in self-preservation. No longer trapped in caveman circumstances, the modern forms of this 'acting out' may include disdainful word to mouth to friends, bad online reviews or a complete refusal to ever revisit your brand.

This means that a plus does not necessary cancel out a minus. Often, it takes many-a-plus to balance one grievance, and sadly, some minuses are irremediable. Not only do negative emotions linger, but they are also powerful interlopers. Fear makes us tense, which makes us angry. When moods are heated, what might otherwise be considered 'water under the bridge' (for instance, exorbitant charges for local telephone calls) can easily morph into yet another subsidiary cause for scorn. This is all in the eye of the beholder to a degree, but, at the very least, once a guest's guard is up, it's not coming down anytime soon. The universal lesson that our biology tells us is that guests' emotional states require extra precaution.

Defeating the Undefeatable Fear Factor

On an interaction-by-interaction basis, ameliorating this subconscious fear complex and its vitriolic manifestation requires a tactful combination of training and on-the-spot negotiation. Whichever staff member happens to be on the receiving end must first be taught to empathize with an irritated guest's distressed state where emotion trumps logic. Understand that this isn't how the person normally acts and that arguing back would only serve to exacerbate the situation. Instead, stay calm, apologetic and proactive with an immediate solution.

Often having a guest talk through his or her concerns can not only elucidate the underlying emotional triggers but also quell the present ire to let cooler heads prevail. Team members don't have to be expert negotiators or psychologists, but they must be people persons, able to read social cues and respond accordingly. I emphasize again the importance of training, with those positions more likely to encounter guests necessitating more frequent instruction.

Harkening back to the point about guest service permeating through all departments, another grievous error occurs when a staff member is approached by a concerned guest only to respond with a fleeting, "That's not my department." Such demoralizing interactions can easily be avoided through educating your team on proper protocols for these ordinary scenarios. In this instance, a good response would be, "Let me see if I can help. Normally, this issue isn't handled by my department, so it may take a bit longer to resolve."

All these scenarios are reactionary, however. The disgruntled guest must first find the courage to lodge a complaint directly with the hotel in order for the staff to actually notice what's wrong. Excluding the budding role of social media as an intermediary option for real-time protest management, often guests will only give you the silent treatment.

Telepathy would be great for these unspoken moments, but we'll just have to make due with the next best thing. With a warm, friendly smile, address your visitors with a, "Hi!" and, if time permits, a, "How are you today?" or a, "Is there anything I can help you with?" Perform this whenever a guest passes by and eventually your cheerful spirit will rub off. These routine questions present affronted guests with a chance to speak their minds as well as provide you with an opportunity to improve a satisfied guest's already pleasurable experience. It really can be that simple. You need only look at various online reviews to notice the cases where extraverted staff transformed an experience for the better.

Double Deviations

If the ideal goal is to never mess up, then the backup plan is to never mess up twice with the same guest. Yes, guests are capable of laying on the fire and brimstone when incensed, but the average person is willing to forgo one mistake. They'll give you the benefit of the doubt. But by doubly deviating from the expectation, it's a confirmation in the guest's mind that your property isn't deserving of their praise.

Think about this from the inner brain's fear factor point of view. Suppose a property's first grievance falls in that special zone of irascibility. The snubbed traveler can then choose to lash out in one of several emotionally-charged ways or the guest can exert self-discipline to allow logical thought patterns to prevail. However, a subsequent offense is inexcusable and can excite many, "What was I thinking?" forms of guilty, angered deliberations. Further, as a guest will have his or her proverbial guard up after the first blunder, the second offense need not be as severe in order to elicit highly memorable discomfort.

It goes without saying that a large part of the solution for these types of situations is to not make a mistake in the first place. But, as with seemingly everything in hospitality, a calamity of events occurs beyond our control. Double deviations can be mitigated via a flagging system and employee empowerment.

If a guest is noticeably grumpy and verbalizes an error on the hotel's part, flag this person as you would a VIP. Inform staff, offer complimentary gifts and do everything within reason to ensure that a second mishap doesn't transpire. Empowerment thus serves to expedite any remedial actions. If a patron ardently complains about a dessert, does a waiter need permission from the restaurant manager to offer a replacement confection? Mandating the involvement of higher authorities would take too long in this case. Front line staff members must know the limits of their power to help buffer an emerging problem before it imprints.

Congruent Guest-Hotel Interactions

Onsite guest-staff interactions are at the core of guest satisfaction, but they're not the only factor. Social media is a demonstrative platform for this as well. To the casual viewer, your online forays will give future travelers a flavor of what to expect. Such networks are also an excellent tool to keep in touch with past visitors. Alas, the elegant nuances for these communication mediums are a topic for a whole other discussion.

What's most crucial for guest-hotel interactions is to ensure that every encounter with your brand, from the print advertisements to the onsite staff and décor, conforms to a prescribed tone. In the opening I said to strip away all these additives and consider only the guest and the staff. Now, bring everything else back into the equation, but treat each and every object as a point of interaction subject to the same scrutiny as your team members. Is the artwork in the hallways evocative? How would a well-placed sculpture add to the ambiance? Can you discern any commonalities amongst your unhappy restaurant critiques?

I consider these inanimate objects as subsidiary to the interactive human touch your hotel provides, but they are nonetheless important. Focus first on perfecting your guest-staff interactions then build out from there. By inculcating you with this mantra, attaining high percentages of guest satisfaction should be a breeze whether you operate at the budget, four star or five star levels.

THE FOUR STAGES OF HOTELIER COMPETENCE

Maslow wasn't a one hit wonder, and, aside from his venerable Hierarchy of Needs, he is often credited as one of the progenitors of another paradigm of behavioral psychology. Rising to prominence in the 1970s, the 'Four Stages of Competence' describes the pathology by which one acquires a new skill from the drudgeries of persistent failure to innate, reflexive action. Needless to say, this time-tested theory is rife with applications for hoteliers, primarily insofar as how we approach contemporary problems that face our properties and our industry.

The four stages are unconscious incompetence, conscious incompetence, conscious competence and, lastly, unconscious competence. Don't let the word 'incompetence' alienate you. What's remarkable about this learning model is that it is not designed to presuppose certain people as 'smarter' or 'better' than any other. As professionals, we are all a spectrum of learned skills with various character traits falling into each of the four labels. In short, nobody's perfect.

Hence, we can all still learn, master or perfect some aspect of our daily routines. The key is to accept the fact that you're not perfect then be open to both personal criticism and new experiences which might widen your perspective. The hospitality industry is so diverse and panoptic that there's always something new the world can teach you.

Unconscious Incompetence

The first part of learning is, at its core, the stage where you aren't learning at all—nor do you already have the appropriate skill (incompetence). In fact, you don't even know there's a problem (unconscious). And not knowing there's a problem can be the biggest problem of all!

How does someone crack out the proverbial defibrillator and shock himself or herself into an existential frame of mind where every thought and action is open for conjecture? The answer to this differs for each person as everyone discovers their own eureka moment at one point or another in their lives.

When I was first running the gauntlet of a rookie marketer at Procter & Gamble in the late 1970s, one phrase constantly bouncing off the drywall was, 'Smart people listen'. Simple, elegant and true. The only difference between someone who learns and someone who remains obstinate and 'set in their ways' is the ability to wholeheartedly listen and approach situations from multiple points of view.

The essential qualities are curiosity and keeping an open mind; two sides of the coin more or less. Furthermore, both are internal beliefs, and, although they aren't entirely immutable, your efforts as a manager to coax, cajole, charm or coerce an employee into your slipstream of leadership pathology will ultimately fail if you aren't promoting change from the inside out.

My recommendation to you and all those who work for you is to focus on inspiration. Lead by example and give your colleagues an aspiration they can see with their own eyes, not one hidden behind the jazz of well-edited television, photography or the written word.

In terms of keeping an open mind, the easiest morsel of advice I can give you is to always be reading. Novels, magazines, newspapers, essays, trade journals, poems or comics—whatever goes well with your morning brew, gulp it down. You'll never know what inspirational factoids you might stumble upon or how a piece of prose might jumpstart a fugue of introspection.

It's ironic that the very people who are most likely to fall into the unconscious incompetent state for one skill or another are also the least likely to read a book like this. Give yourself a pat on the back for making it this far through my omnibus of inked didacticism. You're here because you want to learn, you want to be inspired.

Conscious Incompetence

Now that you've perked a brow at what lies beyond the red velvet curtain, it's time to nourish that seed of motivation into an actionable plan. By its very namesake, conscious incompetence describes the stage at which you know there's a problem (conscious) but you don't possess the necessary skill or skills to fix it (incompetence).

As you well know, one of the greatest causes for trepidation is the fear of the unknown; in this case, not knowing the answer or path to take to get the answer. Much like my suggestion for the previous unconscious phase, one of the keys is reading, or, as it might otherwise be called at this stage, research.

Whatever your problem may be, there is an answer out there, or at least enough nuggets of disparate information for you to mull and coalesce into your own solution. Getting back to the whole concept of an 'open mind', don't just stay within the hospitality field. Instead, think of hospitality as an amalgamation and application of many different but related fields of study including psychology, business, human resources, cuisine, sports, economics and so on. Trust in the fact that there is an answer somewhere out there. You need only be persistent in your pursuit and the needed skill with develop in due time.

Building on the idea of inspirational leadership, when you do happen to come across a worthwhile book, article or instructional website, share it with your colleagues. Even if they are mired in their own flat-footed obstinacy of unconscious incompetence, one of these days they may open one of your hyperlink bombardments. Leadership often does require a defibrillator.

Conscious Competence

This is the meat of the learning process. You know you have a flaw (conscious) and now you have a plan to execute which will, hopefully, remedy the situation (competence). Again, one of the keys here lies with your beliefs. Are you certain that persistence will pay off? How do you know that trial and error will refine your methodology and speed of action to the point where it actually works?

In order to succeed in the long run, 99 times out of 100 you must fail first. But with this failure comes introspection, "Why did I fail?" and the courage to try and try again. This is the phase corresponding to Malcolm Gladwell's proposed '10,000 Hours' where we put in the grunt work in order to make processes effortless further down the road.

Take employee training for instance. When you first attained the rank of manager and were thrust into a leadership role, you might have been a tad nervous about ordering, instructing and reprimanding those below you. You might have even clung to whichever training manual or college textbook said it best. But gradually, the books were referenced less, the dog-eared pages unfolded and a more internally-driven skill emerged.

This third stage is not just about deriving then following a solution from one source or an array of sources, but working through the drudgery of repetition in order to make it an automatic, yet also adaptive to a given situation. And by drudgery, I mean grueling, sweating, aching, shivering, agonizing drudgery, because that's what it will take to log your 10,000 hours in order to reach mastery of a skill.

For some, simply knowing that the next stage is possible can be enough motivation to drive you there. Indeed, modern science has afforded us with a bevy of conclusive research which proves that consciously working on improving a skill can realign your brain circuitry to better execute said skill in the future. For reference, look up the subject 'neuroplasticity'.

Unconscious Competence

This is the point where, in the blink of an eye and without any internal deductive monologue (unconscious), you can intuit the answer (competence). Intuition is the mark of a true professional. Like how certain managers instantly discern what a troubled guest needs to quell his or her concerns, or a marketer who instinctually knows which taglines and promotional materials will generate positive returns. Like how certain wait staff interrupt your conversation at just the right moments to confidently guide you towards the next step of the meal or a chef who can improvise with any ingredients to produce excellent cuisine.

This isn't an echelon exclusively reserved for the upper tiers of managerial skill sets, but permeates all manner of careers, jobs and tasks. My advice: surround yourself with people who have reached this stage in an area of expertise that can help your business then ensure that this tacit knowledge rubs off on the rest of the team.

Regression

There is a debatable fifth step that is often described under the banner of complacency or the motto, "If you don't use it, you lose it." Suppose you used to be a literal accounting machine, number crunching and balancing spreadsheets until your fingertips bled. Then you got off the wagon and segued career paths into the sister field of marketing. Over time, the ability to effortlessly juggle digits in your head slips away until you catch yourself saying, "I used to be able to do that."

Complacency, or the gradual erosion of a learned skill, is a natural part of life. Each stage of your journey necessitates slightly different proficiencies. This isn't something you should fight, but rather, you should 'roll with the punches'.

To describe this phase, I prefer the term regression. Whether due to the stress, the fear or the self-fulfilling fallacy of old age, we grow soft. The thinking goes that in these ever-changing times, the skills required to be a successful hotelier are elusive to the point where unconscious competence is either unattainable due to the rate of technological progress or invalid due to forced obsolescence. Even worse is 'illusory superiority' where you think you're a master, when in reality the world is passing you by.

With complacency, regression or whatever other term you muster to represent this deterioration of learning, the antidotes are the same as someone stuck in one of the first two incompetent stages: curiosity, an open mind and persistence. To put it in more lucrative terms, the more you learn, the more you earn, so keep on learning!

LOVING HOTELS, HATING AIRLINES

Airports and their planes garner a lot of complaints. Airplanes are tight, cramped spaces with limited room to stretch one's limbs, the constant droning hum of the ventilation system and no way to escape the coughs of strangers or crying babies. At six-foot-three, traveling economy as I so often do can be especially noisome—the seat in front of me reclined and jamming into my knees with insufficient tray space to even contemplate opening my laptop.

Airports are a tad better. You can walk around the oftentimes clinical gray footpaths, check out a few shops (duty-free, anyone?) or relax at a restaurant. But all that goes pear-shaped when there are delays, cancellations, hour-long security lineups and last-minute dashes to the boarding gate.

But this all pertains to the trials of air travel. We're in the hotel business, so why care?

Think of all the guests who will arrive at your property via transportation from the airport. Given the elevated number of people who apparently find air travel displeasing, it's safe to assume that a corresponding ratio will arrive at your house in an affected mood. They've just sat through a horrendous flight, and in this ornery headspace one miniscule disagreement at check-in will set them off.

Whereas others might see this as an omen, I see it as one of the best opportunities to form positive bonds with your guests. Because the flight experience was such a disaster, if you do your best to be the opposite, your guests will love you all the more for it. Be warm and empathetic, and definitely train your front-desk staff to recognize the all-too-common scenario of the wearied, irascible airport arrival.

It's all about contrast. Consider the frog in a bathtub example. Start on cold then blast hot water and the amphibian jumps away. But start on cold and gradually add a pinch of warmth and the frog stays put.

For this particular application, you should lean towards the former. When a guest arrives after an exhausting flight (cold), your well-gauged cheerfulness and genuine attentiveness (hot) will blast them into viewing you in a highly positive light. By virtue of contrasts, when a guest arrives after a breezy, uneventful flight (warm) and you bestow them with the same gratitude (hot), it just won't have the same impact, emotionally speaking that is.

Not that you shouldn't be treating all your incoming guests with the utmost of care, but if someone drops a hint that they've just survived a nerve-racking ride in the sky, it's your chance to seize the day. Show them what real hospitality is all about with a generous dose of compassion then win their loyalty and the oh-so-valuable word of mouth as a prize.

FUNDAMENTALS TO BUILD A
GUEST BILL OF RIGHTS

It never ceases to amaze me that some of the simplest gestures can lead to a better service culture. Quality service is not just the domain of those fortunate enough to be sitting in the front of the airplane or those sipping champagne at some five-star lobby bar. Rather, quality service should be considered no differently than water and air. Here is what I consider the core elements of service—a guest bill of rights, so to speak.

1. **All guests are treated with respect.** This means there are no discriminatory practices based on age, weight, religion, race or gender in addition to one's clothes, car, hairstyle or any other personal accessory.
2. **You try to accommodate and respect any special needs.** Is a guest in a wheelchair? Then you must provide a lift and appropriate ADA-compliant rooms. You also try to genuinely empathize. For instance, elderly guests should be assigned rooms closer to the elevator. I say try, because there will be times when circumstances such as late check-in may make this impossible.
3. **You pre-clear all extra charges on the guest folio.** This may seem odd initially, but when you think about it, hidden or obscure surcharges are a disservice. They create anxiety for the guest, foreshadowing negativity that will impinge service delivery. For clarification, this does not mean extras are wrong. Rather, they should be clearly identified before purchase. As an example, claiming WiFi is free then delivering low bandwidth at no charge and high (useful) bandwidth at a fee without advising the guest beforehand is inappropriate.
4. **You value your guest's time.** Long queues for check-in, valet car pickup or checkout are all not conducive to a quality service culture. Again, there will be times when this cannot be avoided. In such circumstances, making a guest aware of the delay—in advance if possible—or providing options such as prepaid checkout are service advances.

5. **You don't add excess (and confusing) technology.** I recently visited a luxury property with advanced iPad controls for each guestroom. There were no instructions and for the life of me I could not figure out how to turn off some of the lights. I ended up having to pull the plug out of the wall. And this challenge is not restricted to electronics. Ever go into a shower and stare at the controls trying to find a way not to be scalded or frozen by a stream of water?

6. **You deliver the basics perfectly.** Here are the six that I slot at this level:
   - A comfortable bed
   - A spotless guestroom and bathroom
   - Clean water, with ample hot water for the shower
   - Quiet HVAC to maintain a guest-requested temperature
   - The ability to effectively close out sunlight (drapes, blinds, etc.)
   - Secure locks

7. **You greet customers when they arrive.** A smile goes a long way. I cannot stress this enough. Be friendly to your guests and they in turn will reward you with good reviews, positive word of mouth and return visits.

8. **You treat your staff as you would your guests.** In doing so, you set the tone for a mutually positive relationship.

9. **If a guest issue arises, resolve it quickly and professionally.** This does not mean the guest is always right. It means learning from each event and sharing this knowledge with your team. By reflecting on each situation with sincerity, there's no way you won't improve.

10. **You provide your guests with free high-speed WiFi.** This seems to be controversial, but it shouldn't be. Many hotels offer complimentary WiFi in their lobbies, so why not guestrooms? I have heard the arguments about the costs of building appropriate bandwidth transmission into facilities and the need to get a return on capital. Frankly, I don't buy it. When your guests need more air conditioning, do you levy an HVAC charge? WiFi is not an amenity; it is a basic right. Failure to provide a basic right is a fundamental service failure.

LESSONS FROM THE SILVER SCREEN

Movies and television are designed as entertainment, but both of these popular visual mediums are also ripe with sentimental life lessons built on universal truths and aphorisms. Occasionally, these two mediums intersect with the hospitality industry and are able to offer us some smart lessons hidden underneath layers of humor and drama.

The following subsection outlines a few examples that I've recently watched and what lessons they can teach us about our line of work. Sometimes it's best to get an outside opinion so we can improve as objectively as possible. And if you're still not convinced of the merits of film and television, here are a few more reasons why you should pay attention:

- **Writers have perspective.** Reality television aside, all fictional motion pictures are scripted, meaning that someone has to write down what happens before they roll the cameras. If a picture involves a hotel, the hired writer might slip in an astute observation about the staff, the setting or the hospitality industry in general.
- **Filmmakers travel.** Everyone travels and hotel guestrooms are a prime place to hang one's hat whether you're in Canada or Cambodia. This alone gives a person experience as to what entails a good night's stay. Filmmakers have the additional benefit of shooting on location. This job perk translates into many extended periods of time away from home and holed up in a guestroom.
- **Hotels are filmable.** Whether it's the exceptional room décor, a scene in a spa or a star-studded shootout in the lobby, hotels can make for some very vivid scenery to set part or all of a movie. Our properties are also sensible locations because they are well trafficked—meeting a client for lunch at the lobby restaurant or visiting a guestroom are two relatively common occasions.

HOTELIER NOTES FROM SEASON ONE OF FAWLTY TOWERS

Sometimes in order to understand what sets the bar for good service in the hotel industry, you have to gaze upon the dark underbelly of what is truly and horrifically bad. It's all about contrast. To know what would qualify your establishment as a lemon, you need only take one passing look at Fawlty Towers, the 1970s 12-episode British sitcom starring the magnetic John Cheese as the titular rural English B&B owner and operator, Basil Fawlty.

The show is a riot, brimming with bashful comedy and ludicrously over-the-top coincidences; all in good fun though. It's as if the writers said, "What makes for a great hotel experience? Good, now let's do the opposite of that." And this is why Fawlty Towers deserves our attention, even some three decades after the second season wrapped.

There are so many delicious nuggets of information for hoteliers in this series that each season deserves its own essay. Keep in mind that given the calamitous nature of the show, many of these are "Do Not's" rather than "Do's"; not ideal for a positive learning experience, but still a patchwork of lessons for your consideration.

1. **A badly run hotel starts at the top and trickles down.** No matter the kookiness of the guests or the state of disrepair of the property, no situation would spiral out of control without a catalyst from the top. May I present the asinine leadership abilities of Basil Fawlty. True, Basil's wife, Sybil, is also self-absorbed and lazy in her duties. And Manuel is an incompetent klutz despite any language barriers. Nevertheless, it's Basil's responsibility to keep a level head and provide a moral beacon for his team to uphold.

2. **Never get impatient.** Part of keeping a level head means staying as cool as a cucumber, even in the face of unruly guests or stressed employees. Nothing can be solved in heated emotional arguments, even if a logical answer is proposed. Instead, take a few deep breaths and become that calming reflection for which people aspire to emulate. Talk in a slow, articulate manner and always be attentive. Give people the respect they crave and they will return in kind.

3. **If a guest insults you, don't stoop to their level.** Leveling insults on another person often says more about you than the person you intend to sway or hurt. Furthermore, in different circumstances or when one's mood is brighter, such vitriol might never occur. Stay calm, carry on. Basil Fawlty doesn't seem to know this principle. Whenever a guest raises his or her voice about the property's incompetence, Basil always fires back. From there, the conversations descend into a hateful, irreprehensible argument; comedy to all except the affronted guest. It's mutually assured destruction; easily preventable if Basil were to keep his cool.

4. **Never make uninformed assumptions about your guests.** Just because a fellow strolls toward the front desk in track pants and not a bespoke suit does not mean that such a person is undeserving of your full attention. Treat everyone with the utmost of respect and they will all in turn find a place in their hearts for your hotel. Oh, if only Basil knew this. Like a swift kick of poetic justice, whenever Basil assumes something about one guest or another from an outward appearance, it comes back to bite him in the pantaloons, and rightfully so.

5. **Don't panic!** Just as Douglas Adams would advise you when traversing the universe, so too must you abide by this simple principle when marching through your own abode. Any curtness or fright you display can be emotionally transferred to passing guests, startling them and filling them with uneasy sentiments. Instead, aim to be the air of grace, perpetually comfortable in your own house, even in the face of disconcerting or pressing issues.

6. **Get to know your guests by their names.** A simple 'Hello' is still appreciated, but a personalized greeting goes a lot further and may even spark a conversation that leads to a better perception of your property or a few chores. This name game works especially well when a guest approaches you needing assistance. Some might be temporarily stunned by the fact that you remembered who they are! It's a matter of respect and tried-and-true formality, so knowing a guest's last name is far more appropriate than one's given name.

7. **Always greet guests.** Building on the last point of the power of name-dropping, this is an old-fashioned principle of hospitality that should remain firm and timeless. When someone currently staying at

your hotel enters the lobby, make them feel at home. Such a renewed welcome will instantly elevate the mood and put one's mind at ease.

8. **Socialize with guests.** Outside of a polite greeting, one or two questions go miles towards building the kind of familial and sociable atmosphere that all hospitality settings strive to attain. In the restaurant, ask how the meal was or offer suggestions if the menus are still in hand. Introduce guests to other regular guests and managers. Remember that part of the phrase 'Make Yourself at Home' implies that a person should know everyone staying in their house!

9. **When guests are in a hurry, drop everything to help.** First and foremost for guest service is just that—servicing your clientele. When guests are rushed, your assistance will be greatly appreciated, probably more so than on other lackadaisical occasions. On the flip side, if you are unresponsive or sluggish towards a hurried guest's urgent needs, you might just find yourself with a new enemy.

10. **Avoid shuffling guests.** Whether it's from room to room or from table to table at the restaurant, switching guests around is tremendously annoying. Although not a death knell, all that movement can precipitate into far more unsettling dispositions. Yes, mistakes are made and there are instances where this is inescapable. But if you find that this is happening with any sort of palpable frequency, then measures must be taken to reduce your error rate.

11. **"He's new" is passable once or twice.** Yes, visitors are people too and everyone has had to receive on-the-job training at some point or another in their careers. Just don't make it a theme of a guest's stay. If you notice that a rookie employee has made one or two minor blunders while dealing with guests, rotate them elsewhere for the time being so that you minimize the risk of further irritating the same people.

12. **Never reprimand staff in front of guests.** Oh, Manuel! If only you'd learn. Basil's hapless servant never really understands what his boss needs of him, but Basil is equally at fault for his impatience and by improperly disciplining such a team member. When someone is scolded in public, they can become embarrassed and demoralized, two emotions which might get in the way of the message being fully absorbed. Take the time to escort such a staff member to private quarters and then discuss the problem in full and with a genial tone.

13. **Never do repairs during peak hours.** This one may seem fairly self-explanatory but you'd be surprised how many personal experiences I've had where maintenance has obstructed my enjoyment of a vacation. I understand that this is oftentimes unavoidable and that managers must abide by shift schedules, contractor hours and union rules, but if you have room to wiggle then do so as much as is humanly possible.

14. **Fire drills are important but highly disruptive.** Visitors will respect that you are performing the fire drill for their own safety, but that doesn't change the fact that it is excruciatingly annoying. Whether it occurs consciously or subconsciously, guests' perceptions of your hotel will drop. My advice is to work with your safety supervisors to comply with fire codes but to make drills as unobtrusive or as infrequent as possible.

15. **Fresh flowers are great.** To end on a positive note, the aromas that permeate a hotel are very important and very subliminal. In Fawlty Towers, Sybil isn't known to be the shining star of the property, but one thing she does right is place fresh flowers in the lobby, coming straight from the garden. True, there are allergy concerns, but overall, flowers bring color and smiles. Isn't that what it's all about—bringing a smile to your guests' faces?

BONUS: Whatever you do, don't mention the war. (For those of you who know the show, you know what episode I am referring to!)

HOTELIER NOTES FROM SEASON TWO OF FAWLTY TOWERS

When I first starting researching—and by researching I mean watching—the 1970s British TV series Fawlty Towers for a 'Lessons Learned' style article, I wasn't too optimistic. After all, we're talking about extrapolating the screwball sitcom antics of a small English countryside inn into something meaningful for hoteliers; managers who are undoubtedly the complete opposite of what the hilariously spiteful innkeeper, Basil Fawlty, embodies.

When the creatives convened to start outlining ideas for the latter six episodes of the series, they knew that, even though it was a sitcom, they couldn't rely on the kookiness of the main four characters for all the gags. Sure, nine out of ten laughs are still the result of abject miscommunication, clumsiness, sarcasm and neglect amongst the staffers, but a few more are coming from the zany antics of supporting characters and one-off guests, thus giving us some keen insights about how to deal with unruly customers.

With that, we dive headfirst into the second coming of Fawlty Towers. And let me remind you that even though the characters on this show are, for the most part, totally incompetent and disgraceful hoteliers, by their very nature they have a lot to teach us about how to get things right.

1. **Stand behind your product.** In the first new episode, Basil and his team are treated with a rather miserly old lady who demands a discount for supposed errors on the hotel's part. Obviously there are occurrences where a price reduction might greatly help ameliorate an aggrieved visitor. But, in cases where you and the hotel are clearly not at fault, you have to first hold tight and discuss the issues in a calm, arbitral cadence. Only then can you discover the true nature of the problem while also placating the distressed party.

2. **Guest prioritization will always be complex and confusing.** At the front desk, if all goes as planned, it's typically first come first serve. But then a stressed-to-the-max guest rushes the desk, interrupting, demanding, commanding, pointing and shouting. Do

you drop everything to quell this concern? Will the person you were previously helping understand your need to shift gears? Now apply similar instances of urgency to the restaurant, rooms and any other frequented locale. My advice: set boundaries for your team, but also train them on how to adapt to individual cases which may require special attention. For the abovementioned front desk example, ask the previous guest if it would be okay to attend to the tense new arrival. Only once you have approval do you strafe over.

3. **Never complain to your guests.** Basil has a knack for infecting his guests with his gripes in casual conversation. Under the studio audience's raucous laughter it's often hard to pinpoint character reactions. Frowns, sneers, snickers and gasps—they're all there. Don't whine or protest your personal problems to your guests; that's their job, so don't steal their thunder!

4. **Never interrupt a guest.** Just like the fine art of complaining, interrupting is also a clear and obvious faux pas. Even if you have something of extreme importance to convey which may completely alter the course of the present conversation, just let the guest finish his or her train of thought before you commence. British sensibility applies in full here: stay calm, carry on . . .

5. **No one likes a brusque waiter.** Haute cuisine is a delicate matter and the more your menu is a wonder to behold, the longer it will take your patrons to decide. Double this allotted time for couples on romantic dates or large parties where there's a lot to discuss. It's a matter of how your waiters frame their approach. Instead of saying, "Ready to order?" start with, "Can I help you with anything on the menu?" The former is curt; the latter is helpful and attentive. The same applies for opening beverages or aperitifs. Ask, "Can I help you decide on a drink to start with perhaps?" rather than, "Something to drink?" It's a subtle but significant difference.

6. **Accrue regulars.** For those following along, the main inspiration for this point is The Major, a veteran from World War II who always seems to be poking his head around Fawlty Towers and occasionally partaking in one of Basil's many snafus. This can apply to the restaurant, bar, spa, gym or, ultimately, your rooms. Hosting regulars elevates the spirits of all around while subliminally demonstrating to other newcomers that your abode merits return visits—yet more proof that a discount for regulars can pay dividends in the long run.

7. **Is your kitchen open late?** In Fawlty Towers, this scenario presented itself as a late arriving couple who missed their late meal and were rather grumpy because of it. All they wanted was some warm food straight before bed. Lo and behold, in their frazzled state, the fact that they missed last call in the kitchen shocked them—it was the hotel's fault, not theirs! Either way, it's a difficult situation. If your restaurant stays open late as a contingency, your costs will climb, but if you close early, you run the risk of ticking off night owl patrons. One simple solution is to be sympathetic and keep a handful of late night delivery services on file.

8. **Surprise parties require extra attention.** In and around a person's special day or other day of significance, he or she can be both highly perceptive and very suspicious. Therefore, when organizing such a clandestine affair, take precautions against some of the more common risk factors and do your best to plan around unforeseen events which might spoil the surprise.

9. **"When will we be seeing you again?"** Much like how you can elicit a better response by posing a slightly tweaked set of questions in a restaurant, the same applies for check out. This particular query is great for jumping into a rapport building dialogue and cuing a departing guest to consider you for next time. Plus, if there was something displeasing about the visit then this may prompt a guest to flesh out his or her disdain into something far more constructive.

10. **Don't let staff conflicts boil over to affect service quality.** In a perfect world, everyone would get along with everyone else fine and dandy. But that isn't the case, so we have to make the best with what we have. If a conflict arises between two or more staff members, it's your job to intervene, lend a friendly voice to the discussion, and then resolve the issues behind the scenes and as soon as possible.

11. **Booting an unruly visitor is always a final resort.** A problem I see nowadays is that even if a guest is the bona fide culprit for certain transgressions on property, banishing him or her does more harm than good. The reason: online review sites. In the immediate postmortem, any past guest can write a semi-anonymous narrative of events and make the hotel out as the maligned party. This puts managers on the defensive, forcing them to provide evidence of their blamelessness. Best to suppress the issue before it migrates online

and convince a guest of your point of view while onsite then find a common resolution.

12. **Smile when you joke.** Basil's 'sledgehammer wit' comes off exactly as his snarky smile portrays it: rude, impatient and crass. However, all would be well and good if he simply adjusted his tone and delivered his sarcastic banter with a big, genuine smile—one which originates from within and not a mere façade. By approaching your own unique brand of humor with a deep-rooted love for your guests, they'll return in kind.

BONUS: Above all, don't forget your spouse's anniversary! Don't do as Basil did by turning this day into a nefarious game of cat and mouse. Make it known that you remember from the moment you wake up.

As a concluding remark, one of the episodes of this second season dealt with a particularly dark and touchy subject matter for you to consider—someone dying while staying at your hotel. Obviously, on the show this was approached very lightheartedly. But in reality, it is a direly serious scenario that you must ensure is accurately covered in your crisis communications binder and training protocols.

Apart from that, I hope you have enjoyed my thoughts on what this classic BBC series teaches us about service. And the next time you find yourself in Torquay or anywhere else in the English Riviera, be sure to stop by Fawlty Towers, which may or may not have reopened after a clever rat made his home in the hotel's kitchen.

LESSONS LEARNED FROM "THE BEST EXOTIC MARIGOLD HOTEL"

After being told by a friend to 'run, not walk' and see "The Best Exotic Marigold Hotel", I rushed to the theatre for a weekend matinee. Despite having been released several weeks prior, the film was still sold out. "Fair enough," I thought, and made plans to see it the following Monday. But it was sold out that day, too!

Clearly, this film was resonating with its audience, and I was now more determined than ever to see what all the commotion was about. After booking tickets in advance (like I should have in the first place!) and sitting in a still-very-packed theatre, I can safely say that the fuss is justified.

Steering clear of all the blockbuster CG effects, droning explosions and ADD-inspired editing which seem inescapable these days, "The Best Exotic Marigold Hotel" focuses on what makes for genuinely great cinema: strong storytelling and well-drawn characters. The movie boasts a cast played by a veritable "Avengers" of talented Brits including Judi Dench, Maggie Smith, Tom Wilkinson and Bill Nighy. The story revolves around a group of retirees who decide to spend their golden years at a hotel in India. They each have their own reasons and there's the quotidian dose of internal strife, yet they all grow to love each other and their new home.

One scene in particular should be recognizable for hoteliers. As they reach the property, it does not appear as advertised. In fact, it's dilapidated. The patrons are swiftly informed that the brochure is advertising what the hotel could be rather than what it actually is. After some debate and hubbub, they decide to stay and make the most of it.

While this is perfectly fair to drive the plot, I cannot foresee this situation playing out in much the same way for a real-life hotel. It's much more likely that a visitor would turn around and never set foot in such an establishment, snickering to all his or her friends on social media about the experience. In a movie, I'm willing to suspend disbelief and assume that the characters will act like hyperbolized people in order to take the story somewhere special. But in real life, I'm pretty sure that paying customers wouldn't be as obliging to this blatant deception.

Think for a moment about your website experience. Examine your guestroom photography. Does it accurately represent your product? Or are there features that are exaggerations of the truth? Compare your professional photography to those taken by guests and displayed on social media. They should be similar, as customers will expect the real thing to be consistent with your web presentation, even with all the proscribed retouching.

There is a lot more to this film than this one scene, of course. Overall, it's a stellar antidote to all of the woes baby boomers are feeling about the trending slates of Hollywood movies these days. The success of "The Best Exotic Marigold Hotel" demonstrates that the baby boomer generation is still seeking a bit of wish fulfillment in much the same capacity as children watching a Pixar animation or teenagers ogling the latest superhero extravaganza. The film works because it begs to ask the question, "What will you do with your retirement years?" And it appears that many recent retirees are on the search for renewed adventure.

Ask yourself how you can translate this nugget of socioeconomic insight into revenue. What makes your hotel appeal to retirees? What specific adventures can you offer them? Think of all the local and unique experiences that may appeal to an energized baby boomer and you're bound to tap into this ever-prevalent demographic. Just make sure your establishment is first and foremost as advertised on your website and in the brochure!

LESSONS LEARNED FROM "HOTEL TRANSYLVANIA"

A breezy hour and a half of bright, colorful fun, this Adam Sandler vessel is great for the young ones, albeit with a rudimentary plot and tame humor. Don't go in expecting "Lawrence of Arabia" and you'll be fine. What I find germane about framing films—particularly comedic ones— through a hospitality lens is that at the core of every scene or nuanced quip is the bare truth about our jobs. I digress; here's what I gleaned:

1. **Lively Lobby.** As one of the principal sets, this towering Gothic hall is never anything but a beehive—effervescent guests socializing, staff forever in hurried motion and live music. A vibrant lobby is a healthy lobby is a healthy hotel. You need only watch the extended scene where each of the key supporting cast enters in style to see this in action. The ambiance is invigorating and intoxicating, bringing a smile to all new arrivals and, by extension, us.

2. **Gregarious General Manager.** More than just a plot device, Adam Sandler's Dracula—who also happens to be the hotel's owner, operator and chief architect—is a constant presence for his maniacal guests, offering sincere greetings and noting specific tweaks to accommodate each monster's idiosyncrasies. Whether it's in the lobby, in the halls or by the pools, Dracula knows every guest by heart. He anticipates their needs and is rarely out of sight. Can this urbane attitude increase guests' affinity to a hotel and better their experiences? You decide.

3. **Rapid Response Staffers.** No matter the mess, the cleanup crew is there in a jiffy. Mind you, we're dealing with supernatural movie logic (witches on flying brooms and a horde of far-below-minimum-wage zombies), but the metaphor holds. Don't make your guests wait. If someone makes a request, treat your response time the same way firefighters and police officers react to their emergency calls—sirens and urgency.

4. **Choose Your Activities Wisely:** In a sequence geared to illustrate Dracula's mothering and antiquated obstinacy, he treats his guests to a soporific Bingo Night only to have them jump at the chance

43

to experience a live band or hang poolside. My thoughts exactly: some activities enhance the social atmosphere, others not so much. Develop programs that will play to what your guests want as well as what's most engaging and energizing.

5. **Exclusivity:** Dracula's property has a monopoly on the monster demographic and undoubtedly runs a ritzy occupancy rate. This feat isn't achieved solely through prudent channel distribution or shrewd marketing, but is intrinsic to the property's core purpose. By translation, what's your hotel's core purpose for existing? What makes your property undeniably unique for all who have come and gone? How will you carve your own niche?

LESSONS LEARNED FROM "DOWNTON ABBEY"

For those unfamiliar, Downton Abbey is a spectacularly produced period drama series set on the titular aristocratic estate just outside of London in the period in and around World War One. The story follows the Earl of Grantham family, the activities of the era and, importantly, the ample cadre of servants with their own explicit hierarchy. As hoteliers, this is a worthwhile show.

Setting aside any spoilers, my focus today is on the lessons learned which are applicable to our jobs even a century after the time period of this show. Without any further convincing or buttressing, let's dive in and see:

1. **Staff and guests do not mix, except in specific interactions.** It's not appropriate for members of your staff to have close relationships with any guests. This does not mean your team is barred from going out of their way to provide assistance, but never should they assume the role of equals. With the exception of senior staff or friendships outside of the work environment, guests should not be casually acquainted with staff. After all, the term 'guest service' implies that we take on a 'servant' role with our visitors. As an example, notice how awkward the staff acted when Tom Branson (played by Allan Leech), left alone for the evening, invites himself downstairs for dinner with the staff.

2. **Every staff member has a specific role to play.** In Downton Abbey, the head butler, Charles Carson (played by Jim Carter), serves as proxy to a general manager position, coordinating all other roles. He ensures that the property runs smoothly with an effective distribution of tasks amongst the team. He manages staff shortages through a realignment of responsibilities, ensuring at all times that proper protocol is maintained. Even amongst footman there is an order that makes for fluid service. As from a rather fun third season episode, notice how just a small deviation to this service order resulted in near total chaos.

3. **There is a lot a GM can learn from having dinner with his staff.** All your staff, not just the executive committee. Each episode in Downton Abbey typically includes a scene at the staff dining room where the butler resides as the patriarch. The flow of information provides the butler with valuable insights in addition to disseminating knowledge to the team—a two-way street. In modern day, a team is far too large to have everyone at the same table, so I encourage GMs to take a sampling of staff for lunch at least every four weeks.

4. **When the house is empty, it's an ideal time for maintenance.** Be flexible in your engineering and maintenance scheduling. Look at year-over-year figures and prudently take advantage of occupancy 'holes'. Further, maintenance shouldn't be compromised due to staff shortages. For an apt demonstration, look to when the Crawley Family departed on a trip to Scotland. The footman immediately thought this was an opportunity to slack off, until Charles Carson reminded them of how great an opportunity this was to clean the silver in bed chambers.

5. **Choosing the freshest of ingredients is vital.** There's no compromising your standards for the sake of costs. Several kitchen scenes in this series explicitly mention the selection of fresh foods over canned equivalents. (Recall in the final episode a discussion with the food purveyor on the difference between fresh and canned legumes and the cooks preference for fresh.) That was 95 years ago; the same applies today. Not only does fresh food taste better, but it has more vibrant colors, making it more appealing to the eyes.

6. **Breakfast is an essential part of every day.** And it's a great opportunity to plan the day for maximum productivity. In Downton Abbey, Charles Carson attends every breakfast with the Crawley family. He doesn't work, the footman do that. Rather, he uses this time to learn about what's happening, allowing him to anticipate needs and coordinate his staff accordingly. Sounds a lot like an executive planning committee meeting, only with wittier dialogue, fewer inconsequential metrics and better food.

7. **Additional guests mean more staff and more planning.** Don't forget that as occupancies rise, seasonally or via special events, staff complements have to be managed accordingly. They get it in Downton Abbey. Do you ensure that staff levels are organized to

balance the needs when the property is full or when major functions are in house?

8. **A female head of house is important for speaking to female staff.** Alas, there is only so much men can do to empathize with women outside of the spousal unit. A female touch is a necessity, both for exemplary leadership in the public realm and private chats. Notice how head housekeeper Mrs. Hughes (played by Phyllis Logan) is able to diffuse issues with the kitchen maids in a way that Charles Carson couldn't even begin to comprehend.

9. **Staff talk about everything.** They'll chitchat and gossip over the good, the bad and the ugly, and especially rumors regarding financial issues. Speculation on the decline of Downton Abbey due to the Grand Trunk Railway mis-adventures of the Earl not only put the estate at risk, but also had the entire staff abuzz. Speculation about finances (bankruptcy, change of owners, re-finance, etc.) within a hotel can be a death sentence for moral. Uncertainty can lead to premature departures and neglecting of duties. As a GM, your role is to ensure that this never becomes an issue, so don't let the rumor mill gain momentum!

10. **Remember that owners make the decisions.** It's their property. As a GM, or as the butler in the case of this show, you might not agree with a decision coming from the top, but ultimately, it's not your place to veto. Rather, your role is to execute the owners' agendas to the best of your abilities. Think of your hotel as a giant ocean bearing ship; the owner is the captain and the GM is the navigator. In this analogy, the owner sets the course while the GM finds the best route to get there, and the two are in constant communication to avoid crashing into icebergs.

"THE GREAT GATSBY": A RETURN TO ELEGANCE

If you didn't catch the latest theatrical iteration of "The Great Gatsby" (2013), be sure to pick it up once it hits the rental market. When you watch it, pay less attention to Leonardo Dicaprio (who plays F. Scott Fitzgerald's Jay Gatsby) or Cary Mulligan, his object of attraction. Rather, cast your eyes on the sheer opulence portrayed in the movie: the costumes, the sets and the food consumption. Note how retailers, from Brooks Brothers to Harrods, have adapted promotional opportunities tied into the movie's premium positioning. The world of Gatsby is one of total excess. Champagne pours like water, cars are only the finest, men wear tuxes, the women are dressed proverbially 'to the nines' and the party never stops.

Contrast this with a trip to a two-star Michelin-rated restaurant in Barcelona. There I was on a weekday night, the only one wearing a sports jacket. Looking around, I noted men wearing sweaters, sports shirts and blue jeans as well as women dressed in pretty much every level of apparel. In a restaurant where the tasting menu is well in excess of $200 (US) per person, if they can't get diners to get dressed up, then what hope does a more typical establishment have in getting customers to do the same? Or, does it really matter?

I know this rumination is a little bit old-fashioned. My hypothesis is that when guests dress up, their moods are elevated and the spending follows. For hoteliers, this should mean more revenue for your upper-tier F&B outlets. Dress codes may be a thing of the past, but they establish an unwritten baseline pertaining to guest expectations and ultimately how much patrons order. Perhaps you should consider giving your property a Gatsby-esque makeover and see how you fare. This is just a small thought to consider for your restaurant and lobby operations— what dress code do you promote at your establishment?

WHAT'S YOUR HOTEL MOVIE MOMENT?

Like many other North Americans, I've succumbed to the decades-in-the-making surge in television consumption. It's now all too easy to be enamored by the crisp, flowing images of a plasma or LCD monster with ear-popping surround sound on top of access to hundreds of cable channels and streaming portals like Netflix or Hulu. You can spend days eating away at program after program, all of arguably high entertainment value and worth the watch.

For me, my specific vices are movies and the occasional sports game. But very few shows ever get my full attention. It's only when I go to the theatre that I give it my all. Most of the time, the television is in the background as I blast out memos, emails and short essays on my laptop; multitasking at its finest.

So one night I'm burning the midnight oil while a rerun of the fan favorite "Scarface" (1983) plays out ten feet away. I had a eureka moment midway through the film when Al Pacino's eponymous character strategizes his next move while lounging on a terrace at the Fountainbleau in Miami Beach. Then it occurred to me, "Can having a portion of a popular or iconic film set in your hotel work to increase your brand appeal in the long run?"

At first glance, no. Or at the very least, the positive effect of this action would be immeasurable or nominal at best. But then I gave it some more thought with particular attention to the inspirational case above still wrapping up its second act onscreen.

Emotional Associations

The Fountainbleau has hit the silver screen many-a-times, notably in "Goldfinger" (1964), "The Bodyguard" (1992) and the opening example which has had remarkable syndication and garnered a definite 'cult' following amongst male Gen Xers and Millennials. Do these appearances 'legitimize' the property as beholding a certain brand mystique in a customer's mind?

There's little doubt that the Fountainbleau needed these movies to bolster its image. The building is stunningly colorful and easily memorable, two traits that producers and location scouts would factor into the mix when settling on where to film. On the surface, it looks to be the other way around: using the Fountainbleau legitimized "Scarface".

Picture yourself as a younger travel shopper, however, and perhaps such 'hotel cameos' could be leveraged to help win a few more bookings. Suppose the Fountainbleau posted the appropriate images from these popular movies under the accommodations or activities section of their website. A fan of any one of these films would instantly form a deep emotional connection. "Whoa! We could stay where Tony Montana stayed," they might say to themselves.

This association to the film can help bridge the gap to a future experience one might enjoy while on property. They liked "Scarface"; therefore they will like staying here. With every hotel in Miami available for cross-referencing at the click of a mouse, the fact that this 80s classic took place at the Fountainbleau becomes a unique, albeit very niche, emotional selling point. Perhaps it is enough of an 'X factor' to sway young travelers away from the plethora of cheaper options in the immediate vicinity.

Further Examples

This same argument could be applied for many other popular Hollywood film jaunts. For instance, the Plaza Hotel in New York City has played host to "North by Northwest" (1959), "Crocodile Dundee" (1986) and "Home Alone 2" (1992), three films that were well-received across a wide range of demographic and psychographic clusters.

Given its traditional, luxurious design, its location abutting Fifth Avenue and Central Park, and, above all, its commitment to outstanding service, yes, the Plaza Hotel would be successful without this trio of Hollywood cameos (not to mention the countless other appearances). But, would it be as successful? The pertinent analytics question is: Did the Plaza Hotel experience a spike in occupancy shortly after these three films reached blockbuster status?

Better yet, picture Las Vegas, a town where movie associations are pretty far down the list of travel considerations after conferences, desert warmth, shows, gambling and all things sin. But, all hotels have casinos, spas, shops, restaurants and bars—taken from a very macro point of view, they are all interchangeable. When selecting whichever hotel a guest might stay at on The Strip, movie associations might play an important but imperceptible role.

The remake of "Ocean's Eleven" (2001) prominently displayed the Bellagio's magnificent fountain, which is already a unique point of differentiation for the hotel. All established loyalty and promotions aside, people might choose the Bellagio over other luxury Las Vegas properties simply to have a front row seat for one of the town's best landmarks. Essentially, whenever the cathartic denouement fountain scene in "Ocean's Eleven" is on television, it's a flashing billboard for the Bellagio featuring the charismatic faces of George Clooney, Brad Pitt, Don Cheadle, Matt Damon et al.—so star-studded a scene it's near impossible not to rubberneck. Subliminally, it's convincing you to stay there.

Next, consider "The Hangover" (2009), which, apart from some shenanigans in Los Angeles and out in the desert, spent a good portion of its screen time at Caesar's Palace. As one of the highest grossing comedies of all time, it's safe to say that this movie touched a fair number of people, particularly those in the Gen X and Millennial bubbles. With all its raunchy jokes and laughs, recollecting "The Hangover" elicits happy emotions; feelings that might percolate through the brainwaves when a younger consumer is researching options for the next bachelor or bachelorette party on any given online hotel booking portal. It's a subtle push, but perhaps enough to sway a traveler towards Caesar's Palace over similarly-tiered properties along Las Vegas Boulevard.

Reaffirming a City's Best

Flying across the pond to Tokyo, we're struck with another unlikely contender in the breakout indie hit "Lost in Translation" (2003). Filmed on a shoestring budget and firmly embracing its arthouse oeuvre, the movie went on to earn over $100 million in tickets with further Oscar prestige and gangbuster rental sales. Looking back on it now, the film is still top of mind across a slew of disparate population groups. Lucky for the Park Hyatt Tokyo, over three-quarters of "Lost in Translation" takes place at their property. And in a similar but much more observable manner than the use of the Bellagio fountain, every syndicated run of this movie is a blaring promotion for the Hyatt that happens to feature Bill Murray and Scarlett Johansson.

Thinking in terms of wish fulfillment, Tokyo is unquestionably a premier travel destination, and I'd wager that many cosmopolitans have it on their bucket lists. Some may have already surfed through tourist attractions, neighborhoods, local cuisine, airfares and hotels. What's exceptional about this particular case is the premise of "Lost in Translation" which follows two Americans in their doldrums visiting the Japanese megacity for the first time, flawlessly intersecting with an enormous, likeminded travel cohort.

Given the movie's popularity, it has most certainly touched and continues to touch a fair number of people. Would this film singlehandedly convince someone to visit Tokyo? Probably not. But, by identifying with the characters on screen, viewers in turn identity with the Park Hyatt Tokyo and this will play a part when it's time to divulge credit card information to one hotel or another. Moreover, considering this is a five-star property, perhaps one's love of the film acts as a 'nudge' for them to splurge beyond their intended price range.

My suspicions here were all but confirmed by the presence of the 'Lost in Translation Experience' where guests at the Hyatt can relive all the best moments of the film spread over a comfortable five night stay. They've passionately espoused this indie hit and the hotel-film connection continues to propagate media attention. On a completely unrelated note, the Park Hyatt Tokyo repeatedly ranks as one of the best properties in the city. Exquisite services, décor and amenities notwithstanding, maybe "Lost in Translation" helps 'guide' critiques to this conclusion as well.

Transforming a Whole Country

And then there is the magnum opus of examples—"The Lord of the Rings" trilogy and "The Hobbit" trilogy. With stunning panoramic cinematography, New Zealand is undeniably Middle Earth, and tourism has spiked upwards by hundreds of millions of dollars to the nation's two main islands as a direct result of the popularity of these fantasy epics.

The whole country has adapted its hospitality approach with various tour groups and hotels catering specifically to the Middle Earth-trotting crowd. In fact, "The Lord of the Rings" is so important to the island nation that when New Line Cinema, the parent studio behind the franchise, threatened to outsource production on "The Hobbit" due to rising costs, Parliament stepped in to save the day with new tax incentives to help keep the movie shoot entirely in domestic hands. I'm sure the rationale for this was less about pride and more along the lines of 'spend more now, win big later', in addition to all the locally-generated jobs.

By kowtowing to the threats of Hollywood bigwigs, the government was firmly set towards long-term gains—millions, nay, billions in future hospitality revenues from avid travelers yearning to visit their favorite Middle Earth locales. Instead of throwing its marketing capital solely towards the creation of a distinct brand image for tourists somewhere along the lines of 'Visit New Zealand Today!', the government decided to also leverage an existing fan base towards its own interests.

Think of Your Property

If a film producer approached you about using your hotel for a shoot, would you jump at the chance? Again, a 'no' is perfectly logical. Even though you'd be paid for your troubles, you'd likely have to close shop for several weeks and the compensation would hardly match that accrued by occupied rooms or the disappointment of those unable to visit. And if you stayed open during the ordeal, you risk infuriating your guests with the disturbance.

But a 'yes' has some powerful advantages that you should at least consider before passing on the opportunity. Chief among them being that your hotel will be immortalized on film, and if the movie performs well at the box office or gains a 'cult' following, you might be reaping the rewards of this investment for decades to come. Mind you, there are a lot of ifs here, but it's not every day a movie studio comes knocking at your door.

Logically, the next question is: What would make Hollywood want to stop by? Distinctiveness in location, ambiance and décor. The sad fact is that 95% of hotels in the world won't make it past the first round. Remember that oftentimes it is more cost effective to film in a studio than on location. Thus, your exterior must offer irreplaceable vantage points and your interior must likewise give the story something that's unfeasible or cost disruptive to reproduce elsewhere. In all likelihood, they'd use your exterior and duplicate the interior.

What does this say about your façade and the impression your hotel bestows on the outside world? Does your property 'wow' guests with stunning views of the surrounding city or countryside? Is there something exceptional about the architecture to truly separate your property from the competition? Is your curb appeal movie worthy? These are definitely things to consider for your next marketing budget and renovation slate. And if your hotel has been fortunate enough to already play host to a film production, is this something that you are, or should be, broadcasting to the world? I say 'yes' in big, bold letters.

BRANDING

The iconic Fairmont Chateau Frontenac in Quebec City is one of the most photographed hotels in the world and its façade is a hallmark for the brand.

INTRODUCTION

The term 'branding' is tossed around quite liberally these days and I'm ambivalent towards this. On the one hand, it means that many people, and especially marketers, have grasped the power of what good branding can do for an organization's growth. Yet on the other hand, the true essence of branding is being diluted by those who misuse the word.

Branding is a lot of things. Branding is how the general public perceives your product. It's the reputation your organization has built over time so people trust you to deliver a quality product. Branding is what your product does to enrich someone's life or make it easier. In its simplest form, branding is a promise of all of the above.

When we talk about good branding, what we are implying is the perception of a quality product. But in a lot of ways, we are also talking about the advertising. That is, how memorable the marketing efforts are or the share of mind that a product has attained with the general public.

Branding within the hospitality industry is a peculiar case because it not only relates to the actual physical product (guestrooms, location and amenities) but also guest services—that is, the interactions between your staff and the hotel guests. It is my hope with this section to not only instill a proper sense of the term 'branding' but also to present how the notion of good branding for hotels is changing based on the evolving expectations of 21st century consumers.

CHOOSING HOTEL BRANDS IS DOMINATED BY EMOTION: PART I

A study conducted by Protean Strategies, partnering with the research firm Hotspex, has shown some very fascinating results as to how consumers engage major hotel brands, giving a fresh perspective on where to take your brand in the near future. Using Hotspex's proprietary MarketSpex™ methodology and a sample survey of 800 North American travelers, the researchers have found that choosing a hotel is dominated by emotional drivers (67% of the decision process)—such as connection, warmth, excitement and pleasure—over rational features and benefits (33%).

When it comes to the hotel landscape, how people feel is far more important than what they think—by a factor of two. Their study also showed that a hotel decision is more emotionally charged than for their comparison studies in choosing an airline, a beer or a smartphone. Moreover, the researchers found that the three most powerful hidden drivers of these emotional choices were excitement, surprise and acceptance, of which hotels are shown to have plenty of room for improvement.

A further derivation of the analysis distinguished eight major hotel chains by class with premium 'inspiring' brands (Hilton, Hyatt and Westin), middle tier 'competent' brands (Marriot, Sheraton and Wyndham) and discount 'familiar' brands (Best Western and Holiday Inn). The study identified what each class was doing right and where they can develop relative to the three chief drivers of emotional decision-making.

With the inspiring brands—that is, ones that already excite and amaze in a way akin to a rousing leader—gaining acceptance is the biggest challenge. For luxury hotels, there's not enough balance between the exhilarating aspects and the personal connection. As such, many brands come off as pretentious and arrogant. In other words, guests feel alienated and intimidated. If your property falls into this category, think about how you can bridge the gap between guests and your services, and ease people into your hotel experience.

For the competent brands, the problem appears to be a dominance of rationality. These middle-of-the-road hotels are perceived as hardworking, discerning and trustworthy. However, while the expectation holds that these brands are of quality value, they are coming off as unpleasant. There's a definite lack of emotional connectivity. They're perceived as generic without anything specific to distinguish each brand's experience. Additionally, more should be done to instill a sense of warmth to foster personal relationships with each hotel.

Familiar brands are almost a mirror image of the dilemmas faced by inspiring brands. Discount hotels relish in acceptance but lack excitement and consumer boredom sets in. The study finds that these brands need to add some flair and rethink how they deliver modern thrills. Such hotels need to be more active and bold in their presentation.

The main inference from this research relates to how you can differentiate your brand on an emotional level. Aside from familiarity, competence and inspiration, other key emotional contexts to lens a hotel through are fun, friendliness, interest, nurture and trustworthiness. As major brands, think about how you can excel in two or three of these categories, and as niche hotels, think about how you can become a leader in one particular stream. Moreover, as a major chain with multiple brands, how does each brand fit into and demarcate itself across one of these seven emotional niches.

Hotel brands are about feelings no matter which way you try and sell people on benefits and otherwise logical choices. Aim to make your décor, staff attitudes, amenities, features, website and advertising copy all congruent around one dominant and emotionally-charged theme. Like scraping butter over too much bread, instead of being mediocre in all seven attributes, strive to give a visitor a strong feeling in a single attribute so that you imbue them with one specific experience to remember you by.

CHOOSING HOTEL BRANDS IS DOMINATED BY EMOTION: PART II

In order to fully clarify some of the counterintuitive outcomes generated by the research at Protean Strategies, I approached Laurence Bernstein, a managing partner, to expatiate on how the study was performed and what hoteliers should be learning.

For those who haven't read the summary report, what were some of the key findings?

Three things stood out immediately. The first is the importance of emotional connection in choosing hotels. As hotel marketers we are so focused on rational differentiators and, lately, price and discounting, that we have forgotten about the emotional, or irrational, component, which the study indicates accounts for nearly 70% of the decision process. In a way, this highlights the commodity nature of the hotel functional experience and accounts for the fact that hotels have become price-driven commodities in many segments.

Secondly, the fact that hotel brands generally demonstrate such limited emotional ratings, less than 50% of the highest rating for a casual dining restaurant chain. For a category that is so heavily driven by emotion, this highlights a serious weakness, or, as we see it, a significant opportunity.

Third of note was the relative unimportance of some of the attributes that we would have thought made all the difference. For instance, the study shows that the relationship between a brand's performance on the attributes 'online rating and evaluations' and 'actual intent to visit' is really low. In fact, the study suggests that 'online ratings' fit into the 'unimportant' quadrant in terms of hotel brand choice. Yet, as an industry, we spend an inordinate amount of emotional energy and time (not to mention money) on trying to manage what people say about us online.

Generally speaking, how do emotions affect hotel brand perceptions?

Emotions drive choice and behavior. Perhaps not emotions in the traditional way we understand the term (love, hate, etc.), but rather unconscious attitudes and perceptions. This is increasingly borne out in studies of choice by economists, psychologists and neurologists. We make brand decisions before we are aware of the options then use our rational mind to execute the choice and, importantly, retroactively rationalize the purchasing decision.

As an example, let's say, for a number of reasons, I have a strong emotional attachment to Hilton. If I am faced with a menu of hotel options for a specific trip and Hilton is one of them, I will try to find reasons why staying at that hotel makes more sense than other hotels, even if it's more expensive, less conveniently located or has some negative ratings.

The problem arises when there is no possible way of justifying the choice. That is, the hotel is outrageously expensive relative to the other hotels, the reviews are so universally negative or it is just too complicated to make the reservation online. When this happens, not only will I stay at another choice, but my emotional connection to the brand will be hurt because I will feel like I had been let down or deserted by a good friend.

Without delving too much into proprietary details, how did you go about quantifying various emotional drivers of intent and brand perceptions?

Our research partner has developed a model based on, literally, hundreds of thousands of interviews. There are eight 'emotional regions', and each emotional region is defined by several hundred positive and negative attributes, including such terms as 'honest', 'interesting' and 'pretentious'. In surveys, we ask travelers to rate each hotel brand according to these attributes, and then, using the black box magic that guides all research, the brand's emotional strengths and weaknesses are plotted on a heat map.

How did you go about determining where hotel brands need to improve? How is this inferred from the research?

That's the $50,000 question. Using the maps we can see what the positive emotional attributes are and we can also see what the negative attributes are. The first stage is to see which negative attributes are the most important in terms of driving (or diverting) decisions.

We start by looking at the derived importance of each attribute; that is, the degree to which the attribute affects the choice of the brand. For instance, if the brand is seen as pretentious, and we see that being pretentious is a particularly strong turn-off for hospitality organizations, we try to understand what the brand can do operationally, experientially and in its communication to ameliorate this perception.

We would also compare the brand to the competition and see where there are strong positive attributes that the brand has and the competition does not. The idea would be to build a strategy that emphasizes these aspects in customer experiences and communications.

The report identified three broad emotional regions for hotel brands: inspiring, competent and familiar. What factors contributed to these delineations?

These are the three emotional regions that the brands came to inhabit based on the ratings given in the survey. Bear in mind that there are a total of eight emotional regions. So, the fact that the brands all fall into only three suggests that there are five emotional regions where hotel brands have substantial room to grow.

If two or more brands fall within the same strata, does this mean they are perceived as the same from a consumer's eyes?

Again, this is complicated. The short answer is 'probably', but it is nuanced. For instance, a brand that falls in the 'Competent' territory could be stronger in some of the positive attributes such as 'straightforward', 'reliable', 'accepting' and 'happy' while another might demonstrate some negative attributes such as 'impatient', 'miserly' and 'unfriendly'.

What emotional drivers are most important for guest satisfaction? Does this differ depending on regions occupied, or are there any all-encompassing traits?

Our study identifies the most important drivers for each category and also for each brand specifically. Generally speaking, making guests excited, amazed and feeling accepted are important emotional drivers. But, drivers are different for each brand depending on the unique make-up of preexisting emotional connections. However, there are strong similarities between brands based on which emotional region they occupy. There would also be strong differences between customer segments such as business versus leisure travelers.

The report identified certain brands as lacking emotional connectivity. What are the indicators of this and how can these issues be resolved?

In the case of one of the brands, respondents did not demonstrate any strong relationship attributes at all. On the other hand, they indicated quite strongly that they felt disconnected and that they couldn't relate to the brand. They were most positive about dry, functional attributes such as competence, but even this was offset by tone and manner. They felt the brand was pretentious and arrogant.

The prescription would be to evaluate the nature of the experiences and to understand why the emotional resonance was so dismal. Also, it's important to understand what experiences the target group would associate with various positive attributes, and then build a new brand experience based on those findings.

Can you explain the term 'Derived Importance'? How do you calculate this?

Derived Importance is a crucial part of the study. Because we look at unconscious emotional evaluations, we need to understand that people don't necessarily know why they do things or make choices. They may think at a rational level, for instance, that they choose a hotel brand because of price. But our study might show that in fact the statistical relationship between price and intent to stay is not all that strong. This would represent the derived importance of price.

On the other hand, as an example, the same person may not even mention 'feeling accepted' as a reason for choosing a brand. But in analyzing the data we find that there is a strong statistical relationship between 'feeling accepted' and intent to stay. In this case, the derived importance of 'feeling accepted' is strong. The study examines each attribute and identifies those that have the strongest statistical relationship—both positive and negative. For instance, being seen as 'pretentious' has a strong reciprocal relationship with intent to stay.

From a derived importance standpoint, simply satisfying guests isn't enough to elicit a future visit. What factors contribute the most to this?

This is interesting. Among the strongest determinants of whether a person 'intends to stay' are things like seeing the brand as passionate, modern, active and happy. Generally hotel brands do quite well on getting people interested, but they fall far short in amazing and exciting guests or being seen as passionate and happy. They do well on making guests feel satisfied, but that is not as important as some of the other attributes and is only one among many.

Your research also had some interesting findings related to how people choose hotels based on price, locations, recommendations and social media. What are the most important determinants here and are there any common misconceptions?

Using the derived importance numbers we look at the more functional attributes in terms of how they fit into the decision process. That is, are they key drivers that strongly influence choice at a conscious level; hidden drivers that strongly influence choice at an unconscious level; table stakes which are important but don't impact choice per se; or simply non-drivers which are just not important in the decision process for one reason or another?

What we found is that functional attributes such as location and price are important (key), while having high online ratings is simply not important. The strongest functional hidden driver (that is, the attribute that drives choice without the person being consciously aware of its importance) is the brand being recommended by friends or family. Attributes such as room design or even friendly service staff are important, but they don't really drive choice. These fit the bill for table stakes—you have to have them, but so does everybody else.

How does a manager go about translating emotional driver shortcomings into effective actions? Can you cite a specific example?

Many years ago at The Plaza in New York, guests felt the hotel was arrogant and pretentious. They did not feel connected and they did not feel the hotel wanted to relate to them. All this was true, in fact. New ownership wanted to change this and make guests feel more at home and comfortable. The problem was that the staff were not trained in relating to guests—they were trained to shrink away when the gentry was around and not be noticed. To turn this around, they needed to have the staff talk to the guests, and the manager understood he needed to provide a simple conversation starter that everybody would understand and be comfortable talking about.

The answer? Recommend the strawberries in the dining room. Whenever a staff member was in contact with a guest, he or she would ask, "Have you tried the strawberries?" The back story was that it was strawberry season and The Plaza had access to the best strawberries in America; a delicacy featured in all the restaurants and room service. The result was not only selling enormous amounts of strawberries in the restaurants, but guests came away with a very different sense of the hotel.

Are emotional drivers of choice changing over time? How is this emphasis on emotional states of mind influencing the future of travel and hospitality?

Neuroscientists are constantly trying to understand the nature of subconscious connections. There is much debate as to whether they are imprinted permanently at a very early age or whether they are constantly changing based on different life stages and external factors. What we surmise is that emotional attitudes and responses are probably different for different generations, but these differences might be more in how they are translated into action rather than the unconscious belief structure.

For instance, a 50 year old might see friendliness in the way a Ritz-Carlton Lady or Gentlemen says good morning, but a 25 year old may see arrogance in this action. On the other hand, the 25 year old might find the off-handed greeting at a W-Hotel to be friendliness personified, but a 50 year old would see it as nothing more than churlishness.

This underlines the importance of looking at this study in terms of the brand's specific market; in understanding who these people are and how they relate to the world around them. Applying this perspective to the learning from this study will enable hotels and brands to develop differentiated offers and create lasting relationships with their guests and the marketplace.

CLEAN THE ROOM OR OFFER A DISCOUNT

Housekeeping has always been a cornerstone of a guest's experience, but now it appears that hotels rendering opt-out exchanges may change the paradigm behind this integral service. Encompassed as a part of the buzz term 'decontenting', this particular entity is when guests are prompted at check-in to opt-out of daily housekeeping services with primary compensations including additional loyalty points, room discounts or F&B vouchers. Many independents and a few major brands, notably select Westin hotels, are already employing this alternative tactic.

Decontenting can pertain to much more than just housekeeping—bathroom amenities as another obvious occurrence, but also think basic cable, breakfasts, newspapers and even the comfort of meeting a person at check-in instead of completing this process via a mobile device. Ask yourself: at what point does a hotel stop being a hotel and become an a la carte service?

The biggest fear is that decontenting will act as a preceding action towards drip pricing accounting models; gradually removing all the content from the product then adding surcharges for their reintegration into the hotel experience. Drip pricing has been widely shown to frustrate travelers and ultimately discourage brand loyalty. You need only look to the airlines as a cross-example of this effect. But decontenting does not directly lead towards chagrin-inducing, opt-in drip pricing. It's a precursor built around the choice to opt-out.

This leaves plenty of wiggle room to argue the merits of decontenting on a case-by-case basis, especially given the spectrum of hotel brands across different price points. Housekeeping is one of the most sensitive cases given the potential for massive labor cost reductions. To help settle this debate, it's handy to know a shrewd marketing and branding researcher already tackling the matter, and that's precisely where I stand with Laurence Bernstein, a managing partner at Protean Strategies (www.proteanstrategies.com).

From a study conducted earlier this year amongst a representative sample of 320 US business and leisure travelers covering the gamut of budget, five-star, boutique and lifestyle hotels, there were many definitive conclusions. First of note is that 24% of business travelers and

13% of leisure travelers have been offered this alternative at some point in the past. This tells us that this topic isn't anything revolutionary, for both hoteliers and for the consumer at large.

Significantly, almost 80% of respondents were willing to barter for the daily cleaning, although sensitivities varied tremendously across all key variables such as hotel type (no frills, luxury etc.), travel purpose (solo business, couples leisure etc.), type of compensation offered (ADR reductions, F&B coupons or loyalty points) and amount given as actual compensation.

Nearly one in three said they definitely would forfeit having their room cleaned everyday in exchange for $10 off the ADR. This number jumps to 45% when the reimbursement is swapped to 1,000 extra loyalty points. When you add together the 'probably would' responses, the affirmative percentages for both of these incentives roughly doubled (71% and 79% respectively). However, when the reward was listed at 250 points, only about one in ten said they'd definitely bite.

The least motivating reimbursement concerned F&B discounts, attributed to the fact that many participants likely don't use a hotel's restaurants or bars when traveling. Outside of extra loyalty points, there also appears to be some stark elasticity in ADR and F&B incentives. A $5 room rate markdown only prompted 42% of both the 'definitely would' and 'probably would' categories. Applied to F&B, that $5 only elicited a combined 38% affirmation from those surveyed. Thinking in general terms, roughly 50% of guests are highly inclined towards this tidiness tradeoff, with loyalty points valued most followed by room discounts, and then lastly by F&B vouchers.

Supplementary questions gave further insights about the declining respondents. Two popular answers were that they weren't involved in the points program, rendering loyalty rewards worthless, and that they were on an expense account, bestowing no personally actualized benefits to monetary discounts. In addition, of those unwilling to consider the housekeeping opt-out, 54% of those surveyed believed that the rooms required daily cleaning and most of the remainder believed that the counteroffers simply weren't high enough.

Of particular importance was the phrasing of the offer, although this didn't necessarily parallel the underlying reasons for accepting the exchange. It's currently de rigueur to wrap daily cleaning substitutions in a pro-environmental envelope, but only 20% of those surveyed accepted on these grounds, the rest came from those seeing the inherent value in the reward.

Regardless of whether they took the offer, the delivery affected how travelers perceived the hotel. One in two of those surveyed felt better about the property because they believed that the hotel was more environmentally conscious; that the rooms pragmatically didn't need daily cleaning; that the cost savings were being passed onto the consumer; that merely having the option was a plus; or that it was just nice of them to ask.

Contrarily, describing the offer in the wrong way can alienate guests. Around 11% of respondents cited this form of decontenting was a vessel to improperly cut corners or a blatant suspect of greenwashing, while 39% were unaffected either way.

Taken purely by the numbers, the overall percentages speak in favor of making this alternative available to guests. Contextually, opt-out services are far more lucrative to those staying at budget properties versus luxury hotels. Business travelers were less likely to eschew the daily maid over their leisure counterparts with double digit spikes in disapproval ratings for both of these broad groupings as the jump was made from economy and three-star to luxury and boutique classifications.

After all, if you're paying upwards of $500 a night, striking $10 off is hardly worth the trouble. However, that same deduction from a $75 ADR is a dramatically greater consideration. This excludes the potential amongst luxury travelers for a hotel to appear as 'cheap' by proffering this exchange. Clearly, decontenting isn't for the affluent.

It comes down to housekeeping and cleanliness as a part of the overall experience and interaction with the brand. By removing amenities, you are removing physical points of interaction and thus, dehumanizing the hotel. Treating services with an a la carte approach means that guests are less prone to discover the fascinating nuances of your full experience—for instance, a special note and chocolate left on the bed with turndown service. You'll never have the chance to sweep your guests away and give them the fulfilling stay they truly desire.

As a more transparent comparison, think of an upscale sushi restaurant. Does such an eatery rise in acclaim for its a la carte sashimi menu or for the savory rolls that only the chefs know how to make? When a friend recommends a new sushi joint, are they more likely to laud the individual nigiri pieces or the special in-house creations? Keep an ear up the next time someone describes a restaurant and note what they fixate on as the distinguishing factor.

I agree wholeheartedly with Mr. Bernstein's dire warning that too much decontenting will commoditize the hospitality industry into something far similar to that of the airlines, and consequently, a far less profitable beast. Housekeeping opt-outs may be logical for budget hotels as their average guest is more price sensitive and hence receptive to these tradeoffs. But as you ascend the ladder, differentiated service becomes a key impediment to commoditization and driver for long-term growth.

DO LOYALTY PROGRAMS ACTUALLY HELP YOUR BRAND?

I've long held the belief that too many major hospitality brands and too many big names operating in the hotel space can seriously confuse travelers. As a result, this leads to less overall awareness of your brand's unique qualities and, ultimately, decreasing loyalty. By itself this is a very loose argument. However, a study spearheaded, Laurence Bernstein, managing partner at Protean Hospitality Partners, has confirmed this sentiment.

For this study, 400 US business travelers participated in an online survey asking them to associate 36 hotel brands not containing the name of their parent chain with one of the following seven loyalty programs: Choice Privileges, Hilton Honors, Hyatt Gold Passport, Marriott Rewards, Priority Club, Starwood Preferred Guest (SPG) or Wyndham Rewards.

Results That May Surprise You

On average, only 20% of the ensuing pairings were correct. Moreover, participants had the option to tick a 'Don't Know' box for each of the 36 hotel brand prompts, of which this selection was made 52% of the time. Either way, this indicates that knowledge of loyalty programs associated with various brands is drastically below where it should be.

Drilling down to the individual percentages, there are some standouts worth noting. Courtyard, when presented independent of its 'By Marriott' namesake, was correctly identified 65% of the time as part of the Marriott Rewards program—the best percentage of the lot. Other victories include Comfort Inn (41%) and Quality Inn (36%) for Choice Hotels; Garden Inn (37%) and Hampton Inn (30%) for Hilton Worldwide; Residence Inn (35%) for Marriott; Holiday Inn (33%) for InterContinental Hotels Group; and Sheraton (31%) for Starwood Hotels.

All other correct matches were in the twenties, the teens and, in three instances, single digits. In several cases, an erroneous loyalty program was identified more frequently than the correct one, most notably for Days Inn (Choice Privileges: 27%, Wyndham Rewards: 11%) and W Hotels (Wyndham Rewards: 25%, SPG: 12%).

Two other participant characteristics measured were annual household income (above or below $100,000 US) as well as preexisting membership in one of these seven loyalty programs. For the former, greater income resulted in better brand knowledge, with correct associations increasing by as much as 14.8% for Hilton Honors (41% overall) and as low as 2.4% for Wyndham Rewards (13.6% overall).

Affiliation also helped awareness. For instance, when asking SPG members in the study which of Aloft, Four Points, Le Meridien, Sheraton, St. Regis, W Hotels and Westin were associated with the SPG rewards program, 39.9% of answers were correct as opposed to 17% when including all participants. This upward trend was present for all seven loyalty programs, though SPG showed the largest increase. Awareness for most affiliated brands also increased with membership in multiple programs.

Consumers Need Education to Increase Loyalty Program Awareness

These low percentages indicate that the majority of business travelers have limited awareness of loyalty programs and, by extension, their corresponding brands. As awareness is a key towards long-term loyalty, and ultimately bookings, this is a grave problem.

Loyalty programs aren't sufficiently educating consumers about their brand families and partner benefits. True, a part of some strategies may be to wholly distinguish a brand from the parent chain—my thoughts here lean towards luxury like Conrad, St. Regis, W Hotels and Westin—but with so many hotel names for a consumer to remember nowadays (in addition to the umpteen other products and trademarks vying for their attention), this tactic might spell disaster in the long run.

Courtyard offers a clear example for how brands can improve. All Courtyard properties' official logos are adjoined with 'Marriott' or 'By Marriott' directly underneath. Hence, every time you encounter the Courtyard logo, it's impossible to ignore the chain association. This tacit knowledge transfer helps explain Courtyard's impressive brand-loyalty program matching score, even without factoring in all the targeted marketing and brand positioning work that Marriott has performed over the decades to build this reputation.

This is hardly a revolutionary thought though. It's 'Hilton Garden Inn', not 'Garden Inn', even though the survey used the latter to better gauge realized familiarity. Likewise, the official nomenclature is 'DoubleTree by Hilton' instead of 'DoubleTree', 'Holiday Inn Express' versus simply 'Express Hotel' or 'Four Points by Sheraton' despite the colloquial abbreviation to just 'Four Points'. But what about, for example, Ritz-Carlton and its vassalage to Marriott? Not very intuitive, even though in this particular case that might be intentional.

I'm not suggesting that multinational organizations perform a company-wide logo alteration to better imitate Courtyard's cognitive success in this study. 'Ritz-Carlton by Marriott' doesn't exactly roll off the tongue. Rather, information on parent chains and sister brands should be conveyed through website copy (across multiple pages and via blog articles) in addition to well-placed hyperlinks, newsletters, brochures and even onsite awareness events. A loyalty program, and the ability to apply points to one family brand or another, can be one of a chain's biggest strengths, but only if consumers are informed on the scope of this benefit.

A corollary proposition would be that, instead of rebranding the hotel chains, we change the names of the loyalty programs. Take W Hotels, for example. Its falsely high association with Wyndham Rewards (as opposed to Starwood) may well be due to the simple fact that the hotel brand shares the same first letter with Wyndham. Rather than try to sign up W Hotel guests to SPG, give them a W Hotel rewards card and take the time to explain to them about all the other hotel brands where it might apply. This way, the W Hotel brand is emphasized as a stepping stone towards other Starwood franchises. In this case, similar branded rewards cards would be employed for Aloft, Sheraton, Le Meridien, Westin and St. Regis.

As Laurence puts it, there's also the factor of 'loyalty vulnerability'. That is, members of one loyalty program having roughly equal awareness for both their existing affiliation as well as that of direct competitors, making such consumers more prone to defection. An inference from this is that such programs are relying too heavily on consumers to 'discover for their own' each brand family rather than broadcasting details straight from the company and cajoling them towards a desired course of action. This might also imply that, on top of the need for more direct education, loyalty programs aren't doing enough to differentiate themselves from one other.

A Note for the Independents

Even though this study only comprised seven major hotel chains and their sub-brands, there are nonetheless a few key inferences that can be applied to independent or small chain operators.

With decreasing awareness of loyalty programs comes less consumer attachment to specific brands. Knowing this, you might find it advantageous to promote your independent or semi-independent status as part of a broader campaign to present your hotel as a 'unique experience' and to distinguish it from local competition.

Furthermore, if loyalty programs are in the druthers as this study indicates, do you really want to board a sinking ship? While this study did not test any of the loyalty programs that are offered for independents, I am somewhat skeptical that the results would be any better. The loyalty programs tested in this study were all 'big names'. If the major chains with their extensive capital support are unable to generate reasonable levels of customer awareness, then how well could those with more limited resources possibly fare?

The Bottom Line

The results from this study are simple: business travelers don't know a whole lot about the major loyalty programs or where they apply. Apathy rules the day. Without any substantial awareness precedence, how can a symbiotic relationship between a brand and its soon-to-be-loyal consumers properly develop?

Moreover, this study was exclusive for business guests—those already primed towards loyalty programs for various reasons such as corporate plans and repeat trips to the same cities. The analysis doesn't even begin to breach discussions of the leisure market, the mixed traveler or even the loyalty-dilutive effects of the OTAs and the general attention deficit disorder nature of our internet-crazed society.

As I got my start and continue to earn a living as a hospitality marketer, I'm inclined to believe that the solution lies in advertising—in other words, supporting the brands by vastly augmenting the communication channels with the customer. Where have all the hotel television ads gone? Why not talk about your loyalty program on the radio? Some colorful yet descriptive magazine spreads can help reach a few niche markets. How about designing a custom plugin for your Facebook fan page dedicated to elaborating on the merits of your loyalty program? Any way you put it, brands need to get the message across about their loyalty programs, and they need to do it loud and clear in order to break through the noise.

THE MOORE'S LAW OF DEMOGRAPHICS

It's often said that a key problem we face in today's labor market is not a lack of job opportunities, but a paucity of candidates with the prerequisite skills. Wrapping this sentiment around the prospects of hiring and training someone from the Millennial generation, I add that there's a scarcity of potential employees with the necessary motivation and passion to succeed at a given position. After all, if someone is properly motivated, they'll put in the effort to learn and exceed the base skill requirements.

I would even go so far as to describe the Millennials as the next 'Lost Generation', sharing many of the same characteristics as the boisterous, tawdry youth of the 1920s. With the internet and countless forms of wireless communication at their disposal, Millennials have every opportunity in the world available to them on top of a life largely free from many of the rigors, diseases, wars, crimes and menial daily chores which have all plagued past generations. And yet the Millennials are lost. Plenty of options and the freedom of manifold choices can often be a surefire means to abject indecision.

With uncertainty, apathy and entitlement as an everyday occurrence, managers with a true passion for hospitality might find themselves unhinged by the archetypical outlooks of this latest bolus of workers. Why bother devoting your resources to a youth who isn't willing to reciprocate in full? Why bother training Millennials whose only purpose at the hotel is to fill the void in their wallets until something better comes along? Rest assured, this is a sweeping issue for which our fair industry is but one spoke on the perpetual wheel of time.

Much like any other corporate enterprise, hospitality organizations need intrapreneurs—those employees with the passion and gumption to go beyond the perfunctory daily grind and innovate for the future. Essentially, they are entrepreneurs without the whole 'leave and start up on my own' approach. The intrapreneurial torch must inevitably be passed on to the Millennials if we are to survive in these ever-turbulent economical waters.

Ergo, the question remains: how do you inspire Millennials to become the next generation of hospitality leaders and motivated team members, especially when there are so many other opportunities and distractions just mouse clicks away?

Inspire Through Empathy

One of the fascinating trends of the 20th century was how different each generation experienced the world relative to their parents. Baby Boomers, Gen X, Gen Y, the Lost Generation, the Greatest Generation—just a few of the terms coined to describe our psychographic shifts through time, largely bound by the major events taught in a fifth grade history class—two World Wars, the Cold War, the Great Depression and so on—as well as punctuated technological advances.

Put yourself in the shoes of an individual growing up after such developments have already occurred. Most boomers never knew a world before the advent of the nuclear bomb, yet they experienced the rise of rock and roll and the space race in a way different from every other population group. Gen X saw the rise of the color television and its gradual creep into every household to the point where now we take for granted the accessibly of our crisp, flat plasma screens. You can even look back further to the 1920s with the advent of such everyday items like the radio, telephone or refrigerator or even to some of the earth-shattering events of the 1960s like JFK's assassination, the Civil Rights Movement and the Vietnam War.

In order to select the best candidates and nurture the best employees from the enormity of the Millennial, and the soon-to-be Gen Z, job applicants, you must first understand their unique perspective on events from the 1990s onward. With the dissolution of the Soviet Union in 1991, no subsequent child or adolescent would ever mature in a world threatened by the outbreak of global nuclear war. True, this peril never even reached full-on paranoia for Gen X and the end of Soviet communism gave rise to a myriad of rogue states with access to highly potent armaments, but nonetheless, as of 1991, the concept of mutually assured destruction was gone.

Then came the internet, email, laptops, DVDs and a host of other monumental gadgets. To inspire the Millennials is to first understand that they live in a world of unlimited possibilities. Science fiction is no longer a parable for an alternate, fantastical universe, but rather the herald of the very near and very real future.

Surrounding all these technological leaps, it's vital to consider not just their impacts, but the rapidity with which they have permeated our daily habits. Simply compare how slow the growth of television was to that of the smartphone. One took decades, the other took years, and with the power of the internet, many trends or concepts now only take months or days to disseminate worldwide and find endorsement from hundreds of millions of people.

For Millennials, life at a mile-a-second is normal. Alongside the belief in ongoing future advancements is one that corporate and personal changes can also occur at breakneck speeds. However lackadaisical or vainglorious this attitude may appear, it's your job as mentors to be empathetic, then slowly but surely, convert such neophytes to the tried-and-true methodology of earnest hard work and prudent, calculated actions. The turtle wins the race after all, not the hare.

Consider Moore's Law

Moore's Law fluently describes an exponential progression of our current advancements by stating that our technological prowess doubles every 18 months. Granting it some leniency, we'll say every two years. This theory is firmly set in fixed, easily transcribed events in time such as the introduction of a powerful new microchip or the launch date of a new smartphone. Given the omnipresent upheaval of many of these dog-eared inventions on the social routines of people in the Western World, a concomitant conclusion is to wonder whether Moore's Law applies to generational divides.

Drawing from familial experience, I'm constantly reminded of my son's journey through college. Born in 1985 on the cusp of the Millennial changeover, he reached university by 2003. By his sophomore year, Facebook was introduced; a novelty at first, but spreading like wildfire throughout his junior and senior years. He was thus at a unique age to experience college life both pre- and post-Facebook as well as the rise of a new online social order usurping so many aspects of 20th century life.

Compare this to a person born in 1987, a mere two years later, who, within months of his or her freshman year, would already be accustomed to Facebook's personal profile, media sharing and event planning utilities. Likewise for a teenager entering this earth in 1989 and college in 2007, Facebook in addition to Twitter, YouTube and LinkedIn were all already table words amongst students as well as their parents. A 1989 baby was also highly more likely to own a cell phone in high school than a 1985 newborn, significantly bifurcating their opinions on proper communication discourse. Ditto for plasma televisions which slid in price formidably during the mid-2000s, changing perceptions on the overall utility of such devices as well as room design. These are but a few contrasts.

From 1985 to 1989; four years apart, yet the first two decades of a person's life in each of these years have scores of enormous social differences. Just as Moore's Law defines technological change on a two year period, maybe we should view generations in the same light. When we think of the word 'generation' we're more prone to conjure images of a vast span of time rather than anything approaching a half-decade cycle, even if this may now be the present reality.

If you are to accommodate and foster successful Millennial intrapreneurs, you must redefine how you approach 21st century generational gaps. Perhaps the term 'Millennial' is itself invalid because it is too broad a cluster to accurately assign behavioral and cultural generalizations. Technology improves at a breakneck pace and so do our generations, or at least the frames of mind that such youngsters adopt these days.

Now Consider Millennials in Their Twenties

Perhaps instead of attempting to anthropomorphically cleave the Millennial generation into the 'Proto-Millennials', 'Middle Millennials' or 'Latent Millennials', we should instead emphatically focus on an individual's exact age. Nielsen, the prominent and trusted surveying company, has it wrong. Sorry, but you can't stick to a rigid 18 to 49 age definition for your prime consumer snack bracket. There are simply too many existential changes that occur during this vast stretch of adulthood, especially nowadays where 'life begins at 20'.

If you can permit my loose insinuation that Moore's Law has a profound effect on modern demographic and psychographic classification that I put forward in the last section, then perhaps you'll also agree that a 22-year-old Millennial bares very little resemblance to the 44-year-old Gen Xer, even if over 99% of their DNA is the same. Contextually, I wouldn't even be inclined to group a present day 27-year-old with a 22-year-old. Both are technically Millennials, but given their differing stages in careers, maturity and exposures to the rolling launches of ever-newer gadgets and gizmos, their experiences and perspectives on life are widely dissimilar.

Thus, when an interviewee enters your office or a résumé lands on your desk, the first detail you must dissect is the candidate's age. A single year one either way may have a profound impact on everything thereafter—what questions you ask in the interview, who you choose to hire, how you welcome such a person to your organization, what tasks you assign and so forth.

My hope for you is to find eager job applicants, and then convert that youthful vitality into passion for your organization's goals and growth. What I don't want is for you to hire someone only to have them leave within three to six months. Nor do I want you to attract those people who view your property as a 'job' instead of a worthwhile career.

As defined below, how you approach each age subcategory will greatly alter such candidates' likelihood of staying on and developing with you as highly productive employees. I've kept the naming of these age ranges as bland as possible so you can assign your own flowery monikers, but also so your actions are directly implied from said names.

- *Early College*, ages 18-19: Vague idea of career path and chosen field of expertise, seeking internships to rule out job possibilities, developing internal values and passions
- *Late College*, ages 20-21: Refining idea of career path and narrowing field of expertise, seeking internships to help decide on career path, still forming values and passions
- *Early Post-College*, ages 22-24: Considering post-secondary education and choosing first serious job, may or may not be wholly assured of chosen career path, passions and broader life goals starting to coalesce
- *Late Post-College*, ages 25-27: Post-secondary education underway or complete, has moved on to second serious job or found happiness with first, the routines of a working lifestyle are firmly in place

- *Early Career*, ages 28-30: Dedicated to a chosen career path which is in line with passions and life goals as provided either by present job or through new employment

Again, this is a loose illustration as there are those who have crystallized their life goals at the outset of high school while others drift until their late thirties. Every person is different, but from this overview, what should, at the very least, be self-evident is the tendency for Millennials, more so than any previous generation, to only devote themselves to a career later on in life. When opportunities abound, it's indeed hard for someone to make a decision that will ricochet through all the years to come. But a decision will eventually be reached.

From a mentor's perspective, your expectations should be immensely different for an Early College and an Early Career individual. I would expect such an Early Career or Late Post-College applicant to know specifically what they want in a job, what they hope to learn, what their strengths and weaknesses are, and where they see themselves in five years. The objective is to determine whether a starting job in hospitality will be the beginning of a flourishing career or just a pastime until another lure tugs them away.

Standard interview stuff really, but this needs modification for Early College and Late College archetypes. Here, you're dealing with younger minds that happen to have a proclivity for hospitality but no specific idea of where they belong within the organization. Are they natural marketers or more prone towards salesmanship? It's your responsibility to help these uncertain youth find their way, be it through internship, co-op, part-time or full-time employment. Give them a flavor of various aspects of your operations and take on a close tutoring relationship to fully guide their aspirations in a mutually beneficial direction.

From Twixter to Leader

Another 'word of the week' for you: a twixter is someone who is twixt, caught between adolescence and the true independence of adulthood. Does this definition remind you of anyone? When discussing the stereotypes of the Millennial generation, this word may now seem more appropriate than ever before. However true it may be, every twixter is simply a tanker of potential energy waiting—yearning—to be put to good use.

Having to play babysitter to a twentysomething may seem like an overbearing workload, but try to turn this negative into a positive. Personally, I take comfort in the platitude that 'life begins at 20' as it means I'm still working with impressionable minds where bad habits haven't already implanted themselves. Millennials understand that the world and the future are at their doorstep. With your helping hand, they might just step through into adulthood and into a job or career they truly love. As for whether Moore's Law actually does apply to our modern definition of generations, this is but food for thought.

APPLYING 'NO-FRILLS CHIC' TO YOUR BRAND

As a frequent flyer living in Toronto, the city's Pearson International Airport is a routine commute. One of the newer additions to the vicinity's landscape has been the ALT Hotel, logo brightly illuminated atop his modest rectangular rise. Passing this structure on my return drive home via the airport expressway is a constant reminder of this emerging brand and my thoughts on how the hospitality industry will segue from the prowess of baby boomer businesspeople to the millennial traveler.

No-Frills Chic

The ALT Hotel brand is a part of a new niche that also includes such soon-to-be-household names like Citizen M, easyHotel, Pod Hotel and Yotel. Catering almost exclusively to the aptly-dubbed 'No-Frills Chic' audience, these brands focus on delivering minimalist product with several near universally-appealing services and all for a very competitive rate.

These no-frills brands appear to have sharpened their allure around the few top-of-mind features that matter to young, independent travelers—comfortable beds, quiet rooms, good lighting, a small workspace and free WiFi. Everything else is extraneous. The rapid proliferation of these newer brands within an overall forecast that we've long considered stagnant proves that there is indeed a market for these stripped-back accommodations, and that less really is more.

There are other doodads these hotels incorporate to better differentiate their brands within the budget caste. Limited, multipurpose, ergonomic furniture keeps the 200 to 300 square foot rooms from inducing claustrophobia. Self check-in and check-out are mainstays, further expediting mobility. Additive services are regularly 24-hour offerings, such as the common area lounges and cafés with their rolling fresh food selections or a gym at an ALT Hotel property. Lastly, drip pricing is a familiar practice; start with only the most elemental features to qualify as a 'night's stay' then trickle in everything else a la carte.

Understanding the Modern Traveler

This genre of hotels has flourished in large part due to their strict targeting of several core demographics and psychographics lionized as the 'Modern Consumer'—young, smart, thrifty and electronically fluent. Let's brush over some of the basics.

Young travelers have manifold choices to select precisely where they will stay. Oftentimes, given income constraints, price is the key determinant, and with inexhaustible online resources, it isn't hard to be scrupulous. By eliminating features to substantially lower the price tag, these hotels streamline the decision on two fronts to further motivate bookings; cheaper rates are easily apparent in any cross-comparison and fewer features simplify this mental balance act.

Apart from being self-sufficient, internet-savvy researchers, this cluster also spends far less physical time in their rooms (an exception being crunch-time computer work). Much like their smartphones, laptops and tablets, these travelers truly are mobile. With 3G/4G services and public WiFi carriers aplenty, the modern traveler has everything they need to stay out and about until the eyelids cave.

And why wouldn't they? When you visit a foreign city, do you remember the city first or the hotel first? No-frills hotels aren't fashioned to be resort-style, fit-for-lifelong-memories locales. They serve a function—give guests some shuteye—and they execute it to a tee.

The entire conceit of the capsule hotel (Pod Hotel a notable provider) is that the guestroom- or guest-closet as a more appropriate classification—is designed for sleep and not lavish vacationing, entertaining, introspective soul-seeking or pampered rejuvenation. You sleep, you wake, you get ready, and then you hit the road. In Tokyo, where capsule hotels have long made their mark, it isn't uncommon for a weary worker burning the midnight oil to rent such a room instead of journeying all the way home. Capsule hotels are typically far closer to the office, and for the convenience of purging the commute times, they are well worth the price.

This raises another important issue: the dissolution of nine-to-five work hours. With email accessible everywhere along with tools like video conferencing and cloud-based group workflows, the modern employee or entrepreneur can fulfill their duties anytime and anywhere. And indeed, if you want to make it in this digital world, you better be ready to do just that!

The notion of leaving work at the office is gone. There are more people working from home, working long, erratic hours and working from their hotel rooms (with variable flight times as a central adjunct to this). This irregularity accumulates, demanding a readjustment of the service industry still in sync with the nine-to-five doctrine. Stores are open later, banks are open earlier and hotels must follow suit. Heed the adage 'Go where your customers are' and you'll quickly realize that sticking to the outdated system of limited hours of operation won't earn you any bankable word-of-mouth. In a world that never sleeps, the 24-hour hotel is king.

More Notes on the No-Frills Chic Success Story

To state the obvious, the binding force of all these progressions is the internet. It's an essential service and providing it for free is a cardinal tenet of the modern traveler, both for business and leisure. These contemporary brands thrive in large part from their simplicity—one easy bill that includes WiFi with no surcharges.

I've harangued on the free WiFi issue at length in the past. So, without digressing too far into this, let me just say: the modern traveler doesn't care about your rationale for charging; all they see is a big, separate bill for internet connectivity and it frustrates them, sometimes enough to deter a return visit. Not offering free WiFi is a great tactic for disenfranchising the next generation of consumers. No-frills means no hassle. And this straightforward approach translates to many other important considerations—too much clutter in the rooms, in-room amenities that add cost and aren't vital, and property amenities that are habitually underutilized.

Mind you, we are really talking economy class and consumer behavior changes dramatically as we move up the stratosphere. No-frills chic hotels get by primarily on their price and the services they deem as indispensable, therein drawing a certain type of traveler—commuters, layovers, transient workers, young urban tourists, backpackers and anyone who just needs a quick snooze. For these traveler archetypes, hotels are commodities with situational convenience and competitive rate trumping loyalty to any one chain in particular. Luxury is a different ball game all together.

The common undertones of no-frills brands also serve to reinforce the statement that a hotel's unique expression of service is rapidly becoming the sole factor of brand differentiation. Able to carve out a healthy base of customers from a crowded space of budget accommodations, brands in this contemporary subclass are obviously highly conscious of their core appeal. Their strategy is wholly geared around what features contribute the most towards increasing occupancy within a firmly defined consumer mentality. The proliferation of boutique hotels follows the same paradigm but with completely different strategies and tactics.

No-frills chic is not without its drawbacks. Self check-in and check-out are fundamental points of human interaction from guest to staff. Psychologically speaking, their absence removes a critical point of 'brand imprinting' on the consumer as well as an opportunity to promote amenities, alleviate concerns or garner feedback. The sparse décor also operates in much the same way; nothing in the clinical furnishings to elicit a strong emotional response. Ditto for the stark lobbies; grand first impressions aren't likely nor are they a company priority. Contextually, these are all conscious tradeoffs to keep prices down and fit the needs of their target market.

Now Think of Your Hotel

What's your core appeal? What's your primary demographic? Really narrow it down. If it's harried business travelers and sightseeing tourists between the ages of 18 and 30, you're in for an uphill battle as these no-frills chic abodes have already plucked some prime real estate and packed each location with enough sardine-sized rooms so that the low-cost, high-occupancy model is actually viable. However, there are dozens of other theatres of war waiting for a revamp that better appeals to the modern traveler.

For application beyond economy hotels, disregard the 'no-frills' but keep the 'chic'. The minimalist approach to furniture can be hybridized to more luxurious accommodations. For instance, a room's workspace might include an extra monitor and a portable keyboard, both readily attachable to an incoming guest's laptop, or even a standing desk. Also, what amenities can you convert into 24-hour offerings? Do you have any truly outstanding features that singlehandedly command attention, like an avant garde spa, a foodie-raved restaurant, a rapid-response social media team, a rooftop bar with a view or a thoroughly resourceful concierge mobile app? If you're lost, then spend a night at one of the abovementioned properties to feel firsthand what they are doing to earn their esteem and what you can adapt.

With the deepening diversity of choices within the hotel space, there are two general actions that stretch beyond any individual market segment.

1. *Continually refine and pinpoint your target consumers.* What's the purpose of your guests' stay and what are their basic expectations from a hotel? What type of guest is your property destined to accommodate? How can your hotel better fit this objective? How is this predefined consumer different from those of your competitor set?

2. *What works for them may not work for you.* If your awareness and loyalty hinge on the quality of services you provide, then simply imitating your competitors isn't enough. This isn't a shotgun approach. Be very selective about what services you offer, scouring a multitude of providers to see what unique points of differentiation they add to these services. Through all the permutations, your goal is to select only the services that work for your guests and perform them to perfection.

HUMANIZING CUSTOMER PURCHASES
AND BRAND IDENTITY

Apple Inc. is big. It's easy to look at such a massive corporate brand and say, "We should be more like them!" Correct, yes, but naïve. After all, what can Apple, a cutting-edge phone and computer company, possibly offer to hotels?

As it turns out, quite a bit. Apple's stores are ergonomically designed to maximize human interaction. The Apple 'geniuses' all wear bright blue and easily-identifiable t-shirts. But that's nothing compared to the furniture orientation. Dominating the front are large and inviting tables with a sparse arrangement of products and pricing details. The stores are filled with employees, all out in the open and ready to talk shop. Last, when it's time to spill bills, Apple uses mobile cashier platforms as a substitute for bulky registers.

The other primary example worth citing is Zappos.com, which posts videos on various merchandise pages of passionate employees explaining what they like about a particular product. Since launching the video campaign in 2009, Zappos has reported a fivefold increase in customer conversion rate. This 'spokesperson video' feature is also common practice in the real estate business. Agents will perform a virtual walkthrough of a house or apartment, all while you follow their effervescent smiles and charismatic voices.

Rapport building, humanizing, enhancing social engagement or giving a personal narrative—call it what you will, but you cannot deny the power of a face and story behind a sale. The central takeaway: a brand is never just a product and a price, whether you are dealing with smartphones, online clothes shopping, property sales or hotels.

Apple and Zappos get it. A brand is an identity and people want to be socially connected to the brands they support on an ongoing basis. This is a major problem I see with selling hotels through the OTAs. There's no identity. Each page has the same layout with different text inserts and image thumbnails. When every page feels the same like this, brand identity is distanced from the consumer. The primary motivations then become location and price, and a consumer will naturally seek the most convenient or deepest discount around. In a race to the bottom like this, every hotel loses.

The key to restoring brand identity is by fostering a personal connection. For starters, why not put videos on your website with an affable manager discussing why he or she loves your hotel? Be on the lookout for passionate team members who can talk earnestly and positively about a specific aspect of your operations. For prospective buyers, such genuine stories might be just the ticket to sway their dollars. After all, visual cues are easier on the brain than reading.

A more time-consuming extension of this would be a live web chat. Once logged on, managers could answer questions directly, sharing their passion and the product benefits throughout. Individual concerns could be dispelled and customers would leave the conversation happier and more likely to make a purchase.

Furthermore, humanizing your brand is not just a cheap trick for first time buyers. It goes miles towards customer loyalty, but most of the heavy lifting has to occur on-property with physical interactions. Your team has to be trained to not only be sociable, but they must also be strategically positioned to maximize guest-staff interactions.

Take Apple again. Their stores are white-walled with beige furniture. On such a matte canvas, the geniuses' bright blue t-shirts pop. Plus, their employees are everywhere and unavoidable. Ask yourself: how do your staff uniforms catch the eye? Your colors should contrast with the décor just enough to stand out without leaning on kitsch. These two are probably out of your immediate control, but where you position the team is not.

Think about removing physical barriers that might impede an interaction. Apple did away with the rows of cashiers in place of a mobile solution. And what's the hotel equivalent of a cash register? The front desk. As customary as it may be, that countertop is an obstacle to customer loyalty. I'm not insisting that you to drag out the sledgehammer, but what if one of your front desk clerks or managers were to stand in front of the aforementioned reception kiosk? Maybe try having staff members check guests in via a tablet.

Subtle but effective, placing your team in unobstructed points of contact is vital to humanizing your brand. It's even more important for directors—those empowered to act swiftly upon individual requests and complaints—to lend their face to the lobby floor. Encourage a social vibe either through polite suggestion or perhaps with something more explicit like a regular manager's reception. For example, host a complimentary late afternoon wine and cheese, with all guests invited to parlay with those managers in attendance. This hits two birds with one stone—improving loyalty and a good team morale booster.

Speaking of food, F&B managers should strive, without being effusively invasive, to open a dialogue with patrons. They may already be in awe of your cuisine and service quality, or they may feel the opposite. By getting in the face time, being receptive to differing opinions and holding a constant desire for improvement, you'll find that visitors will leave happier either way.

Additionally, social media plays a significant role in this process. Gone are the days when you can simply hide behind your corporate logo and advertise with a generic, objective voice. When it comes to fostering true B2C relationships, personality matters. This tenet holds true for both the physical as well as the electronic.

Instead of only hosting one branded Twitter account, why not get every one of your directors on the network with their smiling faces as profile pictures? Then, have them tweet, retweet and reply to items posted on the corporate account and to customers directly—literally putting a face behind the brand. This can also be applied to Facebook fan pages and LinkedIn. Get your managers online and sharing their passion with consumers!

These are just a few suggestions for humanizing your brand. Once you frame every aspect of your operations through this mentality, you'll see that there are plenty of other opportunities to increase both first time purchases and loyalty. And when in doubt, look to companies that continually achieve success in crowded markets despite their higher price points. There are lessons everywhere, but only if you keep an open mind!

WHAT'S YOUR SCENT?

When it comes to depicting a hotel experience, our lexicon usually inscribes a journey primarily of sights—soothing room ambiance, extravagant lobby décor and so on—with glossy, high-res photographs as worthy complements. Next on the list is typically sound, portrayed as crashing the ocean waves, bird chirping peacefully through bucolic trellises or, for urbanites, a quiet space fit for a restful sleep between harried business days punctuated by saxophone harmonics in the elevator. Restaurants and bars excite the palate while bed sheet linens and marble-tiled bathrooms do wonders to arouse the sense of touch.

What's often left out of the picture is the fifth spoke on the wheel—smell. Not that the people who write your promotional materials morally abstain from infusing this, but that there's simply nothing in the room, lobby or hallways to spark a distinct aromatic reaction. Our sense of smell can at times be highly underrated for its powerful psychological effect on people's moods, and more can be done to activate it in a positive way.

For reference, the anatomical terminology of the brain to familiarize yourself with are the olfactory bulb—the processing center for smells—and the limbic system which controls emotions and memories. Both of these are considered evolutionarily old when compared to the likes of the prefrontal cortex which handles complex cognitive processes like problem solving and abstract thought. In fact, smell is often dubbed the oldest sense because of its tightly wired associations with primal emotional states in the limbic system.

Some Cross Examples

Start by taking home staging for example. An age-old sales trick prior to an open house is to bake a fresh batch of cookies. Not only does this mask any unpleasant tangs, but it instills a sense of warmth, nostalgia and even hunger which translate into a better overall opinion of the prospective purchase. It's positive reinforcement. A welcoming whiff can unconsciously enhance favorable perceptions that are consciously formed from visual and auditory stimuli. In this case, cookies makes a house feel like home.

Contrast this to a house that isn't staged this way; perhaps an older abode with a slight moldy odor. Whether you are aware of it or not, certain smells sound the alarm in our minds. For instance, the acrid smoke of a nearby fire spells danger in big, bold letters. Mold might not be as conspicuous as a smoldering blaze, but it activates the same brain centers.

And then I read about how this particular brain pattern was employed by Procter & Gamble to help sell Febreze during its initial launch in mid 1990s. Keep in mind that I myself am a P&G alum and gained indispensible marketing experience with the company. Even with all ingrained loyalty aside, this is nonetheless genius at work.

The impetus for Febreze came when P&G researchers found a chemical that could nullify malodorous compounds retained in fabrics from cigarette smoke, rotten food, pets or any other domestic perpetrator. This alone was a grand discovery with vast benefits, and yet Febreze debuted with lackluster sales numbers, so much so that the product was nearly scrapped. After countless hours of reflection, they deduced the problem: it was scentless.

Febreze's active ingredient only quashed bad smells without producing an enjoyable aroma to confirm to the user that the spray actually worked. Because said consumers were very often accustomed to the bad smells in their domiciles, they needed a positive feedback in order to perceive Febreze as having utility. Once P&G introduced a little perfume into the formula, the product started to blossom and is now a worldwide, billion dollar brand.

Let me repeat. The active ingredient in Febreze would work just fine to undo the damages left by all things noxious, but without the additive bouquet, how would you know that it's doing its job? It's the distinctive smell of this product that signals the brain and tells you in an instant, 'Febreze saw, Febreze conquered'. Perceptions are reality; think of the fragrance as your reward for doing the hard work of aiming the bottle and pulling the trigger.

A similar sensory cross-example is the food coloring added to Coca-Cola or Pepsi. Without it, this soda would still deliver the same freshening blend of caramel, spice and carbonation, as any blind taste test would confirm. The brown dye was initially included for marketing purposes—to visually differentiate the product. Now, after nearly a century of indoctrination, the cola color has become so entrenched with the particular flavor that to separate the two would be blasphemy. This is a case of sight and taste, however, so let's stick to smell.

Scent as Design

It's not like I've stumbled upon anything novel here; scents are shrewdly used around the globe for desirable effects, most prominently in the retail industry. Marketers have even coined the expressions 'ambient scenting', 'scent branding' or 'scent marketing' to denote this type of mood-enhancing (or subtracting if you're not careful) effect. All this is, of course, under the umbrella of 'scent as design' or, more broadly, 'sensory branding'; the grand objective is for consumers to form a deeper connection with products and more esteemed perceptions of brands to increase sales.

Applying these ploys to hotels presents three general scenarios worth discussing. First is when a guestroom has an off-putting stench. For this, expect problems. Just as pleasant aromas can relax and rejuvenate, bad smells can ignite the fear and danger centers in a person's brain, causing discomfort and chagrin. The culprits for such stinks might be something as cantankerous as dirty carpets or old pipes. Regardless of the replacement costs, if you ever want to deliver true guest satisfaction, you cannot have foul odors pervade your rooms.

Next is neutral. A good smell counts for you, a bad one against, but the middle ground, where most hotels sit, offers nothing to activate this sense. As such, hoteliers are missing a key opportunity to foster an emotional bond with consumers. There's only so much you can do to outmatch your competitors in terms of opulent décor, the size of the in-room plasma television, linen thread counts or the noiselessness of your temperature modulators. Add an 'old school' weapon to your arsenal; add scent.

On the positive side of things, I'm constantly reminded of a former client, Ojai Valley Inn & Spa, a five-diamond resort 90 minutes north of Los Angeles. Every guestroom exudes a trail of lavender and orange and their bathroom amenities are likewise infused with these two fragrant elements. Plus, both ingredients are exclusive to the Ojai experience; lavender is grown onsite and the surrounding valley teems with orange orchards. Upon arriving, this pleasurable blend instantly relaxes you (lavender is known to help induce sleep) and completes the in-room ambiance, albeit subtly when compared to the resort's other features and endless scenic vistas.

To this day, I still remember the soft mix of lavender and oranges; a slice of sweet nostalgia yearning for me to return. It's but one more memorable cue that enhances my affinity for the property and no doubt this unique aroma contributes to loyalty amongst other customers.

This is one personal instance, but the hospitality industry is rife with other ambient scenting success stories, even if those victories aren't directly quantifiable. Mandalay Bay in Las Vegas pumps a concoction of coconut, vanilla and spice throughout its lobby, shops and casino floor—a fragrance that is striking yet subtle and pleasant. As well, it's evocative of the hotel's tropical theme and proficient in masking some of the casino's lingering cigarette pungency. Indeed, many other Las Vegas establishments, notably Bellagio, Harrah's and MGM Grand, all use similar ambient scenting to mask tobacco and for branding purposes.

Outside of the casino business, look to the Westin Hotels' white tea perfume or Mandarin Oriental's conference sprays designed to enhance meeting productivity. Many other major chains are worth investigating for their scent marketing including Hilton, Intercontinental, Marriott and Sofitel. Your hotel's smell is big business and now is the time for everyone to get involved, whether you're an international chain or an independent operator.

Apply Scent to Your Property

Building on these examples, start to think of ways to integrate scents for your guestrooms, lobby or spa. Restaurants should already have this one covered in a positive manner (fresh food); although, if they don't, that's cause for a whole other discussion. Spas are likely already performing in this area of expertise as well.

Ideally, you should strive for a thematic infusion—local fruits, herbs, minerals or perhaps a product the region already makes to much applause. You could even consider a selection of different in-room scents chosen by the guest before or at arrival. Or maybe a holiday spirit— Thanksgiving would be pumpkin spice, Christmas a hint of frankincense and Valentine's Day is all about rose petals. There are plenty of chances to get creative.

The key is to ensure that the scent is ambient, pervading the entirety of a space without being constantly perceptible. And there are options to fit your every exact need, from devices that attach to your central air conditioning units to local apparatuses like the Lampe Berger for more localized and readily changeable aromas, or motion control systems that will waft a bit of fragrance when a consumer approaches. As well, there are important considerations for allergy, headache and migraine sufferers who have heightened sensitivities to certain smells—that is, too much of a fragrance might backfire with these people.

The bottom line is that you should be doing something in the scent department. This is a friendly wakeup call for you to brainstorm how this underrated sense can be harnessed as a way to further guest satisfaction and develop a loyal consumer base.

OVERCOMING THE LOYALTY EROSION PROBLEMS OF DRIP PRICING

Are you aware of the term 'drip pricing' for hotels? Market and advertise the base daily room rate then divulge additional, and exceedingly compulsory, fees after a customer has signed on the dotted line. These extras might include anything from standardized resort fees, housekeeping charges, fitness room fees (whether you use it or not) and food coupons to amenity surcharges for local phone calls, in-room internet access or bottled water. Even with most federal laws dictating that these gratuities must be wholly visible and conspicuously outlined, the consensus amongst guests is that such tactics are frustrating and deceptive; not exactly the adjectives you'd attribute as loyalty builders.

Look to two cross examples: airfare fuel surcharges and cruise line port fees, both of which have been officially deemed unreasonable to the consumer and rectified to a certain extent. In the short run, customers bore the brunt. However, regulators had the prescience to look beyond and understand that these actions inevitably hurt vendors by deteriorating brand trust. Drip pricing for hotels follows a similar pathology but with a salient caveat. These compulsory fees are complicated by the pricing models of third-party interlopers.

Lo and behold, we're back to discussing the surreptitious actions of the OTAs. Such sites are engineered towards displaying the lowest prices possible, which also happens to be the most accessible method for potential consumers to favor their reservation engines over, say, booking directly at a brand.com. Marketing 'Cheap!' is, after all, a proven technique, beckoning our impulsive natures to surface. And so the OTAs milk this by only exhibiting the basal daily room rate and keeping the remainder hidden; it's their choice.

Only after a nonrefundable purchase is complete do the applicable fees start to drip, drip, drip to the surface. We hoteliers know this is a serious issue; we are in the business of satisfying our guests, not incensing them. And yet we are hamstrung.

In this race to the cheapest marketable price-tag, properties have no choice but to oblige. You'd lose business to competitors if you didn't follow this paradigm, and desiccating your interactions with such third-party sites is currently implausible. You have to meet customers where they are buying, and OTAs are rapidly proliferating bazaars. They hold all the cards.

The numbers can offer a misleading counterargument. Ancillary levies now account for over $2 billion in revenue in the United States alone. Not bad, but not good either if you are thinking long-term. When a guest doesn't understand the rationale behind an additional cost, do they complain to the OTA or the hotel? When a guest is told that such fees are mandatory and written into their initial purchasing agreement, do they blame the OTA or the hotel?

Give yourself a cookie if you guessed the latter in both cases. Consumers are more likely to perceive hotels as the culprits, and as such, we are the ones who suffer from loyalty erosion, all the while the opacity of the OTAs remains. It's a sad state of affairs and hotels are drawing the short straw. Turn your speakers on to the dolorous Taps melody for a minute, and then think of how we can fix this.

An Example to Elucidate the Broader Issue

Let's start with in-room internet access fees—an issue I've harked on extensively in the past. Your guests know there is a cost; they have cell phones and internet access at home, and the monthly bills never stop coming. Like electricity and running water, it's a 'mi casa es su casa' mentality—an essential service where charging 'extra' is a surefire faux pas. The ideal solution is to charge everyone and bury the expenditure into the daily rate. But it's not that simple.

Budget properties should be commended as they are increasingly offering in-room internet as complimentary. Obviously they are burying the tangible cost as well as its associated markup, the size of which cannot be said for certain without a glance at the accounting ledgers. In addition to this, when you offer internet access 'for free', it may well be perceived as a bonus!

However, incorporating the cost into the daily rate upfront raises the issue of price sensitivity; your product now appears marginally more expensive than your rivals who save the extraneous levy for later. As a result, your listings garner less click-through considerations and, ultimately, purchases. Maddening still is that the consumer doesn't encounter the warning labels for compulsory fees until they are halfway through the booking process. "Well, I've already made it this far," is undeniably a popular inner monologue for such eye-rolling occasions.

This case is intriguing because there's generally less latitude for price increases at the thrifty end of the spectrum and that internet access can be one of the heftier surcharges when considered alongside bills such as additional towels ($2-$4), safe warranties ($1-$3 per night), local telephone calls ($1 per call) or groundskeeping ($3-$8 per night). Taken together, all these little costs can add up, or subtract if you are judging them from a search results point of view.

What This Says About the Modern Consumer

I'll leave the issue of acceptable price sensitivity to the revenue managers and other numbers gurus. As you might have already inferred from the abovementioned examples, nearly any aspect of a hotel experience can be 'dripped'. Therefore, an area to explore in tandem with price sensitivity is modern consumer behavior—which fees are tolerable and which are deal breakers.

Hotel customers these days strive to know what's included with their rooms. They have the wherewithal to research ahead of time and know when they are being cheated, at least from their perspective. Let's turn to the previous example to clarify.

Internet access costs money. It's not that guests can't afford it; it's that they believe the hotels are taking advantage of them by demanding an extraneous levy of $10 to $15 per day. Here's the thought process going through a guest's mind at some level or another: $15 per day is $450 per month, a markup of more than 400% over what even the premium cable packages table per month. In short: highway robbery.

How about the $4 bottles of water and $1 local phone calls? A simple mental calculation is all any guest needs to identify these as ludicrous margins. A common objection cited by hoteliers is that the property should be adequately compensated for giving guests the luxury of ready-at-hand water-in-disposable-plastic and access to a hard line in their rooms. Moreover, others feel as though they can charge for this because customers have the disposable income to cough up. Both of these opinions are maligned.

Believe you me, markups are a necessary part of any business's survival and I'm not advocating any sort of Bolshevist reversal of a trade system that has worked since the dawn of civilization. However, the flip side of market capitalism is that those who charge too far above the perceived value will be logically rebuked with fewer sales. Economics 101.

A convenience store stays afloat by charging $1 per bottle of water because it gives its consumers the utility of not having to drive 30 minutes to a warehouse and buy water bottles by the pallet. But this isn't a 400% markup; more like in the range of 100% to 200%. Hotels should stick to common practice as a $4 bottle of water is sending the wrong message. It's saying, "We are charging you this much because we can get away with it," instead of, "We are charging this much because we must in order to make ends meet."

Many managers talk a big game about how they strive to empathize with guests and deliver warm, compassionate experiences. Right they should; hotels are an emotional purchase and playing the harp string is an irrefutable method for accruing return customers. Yet, miniscule acts of brazen greed can nullify all other positive efforts.

Although the stigma of drip pricing applies to all its encompassing scenarios, there's a wide degree of variation in reactions. Perhaps starting with water bottles and internet access weren't the best choices. What about pet surcharges or discontinuing the complimentary breakfast? Are these met with the same chagrin?

Guests don't like additional payments, at least ones they don't understand. They don't understand the cost allocation structure behind the $4 bottle of water or the $15 internet surcharge. Conversely, it's common knowledge that animals make a mess and that food can have sharp preparation costs. Many will readily consent to fitness center charges if they plan to physically use the equipment, but do so regardless of a guest's intent and you'll meet only scorn.

Bringing It Back to the OTAs

What does all this have to do with the bargain-basement pricing model of the online travel agencies? Simple: their platform for displaying room rates propagates a hotelier mentality in which there's no alternative to drip pricing. A hotel should never treat its relationship with the bland edifice of an OTA as fiduciary. Everyone's doing it so therefore we have to comply or we risk dismal income from this otherwise-lucrative channel. But solutions abound and indeed many properties may already hold the answer.

If part of the rationale behind consumer derision towards drip pricing concerns a gap in knowledge—that is, not understanding heavy markups or ancillary fees—then much of that can be fixed with a proper dissemination of information. Tell your guests why these charges are necessary for you to effectively operate. If your TripAdvisor score reveals numerous tirades against charging for local calls, place a card in every room next to the telephone that makes the price clear and offers a satisfactory explanation behind the price. The same for internet access fees, shuttle services and whatever else isn't blanketed by the daily room rate. Knowledge is power after all.

This may work to mitigate minor grievances, but it isn't a panacea. Ideally, all hoteliers dream of cutting out the middleman, but the OTAs are still fantastic tools for vacation brainstorming and comparison shopping. What I foresee as the real cures are exclusive brand.com deals and best rate guarantees. Make your incentives so lucrative that it's impossible for customers to refuse booking directly with you. And advertise these promises so guests know where to go when they're ready to spend.

Having a price parity policy will do you no good if it's buried (like hidden fees) under a mile of red tape and in the sub-navigation on your website. Rig the home page with big, bold letters. Furthermore, highlight the fact that reward points and specific requests are only attainable via direct reservations. Social media is also an empyrean vessel for divulging this factoid, but the uses of these web networks don't stop there.

Dangle exclusive deals and chances to win gift cards through Facebook. Drop limited-time sales on Twitter. Reward YouTube videos that demonstrate your property's excellence. Discount rooms for those who spread the good word through Instagram. Give back to those who share. Be careful, though, not to offer too deep a discount; just enough to persuade potential guests that booking direct is the only way. In my ongoing battle to determine once and for all whether social media is a pro or a con for hotels, it would appear that these networks can actually help counteract other more malevolent forces.

Many of the major chains have preventive measures underway and it's time the rest of us followed suit. Drip pricing proliferates because we don't account for their long-term ramifications. Knowing your consumers and knowing how to entice them to be loyal to you, and not a third-party, will always be a step in the right direction.

TRADITIONAL MARKETING

The laid back, California-style of Montage Laguna evokes a calm and understated luxury, led by an intrepid team that fully understands branding and marketing.

INTRODUCTION

Writing on traditional marketing is becoming a very finicky pursuit. Given the pervasiveness of internet-born and electronic-dependent tactics for improving your business, methods that don't inherently involve digital systems are often tossed aside. Even though the latest and greatest technologies can enhance your hotel operations, there are still many fruitful approaches that do not directly involve electronics, but rather thinking outside the box.

One theme I try to convey in this section is the need for your property to genuinely differentiate itself from the thousands of other places occupying the same broad category of hotels. This can be done through onsite refurbishments or exceptional marketing tactics and promotions that others are not taking advantage of. The key is to take a step back and analyze where other hotels are disseminating their messages then do something slightly different. Always look for a way to 'nichify' your business so that you can streamline your business efforts and capital resources towards one clearly defined goal. This also works to solidify your base support of loyal customers as they will know exactly what they are getting when they book with you (plus a little extra that you give them to exceed their expectations). Only by being different, from the marketing techniques you use all the way through the onsite experience, will you truly stand apart in the consumer's eyes and become a hotel that they remember.

The latter half of this section is devoted to two subjects: using holidays and seasonal landmarks to your benefit; and tapping into the rapidly retiring baby boomer generation. As a boomer, I've curiously watched many close friends retire and I am certain this demographic is ripe for receiving your message, but only if you know how to target them correctly. As for specific holidays, these are always excellent opportunities to capture new customers and reward those already loyal. You have to remember that everyone else will be marketing to consumers around these times, so your approach must distinguish itself from the rest of the herd.

Regardless of the topic covered, my hope for you is to start to think creatively about how you prompt the community to learn about your property, and then prompt them to actually visit. The following articles are but a few ways to get the ball rolling.

NEXT YEAR'S PLAN: ORGANIC MARKETING

Ask yourself the question: are you and your company going 'organic'? Food, farming, growth, SEO, organizations and now marketing. Everything is 'organic' and applying it to hotel marketing is an excellent reframing tool. But, talk about a buzzword that's breaching on overuse with its real definition slipping between the cracks. Let's start at the beginning.

(Pardon me while I dust off the high school biology textbook.) Organic pertains to something involving an organism. That's the obvious part. So, what's an organism and how does it apply to business terms? Without getting too heavy on the science, an organism is a cluster of molecules that work together for self-preservation, growth and reproduction, all while responding to the environment and maintaining homeostasis.

And it's the latter part where 'organic' marketing takes its cue. Homeostasis is hybridized Greek for describing dynamic equilibrium, which, for those sans mathematics, chemistry or economics college credits, is a fanciful word for active balance. The environment veers left, the organism adapts left and continues to grow. The environment veers right, the organism adapts again; always striving for stability ad infinitum. Effective marketing needs vision, but it also needs day-to-day flexibility.

Start by applying this equilibrium model to the rapidity of modern times. Does it really make sense that marketing plans are formed on a yearly basis? Yes and no. The 'no' is the easy part. It's fast times at hotel high. With so much happening and social media leading the way towards a faster future, oftentimes plans can't wait until next year for execution.

The attitude behind organic marketing is one of knowledge, acceptance and fluidity. Knowledge in that you are keeping pace with all the new research, resources and channels that will help you reach consumers. Acceptance coming from the belief that such knowledge will improve your capacity as a manager and that all the new research, resources and channels will actually help. And, easiest of all, fluidity is the opposite of rigidity—going with the flow of the times, doing your best to stay up-to-the-minute and anticipating customer trends.

The marketing plan is no longer a document carved in stone. It needs a clear direction, but also contingencies in case the world decides to spin in another direction. The best way to achieve this is through brevity. Writing your marketing plan as 150 pages of canon leaves no room to breathe, no room to be organic. Instead, make it a quick, friendly read.

Understanding this 'no' segment might make for some headaches, but hold the aspirin, because the 'yes' portion is still a much needed capsule of fun. Yearly marketing plans should be all about strategy; where you see your department or the whole property in one, two, five and ten years. The focus should be branding and the very essence of what currently makes your hotel great and what you aspire to be. An annual marketing plan is brief and broad, leaving the day-to-day tactics to the manager's discretion and best judgment—organic, as they say.

The biggest changes are often identified by a single, punctuated event or plan, but never forget the minutia of each contributing task. That's where organic marketers find their groove. They have the tenacity to shift gears at will and improvise away from predefined tactics while still moving towards the big fish. Yes, that last statement was a tad oxymoronic, but isn't all marketing to some degree? Think about what organic marketing means and when it comes time to execute the marketing plan, you will be more ready than you have ever been.

TEN DIFFERENTIATORS

Hotels continue to define novel approaches to further differentiate themselves from competitors and other properties. The concept behind this is to deliver one truly unique facet to the travel experience thereby giving guests a common affirmation to draw upon for word-of-mouth, online reviews and return visits. Here are ten highly memorable and personal examples of properties that are accomplishing this objective.

1. *The Guest Robes in Kimpton Properties.* If you have seen one bathrobe, you have seen them all. Except for Kimpton Hotels. Imagine opening the closet to a zebra print and a tiger stripe gown. Whether you are inclined to use it or not, it's nevertheless an eye-turner, not to mention a great photo opportunity. Fun and uniquely Kimpton.

2. *Avari Towers in Karachi.* Here is a pizza delivery idea that's dangerously good and coming out of Pakistan no less. At the Avari, in-room pizza is always free. Just call down and make your selection, give them the time on your digital clock and they guarantee it in 30 minutes. Oh yes, the mineral water in the room is free too. They also have a thorough fitness room, which you'll need after indulging in too much dough.

3. *San Ysidro Ranch's Pet Program.* Not only is this luxurious Santa Barbara property known for its flawless service, rooms and F&B, but the property goes out of its way to welcome their furry friends. Upon arrival, a complete welcome kit is provided including Pawrier and a special gourmet menu (you can order a raw porterhouse steak!). Moreover, dogs-in-house are signified by special signage posted to the exterior of each of the suites.

4. *Wickaninnish Inn's Weather Watch.* Located on the remote western coast of Vancouver Island, the Wick delights with the thrilling experience of watching ocean waves crash onto the surrounding cliff and beach. The property even provides complete rain gear in each room—boots are picked up at the front desk, arranged according to size. This program is instrumental in driving revenue during the off-peak season.

5. *Hotel Berlin, Berlin's Convention Central.* Talk about immersing a property in a conference, this property rivals any in the world. Using video projectors, the entire hotel lobby can be transformed into a visual display to welcome a group. Plus, through a creative approach to F&B, dining areas can be configured to the exact proportion needed for a group so that it's not too big or too cramped. I rarely see this flexibility and efficiency in a facility.

6. *The Hazelton Hotel's Private Screening Room.* Want to be a movie mogul for the night? Or, want a party that makes your guests feel like one? This Toronto property has a private screening room with seating for up to 25 in decadent comfort. In-house guests can book it to watch their favorite football game, too. And having one of the finest restaurants in the city cater your food certainly helps.

7. *Library Collection's In-House Club Room.* Guests to these boutique hotels are treated to complimentary breakfast, mid-afternoon tea, newspapers, WiFi and a range of amenities that the typical hotels would levy as surcharges. All this is available in Midtown Manhattan, making it even more incredible. The results are clear: happy guests and terrific TripAdvisor ratings.

8. *Chateau Frontenac's Canine Ambassador.* It is hard for most guests to resist engaging in conversation about Santol, a Labrador/Bernese cross merrily stationed in this Quebec City landmark property every afternoon. The success of this dog program ensures a high volume of social media traffic as well as bestowing a positive memory to the hotel.

9. *Butler Service.* I have experienced this in several hotels in Asia and Europe. While not something that would be consistent with most property's positioning, target audience or cost structure, the service is an automatic differentiator insofar as the ultimate in client service. Building hotel-guest rapport is always a challenge and face-to-face conversations are one of the best ways to this end. In this regard, a butler is like having a hotel manager at your disposal 24/7.

10. *Hotel Monaco's Goldfish.* It is fitting to begin and end this article with Kimpton properties. When a goldfish (in a bowl, of course) arrives in the room of a solo guest, the idea is to make them feel less lonely. The reality is that this diversion is fun, cost effective and has lucrative social media opportunities.

TEN MOST COMMON MARKETING MISTAKES

Marketing dollars are precious and scarce. No one wants to pilfer resources away towards programs that fail to deliver a solid return on investment. As a general manager, here are ten thoughts to keep in mind as your hotel marketing team prepares to execute this year's plan.

1. *You can't measure everything.* As a consultant, after presenting a concept, the director of marketing often asks, "Yes, but can we measure the results?" The simple fact is this: not one system has been invented that accurately records the results of each and every iota of action. There are so many variables at play that the ability to study the minutia of each and every element is, at best, a scientific anomaly. Mind you, as digital avenues flourish, we are getting better at capturing this enormity of data. But more data can easily bring on more headaches. Instead, train your team to focus on the big picture—month over month, quarter over quarter, year over year.

2. *Retargeting programs are a fallacy.* It seems brilliant. People log on to your website, they're tracked, and the next time they go to a site that hosts advertising, lo and behold your ad appears. A great trick of technology, this is supposedly the cutting edge of cost-per-click online technology. Makes a lot of sense, doesn't it? Superficially, yes, but by the time the retargeting and remarketing occur, it's already too late. We've tested spending here versus the same amount on traditional CPC. Bottom line: I'm a skeptic.

3. *Flash sales won't save your business.* Flash sales programs are alluring: the promise of bringing 'fresh blood' into the property, albeit at a very low trial price. Think for a moment before you plunge. The consumer wants a 50% discount and the operator wants a 10%-20% commission. So, where's the revenue? The answer: there is none! Moreover, these customers are not looking at you; they're looking at discounts, with your business and brand secondary. A few years ago I would tell you that flash sales are like cayenne pepper—just a touch for flavoring, but a pinch too much and the whole dish is ruined. Now, they're simply not worth your time.

4. *Thinking OTA customers can be converted to book directly.* Wishful thinking, indeed. Let's face it. Anyone who is booking your property through an OTA has a different modality, with limited interest in the hotel selection except for location and price. This does not mean that you treat the customer any differently. You may just win their hearts and minds. But it's a slim chance. There's simply so much choice out there that unless you wow them with a slice of celestial pie, they will revert to their established habit of searching and cross-referencing through the rest of the world's hospitality offers.

5. *Eking out another year from that old website.* I know you spent a fortune building your existing website four or five years ago. But the world has changed and your site is most likely not up to speed. The useful length of a website is currently at about 36 to 48 months, and that's a stretch. The technology of today's digital infrastructure is such that your site will look old, and if it does, your hotel will feel old as well. Your home page must echo the same vibe as your onsite experience. It must also fit the contemporary consumer demands of mobile and tablet readiness, seamless booking engines, social media integration and up-to-the-minute information accuracy.

6. *Thinking smartphone is not yet necessary.* Not next year, now! The fact is that the odds of your site being viewed on a smartphone are already at about one in three and climbing. If you're prepared to walk away from one third of your potential business, then keep waiting. If the light has just gone on somewhere in your cranium that these numbers make sense, go for it. Mobile websites are cost effective to build and results are an easy payout.

7. *Failing to give your sales and marketing team tablets.* The iPad, or any other tablet computer, is no longer a novelty. These are hardworking tools that are useful for one-on-one presentations. While you're at it, think front desk, sales, executive committee, marketing, team leaders and trainers. Start replacing printed documents with tablet-based reporting. Software solutions that remove paper from the equation will also help with planning meetings, communication speed, abstract insights and team accountability.

8. *Neglecting weddings.* Weddings are good business. Wrong! Weddings are a fantastic business, both revenue-generating and recession-proof. It's amazing to me that many properties fail to actively support their wedding capabilities—hosting micro sites, targeted advertising, trade

shows and open houses. All of these marketing programs work. Create the combination that works best for your local market.

9. *Thinking some guru can create awesome SEO for your website and propel it to the top of Google.* SEO is hard work. There are no magic bullets. The cornerstones of successful SEO are content and authorship. This means continuous additions through blogs, social media updated religiously, a flair for community-building and meaningful entries worthy of inbound links. The days of some quick meta tag fixes are long over; focus on the content delivery and Google will handle everything else. Tell the guru to prey on someone else.

10. *Having your revenue management team assume responsibility for property marketing.* Revenue managers are a critical part of your executive committee. They ensure that the balance between yield and occupancy is delivered. They monitor your STR reports versus your competitive set. But they are not really trained as marketers. Marketing is not about today or this week, as that's the role of revenue managers. Marketing is about the future of your business, your brand and your position strategized for long-term growth. There is a certain degree of creativity and intangibility surrounding great marketing and that's the exciting part! There is more than enough work for revenue managers in keeping your profitability and occupancy targets in line. Don't allow them to deviate from the real prize.

GIVE ME A BREAK! TEN PESKY THINGS THAT ANNOY GUESTS

"Give me a break!" That's what a guest will say or think when they come across something in your hotel that's outrageous, and not in a good way. These are loyalty detractors; pesky little issues that even a guest, with their limited knowledge of the industry, knows to be outright wrong. Given the increasingly lofty expectations of travelers these days, minutia such as these ten are instant deal breakers. When guests come across one of them, they roll their eyes and their subconscious whispers to them, "I'm definitely not staying here again."

They are also issues that can be easily fixed. So, give yourself a break from negative reviews and bad word of mouth by addressing these ten items.

1. *Overpriced mini-bar and bottled water.* Why exactly is an in-room bottle of water $4? Every traveler knows this is shamefully marked up. It's perceived as an aggressive cash grab for the hotel. You're not winning your guests over with this exorbitant price. In fact, you're insulting their intelligence. Ditto for everything else in the mini-bar.

2. *Weak in-room coffee and tea selection.* It's always highly assuring and soothing to know that there's a warm cup of stimulating beverage waiting for you across the bed, except when that beverage tastes like watered down battery acid. I try to alleviate this insipid rot with cream and sugar, only to my dismay there's only one of the former and none of the latter. A little extreme, yes, but consider your coffee accessory allotment for when you're dealing with more than one person per room. Furthermore, I've encountered some very peculiar coffeemakers that aren't exactly intuitive; they take too long to figure out and produce a cup of scolding ash. The in-room coffee apparatus is your time to shine as a quality hospitality provider and a chance to deliver yet another memorable experience for your guests.

3. *Charging for local calls.* Why are you billing guests a full dollar per five minutes for each completed local call? Anyone who has ever owned a phone, landline or cellular, knows that local calls never amount to such incredulous fees. When you do this, the guest

perception is one of hostility. You're not doing your part to develop the friendship and positive emotional connection between the hotel and its patrons, which is essential if you ever want such a guest to give you an actual recommendation.

4. *Housekeeping knocks too early.* When is the earliest time housekeeping should start making their rounds? How does this vary for weekdays versus weekends? Every traveler has a different routine and itinerary, so this is a tough call. But keep in mind that knocking too early and disturbing someone's sleep is an instant deal breaker. I remember staying at a budget chain hotel where housekeeping knocked at 8am on a Saturday. And then, after I muffled out a half-reply, they proceeded to enter my room! Not only will I never stay there again, but I've been very vocal to advise my friends never to stay at this particular chain. Don't let this be you!

5. *Not enough bathroom amenities.* Towels, soaps and shampoos primarily. Picture this: you are staying in a room with your significant other, getting ready for the day's events, and he or she decides to shower first. Then you shower. Upon getting out, you notice that all the towels have been used. So now, drenched and sparsely clothed, you have to await housekeeping to deliver more of what should have been there in the first place. Not a good way to start your day.

6. *Not enough pillows or coat hangers.* Some people are used to sleeping on one pillow, others two and some even three. Is appeasing the latter two groups really that hard to do? True, a guest can always call down to request more pillows, but why start off on an uneven foot? Furthermore, too often I've entered rooms that only have five coat hangers or less. When this happens, I think to myself, "Do they really not trust me enough to give a full share?" Apart from the obvious inconvenience of having to jockey for coat hanger real estate, this is just one more irritating, little thing to drive a wedge in an otherwise positive guest-hotel relationship.

7. *Noisy air conditioner or heating unit.* Less a problem during the day, but if your guest is a light sleeper and this stops him or her from getting a full night's rest, you're in for big problems. Without their seven hours, your guests will be put in irrational states of mind and they're bound to do anything, including actions like loudly complaining at the front desk, writing derisive online reviews or

making it their mission to tell all their friends about their unsavory experience. Mind you, this one is substantially more expensive to fix and it requires a total maintenance overhaul, but that doesn't preclude its importance. You're going to have to upgrade these units eventually, why not know?

8. *Too many promotional tent cards.* Once a guest is in the room, you don't need to beat them over the head with endless advertisements for your own F&B or spa programs. The worst I've seen is when these cards and papers clog up the counters so much that it prevents a guest from using them. A polite, concise reminder will do. The guest is already staying with you, right? This is one area where tablets will shine as they can get these types of messages across neatly and colorfully without cluttering the room.

9. *Charging for WiFi.* In-room internet connectivity is no longer a value-added service. Charging for this service is highway robbery and guests won't see it any other way. Whatever objections you have—legacy contracts or bandwidth overload, for instance—get over them and think like a guest for a minute. Nowadays, why would I pay $15 per day to use the hotel's internet when I could run down to a nearby cellular store and get 200 MB of data for $2 per day on my 4G smartphone, which downloads at a rate that's on par with the hotel's service?

10. *Worse: no WiFi at all!* Internet access is a necessity for the modern traveler. Your guests will treat the room as their 'home base'— planning the next day, answering emails, posting to social media and unwinding with a quick Netflix television episode. For some, denying them internet access is equivalent to denying them running water. It's a given that travelers will research their accommodations before booking and a lack of WiFi, free or not, can be an instant deal breaker. If you operate at a hotel that doesn't offer internet access, you're not likely to receive any complaints about this, because every discerning guest has already booked and stayed elsewhere.

DOING THE VIP TREATMENT RIGHT

As a member of the 'working hotel team', I am often given an upgraded room, but rarely am I subject to the true VIP treatment. Having recently experienced this at a local winery, I am now more cognizant of the value of these efforts and its implications for repeat business coming from such activities.

First, my VIP experience. I am a regular buyer of Stratus Wines—a boutique winery located in Niagara-on-the-Lake about 90 minutes south of Toronto. My gang of five arrived in the middle of the afternoon and, remarkably, they had set aside a private room for a tasting of six vintages complete with four premium cheeses. They even printed out a personalized menu for the occasion.

Needless to say, I was blown away by their effort taken to make my group feel special. Since I had not expected anything like this, their actions were even more incredible. And there was no sales pitch or expectation of an immediate purchase.

The whole affair prompted me to reflect on the hospitality industry's approach to the VIP treatment. We tend to throw this term around loosely. When asking personnel about how someone is given VIP status, the response is usually a blank stare, as if the information was either confidential or unknown. Here is my take on the VIP situation:

1. *This is a serious classification.* It should not be taken lightly. There should be a clear set of guidelines as to who is given VIP status requiring planning committee level authorization. By making the classification special, it will get the attention it deserves.
2. *VIPs should be coded so the front office knows why.* Some are obvious, but giving front desk some information as to why the person has reached this status might be useful to ensure compliance so that the guest's stay with you is perfect.
3. *Your VIP amenity package should be highly personalized.* In today's world of custom printing, any correspondence and all presentations should be directed at the individuals and not neutral or unspecific.

4. *Don't ask for the order if you are VIP-ing a customer.* There is time afterwards. Remember, this is an opportunity to demonstrate your thanks for their support.

5. *Be memorable.* A personalized, printed menu, which costs pennies, is worth more than complimentary first-growth claret. Creativity and extra touches count more than their physical value. Further, high priced items could be considered a bribe and may be frowned upon, or even illegal to accept.

6. *It's personal.* Show you care. Don't delegate the responsibility for 'meet and greet' to another manager. If it's after hours then make an appearance at another time during the individual's stay to reinforce the personal impression.

7. *Follow up all VIP visits.* Learn from what you have done. Refine your technique and enhance your presentation.

8. *Diarize your VIP activities.* Make sure that what you did is on the guest file so that you do something different and equally exciting for when the guest returns.

9. *Add a 'loot bag' on the way out.* It costs very little to add a ball cap with your logo and a water bottle for a car. If a particular VIP has children, an age-appropriate ware with your logo makes sense, too.

10. *Most importantly, every guest on your property is a VIP.* While some guests may be identified for a special service or amenity, all guests deserve to be treated with professionalism and care.

RETHINKING THE CONCIERGE VIA SPECIALIZATION

Anyone who has taken introductory economics knows the term 'specialization of labor' and its financially beneficial implications. As possibly the most celebrated example, Henry Ford put this principle to good use when orchestrating his automotive manufacturing line. Indeed, specialization and innovation go hand in hand, but you could write a whole book on that!

With this as a thematic drive, I want you to rethink the idea of the concierge and how we can further partition this title to enhance a guest's experience. By giving your patrons an exact channel to address each specific need, you will not only better alleviate any worries, but heighten their perception of how excellent your hotel really is. Here are three contemporary examples for you to consider.

Sleep Concierge

Conceived by The Benjamin in New York City, this person's task is quite obvious from the name. Inventive and pragmatic, the property's Sleep Concierge can arrange for a bedtime snack or an appropriately soothing spa treatment. They even have a pillow menu with a dozen choices!

I would like to thank The Benjamin for pioneering this concept, but I don't believe it's too hard to implement elsewhere. Do you have a late night menu with two or three food items to help a guest doze off? How about sleep-inducing teas? Do you have anything to fit this purpose on your spa menu? Again, a Sleep Concierge doesn't have to be a fulltime occupation for any one staff member, and maybe you could delegate this to the rotating front desk staff to handle.

Pet Concierge

Being pet friendly is big business nowadays. Catering to your four-legged guests will make for happier owners and a more positive atmosphere throughout the hotel. Dealing with every animal requires a specific skill set and extensive retraining may be needed. (I use the word 'animal' here as, even though dogs are most common, you should nevertheless be ready for cats, birds and other friendly pets).

On a personal note, I've experienced the 'Doggie Concierge' set up at New York's Hotel Pennsylvania, a designation that services the property's thousand or so canine guests during the Westminster Kennel Club Dog Show held every February. These animals are the cream of the crop, each necessitating the VIP treatment. You would be shocked by some of the more esoteric demands people make on behalf of their dogs and the times of night that the demands come in!

You might only get one hundredth the number of dogs that the Hotel Pennsylvania entertains during that one crazy winter period, but they are still paying guests and deserve your attention. Simply advertising the Pet Concierge designation is a good way to soothe any anxious owners.

Art Concierge

A new idea to emerge out of The Hazelton Hotel in my home town of Toronto, the Art Concierge is still a very novel concept. The five-star property boasts an extensive art collection and their guests are often curious. The Art Concierge is there to not only lead tours, but to recommend galleries and art museums throughout the city.

The idea of a cultural associate doesn't have to stop at in-house paintings and sculptures. Think of a 'heritage concierge'—a staff member who can introduce guests to the origins of the surrounding region, recommend insightful museums and give tours that showcase the history of the hotel, if the hotel is historic. If hiring someone for this job isn't in the cards, then recruit one or two personable staff members to receive the necessary training.

Where Your Region Counts

My next three suggestions are all explorations of tasks that your regular concierge is already fulfilling on a daily basis. However, given your area, maybe a fraction of the concierge's duties should be partitioned into its own post. The Doggie Concierge is essential to properly service the deluge of dogs arriving for the Westminster Dog Show. In order to have an Art Concierge, first you have to have the art!

Ask yourself: what is unique about your region? Is there any particular pastime that garners more questions or interest than the rest? Consider these three concierge mainstays and how you expound on their traditional duties.

Dining Concierge

I would consider this one a possibility if a hotel was located in a gastronomy nexus such as Paris, London or New York City. A dining concierge could highlight your own restaurant selection as well as offer nutritional tips or simply have a light conversation on recipes from one region to the next. After all, who doesn't like talking about food? By getting more face time with the guest, you might even be able to glean some very critical missteps that your F&B department has made.

As for who should bear this responsibility, your chefs are tied up in the kitchen and your F&B Director is busy with service orders and menu changes. I would put this on a junior manager who's reasonably erudite in the culinary arts and aspires to be an F&B Director in the future. A little youthful enthusiasm will certainly lead to some hearty, mood-lifting banter with guests.

Shopping Concierge

Shopping is a major pastime whether a guest is on vacation or just killing time between meetings. But what are your guests looking for? High-end brands? An outdoor promenade to shop in the sun? The chic street with vintage wares? A culturally-immersive bazaar with regional produce and trinkets?

Every person's tastes are unique and vary day by day. Moreover, it's hard for a concierge to keep up-to-date with all the latest store openings and fashion trends if they also have to stay current with dining, event and nightlife trends. This is especially true for any major metropolis.

Although your guests can do most of their own research on the internet, they will still benefit from talking to a local, and a savvy one at that. A foreign city can be an intimidating place, and maybe your Shopping Concierge could squire guests about the city for a totally immersive retail experience. Or, perhaps you could enlist personnel under a broader definition such as 'Discovery Concierge' whose expertise would also include area attractions, festivals, museums and nightlife.

Wellness Concierge

You likely already have or have heard of a Spa Concierge. Their job is to liaise matters at the spa front desk and ease guests into a relaxing, rejuvenating experience. They should be wholly familiar with the spa product line and be able to assist in sales or clarify what their services can do. A great Spa Concierge is another face to represent the genuine character of your hotel.

Go beyond with a more encapsulating terminology. A Wellness Concierge meanders the line between fitness, nutrition and spa; someone who might map out a guest's day-long experience with a full itinerary including pre-planned healthy meals, spa treatments and gym sessions with a personal instructor. Such a job would be a great addition to resorts looking to breach the 'wellness retreat' market.

The Bottom Line

The term 'concierge' is literally derived from the Old French verb of 'to serve'. And isn't this what their job description is in a nutshell? Why not better serve your guests through specialization? It'll make for a better experience, and that's what this industry is all about!

ON HOLD? GIVE US A BREAK!

You know the situation. You call a restaurant or a hotel and are immediately put on hold, often before you get an opportunity to speak to an operator. Annoying at best, but quite understandable given the peaks and valleys in call rate and recognizing that telephone staff has its limits.

But hoteliers have a way of making a bad situation worse. How? By adding a pre-recorded script trying to sell you on a variety of items offered at the property or to give you details about property features. Because these nuggets of useless information are interspersed with bland music, such sound bites become increasingly irascible—the change from music to voice commands your attention as you anticipate a live operator, then the pre-recorded message twists your hopes into frustration.

Having to put a guest on hold is not what any one of us would call great guest service. Shoehorning in a sales message is what I call guest disservice. An on-hold message is required, but it would be prudent to disregard any further voice scripts.

Whoever sells these pre-recorded message programs has made a lot of money selling something hoteliers simply do not need. This superfluous use of technology does nothing to enhance guest service. I encourage you to test your own call center and listen to the on-hold soundtrack for any such perturbations. In the end, however, you still have to promote your wares. They aren't going to sell themselves. But this is not the way.

Instead, I would recommend that you train your telephone operators to inform callers about new property features or promotions after they've handled the initial inquiry. People are harried and might not want to be haggled with an ancillary sales pitch. But if you're polite about it—for instance, by asking them first—they will respect your efforts. Operators should approach this as an opportunity to continue the conversation first and foremost, and not with the outright intention of forcing an additional sale.

HEARTS OF MONTAGE: CHARITY DONE RIGHT

This isn't anything revolutionary, but it's executed to perfection. Montage Hotels & Resorts' Hearts of Montage package is a quintessential example of how to incorporate philanthropic ventures into your overall revenue stream. The offer is simple for guests to appreciate: book with Montage and 10% of the room rate fee is donated to charity.

And simplicity is what's on full display here. Hearts of Montage, the company's associate volunteer program, has an earnest and catchy name. The package itself is straightforward, providing daily breakfasts and complimentary parking—nothing esoteric or extraneous. And no extra work is required from the buyer; the donation is already a part of the bill. As well, the organization's website has a crisp design that clearly spells out exactly what the program is about with projects both local and abroad.

All said, this is a fluid extension of the Montage brand and a model to surely emulate. We are all well aware that corporate social responsibility is a popular concept for the modern hotel industry, and indeed many customers look specifically for brands that are engaged in this manner. Montage goes a step above in that they make their charitable cause incredibly visible to the consumer and fully integrated with their core brand.

It's not just something done on the side, but its name (which has the hotel's name in it) and the corresponding package are simple for consumers to grasp. Comprehensibility makes it easy to be altruistic, leading to a higher retention rate amongst consumers and thus imparting a greater brand reputation. In its ideal state, this program structure also encourages customers to book directly with the hotel and it propagates the brand perception as a contributing member of the community.

Does your property have a charitable cause? If yes, think about how you can simplify and streamline your hotel's charitable cause in much the same way as you should for your overall brand perception. If not, why not begin today? Better results will surely follow.

GIVING BACK TO THE COMMUNITY, MONTAGE STYLE

Anyone who lives or works in Southern California is well-aware of the two ultra-luxurious Montage properties in their midst, located in Laguna and Beverly Hills. In its ten short years since the opening of their Laguna property, Montage has worked hard to deliver one of the finest accommodation experiences in the country, rivaling brands many years their senior. Clearly, in their halls and rooms are numerous applicable lessons for hospitality management that deserve your appreciation.

The company's approach to their tenth anniversary celebration was especially interesting. It identified community support as a priority under the banner: Montage Memory Makers Contest. This program targeted adolescents aged 13 to 17, deemed as 'young humanitarians', to win one of five $10,000 college scholarships. By submitting a summary of their efforts to inspire and provide community service, entrants were judged on key criteria such as creativity, impact of their achievements, service and inspirational value to others. Ten finalists were selected and the five winners were then chosen through a customized social media platform which allowed for open voting across the US.

I spoke with Alyssa Bushey, Montage's Corporate Director of Communications, while having a coffee at the Loft Bistro at Montage Laguna. As we talked, I couldn't help but notice the many families with young children at the restaurant, all of them remarkably well behaved for their age. My first thought: this celebratory contest was a continuation of Montage's already outstanding track record with families, who seem to be a dominant demographic.

Of course, the contest did not exclude the parents. Winners not only got the scholarship along with a detailed write-up in Montage Magazine, but they were also able to travel to Montage Laguna (accompanied by a parent or guardian) for a presentation of their award by the Founder and CEO of all Montage properties, Alan Fuerstman.

That's a pretty good incentive for anyone, child or adult. But place yourself in the former's shoes. It's nostalgia; the vacation experience that hotels create for younger, more malleable minds can help shape things to come for many, many years.

I see the Montage Memory Makers Contest not only as a community-building tool but a brilliantly effective marketing campaign as well. Yes, Montage has changed and improved the livelihoods of those kids who win one of the five scholarship bursaries. Plus, consider all the entrants, not just the winners, who, through merely putting in the effort of submitting, were learning the valuable skill of applying one's self. Through all this, Montage is also building its next generation of devoted fans; those who will take their families to Laguna decades from now.

As takeaway ruminations, consider what efforts your hotel has undertaken to give back to the community. Are any designed to help kids in such noble pursuits as attaining a higher education? Moreover, how are you building loyalty amongst the Millennials and subsequent generations of travelers?

MARKETING IS DEAD: A REBUTTAL

With the proliferation of social media and the manifold forms of digital communication, I've heard the phrase 'marketing is dead' tossed around as if it's a foregone conclusion. There is much to argue, however, and so argue we shall. While it's quite egregious to say outright that traditional marketing channels like newspapers, magazines, television and direct mail are useless, it is right to insinuate that the cumulative impact of these channels is diminishing. The real question then is how much they are diminishing.

The problem now is that we've overestimated the importance of new electronic channels, while simultaneously relegating traditional channels to the sidelines without the proper evidence to justify such a shuffle. When it comes to this false frame of mind, we hoteliers are guilty as charged, probably more so than in other industry circles. Perhaps by refuting some of the evidence surrounding this bold claim, I can restore the balance between old and new—a balance that actually works.

To start, buyers do in fact pay attention to traditional marketing channels. It is just that they are more skeptical and inquisitive than ever before. They will listen to traditional mediums, but they will cross-reference your products and their purported benefits via the internet. It's your job as marketers to be flexible and meet consumer needs or concerns in a manner that's appropriate for each channel.

Further, community marketing has already worked in tandem with traditional models for positive results. Ever heard of the term 'grassroots'? Rarely do people take salespeople at their word 100% of the time (unless of course you also believe that the word 'gullible' isn't in the dictionary). Cross-referencing and fact-checking have been common practice since the founding of commercial trade nearly 10,000 years ago.

Mind you, the notion of excising traditional marketing is not all hogwash. In this rapidly changing economic landscape, building social capital and involving customer advocates are worthwhile processes. This social capital, as well as the fostering of a dedicated fan base, will help you get external (and hopefully unbiased) feedback to refine your product offerings. And this is a function for which internet-born channels excel over the more traditional siblings.

As a hypothetical case to ponder, let's suppose Coca-Cola dedicated its marketing budget entirely to social media and banner ads while Pepsi maintained its channel mix. How do you think the two beverage giants' market shares would compare after two years?

What I propose is nothing new; nothing revolutionary. It's called synergistic marketing, combining traditional channels with websites and social media networks. However, the concept here goes beyond simply finding a balanced channel mix by which to advertise and sell your product, but a mentality shift away from absolutes and rigid thinking. You need to be open to change in order to correctly adapt. As a crude example, seeking out customer influencers via Twitter might be a plausible tactic today, but who's to say Twitter will have the same preeminence five or ten years from now?

The ironic twist for hotels here is that you can't watch the evening news without running across a flashy commercial for an OTA, which technically falls within the scope of tradition marketing. If the old channels were truly dead, then why would a digital distribution channel use them to disseminate its message? Maybe they realize the power of television advertising which is nowadays considered a traditional, yet still quite powerful, channel. Or, maybe the OTAs are just wasting their money. You decide.

PLANNING A MEETING AND POINTS DON'T MIX

Within the past year, I came across an offer by a major hotel chain aimed at meeting planners and companies looking for a meeting location. The promotion offers triple the quantity of loyalty reward points if you book your meeting at one of their hotels during a two month period at the end of the year.

It's simple: give perks to secure more meetings business. On the surface, this seems like a crafty way to create an edge in the RFP marketplace without spending any real money to do so. The points cost little, but they're worth little as well. So, does anybody care about points when it comes to meetings? What are they really good for?

To fully answer this question, you have to first look at who benefits from receiving such points. In the case of meeting planners, their contracts very often stipulate that they cannot accept these types of points or that they have to give them back to the client. If this isn't expressly stated—for instance, when a meeting planner is independent—then there might be some impetus to use such reward points. But, it's often the case that meeting planners will not want to stay at the same hotel as their clients.

Second, points are individualized, which means they cannot be distributed to a general company account but must be attached to a person. This treads on some very unethical fibers, especially when the company is publically traded and an employee cannot legally accept gifts with a value of over $25. So, if not the meeting planner and not the employee, then who is being incentivized by these points?

Consider this example. When helping plan the P&G alumni meeting in my home town of Toronto, we received just over 100,000 loyalty points for booking with a certain major downtown hotel. Not only did the points only garner an iota of our interest when planning the site, but no one could ethically accept them after the fact. We ended up having a raffle for the planning committee and the points were proffered as one of the prizes. Moreover, the winner of the points later told me that such a hefty accumulation only netted him a free weekend's stay.

Not only were these loyalty points a trivial bonus, but they weren't even anywhere closer to a top consideration when booking. Why is that?

By and large the most important aspect of deciding where to host a massive symposium is availability. Does the site meet our needs when it comes to ball rooms, guest rooms, breakout rooms, catering and other miscellaneous features? Being able to bring hundreds of people together from all over the world into one building is no small task. It requires expert precision and a variety of room types. Then, and only then, does a meeting planner consider other aspects such as hotel brand, cost structure, proximity to city attractions and, on the bottom rung of the totem pole, points.

So, I wonder who is swayed one way or the other by an offer of triple points. To me, it seems like an empty offer and a waste of marketing resources. Instead, to go about your meetings business, you should start at the top of the totem pole and focus on delivering the best possible site a city can offer.

MICROSOFT'S NEW STANDALONE STORES OFFER KEY INSIGHT FOR HOTEL BRANDS

Microsoft has recently opened its first international standalone store in a popular mall in my hometown of Toronto. This move was part of a much larger strategic vision that no doubt involved numerous store launches worldwide.

The tech giant is indeed warranted in this action as they need a physical outlet to properly demonstrate their myriad of hardware products such as the Surface tablet, the Dune, the Xbox as well as their full line of software merchandise (namely Windows OS and Microsoft Office). Microsoft's plans follow a similar model by Samsung, where both corporations need only look at the rousing successes of Apple's and Sony's chic retail outlets to see the potential in this move.

Overall, Microsoft's goal is the same as the other hi-tech giants—reach consumers directly to reinforce brand image and heighten sales. Standalone locations in major shopping centers enable consumers to interact with the products, enhancing the buying experience. These retail outlets are staffed with knowledgeable professionals (much like Apple's Geniuses) to make sure that each customer gets exactly what they want.

What can hotels glean from this? Think about how your brand is presented to your guests. Compare your points of differentiation as presented on an OTA versus your own website, or that of your parent chain.

Apple makes outstanding products. Apple Stores create that fan buzz which drives fierce brand loyalty as well as offering a hub to tactilely introduce new consumers. I don't believe that they would be in the running for the number one publicly traded company in the world without establishing a physical point to build this relationship.

Simply put, it's not just about the purchase but the experience of the purchase. And how does the buying experience differ between the acquisition of a room directly from a hotel website and the acquisition of a room through an OTA? Given the tremendous effort you put into your brand.com site, I'll wager there is a significant difference in terms of your product's positioning.

True, the OTAs are a channel and you have to go to where the consumers are. It's all too easy to shrug your shoulders and just go along for the ride. But, the purchase of an accommodation through an OTA does not bolster any hotel's brand image; it bolsters theirs.

You can continue living in the present or you can start planning for the long-term future, one where your exceptional brand qualities are showcased across every consumer channel you operate in. If you believe in your brand, those channels where your property is commoditized are not the place you want to be.

Microsoft's strategy is bold, but I believe it will pay off. I'm not suggesting that a hotel chain open its own retail outlets. Rather, it would be prudent to think of new ways to palpably augment the buying experience. How do you market your brand's unique qualities across traditional and electronic mediums? What can you add to your website's reservation software to assure guests that they are making the right choice?

TEN QUICK WAYS TO GET THE MOST OF THIS SUMMER SEASON

Ah, the long hot days of summer. Plenty of sunshine, plenty of heat. While many properties are hoping for their best few months, here are ten ideas to consider as ways to step it up a notch and invigorate your team.

1. *Set a personal goal for yourself.* It starts with rumination. Then, write it down and commit to having it completed by Christmas. It doesn't have to be big. My top one for this season was learning how to welcome a guest perfectly in Mandarin. As another example, if you are one of those few who have not embraced a tablet computer, buy one and learn everything you can about where this hybrid technology is headed.

2. *Exterior photographs.* Unless you're in the throes of renovation, late summer brings with it magnificent lighting conditions and bountiful foliage. Now is your chance to get those great exterior pictures you've been meaning to take but have somehow forgotten.

3. *Reward your best group.* Everyone needs a vacation, even if it's a mid-week night or two. Once your corporate customers arrive, give them some peace and quiet. No sales pitches or no business breakfasts; just a welcome amenity and a personal thank you letter.

4. *Throw stuff out.* This one's great for GMs. Walk into the sales office and ask to see the store room. Is it tidy? Or, does it look like a high school locker? Strongly encourage your sales team to use the quieter summer months to throw everything out that's outdated, outmoded or never used as well as everything with the wrong logo, wrong color or wrong design.

5. *Seek departmental input.* Ask each department head for the single task they feel is most valuable which they just didn't get a chance to tackle, but if the opportunity came about, they would pounce. Review them all; authorize only those within reason. In doing so, make the individual who introduced the idea responsible for implementation and reporting the results.

6. *Host a spectacular summer party.* Have the chef prepare new menu items then give everyone a chance to test the menu and write their notes. It's also a good time to improve your children's menu as you have an incredible focus group that's out of school and available.

7. *Walk the grounds.* As a biweekly routine, wake up one morning before sunrise and walk your property. Shake hands with all your night staff. Reward them with small gifts ($25 or less for tax reasons) and personally thank them for their work under these often strenuous conditions.

8. *Streamline your planning process for next year.* With over half the year done, it's already time to start thinking of the next one. So, make vows. Vow never to produce those redundant, and somewhat useless, 100-page plans that no one looks at. Vow to make your planning process better so your results truly shine.

9. *Hire a student.* If you don't have an intern program, consider hiring a student part-time. Don't advertise. Use word of mouth; your planning committee, department heads and team leaders can get the word out quickly. A little youthful vitality will go a long way.

10. *Give that student a meaningful task.* This is not just clean-out-the-storeroom time. Rather, it's an opportunity to imbue your life-long passion for hospitality into a new generation of hoteliers. For example, have them look at your brand.com website in comparison to your competition's site on a page-by-page basis with an evaluation of strengths and weaknesses. Get them thinking critically—a crucial step towards passionate resolve and action.

And above all, spend some well-deserved time with your family. If you have children, devote time to them without staring at your smartphone every 15 minutes. You will find that your corporate manager and owners can indeed live without you for 48 hours.

SUMMER'S OVER: GET BACK TO WORK

I hope everyone reading this had an excellent Labor Day vacation. This holiday typically marks the end of summer, but officially the season still has another few weeks to go. So, with the summer season behind you, spend a few minutes taking stock of your situation and planning your push through to the end of the calendar year. Here is my 'Top Ten' list of items that should be on your radar as we drive towards the final quarter.

1. *Reflect.* Where do you stand through the end of August in terms of GOR and occupancies? What is the current forecast for the balance of the year? How close are you to being on track with budget? Are your promotions and other marketing programs meeting expectations? Are you getting any insight from your STR reports into competitive rates?
2. *Review capital expenditures versus plan.* Often adjustments are needed to reflect unforeseen situations or delays. No one likes year-end surprises. Better to get these changes addressed now.
3. *A property walk should also include that of your key competitors.* A little bit of field research can go a long way; maybe inspire you as well. And while you're at it, does your property still say 'summer' on in-room and in-house collateral?
4. *Talk to your sales team about the year's rates.* You need to build your base of meetings and conference rooms for next year. While your budget may not even be finalized and targets not yet established, rates and bookings through the fourth quarter are critical to succeed in the first part of next year.
5. *Time to ensure that all your rates are loaded for online bookings.* I understand that you do not even have a marketing plan yet, but you need to have rates available for FIT at least 366 days in advance. Rates can be changed, but customers who can't book your property will be off scrutinizing the next hotel.
6. *By this point in the year, you're already late with your marketing plan.* Remember my previous comments and suggestions: brevity is key. You are out to grow your business, not kill trees for photocopy paper.

7. *Thanksgiving is coming.* Begin your plans for this late-year program now. The earlier you get your program established, the earlier you can spread the word and get bookings.

8. *Along the same lines as Thanksgiving, start thinking Black Friday.* It is the number one retail day of the year and you will want to ensure you get your fair share. At the very least, brainstorm ideas with your team.

9. *Give some initial thoughts to the pre-Christmas period.* For most, this is traditionally a lull before the winter holiday boom. Advance planning and special incentives can serve to build revenues. Don't forget to tie a charitable cause into your Christmas program.

10. *Plan an end-of-year thank you for your past guests.* This doesn't need to be a particularly grand gesture, but something of value and definitely something with a little more punch than an email. Physical is always better as it activates more senses than just sight. Perhaps a small end-of-year gift basket for your key customers and a mailed coupon on future purchases for everyone else? Just something to show that you truly care.

AUTUMN RESOLUTION: YOUR COMPETITION IS YOUR INSPIRATION

Everyone makes New Year's resolutions. They're fun and they're a promise for change (and nowadays they're almost compulsory). But with summer winding down, perhaps there's time to holistically reevaluate on a seasonal basis. September is the back to school month. Ergo, autumn resolutions make total sense. After all, real change happens in baby steps and a quarterly refresher can go miles towards maintaining the levity and practicality of the impending New Year's wish list.

This year in particular, I've been blessed with the freedom and opportunity to travel all over the world for business, staying in accommodations both noble and no frills. One observation I've made is that despite all the resources and online media within arm's reach, many managers have contracted an acute case of tunnel vision. People know their property or their chain, and that's about it, something especially true for those curtailing holiday time or consistently vacationing close to home.

Examining how other hotels, including your competitors, work is a vital exercise towards self-improvement and, ultimately, ongoing success. And you can't do it by just surfing the web and its abundance of multimedia. You have to get on property, view the operations in full and observe any intangibles. Here are a few options:

1. *Go by yourself, unannounced.* Check-in, eat, relax and be a fly on the wall. Don't let your insider knowledge get the better of you. Try to think like a consumer, discerning yet hassle-free, and let the experience wash over you. What you're looking for are all the minor touches that complete the narrative. And those minor touches are everywhere, from the décor and in-room amenities to the staff demeanor and attention to service.

2. *Go as a couple.* Treat your significant other to a weekend getaway. Do as you would if you were going solo but fill in the itinerary with a few activities. Above all, recognize that each person's experience will be different and therefore each person's inspiration will be different.

Talk it through to see how your interpretations of events differ and where they coincide.

3. *Comp a few other managers.* Form a team from across multiple departments that you are confident all have expert and incisive opinions. Your mission, should you choose to accept it, is purely reconnaissance. Send those managers and yourself into a competitor's lair at various times during the week and see what you can dig up. Then have a meeting to compare and contrast.

Again, what you are looking for are the minor touches, not the broad strokes that require a full forearm into the budgetary cookie jar to make feasible. You want details where you can say to yourself, "Why aren't we doing that? We should be doing that. We can do that!" Here are some inquisitive examples of the playing field we're dealing with:

- How does the hotel staff welcome new guests? How many people are outside and how many are inside? What's the procession of events?
- How are you treated by the front desk clerk? Is there anything specific that he or she mentions or offers? What objects are present on the front desk countertop?
- What's the ambiance in the lobby? What extra décor items do they add to promote this feeling? How's the general flow of people through the lobby?
- What's your first reaction to the guestroom? Were there any notes or food items personally addressed to you? What features dominate the room?
- How's the bed? Do you like the pattern on the linens? How many pillows do they provide? Any other comfort accessories?
- How's the washroom? What hygiene products do they provide? Is the shower easy to use? What extra features does the washroom have?
- What was your initial impression of the restaurant? How were you greeted and seated? What feeling does the menu exude, both in food offered and in format? Were there any exceptional cuisine items on the menu, ones that you had to try?
- Remember to use your smartphone camera. Take photos of everything. Transfer these photos to your tablet or laptop and

project them at the next planning committee meeting. Share your insights visually; it's a lot faster than writing a mega-report.

These questions obviously exclude dozens of other facets that go into the making of a successful hotel visit—ones you can only truly feel once you're there. I stress the old adage that you'll never know until you try. Get out there, experience your competition and let them inspire you with new ideas that you can act upon and act upon post haste. Make your autumn resolutions all about the smaller adjustments, leaving more wiggle room to accommodate the grander changes you will propose come January. Given that it is a budgeting time of year, this approach makes more sense than at any other time during the year.

MOVIE NIGHTS: HALLOWEEN AND BEYOND

Hotels make for fantastic event venues. We all know this; we're all proud of our facilities! They're flexible, spacious, beautifully decorated and chaperoned by attentive, qualified staff.

One of the simpler, yet quite effective, ways that we demonstrate this around this time of year is through a Halloween-themed movie night. Often held in a ballroom fashioned into a makeshift rear-projector theatre with freshly prepared snacks on the side, these events are great for bringing travelers and the community together for a night of spooks, thrills, chills, gasps and maybe even some laughs.

Certainly it helps to build the Halloween buzz if your property is already whispered about in popular urban legends, or if it is indeed rife with paranormal activity. For these notorious properties, a movie night or a ghost tour is already a bona fide best seller. But such supernatural exploits are relevant for only an iota of the properties out there. For the rest of us, think of this as an event to celebrate and thank the community for the support.

By now the concept of the Halloween Movie Night or Scary Movie Marathon is de rigueur for hotel marketing teams. It's a breeze to organize and far less burdensome than, say, crafting a haunted house experience. If a movie night is so easy to put together for one commercial holiday, why not extend the concept for a few others?

How many movies can you think of that take place over Christmas, Thanksgiving or Valentine's Day? Certainly there are enough to fill a four or five hour timeslot. Why not develop a movie night for all three holidays?

Start by browsing your options using a combination of Google searches, IMDB and Wikipedia to find a good mix of films as well as their MPAA ratings and runtimes. Next, the most important aspect of this venture to investigate is film rights. As you are using the motion pictures for commercial gain there will be a licensing fee. Yes, even if you are charging no admission, it is still considered a commercial undertaking.

I would suggest contacting both the home entertainment division of a major studio as well as your local film society about this. Perhaps this is why I have chosen to broach this topic now, on All Hallows' Eve, as both these entities may take a while to get back to you.

And there's good reasoning behind each of these parleys. Every major studio owns a vast library of films for you to choose from, giving you the breadth to accurately pick enough content to fill an evening's worth of appropriately themed, family friendly content, and maybe even a forgotten gem from the 30s or 40s. Fostering a healthy relationship with your film society is equally as obvious. They can advise on legal issues, give recommendations and help promote your event within their circles of the community at large.

Next, get your kitchen involved. The food for Halloween shouldn't be the same as that for Christmas or Valentine's Day. The more eccentric the screening's theme, the more fun your creative culinary team will have conjuring up tasty goodies for game day. You could even use such a hypothetical event as a team-building exercise to see just how ingenious your chefs are. For instance, besides candy eggs and bunny-shaped chocolates or cookies, what other confectionaries would be synonymous for Easter?

Don't think that the movie night is restricted to public holidays either. Consider making it a monthly or bimonthly gig. For instance, Ojai Valley Inn & Spa used to run an outdoor film classic series featuring Golden Age masterpieces followed by a Q&A with one of the actors. Unfortunately, the Q&A portion is a luxury that only SoCal can deliver with any consistency. Sadly, there are few independent theatres that screen movies from the 50s, 60s and 70s these days (especially with the mandatory shift towards digital projection), and yet there is still an audience for such fare. Given their relative scarcity, the classic film conceit from this example can easily be adapted for your property.

Perhaps this is a niche—and by niche I mean a crevice of a niche— where you can grow your local market, but it's still a worthy action void of ignominy. Think advertising a paltry $5 to $10 entry fee and a discount for loyalty club members. At the end of the day, films are fun for everyone, and you may just earn a buck while you're at it.

LOVE IS IN THE AIR, ALL MONTH LONG

Love is in the air, and when you're feeling this good, why limit it to just one day? Most of you have already hopped on this Valentine's Day bandwagon, but for those heretofore naysayers, I stress that any romance package or likewise themed offer should last for the entire month of February, not just for the day of the 14th or the encapsulating week.

Contextually, Valentine's Day has a very significant advantage over other holidays. It is very lucratively distanced from other commercial entities which might hope to steal the stoplight.

Take the Commonwealth's Boxing Day for instance. Occurring annually on December 26th, here in Ontario it is a statutory holiday and a mammoth day for retail sales. But alas, one extra day was never enough to sate vendors' pockets, especially given its proximity to Christmas. To appease the plebs still suffering from turkey comas, Boxing Day magically morphed into Boxing Week. Marketers everywhere smirked and high-fived one another; now their promotions and advertisements could be leveraged for a seven day stretch, not just one measly 24-hour rush.

The shift from 'day' to 'week' was a strategic ploy so companies would have more time to differentiate their promotions from those for Christmas. Recently, I have even seen some vendors execute a 'Boxing Month' approach. Along these same lines, Cyber Monday emerged from the fires of Black Friday so that certain online retailers could distinguish themselves from all the white noise and hustle before the American Thanksgiving.

Back on topic, what holidays surround Valentine's Day as potential competitors for a consumer's attention? Here in North America, this would include Groundhog Day (which is celebrated for all of five minutes everywhere outside of Punxsutawney, Pennsylvania), the Super Bowl (happening two weekends before) and President's Day (which doesn't exactly have the 'let's splurge on a getaway' zing to it). In order words, nada.

Elsewhere in the world, first to mind are Mardi Gras and Ash Wednesday, both concurrent with Valentine's Day. Unless your hotel is in a predominantly Catholic region with a proven track record of ignoring Valentine's Day, then your marketing and advertising efforts for the most romantic holiday in February will have a substantial reach and vast influence regardless of religious interference.

It's settled then that you will consider Valentine's Day as a month-long venture, yes? Great! Next up is the concept of romance and how you can use the holiday's pretense as an opportunity to add some excitement throughout your property.

This is less about the grand gestures and more about the nuances and romantic spins that you imbue into your regular operations. Gifts for your guests shouldn't be expensive; it's the thought that counts. For instance, add a half dozen roses to rooms of newly arrived couples. Dip some strawberries in dark chocolate and offer them as an amuse-bouche for all patrons to your restaurant. That one works great for dinner as well as brunch! Even a Valentine's Day card and handwritten thank you note can go a long way towards winning your guests' hearts.

And if you're worried about your Valentine's Day promotions or activities getting stale over the course of the month, consider changing the theme slightly week-over-week. Maybe February 1st through 7th can be the 'spices of love' (cinnamon, vanilla, lavender, spearmint, etc.); February 8th through 15th can be romantic fruit (cherries, passion fruit, pomegranate and, of course, heart-shaped strawberries); then for the remaining two you'd be wise to shoehorn chocolate somewhere in there. I'm aware that I'm thinking with my stomach, but it's a good touch off point for other ideas in the same vein.

Make it a creative exercise with whatever team is involved and that excitement will reverberate through to the final presentation. Work with your marketing department to develop different packages for each seven day period. As well, F&B can have a lot of fun with this as they brainstorm and craft unique mains, desserts and cocktails for each week's theme.

These are just a few ideas that you can use to invigorate your team for this year, next year and beyond. With any luck, the magic of Valentine's Day can transport your hotel from red to black for this oft-lonesome month of February.

A NOTE ON BABY BOOMERS

I am a baby boomer. I have gone through the gamut of youthful adventures and trying everything new, and now that I've settled into the latter stages of my life, I have a strong loyalty quotient. That is, I am loyal to a number of establishments and brands based on their repeatedly acceptable or great past performances. And now I have plenty of points, or clout, to throw around.

Take restaurants, for example. My kids often criticize me for going to the same restaurants month in, month out, instead of being more adventurous and going to the latest opening. My rationale for the tried and true is straightforward. My regular jaunts provide all of the basics—great food, fine atmosphere and a good wine selection—but also something more: recognition. From the moment I am welcomed inside, through the course of the meal to the time I leave, I am treated with respect and preference. In addition, on a random basis, I get extras, such as a complimentary dessert, drink or appetizer. This leads to me tipping the waitstaff anywhere between 20% and 25%. I have established relationships with these places. I'm comfortable there, and I know more or less what I'll be getting.

While the frequency with which I visit my local restaurants is far greater than that for hotels, I nevertheless have hospitality favorites and a strong loyalty to them. Remunerating on why these properties merit my return and my positive word of mouth, it is not usually the obvious, such as the size of the guestrooms, the amenities or the location, as these core elements are usually available at many other properties in the surrounding area.

The reason I select one property over the other is because of the way I am treated by the staff. This is by and large the only unwavering distinguisher. These seemingly small, intangible efforts drive me to return, time after time. Examples abound: a warm greeting from a doorman; recognition by the front desk thanking me for returning; a bellman who anticipates my needs; and housekeepers who do their job seriously and professionally. It's always a relief to know there are people who are 'on my side'. It helps give me comfort amidst a swarm of daily emails, meetings, conference calls, RFP submissions, pitches and all the other stressors.

Who in your organization generates this positive guest rapport—the type of relationships that actually generates loyalty? The answer: your line staff, and not necessarily your managers. Yes, those team members who are probably amongst the lowest wages per hour. And yet, they hold the key to your guest loyalty quotient. Think of this the next time you are evaluating your hiring criteria, planning a service training session or even negotiating with your unions.

The next few articles are devoted to baby boomers, who, as of the turn into the 2010s and decades beyond, are rapidly approaching retirement. This generation might not hold the reins that it once had in the 20th century, but it is still a commanding force in terms of consumer expenditures and a potent demographic for you to surmount.

REMINISCING ON RETIREMENT

This short note is for general managers and other senior managers over 50. If you do not meet these two criteria, please discontinue reading right now. On second thought, this serves as a great head's up for anyone of any age in the business.

Having reached the prime age of 60 last month, I am told by many that '60 is the new 40' or '60 is the new 50'. Not very reassuring, as the aches and pains of every sport injury of my youth reacquaint themselves with my joints.

Many friends of mine have retired and are urging me in this direction. Still others have left their employers of many years and are starting new businesses or consultancies with a vim and vigor that defies their age. These folks are passionate about their new work, their clients and their relationships, and are determined to do great work.

It used to be that by age 65, a manager would be proffered a shiny gold watch and proverbially sent out to pasture. I can recall when my grandfather retired from the railroad at this milestone. To me—at the time I was a teenager—he was old, outdated and obsolete! But now, that's only five years away; the ravens of ironic foreshadowing hungrily perked on the telephone wire outside my office window.

Today there appears to be no real age when you can retire, or choose to do so. Those who are in senior positions often have the luxury of choosing the date to step down, and can do so if their business lifecycle and finances allow them to. For those who have a corporate pension plan, the financial side of the equation is usually simplified. However, in canvassing the senior clients I work with, surprisingly, most do not have a very strong pension program. Thus, financial issues are a critical factor in their retirement decision.

Getting Your Own Financial Plan in Order

Most GMs are experts at planning and executing multiple budgets for their operations—revenues, expenses and capital budgets all seem to be managed with empyrean acumen. But, I am wondering how many of these individuals have the same command of their own financial state of affairs. In discussions, I have heard descriptors of personal finance as 'scary', 'not enough' and 'not sure'; far more often than positive remarks. The 2008 US property meltdown did not make things any easier. I find this tremendously disconcerting.

If you are managing a luxury property, you are surrounded by guests who likely rake in more than you do. It probably never ceases to amaze you how money can be spent with frivolous abandon. Separate yourself from this influencer and recognize that your fortunes are somewhat different than your guests. You don't know their circumstances, so don't let their spendthrift husk dictate your outlook.

This is not a matter of whether you want to retire or may never retire. Rather, it is a case of management. If you are in control of your financial house, you are in control of your destiny. Use the skills that you have honed in running your property to run your own finances. The relationship between revenue and expense has to be understood. Often, difficult compromises must be made. Capital expenditures (your mortgage, car and major home improvements) need to be effectively balanced. You know what to do; set the plan and stick to it.

If you are currently in dire straits, your primary goal is debt reduction. I'm not a certified financial planner, but it's self-explanatory that increasing your debt is generally not the solution. You should always secure help in this regard.

Finances are in Order, Now What?

For those who do have the wherewithal to make the retirement decision, be aware that this is not easy. Remember, you've been working in a high stress environment. You cannot easily move from this to only playing golf every day. (I said easily, as some will find this transition to their liking.) Still others will be looking for something to keep their minds active and their 'fingers' in the business, at least on a part-time basis. Again, planning a stepped approach of emeritus involvement may be prudent. Volunteering with a local charity, may also make good sense.

Then there is the issue of when. A good friend of mine, who also just turned 60, said he would give it another 10 years: five years full-time and another five part-time. He has no real financial impetus to continue, yet likes the stimulation of his work.

Several other friends have segued into consulting. One friend even bought a company so he could work as their CEO. He was just that bored with golf. Yet others, all my age, have fully retired and are enjoying not having to follow schedules or respond to bosses or other stakeholders. For all of these individuals, none have to work to make ends meet. It's a personal decision to persevere and never stop dispersing their expertise unto the community.

In my own case, I am privileged to have a great team and belong to some excellent hotel consultancy groups. I am also told that writing is one of those skills that only improves with age (fingers crossed). All good news, as retirement for me is not on the immediate horizon. Another ten years in the business or maybe another 20, I haven't decided yet, and frankly, I think that's a good thing.

MORE ON THE R WORD

It seems as if this topic is a bit touchy. I imagine that for many early boomers such as myself the thought of retirement may not necessarily be first and foremost, but at least on the radar. It's looming, lurking and can be quite frightening because it requires a complete overhaul of your daily work schedule and routines—a holistic change, and change is scary.

The reality of retirement is actually straightforward. If you work for someone, be it a private owner situation or a corporation, the time will eventually surface when you must step aside. Whether that is at a mandated age such as 65, 67 or 70, or by some unwritten rule, you have to move on. Change is inevitable. (For those who own their own property or company, you are the one in control. You can stay on obviously, but sooner or later, it will be time.)

Whatever your age, at some point you have to realize that your 'day job' is no longer. With this in mind, what should you do in preparation for this change?

Loss of Self Esteem

Right now, if you are a general manager or senior executive, I am sure that you get a daily dose of ego boost from the respect that your position commands amongst your office peer group. This disappears the day you check out. You are no longer instantly seated at the head of the table.

If you drop by for a visit, sure, you may get a few thumbs up from the team, but the second you no longer sign the pay cheques, be prepared for an attitudinal change. And if you were one of those bosses who survived through intimidation or fear, you better not persevere in this manner when the office is no longer your stomping ground. For that matter, hanging around the old office for any retiree is pretty much over. The new guy has no chance of success if you're playing helicopter parent. Short visits should be few and far between.

Loss of Sense of Purpose

You've probably spent more than 30 years going to an office. The routine of waking up, getting ready, fighting traffic and a reverse commute at the end of the day is over. To some, the idea of being on a 52-week vacation seems like paradise. To others, not having 100 urgent emails a day is nail-bitingly problematic.

Surprising to some, but there is a potential risk of depression, as each retiree wonders what to do all day. Of note, the most interesting feedback I received was from spouses who confided in me that they were worried about their husbands hanging around the house with nothing to do. Since first being clued in to this psychological transformation, I've asked others and it is not something exclusive to the male gender.

Loss of Relationships

Think about it. Probably half of our waking time is shared with office colleagues. Relationships with that peer group, be it over lunch, through meetings or general office banter will draw to an end. The common bond with these individuals might have been the work, or what I call 'banding together in the light of situational adversity'.

Once you are no longer part of this sphere of influence, you might find very few mutually shared interests with your office buddies. A similar situation occurs when you move your residence: are your old neighbors still friends?

Realize that maintaining relationships is a lot of work, and it's not out of scorn that your erstwhile colleagues are neglecting you, but that they are busy. Just don't get hung up on this aspect of change; be happy for your time spent at the company and be grateful for whomever makes an effort to prolong the relationship after you've lost the mutual confinement of an office environment.

Loss of an Expense Account

You might plan for the loss of a salary, and with pensions, have a retirement plan that pays you a calculated percentage of your former pay. That's fine, especially when the pension allotment is reasonably sizeable.

But I bet you have not calculated for the loss of ancillary perks: lunches, health insurance, dry cleaning, parking, company car, client gifts, company parties, country club dues and subscriptions all add up to a tremendous monetary figure. Many of my retired friends tell me that the loss of their executive expense account hurts more than not drawing a monthly cheque.

Loss of Support Services

Need to make an airline reservation? Call over to travel services. Having trouble setting up your email or downloading a security patch to your computer system? No problem, bring in the guys from IT. Need a restaurant for dinner this weekend? Your assistant will handle this easily (she knows everyone by first name and handles all of these for you). This goes even further for the corporate guys, who may have fleet plans to buy their automobiles and corporate tax advisors.

Once you leave, you're basically on your own. It is really funny to see a former CEO with his or her own personal laptop and not even knowing how to set up a new Gmail account. Compound this with fact that all of said retiree's friends still contact him/her via the old office email address, which now forwards to the successor.

Some Solutions: Be a Retirement Entrepreneur

If you are savvy enough to make it to the ranks of GM or higher, then you should be sufficiently smart enough to start planning for this eventuality. Don't be an ostrich with your head in the sand and blind to what's on the horizon!

You need to become a retirement entrepreneur. It's your life and the sooner you start to prepare for the eventuality of retirement, the easier this transition will be. A one or two-year preparation schedule would not be uncommon. Putting aside the financial aspects, other preparations include:

- If you haven't done so already, get your own Gmail account and your own laptop/tablet. Fully segregate personal and work communications. Move all of your personal communications to this email address. Learn how to back up your documents to the 'cloud'.
- Start making your own reservations, and get all of the planning information from your support team. Develop a deep dossier of

all of the appropriate information that runs your life. Set up a file on your Google Drive (accessed through Gmail) to store all of this information.

- Go beyond golf. Rekindle interests like taking up doubles bridge, fine art or another sport with a little more physical exertion like tennis or sailing. Golf is still a great pastime, of course, as long as you're mobile.

- Maintain your health. Making sure your health club membership is portable is paramount. If it's not convenient to where you live or travel then you're all the less likely to go. And it is more than just a membership; you have to use it! Watch the diet and keep your medical visits in order. While still fully covered, get all the latest and updated vaccinations too.

- Get involved. Channel your energies into education, charities and giving back to your community or church. Plan to utilize your time every day, just the same way as you did when working.

- Share the joys of retirement with your spouse. You will be spending more time with him or her during this next exciting phase of life, so finding the right activities to do together are all the more important.

- Expand your mind. Without the morning grind of getting to work and the daily brain drain of a nine-to-five, the sponge that sits above your eyes and below your scalp will be getting hungry for more juice. Personally, I've made an effort to read one book a week, alternating between fiction and nonfiction. That's with a job, too. I don't see any reason why this can't be accomplished for retirees. So, pick up a book; you never know what you might learn about the world or yourself!

WHAT'S YOUR NUMBER?

Several months ago, I saw an advertisement for a financial institution where various actors walked around haloed by a three-dimensional dollar figure—their savings target for retirement. The concept was sound, encouraging viewers to focus on saving for the future with each individual having a different financial goal. It's a great ad with an important message.

Giving this so-called fiscal 'number' a minute of thought isn't really the priority for those not facing the imaginary wall of retirement any time in the near future. With housing bills, car payments, kids' tuitions and the like, looking at the 401K in this grave light is not yet in the cards. But, once the dust settles on familial affairs, this number creeps into an overriding question; a barometer of sorts to how close or how far one is able to consider retirement and maintain a peace of mind about it.

As the commercial eloquently demonstrated, not only is there a different satisfactory number for everyone, but also these monetary figures change with time, taste and circumstance. Retirement is no longer a binary 'yes or no' financial achievement. The number that each person needs, or thinks they need, is fluid, making adherence to a rigid plan or goal highly impractical.

Here are some simple considerations:
- The greater the age you call it quits, the lower the financial goal for retirement. It's a matter of life expectancy charts and, even though I foresee these statistics to rise substantially over the next few decades, mortality is still something everyone must face.
- Many of us will probably continue to work in some sort of capacity for a number of years after retirement. This tiered approach, where there is less income rather than not at all, also reduces the strain on a rigid fiscal goal.
- Interest rates have a significant bearing on your number. We are in a period of strangely low rates. It used to be that you could safely look at a 5% rate of drawdown on savings as a benchmark for an annuity. Drop that figure by 1% to 1.5% and you have to ratchet up your number by a quarter. Meeting with a financial

planner to thoroughly understand this cause-effect situation is highly advisable.

- For many, the equity in their home is a critical part of their savings plan. While the housing market is showing signs of resilience, for many markets, there's still a long road ahead to restore the values attained before subprimes went belly up. By that time, any home will be a decade older and may require considerable renovations or tech upgrades to stay with the times. Also be mindful of the natural boom-bust cycle which has sharply affected the housing market since the proliferation of modern economic practices.

- Families put pressure on savings. It is no longer a guarantee that your children will get high paying jobs immediately upon graduating from high school, college or any other post-secondary educational pursuit. Continued support in at least some capacity is becoming a defining factor of the millennial generation. You might also be responsible for aging parents, putting further pressure on your strict financial goal.

- Different cities have different costs of living. This applies to your monetary plan of course, so changing locations can have a major impact; one that you might not wholly realize until the move is already completed.

When I was just starting my hospitality consulting firm, I asked a CFO client about the topic of retirement. Even though I was nowhere near the half-century mark, I wanted to know what he thought. His comfort factor (remember, this was some 20 years ago) etched in at $8.3 million. How he got that figure, I will never know. But, he said with all confidence that this was his goal, and once he achieved it he would no longer be working.

Fast forward to now, he's living the retirement dream while I'm still working. Perhaps thinking long-term and solidifying your number earlier on can help guide your work life and motivate you to reach a loftier goal. So, what's your number?

GRAY IS THE NEW GREEN: PART I

Gazing ahead, much of the discussion in hotelier circles pertains to the impact of technological changes on the modern consumer, and indeed I'm no exception. The image of nouveau travelers evoked by managers and hospitality marketers such as myself is generally one between the ages of 20 and 60 who 'gets it'; someone who intrinsically understands technology, using the power of electronic devices for research, deals and everything in between.

The point that we hospitality writers are trying to hammer home is that properties must adapt to meet the buoyant expectations of the laptop and smartphone generations. One of the primary intents to provide hoteliers with a 'digital age' perspective on what these travelers look for in a property that merits their loyalty. I vehemently emphasize loyalty because it is much easier to keep a customer than it is to get a new one—doubly true given the manifold options a consumer has to find another suitable operator.

This is a long-term mindset, preparing you for the future of travel that will define the next few decades. In the short run, however, all this talk of technological evolution and modernization can naively overlook the glut of baby boomers, myself included, fast approaching the threshold retirement age of 65. People at or over this age currently represent roughly 13% of the US population, but by 2020, it's estimated that this percentage will climb to between 16% and 19%. Japan, most of Europe and the rest of the developed world abide by this sexagenarian trend, although exact statistics vary nation by nation.

The idea of reaching the coveted age 65 is very different than what it was 10, 20 or 50 years ago, and baby boomers are hardly immune to most of the concurrent changes within the younger demographics. For starters, why 65?

This preconceived demarcation was largely established based on average life expectancies figures and the 20th century nine-to-five punch clock workplace model. The current lifespan estimate for a North American is roughly 78 years (75 for men, 81 for women), making 65 a fairly appropriate age to send a career worker out to pasture to enjoy their final decade or so in peace. I find this appraisal at 78 to be maligned for the incoming boomers as it is an extrapolation from older generations less enlightened towards the ways of healthier diets, consistent exercise and cigarette-free respiratory tracts in addition to the fruits of new life-enhancing pharmaceuticals and medical procedures. All fingers point to longer life expectancies.

Furthermore, the very definition of retirement has grown a newfound plasticity. People increasingly recognize that staying active through regular mental exertion is a foremost means to extend life. Thus, 65 is no longer the age when every person has to stop working altogether. Rather, many are transitioning into yet another chapter of their careers. The hours may become flexible and the checks may thin, but a job is nonetheless a daily regulator of health.

Perhaps Japan, the nation topping the worldwide life expectancy charts, provides more evidence of this. You could argue it's their habitual diet supplemented by cleanly prepared carbs, fish (healthy omega-3 fatty acids) and ample green tea (antioxidants), but there's something more. The traditional Japanese culture values their elderly to much larger degree than in European-born societies, bestowing the oldest family members as heads of the household and cherishing their sagacity with extended decision-making responsibilities. When the mind loses purpose, the body gives up, and members of the developed world are rapidly following the Japanese to avoid this mental stagnation precursor brought on by retirement.

Returning to the digital side of things, it would be unequivocally false to stereotype baby boomers as technophobes. Maybe they aren't the early adopters and maybe text message shorthand isn't second nature, but this doesn't preclude them at all from owning smartphones or tablets, or being regular users of social media. Perhaps the only omnipresent distinction that can be made is that because this demographic existed before the outset of computers and the internet, more contemporary channels of communication aren't top of mind. We'd rather phone a friend instead of text, or email instead of message over Facebook or Twitter, although we're still fully aware of the latter route in both cases.

What does this all mean? Yes, it's an aging population, but the adage 'You can't teach an old dog new tricks' should now only be attached to canine contexts. Boomers are not a generation that will fade quietly into the night. Many of us will continue the daily grind long past the

65 presumption. We are also hard at work adjusting to the conveniences and rapidity of a social media and internet-centric lifestyle.

On the marketing front, this means that our wages will still be a dominant force for the next decade. Some of us are retiring and looking to spend, others are still working (and possibly traveling for business) but nonetheless in need of some vacation time. Mobile, tablets, OTAs, social media—all trends that apply elsewhere also apply to us, albeit with less immediacy. So, in order to win our dollars, you must tactfully deliver the balance of both old-fashioned appeal with an experience aimed at those still young at heart.

GRAY IS THE NEW GREEN PART II

As a resident baby boomer writer, it's time once again for me to chime in with a few thoughts on a great demographic shift unfolding before our eyes. First, a statistical recap: boomers born in the post-WWII years from 1946 to 1964 comprise a total of roughly 78 million Americans. Aging is inevitable and, if you're lucky, you and your hotel may well find yourselves in greener pastures by thinking like a 'gray'.

In the past few years, I've had many discussions with people my age; those of us entering the sexagenarian twilight years of a long, industrious career. From this anecdotal research, what's most striking is that retirement is now less of a guaranteed guillotine at age 65 and more of a transitional phase. More and more people are realizing that work is an important aspect of one's life, for disposable cash as well as for health. So, why excise it in its entirety?

Nowadays, retirement presents the opportunity to enter a second career, albeit in a part-time consulting or emeritus role. After all, a brain with nearly half a century of practical experience and intuition still has bountiful residual value, regardless of what new technology or hungry young whippersnapper enters the scene.

As well, a weighty factor for this wind down as opposed to a complete withdrawal relates to fiscal concerns. The cost of living has skyrocketed and so have average life expectancies—two elements that compound to largely negate the 20th century age 65 retirement paradigm. For most, it's no longer monetarily feasible to stop the cash inflow outright at this age and expect to reap the highlife for two or three extra decades.

As it relates to hotels, this points to a different type of travel behavior than what is currently archetypal for retirees. Boomers are no longer a sedated mass of gullible cheapskates. We want adventure, we want spectacle. We are very keen on travel—a necessity even—and we will exercise that right en masse. But boomers continuing to work will have less time for extended leisure stays and instead will be on the lookout for shorter, more productive vacations as well as the occasional business excursion.

Slowly but surely, this demographic has tuned its fork to align with the Gen X and millennial generations who already understand how to optimize their travel time and their wallets. Boomers are now wise to the ways of modern technologies—smartphones, tablets, internet research—and are using such tools to minimize costs and maximize time. Expect boomers to seek out the most bang for their buck overtop of absolute loyalty to one brand or another, albeit with a different rhythm than that of their younger counterparts.

For them, it's a matter of function over form, personal memories over image. It's a creeping sense of time deprivation that implies less about the status of associating with a hotel brand and more about what experiential benefits will be gained. For example, when describing a spa package, focus first on the effectiveness of your stress-reducing treatments. For a restaurant, weave your narrative around unique aspects of the cuisine, with the ambiance as a clear second, and rubbernecking opportunities as a distant third. Yes, we crave sophistication, but it should never compromise the taste of the food. To build loyalty, think of ways where you can step in to complete rudimentary tasks for guests (such as prearranged walking tours or dinner reservations) so that boomers can remain as carefree as possible while on vacation.

Despite any hints of frugality suggested in these previous paragraphs, many boomers are still big spenders. They want luxury and they are willing to pay for extras that will maximize their enjoyment while traveling—the extras that add value through convenience. Individual car services make your hotel look like a star. A solid and efficient concierge service is also a huge plus—something I take particular note of when researching a potential hotel to give my credit card information. Or, consider two alternatives to this, one in the form of a native mobile app to streamline local recommendations, and two in the luxury marker of a private butler service.

On a personal note, I liken this new way of boomer thinking to more of a 'Work Hard, Play Hard' approach than what is typically bestowed on the lackadaisical retiree. When I go on vacation—something that is definitely happening more frequently as I get older—I go all out. This not only means that I'm considering luxury properties for my time, but that prior to my departure, I am constantly researching local attractions via google and fine-tuning my itinerary so that there's never a dull moment in my journey.

And once again, it all boils down to the onsite experience. Prior to any booking, I'll know if a region under consideration has enough local activities and attractions to keep me (and my wife!) engaged and amused. But what makes me book with you versus one of your competitors will be the services, expertise and knowledge you bring to the table to help make my journey as relaxing and work-free as possible.

GRAY IS THE NEW GREEN PART III: POINT HOUNDS

Loyalty programs are a luxury that many take for granted nowadays. This wasn't always the case, and much like the advent of the television, loyalty programs and their associative reward points are something that rose to prominence right as the baby boomers reached adulthood.

I still recall the unveiling of the American Airlines AAdvantage program in 1981, the second official loyalty program in the whole world right behind that for Texas International Airlines (which is now technically a part of United Airlines). What was once a very unique 'miles for points' selling advantage has been universally applied for airlines, hotels, retail outlets, gas stations, credit cards and so on. Nowadays, such programs are expected and hence it takes an increasingly lucrative points-to-reward ratio to spark any sort of consumer excitement and, in turn, loyalty.

But there is an interesting opportunity within the aging boomer masses. We matured alongside the novelty of such programs and, whether out of respect, habit or stubborn nostalgia, we are the generation most correlated with the concept of 'point hounds'—those who ardently seek out desirable rewards and make a plan of redeeming them.

Given the boomers' leading spending power accumulated through decades of career life within some of the most prosperous decades for the North American economy, we have likewise accrued the most points on average of any generation. Now, because of retirement, we are ready to cash in our points en masse for the best deals, and we have the time to book a year or so in advance as mandated by many of these points programs.

This has both pros and cons. First, most properties don't obtain a direct monetary stimulus from point redeemers. For the most part, it's a cost the hotel has to swallow. Never forget about the immeasurable secondary benefits: word of mouth and upsells. Also, the principle of 'a full house is a happy house' applies here; this group can help you raise occupancy levels during traditional low seasons.

Typically speaking, point hounds are a rather thrifty lot, but that doesn't mean they are immune to the emotional sale drivers a marketer might use on property and through the website to help capture a bit more revenue. The hospitality industry boils down to the creation of special experiences and memories for guests. Play up this fundamental objective by appealing to a boomer's desire to make each moment count, whether it's through food (buy one get one free desserts, for instance), beverages (special aperitif menu for loyalty program members), spa (retiree-only treatments) or rooms (upgrade at half price pending availability).

And then, of course, if a point hound likes what your hotel has to offer, word of mouth will bring more fellow baby boomers in and further opportunities for upsells and loyalty building. Some of that word of mouth may even trickle down to Gen Xers and Millennials, propagating your brand awareness into future generations of consumers. The bottom line is that even though the concept of boomer point hounds may seem discouraging, always be on the lookout for creative ways to turn this gray into a potential new source of green.

WHAT DO YOU CONSIDER TRADITIONAL MARKETING?

Given today's rapidly changing landscape of hotel marketing, it's all too easy to get caught in a rigid frame of mind in terms of how you classify your sales channels. As a result, the term 'traditional marketing' needs constant revision in accordance with how long a given channel has existed and its relevance to the current cash cows.

Off the top of my head, I would group under traditional marketing the following: print media (magazines, newspapers), brochures, radio, television, trade shows and travel agencies. From this, one could easily assume that 'traditional' encompasses everything physical as well as electronic means that do not revolve around the internet. Therefore, under digital marketing you could put: e-newsletters, OTAs, SEM, SEO, flash sites, social media and so on.

Where then would you place banner ads and any associated re-targeting? Both are wholly dependent on internet traffic and yet they aren't anything new. In terms of efficacy, banner ads are abysmal compared to other traditional channels like magazines or even television. I'd say that the word 'traditional' needs some redefinition.

First, I would encourage you to think in terms of categorizing social marketing channels as a separate entity. This comprises any and all social networks like Facebook, Twitter, LinkedIn and Pinterest, but it also can include nearly anything where there is an interactive component with guests. Think online review sites like TripAdvisor or Yelp in addition to your voice channel where your service reps have the opportunity to directly impact a consumer's level of appreciation for your property.

In the past, I've advised against thinking of social media as a marketing channel. Instead, they are relationship building tools. Now, I've come to believe that relationship building is marketing; it's just not as overt as you would find in direct, 'traditional' channels where there's no room for any back and forth. What I'm finding more and more is that not only are the channels themselves evolving, but likewise are the ways in which we cluster those channels, subtly altering the ways that we approach such groupings.

And so I leave it to you. This article was intended to get you thinking about how you judge and classify channels—new, old or not even available yet. Where do you draw the line between traditional, digital, social and whatever other term you use?

INTERNET MARKETING

Part of the Las Vegas City Center, ARIA has, since its launch, been considered among the finest and most distinctive properties in the city.

INTRODUCTION

The internet is all the rage these days, and rightfully so as there are numerous ways that it can be utilized to enhance your business goals. Rather than carry on explaining the obvious and preaching on the benefits of optimizing your digital channels, the following section comprises select topics and electronic products that demonstrate some of the more fascinating (and alarming) ways that the internet is being used for corporate and personal gain.

The articles in this section explore various aspects of internet-based marketing that are affecting how we conduct ourselves in the hospitality industry. There will continue to be many new entrants to this field of expertise and many new opportunities to reach consumers in interesting ways. It's your job to think critically about what's really important and devote your resources to only the most beneficial endeavors.

Underlying each new product or channel is a psychological principle at work and if such activities do not stimulate a person's emotions in a positive way then perhaps your time and energy would best be spent elsewhere. No matter how colorful or snazzy a product looks, it all boils down to how it affects a consumer's emotions. As long as you keep this on the back of your mind when evaluating technologies designed to work in the realm of internet marketing, you can't go wrong.

IN SEARCH OF THE HOLY GRAIL IN A PERFECT WEBSITE

I recently had the privilege of judging entries for this year's HSMAI (Hospitality Sales and Marketing Association International) competition. This annual program calls for hotels and their agencies to submit their marketing efforts to be ranked among the best in the world. Competition is fierce and this year well over 1,000 entries were received. Judges can choose to examine any number of entry types. I chose websites, as more than 150 different entries were posted.

The goal of any judge is to be fair and above board in basing decisions. In doing so, we are provided with a summary of communications, all with the identical format, and a scorecard which ranks five core attributes on a scale from 1 (worst) to 10 (best). The attributes are straightforward, including creativity and results. After reviewing about 65 different individual hotel sites (I chose not to judge sites from CVBs, hotel chains and other related entities), it was clear that several did rise to the top. Hence, lessons for all.

Establishing a Criteria for Judging

Judges are left to their own devices insofar as what criteria they use to make decisions. The approach I took was an attempt to emulate the potential guest. In other words, I attacked the site from the standpoint of someone reaching it through search or referral, but with no prior knowledge of the property. On this basis, my goal was to see if the site could accomplish the following:

- Can the viewer find the guestroom section, look at a selection of accommodations, understand the differences between these room types and quickly get to the booking engine? (I did not rate the booking engines themselves, as that code is not really part of the front-end presentation.)
- Would a leisure visitor be able to easily find out what there is to do in and around the property? Was the information up-to-date

and available by at least four to six weeks ahead of time (a typical leisure booking window)?

- Was the site fluid when viewed on my iPad as well as my 15" laptop? (I didn't include my iPhone due to lack of time, but will definitely make this mandatory next year as mobile is a critical channel.)
- Was the site effectively linked to social media?
- How effortless was it to navigate through content? And, if I got to an area such as a blog or a downloadable menu, could I get back to the main page?
- Was there anything special about the site and its portrayal of the property that had me in awe and salivating for a visit? This query encompasses that certain 'X factor'—that intangible allure. To complete this assessment, I quickly looked at the target audience and tried to place myself in the mindset of these individuals.

Uniqueness Counts

Not surprisingly, most of the sites I reviewed scored well on the first five of six criteria. There were some with programming glitches (404 errors, 500 errors, etc.), and a few sites did not have any social media—rather surprising in today's Facebook and Twitter-driven landscape. Some had problems on the iPad. Still others had so much content that the site became cluttered with confusing navigation.

But the separation of the wheat from the chaff came in the area of uniqueness—the X factor. Disappointingly, many of the sites appeared to be cookie-cutters, using an identical template from other sites with minor tweaks to the fonts, colors and names of some of the navigation elements.

These sites covered the bases and worked flawlessly, but failed to differentiate their product on an emotional and subconscious level. And they generally scored well in everything but this last point—creativity. I'm sure they saved the property some dollars on their online construction, but really, how can you tell the world your hotel is better if you don't invest wholeheartedly in your own website?

With traditional advertising costs prohibitive to all but a few liquid brands and operators, how are you going to set your property apart with this, the kernel of marketing elements? Is this a pennywise and foolhardy approach? Hardly.

Photography is the Cornerstone

The other aspect of this process was photography. To make a great site, you need great photos. Not surprisingly, some of the sites I rated higher also had the best photography. Here is a rule of thumb: 50% of your web budget or more should go into photography. Good photography sells rooms. Great photography sells the vision of a fantastic vacation and gets the buzz started before the trip even begins. A picture really is worth a thousand words.

The Results

Of the 65-plus sites I personally reviewed, five clearly stood out as exemplary. Want to find out who has the best site? Guess you will have to look them up!

A NEW SCAM EVERY MINUTE

The success of electronic marketing naturally invites a criminal element. Our IT Departments, whether in-house or outsourced, are the ever-vigilant experts on fraud detection, not out of want, but necessity. Yet somehow, all of this prevention often moves such less-than-honest individuals to even more creative endeavors. Here is one such tale.

One of our Agency's clients is the prestigious Hazelton Hotel in Toronto. This exquisite, independent, 77-room property is uber-professional and impeccably run by a highly trained staff. The property's website (www.thehazeltonhotel.com) is commensurate with the Hazelton's cachet—understated with a focus on ultramodern decadence.

Recently, the Hazelton Hotel received a social media inquiry from an individual who wanted to know about employment at the property's 'sister' hotel in London, England. This note was immediately red-flagged. Sister property? We asked the Facebook respondent, who then forwarded a comment that boasted the Hazelton Hotel in Britain as an offshoot of the genuine property here in Canada.

Sure enough, a new website was created at www.thehazeltonhotel. co.uk. A cursory visit to the site was interesting. It was a beautiful property with magnificent guestrooms, dining, pool and scenic vistas. But something was wrong. Then, a double take: no hotel in London that we know of has a view of the Hong Kong waterfront, and no pool in London has palm trees and cabanas! Another oddity was that the site did not take online reservations. This is not unheard of, but rare in today's electronic environment. Of note, nowhere on the site does it refer to or link to the Toronto property.

A bit more digging. A quick look at the WHOIS data showed that the site URL was registered only in late July 2012 . . . in Nigeria. Quite logical for an esteemed British hotel, no? The photos were all sourced from interior design magazines and, for the most part, not sized correctly. Further, the English copy reflects that of a second language user. The site has no meta or keyword tags and is not wholly Google optimized. A Google Street View of the address given didn't reveal any prominent hotel edifice either. And lastly, the telephone number on the site goes straight to an answering machine.

But don't just take my word as bond; have some fun with it. Give them a call or drop them an email, and then see what happens when you prod for more details.

Okay, so why did the fraudsters go to all this trouble? What value would anyone have in replicating the name of an independent property? All we could surmise was that the London site was designed to phish the identities of unsuspecting employment applicants and potential guests who submitted requests for guestrooms. Indeed, emailing this 'property' brought forth a hasty and affirmative reply; no doubt the lure for subsequent inquiries about more private information. Worse yet, imagine what these charlatans could do with a newsletter email list.

To me this raises 'buyer beware' to a whole new level. And while this has happened to the Hazelton Hotel, our Agency's programmers believe that a replica site built on a URL-variant like this case could be created for any hotel in the world in about 40 hours, perhaps less when using a pre-coded WordPress template. While we took steps for the Hazelton Hotel to ensure its integrity, if you get some odd social media query of this nature, don't be surprised. In any event, what would you do in this situation? You might also want to contact your lawyers to protect yourself against any impending malevolence.

NEW PHOTOGRAPHY FOR A NEW TECHNOLOGICAL AGE

A picture is worth a thousand words. Photography is an essential part of selling your hotel, both in terms of displaying features and creating the emotional sale. We all know this, but it seems the message is getting lost under the weight of smartphones and the ability for anyone to snap off a half decent image. Standing in between management and guests are the professional photographers, and it's important to hear their point of view. That's why I approached Darren Edwards, a professional photographer who I've worked with in the past, for a quick interview, offering some pointers for managers on what makes for good pictures and how to better prepare a shoot to reduce the budget.

Photography generally starts as a hobby. How would you make this a career? Why hotels?

I got into photography when I was in high school. With my first paycheck from my first real job at age 15, I went to the drug store in Soldotna, Alaska and bought an Olympus OM10. I remember that day very well. I was hooked from day one. A few years later, after my high school photography teacher suggested I consider making this my career, I decided to attend Brooks Institute of Photography in Santa Barbara. It's the only thing I've ever wanted to do.

After Brooks, I moved to Vail, Colorado, and assisted for an architectural photographer there while also working in the hotel industry. I really enjoy working with hotels because it allows me to shoot a wide variety of subjects within one genre. From lifestyle and food to landscapes and architecture, hotels need it all. If I can provide exceptional work in all the areas they need, it makes the process easier for the client and keeps the jobs interesting for me.

Describe your typical hotel photo shoot. How long is it? What equipment do you use? What crew do you usually work with?

Every hotel shoot is different, which is great. Sometimes they simply need some updated room shots, but others are just opening or have just completed renovations, so these can be much longer. On average, we complete most jobs within a few days. The days can be very long or with strange hours, however. Unless the hotel is brand new, they are always open with guests everywhere, so we really have to take advantage of the overnight times and dawn when things like the lobby and restaurants are typically empty. I love getting that dusk or sunset light, but in the evening when that's happening, so is everything else at a hotel.

I bring a lot of gear to most hotel jobs. We always end up shooting a wide variety of subjects and often have unforeseen situations, so you never know what you're going to need. I have acquired enough gear through the years to light up just about anything a hotel can throw at me, indoors or out. I do, however, have the ability to travel fairly light, (if you can call 198 lbs light). I have my travel gear at exactly one pound under the limits for most airlines, so that helps save on the budget side.

I can get most of the work done with just one assistant, but it's always nice to have two or more. Having that extra body or two to move gear around the property, through the airports and in and out of rental cars makes the process so much easier. Besides, because of the way we light things, it's nice to have a dedicated digital tech and a lighting assistant. I completely understand, however, that most times it's all about the budget, so we work with whatever we are able to bring. Hotel photography is all about being able to adapt to the situation. It seems there are always unforeseen problems that arise, but when we overcome them with creative solutions, it keeps everything on track and the client happy. Extra people always help that process.

What are the most important aspects for hotel photography to showcase?

Hotel photography obviously has to showcase the main areas of the property, guest rooms, restaurants and spa. But beyond that, I think the focus should be on the guest experience. Too many times hotels get caught up in what they want and aren't looking at it from a guest perspective. The customer wants to envision themselves in the photos, so exceptional photography is one of the most important parts of a hotel's website. It needs to sell the experience of the property in order to entice the guest to want to choose them out of all the options they have.

What steps do you take to prep a guest room?

Two words: clean and crisp. In most cases, if the hotel is prepared, the rooms are shoot-ready when we arrive. We have, however, pressed sheets, fluffed pillows or moved things around for the best composition. The room has to look spotless, so we also hide cords, clocks, cards, menus or remotes to make it look as clean as possible.

How do you go about using lighting and framing to evoke a certain mood or feeling? What's your favorite time of day to shoot?

Lighting is one of the things that sets us apart from many other photographers. We'll light every scene in a variety of different ways in order to have all the options we want for post production. I generally see images in terms of how it will be put together, rather than in one shot. This way, we can create just about any look we want after the shoot is over. We like everything in the image to have depth, so lighting may come from many different directions. It will often depend on the mood or feel the hotel is trying to achieve. Some really like the over-lit look, while others prefer more of a journalist, natural feel.

My favorite time of day to shoot is almost always dusk and dawn. Even when they are not asking for it, I will often just go out and shoot during that time to see what I can get. I like to over-deliver and often these are the shots that can make the difference.

Are there any avoidable setbacks that you typically encounter?

The biggest avoidable setback I usually see is simply having the property prepared for us. The rooms need to be spotless and the staff needs to know we're going to be there. If areas of the property need to be closed, the guests need know well in advance. Having a hotel contact constantly with us (that has the authority to get things done quickly) is almost always necessary and unbelievably helpful. Waiting around to reach maintenance or get approval from different managers just ends up wasting valuable time and money.

A common complaint I see when reading online reviews is that the rooms do not look like they do in the photographs. Do you believe that a room should be as accurate as possible, or are you an advocate of enhancements such as floral arrangements?

I believe hospitality photography is about selling the fantasy of the property and not necessarily the reality. When was the last time you got a burger from a fast food restaurant that looked like the picture? The images need to show everything in its absolute best light in order to entice customers to choose that property. There are so many options out there and often the photography on the website can be one of the determinant factors to a potential guest.

Given the extra costs involved, what's your stance on using models to showcase the room, dining area or lobby?

Personally, I like using people for some of the scenes. I think it gives a mood and feel that a static image just can't match for certain areas of the property. However, there are usually corporate guidelines to consider in terms of using models and cost is always a factor.

Some shots work great without people, allowing the viewer to imagine themselves in that scene, while others are meant to show the atmosphere and really need people to complete it. Most jobs we've done include both. Besides, the way we shoot with people, we generally get the room or scene without them too, so the client can get both options. It does take longer and costs more, but the upside is a mood you don't get otherwise. Smiles mean a lot.

What is your position on using hotel staff in photography? Under what circumstances would you use staff members in lieu of professional models?

I always prefer to use professional models whenever possible. They bring a comfort and natural look to the images you just can't get from hotel staff or friends. They've usually done it before, are not shy and take direction very well. You can also predetermine your demographic, clothes choices and make sure they have the right look to give the feel you want. With everyone else, you are sort of at the mercy of what you can get. We always prefer to have as much control as possible, but also completely understand when the budgets don't allow it. Usually we end up with a few pros as our key players and put the staff in as the smiling service people or in the background to fill the scene.

Is there anything specific that you do to match a hotel's photography with its marketing strategy and target demographics?

I always try to have a creative meeting with the hotel managers or agency people prior to the shoot to get an idea of the look and feel they are trying to achieve. This can make all the difference in the planning process, not only in the shot timing, but also in making sure we are consistent with current work and the target market.

By your estimate, what percent of your photographs are used exclusively for the internet?

I would say the majority of our work ends up on the internet sooner or later. In this day and age of photography, we generally give, and most clients expect, unlimited rights. This gives our clients the ability to use the images anywhere they want for as long as they want.

Hotels are in constant need of new photography, so the life of an image is relatively short anyway. If we can provide an exceptional product and combine it with the same great service the hotels give their guests, they will call us back first the next time they need updates or new work.

How are you keeping pace with the current technology? Have these advances freed you to get better results?

I'm always working to keep up with the ever-changing world of photography by attending classes and expos, and by being involved in my local photo community. I started in the film days, so the digital world has opened up everything in terms of workflow and output. The photographer became the lab in the process too, so although it added a ton of work, it also creates unlimited and constantly changing opportunities for the creative process.

How has social media changed the nature of your business? Do people nowadays undervalue the importance of professional photography?

Social media hasn't really changed my workflow in terms of making beautiful pictures, but it's certainly changed the way we view and share them. We post a new picture each day on Facebook then add links to Twitter and LinkedIn. I think it's just easier to get your work out there than it has ever been before.

That being said, everyone with a camera is a 'photographer' these days, so in order to stand out as a professional, we have to do things that every other person with a camera can't do. With intimate knowledge of light and equipment, a trained eye and the experience of major jobs to deliver under pressure, the need for professional photographers will always be there. Most hotel shoots are far too important to the survival of the property to be left to amateurs. Having a good camera gives you a great picture about as often as an oven makes a great meal or a keyboard writes a great novel. It will always come back to the skill of the user.

LEVERING LEISURE CHANNEL ACUMEN FOR YOUR CONVENTION BUSINESS

Online travel agencies are primarily geared towards FITs and leisure travel, but such websites do not intrinsically broach the meetings and events marketplace. That's where companies like Cvent and other similarly designed electronic platforms are making strong inroads. Like everything else, the meetings segment has been turned upside-down amidst the digital revolution. Meeting planners and salespeople now rely, to a great extent, on e-RFPs to govern their transactions and the use of this electronic conduit is bound to take over the lion's share in quick order.

In the past, I interviewed Cvent's Founder and CEO, Reggie Aggarwal, and gleaned some astounding statics. The company's sales are growing exponentially with 2012's final cume at over $7 billion in e-RFPs booked through the Cvent Suppler Network, as tabulated from guestroom sales and ancillary charges (87% of RFPs include sleeping rooms). Cvent is currently engaged with 43,000 unique organizations and with $9 billion in meetings sourced for 2013 with 30 million guestrooms purchased. This and their reach has yet to officially expand beyond that of the USA; an inevitability in the very near future given Cvent's already strong inroads into this salient marketplace.

Here's the kicker: unlike with the OTAs, Cvent sanctions paid-for prioritization, allowing hotels to promote and differentiate their product offerings. Drawing on parallels again, as a hotelier, ask yourself how you have established a goal of domination within FIT search. Perhaps fine-tuning your organic SEO with a paid-for-search adjunct? Think analogously for the meetings space and that is where a synergistic relationship with Cvent can exist. To quickly brush over their advertising slate, the company uses a four-tier diamond rating to choose how a property is displayed. The basic is one-diamond; more advanced is two through four-diamonds.

Reconnecting with the Cvent brass, I was eager for an update on their progress and to hear the firsthand perspective of a satisfied client—in this case, Hotel Del Coronado in San Diego and La Costa Resort & Spa about 30 miles north, collectively represented by their joint Director of Sales and Marketing, Barry Brown. To clarify, the Coronado and La Costa are managed by KSL Resorts, although the properties maintain separate ownership. Both properties utilize Cvent's four-diamond listings, the highest placement available.

And what does that top dollar get you? 'Share-of-screen' is the buzz, and very apt, term casually slipping from Barry's mouth. With sturdy investments for these two SoCal resorts, Cvent delivers prime placement on the results pages from user searches; searches queried by members of the Cvent Suppler Network who are already accessing the site with the intent to buy.

Raised in the old school world of traditional marketing at Procter & Gamble, the canon for me was always that share-of-voice presages share-of-mind—the internal brand awareness amongst the general population. More specifically, the percentage of advertising spent in relation to your direct competitors would equate over the long-term to your market share. This is marketing 101.

It appears, however, that the contemporary equation is: share-of-screen equals share-of-mouse and all therein implied, namely share of click-throughs and share of bookings. Hence, if you dominate the visual display of a browser page, a consumer—specific to this case, a meeting planner or event manager—has no choice but to investigate your offer via click-through, or at least remember your name. Think about how this 'screen superiority' applies for Google searches or TripAdvisor results. The ones at the top naturally get more clicks. Thank you, Barry, for putting this so clearly.

Bantering in generalizations is all well and good for hospitality school, but I was even more impressed by the results Barry presented. The initial objective for utilizing Cvent was to dominate the website's share-of-screen for event searches in the greater San Diego area. Undertaking this partnership in 2009, with only 30% of leads coming in the form of e-RFPs at the time, the two hotels' prospects doubled within a year. At the present, both properties are approaching five times the number of leads they had in 2009.

The causal link between advertising and real-time sales can at times be rather tenuous. Cvent believes that quality traffic can be 'triaged' through increasingly enhanced search criteria. Hence, the system works fluidly for those toiling in the mainstream of groups business; paid-for share-of-screen is increasingly viewed only by prequalified consumers and those with intent to purchase. Further, the company likens itself as the perfect hub for the nontraditional planner—those unencumbered by any particular association or licensing agency—and for properties seeking an unconventional means to penetrate the market.

A logical jump from this is to ask about the e-RFP's function to supplant traditional marketing efforts such as tradeshows, travel publications and direct mail. Although this would be a natural conclusion of this electronically transformative era, the truth that Barry reinforced is that Cvent's channel acts as an augmentation for his organization; not a replacement, an adjunct.

The lesson for hotels is, much like the maxims for other digital advents like social media networks, you have to capitalize on your share-of-screen on all committed channels. Apply your resources in full and not as a cursory aside.

IF YOU LIST IT WILL THEY COME?

Consider the niche booking website eVenues and its potential for helping hotels further tap into a hidden area of meeting revenues. For this, I enlisted the help of the company's president, David Jennings. He identified the problem back in 2007 while working on a social dating platform that needed to dynamically or electronically schedule meeting venues only for its classes.

After awhile, it became clear the idea was very simple: to create a means for any individual to easily find and book small meeting space without the need of a meeting planner. The system David and his team went on to build addresses this fundamental need, but also provided a stronger platform for all types of additional services to get access to venue directory and availability information. You select your city, choose a location from the hundreds shown (with prices and restrictions in full view), and then make your booking.

Interestingly, the original eVenues system was not RFP-based, although this is now an option for some venues. Yet, the renter is in complete control, being able to make a selection based on location, attributes and price. Moreover, eVenues is location and building agnostic, covering everything from conference centers and boardrooms to schools, churches and hotels. In essence, any venue with meeting space is eligible to participate.

It costs nothing to advertise your property on eVenues, which generates its revenue exclusively from a 10% to 13% commission on confirmed bookings and pre-qualified leads it generates from the site. For this, there are two options: have eVenues send you pre-paid reservations for your meeting space that you can 'accept or reject'; or have eVenues send you prospective customer leads for venue sales to work.

For hoteliers, eVenues seems to be a logical extension to the meetings business slate by listing every space you offer using their 'accept or reject' booking system. You can always decline the booking should there be a schedule conflict, insufficient accompanying F&B earnings or room revenue.

When it comes to short-term, last minute bookings, eVenues really shines. It's an Expedia or Airbnb for meeting venues. Here, you can place real inventory availability into the system, propelling your space to the top of the eVenues list. With the ability to select desired price by the hour or by the day, the choice is totally up to you and fully manageable through an easy-to-use interface.

Many of us can recall the early days of online guest room reservations programs and the skepticism many hoteliers expressed towards their efficacy. I even remember a noted hotel owner who laughed when I suggested that, one day, online bookings would become his property's primary method of guest room revenue.

Oh, how technology changes everything! eVenues is an extension of online guestroom reservations into the meeting room arena—a logical evolutionary next step. The question therefore is not whether you support this program with inventory, but rather, how fast you implement eVenues or a website of its ilk as an ancillary force for your sales team.

HOTEL TONIGHT: A MOBILE APP EXCEPTION TO COMMODITIZATION

By this point in the book, you probably have an idea of where I stand on various issues. I'm hopeful and at the same time very cynical of many internet trends that are sweeping our industry, particularly internet-driven room sales. Selling inventory through online channels whose primary purpose is to offer customers the cheapest price can severely weaken customer loyalty and brand identity. The term I use for this is commoditization and mobile apps are no exclusion.

The way I see it, without emotional factors to differentiate one brand from another, it's a race to the bottom. My greatest fear is that one day consumers will only bid for the lowest cost per room and disregard the rest-rooms becoming a commodity traded on the open market in the same way as minerals and agricultural produce.

There are many factors driving the industry down this road, but there are many exceptions as well. The World Wide Web is here to stay, so despite my bickering, I'm always on the lookout for internet-based solutions that will actually work to boost long-term revenues, brand recognition and loyalty. I've highlighted some of these in the past and today I bring you the mobile app Hotel Tonight.

As implied by its name, Hotel Tonight, only available for Apple and Android mobile products, is a same-day, last-minute reservation program. Hotels upload leftover, unsold inventory to the system at noon and customers can then only book rooms for that night, albeit at a fraction of the cost incurred through regular travel agencies. From there, guests can choose to extend their stay by one or two nights.

Founded in 2010 out of San Francisco, the app is live for dozens of major metropolitan regions and airports in Western nations amounting to thousands of properties. Hotel Tonight's layout keeps it sleek and simple with limited information and clutter to make for faster purchases. Additionally, the company curates hotel profiles itself unlike other online booking sites. And as of the end of August 2012, the app had already accrued over three million downloads across all platforms.

At first glance, you would think that the functionality of this app is directly in tune with my rant against commoditization. Hotel Tonight is a flash sale channel. But it's imperative for this argument to consider the mentality of consumers who will use Hotel Tonight.

These are people who are already planning to travel, or are perhaps well on their way, and haven't booked a room yet. Consumers with preexisting allegiance to one brand or another will go through the major chain's native channels to complete their reservation. I sought this app out only for a trial run because I like to plan well in advance. But I imagine it is quite suitable for whimsical or desperate travelers as well as those who are principally deal-savvy.

For the latter, you're dealing with the constantly-cross-comparing crowd; people who aren't easily wooed into loyalty because it's ingrained in their mentality that a better deal is always on the horizon. I likened this psychographic to 'hotel mercenaries', perpetually buying their itineraries from the lowest bidder. True, you will add some short-term revenue from these consumers, but don't expect conversion at the drop of a hat. This psychographic is heavy on the social media savvy, which means you're bound to receive an influx of tweets, likes, posts and check-ins, only for the night they stay with you though.

A good question to ask in this analysis is: "What sort of person leaves travel plans to the day of departure?" Spur-of-the-moment vacationers, adventure-seekers, those traveling due to an emergency, procrastinators and all those in-between. The thought of not having a bed before I arrive in a foreign city is enough to give any boomer like myself an aneurysm, so rest assured, it's predominantly a young person's game. The much-vaunted example of Hotel Tonight's usage is for when you find yourself out partying with your friends in New York City well into the night and suddenly need a room—not exactly the portrait of someone there on business or traveling with his or her family.

But this is the exact case where Hotel Tonight serves to benefit your property. Other book-well-in-advance online travel agencies can act as direct competitors for your own reservation portals, but this app operates in a niche where prior loyalty and brand awareness are a nominal part of the equation. If consumers were already faithful to your hotel, they would call ahead or visit your website first.

Converting first time customers into repeat visitors is always a gamble that's exponentially more dependent on the onsite experience—in-room features, amenities and guest services, for example. Hotel Tonight is another tool in your arsenal to get them through the front door. Such guests may become loyal and praise your name, and then again they may not. But, these are unsold rooms you wouldn't likely sell otherwise, so you might as well try and offload them while also increasing your brand exposure. Hey, you never know, right?

PSYCHOLOGICAL MUSINGS
ON BACKBID.COM

Are you familiar with www.backbid.com? If not, give it a quick browse, mull over it for a quick minute. If yes, would you consider using it to attract new customers?

Although it's a relatively small piece of the pie, this website's model is demonstrative of a contemporary shift in consumer mentality and its perils. On Backbid, consumers post their existing vacation itinerary or ideas for the near future, and then it's up to the hotels to tender those travel plans with better offers. You solicit the customers, not the other way around. With the reversal of the conventional patron-to-business sales paradigm, the foremost and righteously executed goal of Backbid is to engineer the best cost savings for the consumer.

Not that I have a problem with cost savings, but I do have gripes with this inverted model. By lauding how much money they can safeguard for a user, Backbid is, in essence, diluting the sales pitch down to only one element. And this does not bode well for proprietors. As hoteliers, we know that the hotel experience goes far beyond what a lone price tag reveals. Rest and relaxation, adventure, new locations, new food, fun, memories—all are quintessential and highly inelastic facets of a desirable vacation. For the business traveler, this list of qualities is probably less critical yet still part of the consideration process.

That's why marketers and managers devote inordinate amounts of time to such routine items like brochure layouts, advertisements, promotions, public relations, sales videos, e-blasts, sponsored events, website designs, blogs, Facebook fan pages and Twitter public messages. The purpose is to draw potential consumers into the experience and convey a hotel's unquantifiable aspects for before, during and after a stay. For all these ancillary tasks, what may seem routine on the surface is in fact an orchestra of finely tuned instruments acting in unison to tell a hotel's story correctly.

But in the end, even with all our cajoling, it's still in the customer's power to seek out exactly what they want and initiate the exchange. Consumers come to you and pay the price as listed. That's the norm.

And by the time consumers do reach you, half the battle is already over. Beneath the surface there's a fundamental psychological dynamic at play. Out of all the possible options and by whatever miracle, the customers chose your property. Whether through adept marketing or old-fashioned word-of-mouth, you have already earned their respect enough for them to vote with their wallets. People are proud of their decisions and the more they research and examine beforehand, the more committed and attached they will feel to the final selection.

Call it emotional investment. I argue that this underlying pride is a very early contributor to both heightened guest enjoyment and, with any luck, a repeat visit. The loyal relationship with your patrons starts even before you've officially met. Those guests that find and choose you are already primed for your charms, your panache and your vision. Don't disappoint.

This cognitive bias is hardly exclusive to the hospitality industry. Notice how it's much easier to nitpick food on your plate when you're at a buffet than when ordering off the menu; how the shirt you bought for yourself at the mall is better than the one received as a gift, even if they are the same. And then if you realize a purchase you made wasn't the bee's knees, the denial and guilt are all the more intractable.

Contrarily, what happens in the 'you go to them' model where the customers hold all the cards? Do they have the same underlying respect for you (if they do in fact decide to stay with you)? Do they pride their own research and execution prowess? Or, are such customers simply 'settling' among the tendered offers? The chase for the best hotel is a part of the eventual reward of staying at that hotel—no chase means decreased satisfaction. The bottom line: if you offer a good product, people will find you and be all the more happy for it.

There's good reason for the hotelier to remain as the pursuer aside from any broad psychoanalytic cues. Simply put, it takes too much time for managers to bid on every individual customer. You set your prices, and then let any negotiation take place after this precedent. True, you could merely post the same best-rate package that's available through your own booking engine, but then why wouldn't you just focus your efforts on the primary channel? After all, your brand.com is where you have the most control over the delivery of the hotel's story and this channel can handle far more transactions per hour. With only so much energy bestowed to you for each working day, I advise you to put it towards what's most efficacious.

I know that I'm being hard on Backbid, but it does have its uses. Looking ahead six months to a perennial low season and a hypothetical dearth of reservations may present a viable scenario for perusing this website. Just as I would advise for flash sales, proceed with caution and employ only very sparingly. Backbid provides a fresh method to reach new consumers you otherwise wouldn't encounter. But if you have to choose between this and spending time revamping your marketing plans, the latter has far greater potential.

To reiterate, Backbid and any other website like it underlie the imperative to reach consumers on qualities outside of price. Not only that, but with new channels, new tools and new social media popping up every week, you must judge your time on a draconian opportunity cost (time) basis and remain forever vigilant about how you spend it.

MOBILE FRIENDLY E-NEWSLETTERS

New is cool. I get it. With the exponential growth of social media, mobile and all in between, many have prognosticated the extinction of print and even some 'traditional' forms of electronic communication like the telephone and email. To clarify, I lump email into the traditional category because it has been around for over 20 years now (time flies doesn't it?).

Although some mediums have waned and usage percentages have shuffled, nothing has really 'died' per se. These channels all more or less find a new equilibrium of coexistence as older channels adapt to new niches and utilities. Take radio for example: many thought television would slay it outright. True, the vast majority of people would now rather come home and pop on the tube than sit around the old RCA boom box for an NPR fireside chat. But, look how well the sound waves work for cars and its surging contemporary iteration—satellite radio. Mediums don't die, they evolve.

So, even with rampant Facebook messaging, tweets, blogs, forums and smartphones, email still has many justifiable uses, especially for hotel marketers. To kick off our talk though, let's discuss some mail of the more physical kind.

Direct mail advertisements hurt trees and hurt marketers' wallets from targeting and design all the way through to mass printing and postage. With the advent of email where both these problems were drastically reduced, what prevents the total collapse of the snail mail machine? For one, its response rate year-over-year still delivers better results than many other consumer mediums—2% is often used to distinguish a 'good' direct mail campaign, 4% or more is considered a runaway success.

Is there a foreseeable day when direct mail will become extinct? Sure. The axe could come from new green legislation, postal service restructuring or a myriad of other factors. Until that time, marketers will continue to fell trees as long as it's an effective method to sell their products. Despite environmental protests and the dated persona, at the present, direct mail is going strong. Furthermore, direct mail specialists are embracing reams of purchase data—previously too complex or expensive to analyze—to fine tune mailing lists, tweaking their conversion rates and keeping one step ahead of permanent retirement.

Another channel allegedly on the down and out is email. Regardless of whether you believe this statement to be true or not—I deem it to be false—there is considerable evidence and competition to suggest email's eventual decline (but not demise), particularly from somewhere in the domains of social media messaging and mobile-centric communication. In 2006, email marketing saw a rate of return of roughly $52 for every dollar invested while five years later, that same ROI fell to just over $40 for every dollar spent. It's less of a fiscal cliff and more of a pecuniary softening.

Newer is cooler after all; it's only natural to assume that social networks with billions of cumulative users and big data on top of all the other internet-based communication outlets would inexorably render email obsolete. As it stands right now though, email marketing is still one of the most effective and preferred ways to reach consumers, even more so than direct mail in a lot of cases. Rather than abandon email all together to stay ahead of the curve, why not reinvent it to fit what's out there and what's coming?

I've always been a fan of e-blasts (or e-newsletters). They combine the professionalism and simple eloquence of email with many of the artistic virtues of direct mail advertising. Use whatever 'spam' label you deem necessary, consumers opt-in to this channel and tacitly want to receive your message—half the battle is already won! And in terms of what's out there, top of the list is obviously the proliferation of tablets and mobile. Don't just think smartphone and tablet or Apple and Android OS; also throw in the Kindle, Nook, Microsoft Windows-operating products and whoever else still uses Blackberry (as a Canadian, that pains me to write).

Essentially, what's needed for adaptation to present times is a responsive e-newsletter. Just so we're clear, when I say 'responsive', I'm referring to Response Web Design (RWD), the colloquial term describing the ability for a website to detect whatever device is accessing the information and automatically rearrange its layout. Responsive email design is a fancy and more encapsulating way of saying 'mobile friendly'.

No doubt some of you already have the trepidation of recipients deleting your well-crafted e-newsletters without reading them, of automatic e-blast transfer to the spam folder or of rampant unsubscribes.

Now add to that a growing number of people accessing their email through mobile or tablet devices in addition to those same people becoming highly accustomed to seeing their favorite websites bend to whatever device they're using. If your e-newsletter isn't ready to flex or contract to these new channels—leaving your message harder to unscramble—your delete-without-reading frequency is bound to increase.

If you're not wholly convinced about the imperative for responsive design—in all things electronic, not just e-newsletters—then perhaps some psychological musings can sway you. Consider how people use their various devices and how functions can be segregated between mobile and desktop or laptop. Standard computers are rapidly becoming the 'work' machine where mobile is morphing into the 'play,' or 'quick peek' counterpart. If a consumer opens your email while on their cell phone, they're likely to be in a more receptive 'play' state of mind to better ponder your product, whereas while in 'work' mode, people are focusing on other tasks instead of possible hotel room consumption.

As well, your brand identity can only be accurately conveyed on mobile if the e-newsletter is mobile friendly. Otherwise it's straight to the trash without any subconscious imprinting that brands need to proliferate. People are simply too busy (and are too well adjusted to RWD) to squint and scroll to decipher your message.

Problem: responsive e-newsletters aren't easy to setup. Nor are they ubiquitously supported by all firmware or email portal apps. Rest assured, this tech upgrade is on the cusp and we'll be seeing lots more chatter about it in the coming years. You also must be prepared to work with an expert to reconfigure your template programs and website for HTML5, the markup language most widely accepted for RWD. All said, this might be the edge you need to kick start your email marketing campaign back into fifth gear.

The other primary concern here is cost. Think of RWD as a railway switch; crank it one way for a laptop, the other for Android OS, and then another for iPhone. But separate track has to exist for the continuation of each possible route in order for the train to go anywhere. Such is responsive email: you must build multiple templates or skins for the same e-blast, equating to more time and money dropped for each letter. Along the same lines of maintaining your tech savvy status, it's important to inquire about such auxiliary modalities as social media integration, video embedding and, above all, analytics tracking.

This last one is vital because, in the end, once you have updated the context of your email marketing program, it will boil down to the content you deliver. People sign up for e-newsletters because they see value in hearing your brand voice and potentially spending money with you. You've earned their trust; now it's your job to not abuse it. If you don't consistently deliver utility to your fans, then you may find yourself with a spike in unsubscribes. Monthly analytics checkups are a good starting point to assess which messages are working and which are duds, all for the inevitability of generating sales.

One tactic where I've seen analytics and consumer data put to outstanding use is in triggered emails. That is, you know from your records that a guest visited you in the near past for a wedding, conference, honeymoon, golf tournament, birthday, anniversary or celebratory party. Why not send them a timely email triggered by reaching a set date after such a guest has left? This isn't something exclusive to the hospitality industry, but it works so elegantly for us because of the versatility of events that happen at a hotel.

For now, be on the lookout for responsive design coming to an email near you. Then combine it with such previously established tactics such as specific targeting, triggered emails and quality content, and you are due for greener pastures.

THE BRASS TACKS ON CHINESE TRAVELERS

Chinese travel is booming and has been for coming up on 25 years now. As you would expect from that, there's a proliferating bourgeoisie that demands great traveling experiences. With a population of over 1.4 billion, this nouveau middle class is a demographic that should pique any keen hotelier. And yet, as a nation, China is shrouded in mystery; one perception to the outside world and something else entirely to its own citizens.

But China does not have to be an enigma, nor do its travelers. Here to help bust some myths and inform on reality is Joseph Cooke, the North American Director for Web Presence In China, a company that specializes in helping Western organizations get their names out on the Chinese internet.

To dispel any naysayers, could you give some metrics on the growth of outbound travel in China and the importance of appealing to Chinese travelers and where they are searching?

One can Google terms such as 'China Outbound Travel Market' and come up with no end of articles. Key findings from this: bigger than US market, 30% of international tourism growth, 80 million travelers, $20 billion market (as of end of year 2012). Given this, it may be instructive to examine why the naysayers are saying "Nay", why they don't see the evidence of this China outbound tourism boom more directly:

- The majority of this international travel is still to Asian destinations such as Singapore, South Korean, Taiwan, Thailand and Japan. This is partially due to the distance, convenience and breadth of direct flights. It partially explains why Australia has no credible naysayers of the Chinese tourism boom, however, nor do foremost European cities such as London and Paris.
- The majority of Chinese, like travelers the world over, want to visit places where they can be understood and enjoy themselves without too much extra effort. The profusion of Chinese signage proceeding from the Melbourne airport indicates why Australia

is viewed as 'China friendly'. Vancouver, for obvious reasons, enjoys a lot of Chinese visitors, who are organically building the destination's reputation online, although the city is doing much on the Chinese internet to boost its profile further. Moreover, on the Chinese internet, word-of-mouth rules, and destinations which aren't actively engaged in influencing the conversation and building advocacy are going to wait longer than others to be perceived as 'China friendly and convenient'.

What makes Chinese travelers unique? Elaborate on a few key points.

Nothing, but our insistence on perceiving them as aliens from another world is a unique situation the wise can exploit to the detriment of their competition. The boorish, nouveaux riche Chinese tourist vilified in European press a few years ago had nothing to concede to the Russian boorish nouveaux riche tourist. Now, with the age of the massive Chinese tour group coming to a speedy close and self-planned traveling on the uptick, the differences between the Chinese and Western tourist are likewise rapidly diminishing. The global tourist is becoming as generic as the global tourist destination, the obligatory no-car street where all the tourists mill to see what KFC and Starbucks in other countries are like.

This means that the wise will follow the contemporary golden rule: don't pander to the Chinese tourist, but give them an authentic, friendly experience. There aren't many westerners who would take the trouble to go to China, only to be led to westernized locales where only forks are available to eat with, the teahouse is playing Celine Dion music and the minority dance troupe is doing the Harlem Shake. The Chinese, too, want as authentically Western an experience as possible if they've come all the way out for it, with, of course, a modicum of Mandarin-communication available to enjoy this experience to the fullest. Chinese food options should be available with Western ones, too, but in this the Chinese tourist is just like his western counterparts in China, who after two days of the local cuisine are desperately seeking the nearest McDonald's for some comfort food.

What are some simple changes hotels can make to better appeal to Chinese travelers?

At least one fluent Mandarin speaker with competent customer service skills at hotels with over 100 rooms. Mandarin on the menus, and, rather than bilingual everything for signage, a Mandarin pamphlet which takes care of as many concerns as possible: power conversion, check in/ out rules, concierge service, info and rules for business center, gym, etc.

Anyone who has experienced five-star Asian hospitality knows that it is superior to that of the Western world in many significant ways. What differences have you noticed?

If we're using the term 'hospitality' in the most general sense, then yes, you will find yourself treated far more kindly as a foreigner in China than a Chinese person will in the West. If you're doing the five-star circuit in China, you will find prices for personal services (such as at the spa) more reasonable thanks to low labor costs. But the average three or four-star hotel in China resembles a motel in the West—one not particularly interested in keeping its doors open much longer. Once you've gone into your room in that average Chinese hotel, the feel is unhygienic, bathroom plumbing is a fright and complaints are addressed with much less than what would pass muster in a western hospitality organization with dedicated management.

There are many reasons why Chinese hospitality in the commercial sense is in fact inferior to hospitality in the West—newness of the industry in a recently socialist society, for starters. What's important to note is that, in terms of service standards, China is definitely a pupil to the West. The form is filling in rapidly (gilded foyers and in-room sale-ables), but certainly not the function.

Am I right to suggest that this disparity all boils down to labor costs?

China's famously low labor costs are actually a factor in China's continued lag behind international-level competence. The many employee cogs who make a good hotel run smoothly are all aware of how replaceable they are. The attraction of marginally-skilled labor ("We'll just train them up!") overwhelms the good sense of hiring people with educations and good language skills for foreign customers then paying them for what they are worth. As a result, revolving door staffing is the norm, and talented, dedicated professional Chinese staffers below the managerial level are rare.

If Eastern labor costs cannot be beaten, what other key marketing strengths does the West have from a Chinese perspective?

Quality always beats quantity. China itself is first to acknowledge this, as it is doing everything in its power to transform itself from an export economy to a skilled-labor, consumer-led one. Just as Chinese tech companies do all in their power to model their techniques to match Western best practice, so do Chinese hospitality businesses seek to replicate the organizational excellence of Western hotel brand leaders. An example: any savvy Chinese domestic traveler knows that a stay at the Xi'an Hilton will surpass nearly everything available from a local Chinese competitor, and those with the travel budget behave accordingly.

Which of these Western strengths are top of mind for Chinese travelers?

Service standards, every time. Chinese travelers know a big brand Western guestroom will never have strange stains on the rug or bedding; that water pressure and temperature will not be issues; that there is a whole system for demonstrable actions behind brand promises absent from the boasts of Chinese hotels. In broad terms, the Chinese still idealize the West in terms of brand excellence, product value and service standards.

How would you go about conveying and marketing these broad points of differentiation to Chinese travelers?

Superior service is something that must be experienced. Chinese travelers are just as leery as their Western counterparts towards commercially centered messaging. Here's a tip: list on the Chinese version of TripAdvisor called DaoDao (www.daodao.com). Make sure the pictures are clear and the descriptions accurate. Consumer rating can almost be considered a national pastime in China. If a Chinese traveler has a good experience with you, that's the most likely (and easiest) place you'll be found and then commented on by objective third parties—the only kind of messaging the internet generation really trusts.

What are the most important social media networks in China to reach consumers?

Travel is the key inspirational activity in China. Therefore, there is a huge and diverse layer of the Chinese internet featuring all aspects of it. That's why the forward-thinking western hospitality organization will de-emphasize official travel news portals, which only fellow industry workers pay attention to. Weibo as well, the Chinese version of Twitter, is no channel to emphasize promotional efforts on, as standing out with messaging among the hundreds of accounts the average Weibo follower has is a hopeless task.

Instead, consider sites such as www.mafengwo.cn. This site's runaway attraction is picture-focused travel blogs from people who have been there and who interact through the comments section, not by asking for emails and phone numbers. Such sites are a locus of consumer advocacy that can be leveraged by organizations willing to invest in honest communication rather than ads and more traditional branding efforts. A resort in British Columbia, for example, that posted regularly with varied themed photo-sets of the surrounding nature, the food on offer at the lodge, people enjoying the activities and running descriptions through Google translate (including follow-up comment Q&A) would get far more traction from the effort than a far more expensive campaign of ad banners on more well-known social media sites like Weibo.

What special precautions must hotels be aware of when trying to do commerce in China?

- Your Chinese partners will not be invested in long-term scenarios.
- Loss of a little control of your branding and distribution will be a total loss of control.

- Contracts are worthless for the westerner, so is pursuing justice in court as a corollary. Your relationships and superior offerings are your protection.

Is marketing in China something that is only really available for those hotels or management firms with lots of capital, or can independents also get in on the action?

Independents willing to tackle the language barrier have a greater prospect of ROI, in relative terms, than the large firms. One Chinese intern from a local university spending a few hours a week posting picture sets with descriptions and following up on comments will bring in more leads for the effort than a traditional, pricey media blitz wherein the Chinese tourist is held at arms length with a barrage of marketing bluster and no firsthand look with one-to-one follow-up. Those travel-focused social media sites are also ideal for forging relationships with Chinese travel agents, who naturally are all over them.

What destinations will be most influenced by the growth of Chinese travel?

Alternative destinations within a day's drive of traditional or established hotspots: the wine country near San Francisco, Whistler and nature resorts outside of Vancouver, and so on.

How do you see Chinese travelers influencing the marketplace in a decade's time?

The Chinese government's stated goal is to bring 600 million Mainland Chinese to middle class status by 2020. Without going into the many shortcomings of the Chinese government, we can say that failing to deliver on economic growth is not one of them. If this goal is only partially realized, we can expect a Unites States' worth of Chinese with the means to travel internationally as well as a much greater burning desire to do so than the average American (who has so many more world-class destinations domestically) from a fun and leisure perspective.

OPERATIONS

The Timber Cove Inn, located in Northern California, is a four-hour drive from San Francisco, necessitating some very innovative operations adjustments.

INTRODUCTION: I LOVE MY DOG

If this headline grabbed you, then you probably belong to one of the nearly 80 million households in America that owns one of these four-legged pooches. No doubt this stat blooms substantially when tabulating worldwide numbers. I too am one in this category, being the proud 'father' of a 120lb or 54kg bundle of fur named Caesar—a somewhat overweight, spoiled Bouvier des Flandres that entered our family's life six years ago.

Caesar is not just a dog, he is an important member of our household. Many of you may roll your eyes, but a full quarter or more of those reading this will nod in agreement. So, do you accept dogs on your property? And if not, are you missing a significant revenue opportunity? These are the sorts of questions posed in this section dedicated to helping you rethink how you approach some highly specific aspects of your hotel operations.

Getting back on topic, my experience with properties that allow dogs ranges from tourist class to 5-star luxury boutiques. In all, the GM's responses have been unanimous: having dogs on property presents no major problems, and in many ways, dogs are better behaved than their bipedal masters.

When a dog is a member of the family, you have two options: a dog sitter or pet-friendly accommodation. Given Caesar's size, he does not fly, so our kids take on dog-sitting duties. Thankfully, most dogs aren't the size of teenagers, allowing for easier transport. That means dogs are going on holidays alongside Mom, Dad and the kids with increasing regularity. So, if you are not pet-friendly, your property is off the list. People traveling with their pets is but one of many trends on the rise and you have to keep your operations flexible if you are to survive.

Sure, there are going to be issues that arise with having animals onsite, but the advantages outweigh the negatives. Your guests will adore the furry little friends scurrying about the property. Think of dogs more as an additional feature for your guests to emotionally connect with your hotel—one extra detail to brighten one's day. Such a reframing technique should be applied to all novel tactics awaiting introduction to your hotel's operations.

Accepting dogs is not something that is overly complex, but it does require some operational planning. Often, a series of rooms, floors or sections are reserved exclusively for guests with animals. A guide is required, providing the following:

- Dog menus
- An understanding of all charges
- List of local vets
- Map of walking trails and off-leash areas
- A liability waiver for the guest to sign

Once you're ready, make sure you manage the reservations component. There are also many directories of hotels that allow dogs, and in order to tap into this travel niche, you need to get on that list. And as you can tell from the bullet points above, incorporating dogs, even with its proposed benefits, is not as easy as waving a magic wand. In order to get a functional system in place, a lot of groundwork must be done before marketing efforts can be initiated.

All together, this is the running theme of the following section. Consider adjusting an established aspect of operations or adopting an entirely new element. Then when a decision is made, execute it with all your effort so guests can actually find utility in it and so that it can weigh into their emotional state of mind when it's time for a recommendation.

HOTEL GERM SPOTLIGHT

Here in Canada, our government-based TV network is the CBC, the Canadian Broadcasting Corporation and our counterpart to the U.K.'s BBC. The network treads in a more Canada-centric fare than others which lean towards syndication of US programming. I say this because a program airs on the CBC focusing on 'dirty' Canadian hotels, a subject not likely to raise many eyebrows south of the border.

The long and the short of it is that CBC, a national broadcaster renowned for its highly credible reporting, has produced a show potentially sullying the reputation of some of the country's finest hotels—six major chains and 54 rooms in the heart of Montreal, Toronto and Vancouver. CBC beams into every Canadian home and they've now made it a recurrent, primetime habit to disparage leading downtown properties with actual photographic evidence. Aside from any bloodcurdling yells echoing from the damage control departments at the implicated hotels, there's a very essential lesson that permeates the longest unguarded border in the world.

Dirty guestrooms are poison for hotels. The internet is written in permanent ink and many prestigious names have been tarnished. Unless a clever lawyer is able to sneak an injunction past a judge, which may take years to formally process, this vilifying website will be available to the public for a very long time and hosted by the CBC, a trustworthy and heavily trafficked domain name. It's all just another reaffirmation that cleanliness is godliness.

Think about it this way: you have to crawl before you can walk. In order to attain a positive review, start first by eliminating the negatives. Before you attempt to satisfy a guest's higher desires for an incredible, wholly memorably vacation or a breezy business trip, you must first satisfy their most basic of needs—running water, safety, heating, air conditioning, insulation, that sort of thing. Room cleanliness is the epicenter of this foundation; disrupt it and the house crumbles.

The latest CBC reports serve as yet another wakeup call to show how vital and sensitive this issue is for guests. Too often I see TripAdvisor reviews where the writer deems everything agreeable but then gives a lousy one-star rating because of two or three untidy aspects of the room. Clearly, the housekeeping department needs some bolstering.

Moreover, you cannot rest halfway with the belief that what looks clean is actually clean. The CBC investigators used hidden cameras, ultraviolet flashlights and an array of other gadgets to pinpoint all the areas overlooked or improperly sanitized. A neat bed doesn't mean there isn't garbage underneath. A vacuumed floor or carpet doesn't preclude microbes from clinging to the telephone receiver or remote control. These under-the-surface troublemakers won't be readily visible to your guests, but if a journalist with an upcoming editorial on dirty hotel rooms ever comes your way, they might as well be painted in eye-piercing neon.

Don't let this happen to your property. A good first step is to hire an unannounced, independent, external auditor capable of elucidating your housekeepers' shortcomings and suggesting more hygienic cleaning procedures. From there, it all boils down to training and reassessing for improvement. This falls into the hands of your Executive Housekeeper, so ensure that this manager fully understands the imperative of ongoing vigilance and continuous improvement towards perfection.

Particularly as it concerns housekeeper training, there is one tricky matter that comes to mind. For their wages and what is required of them on an hourly basis, housekeepers are often too hurried to perform their duties entirely up to code. If they are cutting corners, it is more likely due to time constraints than malicious intentions against the hotel.

Say you set a quota of 14 guest rooms per shift and with properly thorough technique a maid can only finish 12. Fearful of reprisal, this maid then rushes through the last half of the day to stay on target with expectations. Part of the staff education should include not only a fair allotment of rooms, but also a long chat that stresses quality (meeting standards) over quantity (sacrificing standards). If a room needs more attention than normal, housekeepers should be comfortable taking longer to complete every detail (or calling for support) without the worry of quotas or insensitive bosses.

Regardless of what steps you take behind the scenes, in the end it boils down to guest satisfaction and any preconceived notions of whether such an ideal is attainable. Clean rooms leave guests content; the opposite can have very dire consequences. This is not the first time this issue has come up and it most certainly will not be the last. Just make sure your property isn't in the slug line.

THE AVARI TOWERS' 5@5 CLEANLINESS APPROACH

Reports like the CBC's Hotel Germ Spotlight serve as a chilling reminder that cleanliness is godliness. Guests expect celestially pristine rooms or they will take their frustration out on you with bad word of mouth and negative comments in the online realm. There's no cutting corners on this one. Housekeeping is integral to a quality experience and overall guest satisfaction.

Obviously, the call to action here is to take steps which ensure your cleaning services are topnotch and continually improving. The CBC hired private investigators to spruce up their exposé with hard truths and 'dirty' facts for each hotel, so why not beat them to the punch by appointing your own external auditors? That way you know exactly where you've gone wrong, and hopefully this gives you the time for necessary corrections prior to any reputation-damaging critiques hitting the web.

That's one very practicable (but expensive) solution to complete with a steady frequency. But after discussing the matter in a little more depth with my friend Gordon James Gorman, the general manager at the Avari Towers in Karachi, there is perhaps another solution that entails quite a bit more fanfare.

The key to their success lies in good old-fashioned service and their housekeeping quality control definitely fits this profile. The Avari Towers enjoys the best ADR and RevPAR in the country and is often boasted as the cleanest establishment in the country. Take a look at their TripAdvisor comments and see for yourself.

Within a week of taking on the GM role at this property, Gorman instituted the 5@5 program whereby he and four other senior directors assemble everyday at 5pm to inspect five rooms at random. Once every room and suite on property has been examined, the process begins anew. These inspections are followed by a systematic reporting system where managers must coordinate any required changes immediately afterwards in addition to a follow-up discussion of faults with the respective teams the next morning.

Whereas hired guns take the clandestine approach, this quintuplet of managers is fully visible for staff and guests alike. They might not use all the latest in high-tech gadgetry to uncover any missed microbes, but this noticeable quality assurance team sends a clear message to guests—the senior level believes wholeheartedly in cleanliness and room maintenance.

And this belief will percolate down to every worker throughout the organization. If the directors are committed to supporting the executive housekeeper in recognizing the importance of proper cleanliness, then so will the rest of the housekeeping team. The random selection of rooms serves to only further propagate voluntary adherence to the highest of sanitation standards. As additional incentive, the top performing housekeeping team receives a cash prize and a special lunch at one of the Avari Towers' premier restaurants with Gorman himself to discuss their successes as well as any ideas for future improvements.

This 5@5 system no doubt takes up a fair portion of management's time, but the results speak for themselves. The staff care about the guestrooms because their supervisors do as well—leadership at its finest, as well as a great example of how a small change can go a long way towards guest service perfection. Gorman says you are free to use the 5@5 system in your property, so take him up on his offer!

DO HOTELS NEED GHOSTS?

I am stating the obvious when I say that online hotel reviews have revolutionized the way we do business. Every consumer is a potential consumer watchdog. The margins for errors are now so thin and expectations so high that all it takes is one mistake to wedge a hole between you and future business.

Most of hoteliers have already adapted to this emerging trend and we now ardently listen to our online feedback. The problem is that guests aren't always very articulate about what drives their own grading scales, which are often subjective and largely emotional. Like a magic show, they can only rate what they see or what dazzles them and not what's actually happening behind the curtain to create such a spectacle.

This in turn implies a need for knowledgeable criticism—like having a fellow magician review your magic show to offer constructive pointers a layman can only fathom but not elaborate into words. GuestGhosts is one such firm, deploying incognito 'Ghosts' to a contracted hotel for some in-depth advice. Here's what president and founder, Jason King, has to say about the state of independent hotel consultants in this online-review-dominated world.

With the advent of online user-based hotel review sites like TripAdvisor, has this impacted the need for anonymous ghosts?

Absolutely. TripAdvisor is a great source for hearing comments directly from the consumer. It's critical that we address the problem areas detailed online so hoteliers can correct themselves and have consumers rave about their services. In effect, it's made our jobs more transparent and actually made us better at what we do!

What advantages do knowledgeable hotel consultants offer overtop of firsthand guest appraisals?

We have found through tons of research and focus groups that the 'average' consumer does not write their complaints down online or otherwise. They also usually do not complain directly to hotel management. It's the silent treatment; they simply decide not to go back to a property or chain again. Hence, getting an in-depth appraisal from an impartial professional helps elucidate many of these lurking grievances.

As the old adage goes, 'The customer is always right'. What are some things that online guest reviews get right and what are some things that they frequently get wrong or misinterpret about a hotel experience?

Funny question, to us every review a customer presents is right. "The customer is not only always right," predicates a more appropriate belief system along the lines of, "The customer may not always be right, but the customer is always king!" The biggest problem is that too many hotels do not listen to their customers. Like, truly listen, as well as understand the imperative of constantly improving and retooling.

A lot of this comes from reading between the lines on reviews. Guests are busy people like everybody else and often don't have the time to flesh out a 2,000 word essay that nitpicks all the minor issues they had with their stay. What is mentioned in a guest review is likely an item that has had a lasting impression, for better or for worse.

From your perspective, what are the most common problems or mistakes you see hotels make?

Not taking it seriously insofar as the only way to ensure guests keep coming back is to utilize the absolute best training, hire the best personnel and have daily maintenance inside and outside their properties.

What are some easy mistakes that hoteliers can fix right now?

Evaluate departments and each department head, then sit down and go over all goals and benchmarks. Make your department heads take ownership and believe in what they are trying to accomplish—and always hold them accountable!

Sometimes issues can arise not from physical problems but from a bad attitude in the management. In the rare instances that this is the case, what remedies do you recommend?

Easiest question and solution: get new management. Many managers have been trained by 'old school' techniques, most of which are good, such as strong customer service. But even well-schooled managers forget the need to continue training not only their staff but themselves as well. You must always be learning and improving. New techniques are always available. Old school managers need to be flexible and adapt to new changes in automation and technology as well as CRM and the like.

How would you approach a senior manager about changing their style of leadership in order to improve a hotel?

First order of business is we need to establish what their leadership skills are. This can be accomplished through in-depth interviews and testing. Once you establish their style by doing the latter and by also talking with their peers and subordinates, a good consultant creates a 'Plan'. The plan would be tailored to this particular senior manager. It would encompass coaching and development as well as retraining and much more. If the senior manager is willing to learn they will succeed, if not then they better start putting their resume together!

Any specific success stories you can share with us?

Most of our clients have us sign an NDA because they do not want anyone to know they are using a service such as ours. However, I can describe a recent personal occurrence while on a 'mission' at a hotel.

We left a wakeup call for 5 AM, went to bed early, and were then awakened by an extremely loud knocking on the door at around 10:30 PM. Scary. It was a man in a red, white and blue uniform delivering pizza. We told him we did not order any pizza and told him to leave.

In the report to our client, security measures were addressed. We recommended that all delivery persons be stopped at front desk. Guests should then be called by front desk and guests should come out for the delivery or the delivery person cleared to meet the guest at their door (with access granted by the front desk personnel). It was strongly suggested that, in the future, guest room hallways (and elevators) be accessed by key cards, much like the rooms.

This was only a small mistake but if hoteliers allow guests to call for deliveries, they must also take the responsibility to ensure that all guests are safe and not bothered by these types of mishaps. On a side note our 'Ghost' never got to sleep properly that night. Even though this wasn't exactly the property's fault—it was probably the person ordering or the pizza company that jumbled the room number—the hotel would nonetheless take the brunt of the fallout because they let the delivery man through. It's the little yet irreprehensible mistakes like this that deter the 'average' consumer and are likely never brought to a property's attention.

BATHROOMS MAKE OR BREAK

Grievances with a guestroom's physical space can include nearly anything and the onslaught of online reviews has certainly helped broadcast our pratfalls no matter how subjective or esoteric. Sometimes they're complaints about issues you simply cannot fix without a bulky capital infusion. Other times these pesky problems are the elusive obvious, staring right back at us through the mirror.

Today, I want to address the bathroom. It's a private, personal space, and therefore, its design can evince a highly emotional response. Given this parameter, there are dozens of reasons, whether cognizant or blindly irrational, where you can go awry and hamper a guest's overall experience. Some of these are blatantly simple, snap-your-fingers fixable. Others should be tallied and red-starred onto your long-term renovation slate. Either way, by impeding a pleasurable bathroom experience, you're embargoing return visits and positive word-of-mouth.

For starters, let's talk cleanliness. If a guest is going to turn up their nose in disgust or write a hygiene-centric diatribe online, it's most likely to occur as a result of less-than-flawless housekeeping. And such posts are typically deal breakers; guests leaving unhappy and unlikely to return with only a glimmer of a tepid recommendation. Think small, yet incredibly irritable entities. Smudges on the mirror. Hair snaking out from the shower drain. Orange-brown rust stains in the porcelain toilet bowl. Jaundiced mold crusting over grout.

You are probably saying to yourself, "Not in my hotel." But when was the last time you conducted a personal inspection? Use TripAdvisor and other guest review sites to identify problem areas. The goal is obvious: absolute flawlessness.

Second, let's discuss supply; headlights on the towels and cleaners. The former is a straightforward issue with one or two small puzzles. Everyone knows that towels should be in ample stock, yet many rooms just aren't making the cut. What if there are two people and both plan to take multiple showers per day? That's four towels minimum, plus two more for drying the hair separately. Of course, turn down service (if you perform this) may reduce the in-room inventory requirements. At no point should a guest be interrupted while half-naked to call down for extras.

Two other concerns are hand towels and floor mats. The former here follows the same logic as their larger counterparts. Big faux pas if guests have to rummage through soggy washcloths to find one that may be clean and dry enough to wipe their hands. Bathroom mats are a tad pricklier as safety becomes a key issue. Materials should be thick, large, absorbent and adhesive to the tiles. Keep a spare as well so guests can replace a damp one on the fly.

The main objection I've encountered to stocking excessive textile is that it crowds the space. For this, I leave it to your discretion; you have to work with the allotted space. Think of a smart way to rearrange or use the closet for storage surplus, much like you would for bathrobes and extra pillows. Ultimately, when it comes time for a large-scale remodel, plan for additional cabinets to be installed.

I have often been asked just how long a towel should last. Clearly, anything frayed, ripped or damaged is a natural candidate for the trash. The approach I recommend for ongoing usage replacement is simple: keep one of each towel as a comparative standard. When a towel has noticeably deviated from this original, it is no longer of use.

Moving on to some more pet peeves that deal with the more immovable aspects of this oh-so-crucial room. The cardinal rule for all of these is: function trumps fashion. If you're renovating or building, don't let a flighty interior designer get the best of you. Stand firm in your demands for ergonomic space. The space must be copacetic before it can be cool.

Here are a few examples of what really irks me:

- *Poor Lighting:* This is kid's stuff. Bathrooms should be bright with the correct hues and a focus towards the mirror. If you are looking to upgrade, think halogens and LEDs as they are very radiant as well as energy efficient.
- *Small Mirrors:* The partner-in-crime for poor lighting, it's always nice not to have to twist and writhe every half-second to see what you're cleaning or grooming. Women may also require a suitable vanity mirror at the right height. And need I mention that small mirrors are a strain on the lower back?
- *Cramped Countertops:* Is it too much to ask for a little space to spread out the contents of two cosmetic travel bags? The biggest

culprits here are small washrooms, terribly dominant sinks or a lack of cabinetry.

- *Perplexing Shower Heads:* Which way is hot, which way is cold? No guest wants to spend ten minutes figuring out how the shower works before he or she can use it. Some are so radically counterintuitive that signage or a user guide should be provided. I've even come across Cerberean two- or three-headed spouts.
- *Always Hot or Always Cold:* I don't want to play goldilocks with my shower or faucet. Give me one that can deliver a range of temperatures with sensitive enough controls so I won't be immediately scolded or scaly from pseudo-frostbite.
- *Difficult Doors:* A struggle to close, a struggle to stay closed or partly see-through. This seems to be more of a problem for sliding bathroom doors, as every time I've encountered one, whether by design or by lack of lubrication, they are an utter chore to move—and I work out, too!

These six obviously necessitate a much larger commitment than increased housekeeping oversight. But that doesn't mean you should dismiss them. For each of these six instances, I felt compelled to lower my overall rating of the accommodation based on a tiny inconvenience. Think about it: what are your washroom pet peeves?

A final note: we live in a world of infinite competition. Why would a guest return to your property if the lavatories—a personal and emotional space—aren't up to par? Don't give them a reason to shun you; don't give them a shoddy bathroom!

REINFORCING THE VALUE OF GREAT HOUSEKEEPING, MONTAGE STYLE

I liken them as the unsung heroes of a hotel or resort. Cleanliness is a facet of a guest's stay that, when done properly, goes unnoticed, and when neglected, becomes a rally point for scorn in an online review site of choice. Overlook your housekeeping at your own risk!

Victor Aburto is the Director of Housekeeping at Montage Beverly Hills, a five-diamond property in the heart of Los Angeles. Victor has a passion for housekeeping and that's why I sought him out for an interview after my stay at his luxurious and impeccably clean hotel.

Tell me a little bit about your background and your career.
Having started at the Ritz-Carlton, Cancun, I held the Overnight Front Desk and Overnight Manager positions for just a short time before finding my groove in the housekeeping department. It was there I was given Leader of the Quarter and Leader of the Year awards. I then continued with the Ritz-Carlton in Orlando, Bachelor Gulch, Washington D.C. and Laguna Niguel. In total, over 18 years experience in the industry.

What are the broad changes you've seen in your 18 years of housekeeping experience?
It hasn't changed that much, although it's importance is definitely recognized much more today. I feel General Managers today are now more supportive and appreciative of their housekeeping teams. They see the value of the role housekeeping plays to the core product.

When interviewing a prospective housekeeper, how can you discern if they are 'right' for the job?
I look for the right fit based on their skills, knowledge and talents. I also place high importance on the person's attitude. The job is straightforward and anyone can do it or learn it. But we can't teach

someone to smile. We can't teach someone to want to serve. You can't teach personality. What we can do is hire people who have those qualities and we can teach them about our culture.

How do you keep up with ecological requirements, and yet, remain able to ensure sanitary and cleanliness standards?

At Montage Beverly Hills, we have an 'Environmental Impact Committee' and our goal is to be aligned with the ecological requirements of running a Gold LEED certified hotel. Our focus is to improve and do better practices in all aspects of our operation; save energy, recycle, use biodegradable chemicals for laundry and housekeeping, and use eco-friendly paper to print everything in the hotel.

I'm sure you work in two languages. How do you train staff under these circumstances?

Our primary language is English and we translate as needed for our associates in Spanish. The way I see it, any language barrier is not an excuse to provide an exceptional service.

How do you reward housekeeping staff for exceptional service? For average service?

We have a recognition program which allows us to recognize our associates with 'Magic Cards', which are a simple way to say thank you to our associates for their support and hard work. We also award several associates per quarter as 'Montage Masters'. This award recognizes an associate's performance, attitude and exceptional contribution on a day-to-day basis. A Montage Master should reflect the highest standards, images and ideals of the Montage brand, based on our established company values.

With cleanliness as such a critical component to guest happiness, how do you make sure everything reaches Montage-level perfection?

I can say that we not only make the guest feel happy, but feel safe as well. One of the key drivers for guest engagement is that our environment is stunningly clean, which implies safety because cleanliness requires constant grooming in the form of patrolling staff members. It becomes very difficult for our guests to focus on the experience if it does not feel and look clean. Cleanliness is an unspoken expectation, which may not create a memorable experience, but the absence of it can definitely take away from that same experience. Wonderful new bed linens with stains in them, or expensive marble, crystal and chandeliers that aren't clean and well maintained will severely disappoint our guests. We stress that this is fundamental to everything else we do.

How do housekeeping staff members help manage the ever-vacillating, individualized requirements of Hollywood glitterati?

The rooms division has two meetings every day. We review all guest arrivals and we filter all specific requests to make sure that they are properly handled. If a guest has a new request, we change his or her profile in our system to ensure that the next time he or she is with us, we know exactly what's needed in advance.

Do you give housekeepers and their families an opportunity to stay on property for a night or two?

Yes. We have a family rate discount to give our associates the opportunity to experience our properties. This is based on availability and approval from the General Manager.

How do you manage costs in escalating, pressured-for-profits conditions?

We focus on refining our efficiencies, maximizing our time and constantly considering new processes. We pay close attention to our daily operation costs and labor based on our productivity, but always without affecting the quality of our service.

How has automation and computerization become part of your routine?

I see them as important tools to support our daily work, but in our department we have to be out in the field checking hotel areas and guestrooms. I wish we could clean rooms with the click of a button, but this is not possible and would take all the fun out of it!

How do you provide excellence, everyday 24/7? What standards have been established?

My favorite value is integrity. We are in the winning business; everybody wants to be part of this winning game. The ticket to get in this game is integrity, and your guide to win this game is your mission statement. Everything that we do stems from there.

TOP TEN TO CONSIDER FOR MEETING SPACE DESIGN

One potent offshoot of the exponentially swelling internet is choice; choice in hotels, choice in dining, choice in meeting venues. In this buyers' market, customers demand nothing but the best in everything they purchase. Hotels are no longer the only entrants in the octagon for conference revenues, but the cage has been opened to restaurants, universities, museums, churches and unused office space.

What's more, the very essence of business meetings and conferences is itself in a volatile state. Laptops, video chats, webinars, smartphones—people can work from everywhere nowadays. And they are. Many don't even have an office away from home to call their own.

This is nothing new and reassuringly, at least in the near foreseeable future, nothing will replace quality face-to-face time. It's still the best means for effective teamwork. However, the combination of technological requirements and increasing choice has changed consumer expectations, particularly when discussing the physical attributes of the meeting space.

The key buzz term is flexibility. To conduct business, spaces can't adhere to fixed schedules or rigid design allocations. To meet modern work criteria, meeting venues must be both large and small, with looser structures and separate, comfortable spaces for private work. As well, people now recognize that psychological principles of design play a substantial role towards the overall quality of conducted business. Consumers are shrewd, informed and know what to look for in a venue that fulfills their individual requirements—space that at one end will enhance concentration and at the other facilitate quality interactions. This shift may not necessitate a full-blown renovation, but here are ten relatively frugal investments to consider, starting with the abovementioned hi-tech upgrades.

1. **WiFi.** I would call this one 'The Never-ending Story', but that's trademarked. Many hoteliers continue to pretend that guests are okay with paying for internet connectivity. Meanwhile, every consumer, especially those on business, understands the need for it

to be free. Businesspeople are especially crusty in that they demand a strong signal in all rooms with an easy login and enough bandwidth for manifold devices. Remember that meetings are mostly face-to-face, but face-to-screen is still common. One nifty solution to consider is to offer free connectivity once guests sign up for your loyalty program. Still charging for slow internet? Get with the times.

2. **Cellular Reception.** Can you hear me now? "No!" is never good. People shouldn't have to hike a hundred yards when matters are urgent. As a former civil engineer, I can say with confidence that gutting concrete support beams for this purpose isn't advisable. If you find your venue armored like a fallout shelter, consider installing a repeater or two. And as for the 'No Reception Sharpens Focus' naysayers, there's a solution for that, too—the off button.

3. **Tablet Friendly.** They are here to stay. You'd best be welcoming. Offer stands, styluses and attachable keyboards on loan for your business guests. With laptops, mobiles and now tablets chewing at the grid, you better review your power supply and bandwidth capacity. Does each room have enough plugs? Are they conveniently located for wires to reach them? Quite a few portal systems collapse under the weight of multiple devices accessing the web via the same IP. As these tertiary machines proliferate, be ready to not only offset the internet drain, but also offer a trouble-free connectivity route so you don't frustrate business guests.

4. **Technicians.** Many places rightfully advertise that they have a 24-hour, highly trained techie on call to address all problems and dispel any concerns. This is always a good thing and I'd suggest following their lead. Make sure your technicians are able to respond hastily and that your business guests know how to reach them. Next, ensure that they have adequate supplies at the ready in case anything breaks or if they have to provide extras (like an additional power bar to accommodate more electronics). Above all though, with the heightened pace of technology, your technicians must continually refresh their knowledge and skills.

5. **Food.** We run on our stomachs. Give us the right foods and we'll run faster. Give us the right foods at the right times and we'll sprint. The concept of food for meetings has evolved twofold. First, the rigid structure of snacks during break time is gone. Work towards a continuous break system—food on demand for whenever guests get

peckish. Second, healthy, clean cuisine improves brainpower. Now that the science corroborating this statement is mainstream, more planners specifically seek locations catering to this health-minded audience, and in turn, more people specifically request such venues.

6. **Windows.** This one's a push-pull . . . but not in a literal sense of the term. Natural light can be inspirational and help stave off those dreary, mid-afternoon lulls. On the other hand, sun glare obscures the weak glow exuded by computer monitors and projectors. A simple problem necessitates a simple solution—curtains or blinds, and make sure they're clean of dust.

7. **Table Orientation.** The shape of the table can determine the level of interaction and the dynamic of the room. A long, rectangular form creates an intrinsic imbalance amongst seated delegates and can hinder open discourse, whereas at a circular table, everyone is equal and in plain sight of one another. Furthermore, with the dirge of devices one brings to a meeting these days on top of folders and handouts, one needs a lot of space to spread out. If the center board can't be expanded, consider a few well-positioned side desks for extra countertops.

8. **Chairs.** Another push-pull. You want them to be ergonomic and comfortable, but not too comfy (read: midday nap). Match your chair type to the room's purpose. If it's a boardroom, stock it with armed, upright and leather-backed chairs. If it's a lounge, consider a softer, more cushioned fabric, or even a few sofas or divans. A big pet peeve of mine is when the chairs are too wide, impinging the crucial gap between seats—doubly important for swivel chairs.

9. **Flexible Space.** The grand speeches in large auditoriums with uninterrupted sightlines are always inspirational, but for the most part, the modern meeting hinges on technology-intensive skunkworks—highly collaborative projects with small, dedicated teams of three to eight people. Aside from breakout sessions and pre-fitted hotel rooms, consider caching apparatuses that can divide ballrooms or expansive halls to create smaller, interactive pop-up workspaces.

10. **Identity.** Much like the experience emanating from your lobby, rooms, spa or restaurants, your conference space needs to be memorable. However, don't misinterpret this word. 'Memorable' does not mean gaudy or distracting. The primary focus is, and will

always be, the meeting. Contrarily, that doesn't mean the décor has to be sterile. Make it pleasing to the eye and fresh enough to engage delegates while they are in between sessions. Given that your location is static, this is one overarching attribute that's fully in your control. Consider a theme that's culturally relevant to enhance your décor as a distinguishing feature.

As you can tell, the recurring theme through these ten pointers is a shift towards more informal, hybrid meeting spaces. The market for venues is fragmenting with greater expectations for ad hoc configurations. Addressing the increasing demand for 'smart rooms' means outfitting rooms with built-in technical features and accommodating the ever-expanding technological needs.

Along these lines, you should strategize about what niche best suits your existing space (after you upgrade, of course). The tactics behind whatever plan you follow must also involve new forms of channel distribution. Lastly, look to the majors like Sheraton, Marriott and Hilton, and some of their latest programs. All are leaders in coalescing work and fun into their hybrid workspaces as a means to stay with the times and steer the future.

LET'S TALK BOWLING

Is your hotel fun? Ask yourself honestly. Your chef's creations might excite the senses, and the surrounding area might present a smorgasbord of enjoying daytime activities and nightlife. But what is there—physically, onsite and within reach—to entertain guests?

Maybe it's a private golf course. Or an adjoining beach, a flashy pool area, a trendy bar and in-room entertainment systems (Playstation, Xbox, Wii, etc). What about the games room? Often an extension of the bar with a couple of billiards tables, foosball, darts, shuffle board or ping pong, this area could do so much more to encourage guest interactions and incite a positive vibe throughout the hotel.

As the timeless hotelier adage goes: a happy guest is a returning guest. Any and every effort towards this end will bear fruit. Why not rethink a part of your property that hits the fun factor right on its head? Bowling might just be the answer you've been looking for.

Mind you, this is no small consideration. Bowling alley lanes are a pricey refurbishment, and yet I'm seeing them crop up in hotels all over the world. To name one, Fairmont's Banff Springs Hotel—practically an icon of the hospitality industry in Canada—is notorious for its four lanes of spin bowling tucked away amidst grand ballrooms and Rocky Mountain vistas.

Or how about the Meritage Resort and Spa? Set in the heart of Northern California's wine country in Napa, the presence of luxury bowling lanes isn't really what you would expect. Maybe that's why it works; a good counterpart to the more languid viticultural experiences the area offers. I'm also told that the lanes use a Vollmer string system—cutting edge in Europe—where the pins are held on a string and lifted back into place when struck, meaning less noise and maintenance.

Is this just a fad, or will bowling alleys become a common concept for new hotels and future remodeling plans? More importantly, what's the appeal of bowling anyway? My answer: social, physical gaming. Like darts, billiards or foosball, bowling brings people together in a situation where they can be semi-active and enjoy each other's company. There's a dash of dexterity required (but not too much to exclude beginners) and there are intermittent breaks for people to talk, relax or grab a drink.

Probably what makes bowling so catchy is its rarity. A pool table can be found in almost any bar or home anywhere. Same with darts and foosball. All three of which fit the same profile of social, physical gaming. To bowl, however, you have to go to an alley and rent a lane. It's an event activity, like golf, jet skiing or going to the spa.

That's why I commend the hotels that have put bowling on the upswing. It's a unique feature that guests will remember and it will genuinely uplift their experiences at your property. At no point should a guest be aimlessly scrounging for ways to spend his or her time. Give them something fun; give them bowling!

In case dredging up the games room isn't a serious part of the remodeling budget (likely the case for most of us), consider lawn bowling or bocce ball. The chief requirement of both is a flat patch of groomed grass along with half-decent weather. Also, a professional set of bocce balls shouldn't cost more than $100 US—very affordable if you have the land already set.

The key takeaway from all this is that bowling is simply a launch point for evaluating what interactive entertainment you provide. Be it indoor bowling or outdoor croquet, there are plenty of creative and intriguing gaming alternatives. For instance, if you have an onsite golf course, why not install a virtual golf simulator preconfigured with your course? That surely would make for an excellent 'rainy day' solution. What other fun activities have you come across while staying at a hotel or resort? What do you have on your property to entertain guests?

DEAR PRUDENCE

As a conclusion to this section, allow the following story to serve as a lesson in prudence, and please consider its legal issues as they pertain to personal privacy.

This past year, I sat down with an old friend employed as the GM of a boutique hotel in the American South. He was in town on business, so we met at a café not far from my office. Immediately after we exchanged pleasantries and ordered coffee, his head collapsed into his hands and sweat beaded around his temple. A deflated groan followed.

"Everything alright?" I asked.

"We've just had an outrageously horrible experience with a guest," he said, "And I'm afraid he may file a lawsuit." As he proceeded to divulge the facts of his case, my eyes grew wide as saucers and my jaw slowly dropped to the table.

It began on a typical evening of a typical day, at the front desk of all places. The phone rang. "Could you transfer me to John Doe, please?" asked this caller. "He's a guest at your hotel." The man sounded courteous enough and the front desk had no reason to suggest that this caller was anything but a friend or colleague to the guest in question. The call was promptly transferred.

As it turned out, the caller was not a friend, but a reprehensible criminal. As soon as he reached John Doe's room, the caller fraudulently misrepresented himself as a front desk employee! "Hello, John," said the caller, "I'm at the front desk, and unfortunately the computer system has crashed. Your information has been wiped. If you could please provide us with your credit card number, your social insurance number and your date of birth so we can correct this error?"

John Doe complied without question. After a call from his bank the next morning, he quickly discovered that thousands of dollars were missing from his account. Needless to say, he was flush with anger, and the hotel was about to receive the brunt of it.

He accused the staff of being party to the crime. Even if they weren't complicit, they were still to blame for transferring the call to his room. The hotel staff expressed their sincere apologies and offered to help liaise matters with the bank. The GM also heard the story and, as an immediate palliative action, John Doe wasn't charged for the night's stay.

This was not enough to appease John Doe, however. He stormed out, and soon found a new drain for his frustration—the internet— where he wrote a lengthy diatribe against the hotel; one filled with hateful rhetoric that often strayed far from his immediate problems involving credit card fraud. Is John Doe right to blame the hotel for his misfortunes? Or, is it his responsibility to act with reasonable foresight before relinquishing personal information? Most importantly, is there an all-encompassing remedy for situations like this?

Let's analyze this from a legal point of view. According to the facts, John Doe never expressed his desire to keep his stay confidential. He never expressed his wish to the hotel that he did not want calls to be transferred to his room. There is no proof that he held a subjective expectation of privacy barring calls from reaching his room. It is unfair for him to push the burden of guilt onto the hotel.

Technically, the property is not at fault. But legalities and logic will barely play into the equation once civility is thrown aside and emotions reign supreme. Hiding behind red tape will not save you from defamatory online reviews. To avoid situations like this, I humbly put forth a suggestion. Upon check-in, the concierge should dutifully inquire as to whether or not a guest would want his stay to remain confidential. If guests affirm their privacy, then it gives the front desk a reason to deny transferring calls without appearing as rude or disrespectful to either party.

In the hospitality industry, prudence will always be a formidable virtue and a simple question like this could easily prevent many future headaches.

FOOD & BEVERAGE

*Located in Tofino, British Columbia, the Wickaninnish Inn
satisfies guests not only with surfing, hiking and wave watching,
but fantastic cuisine and an unrivaled whiskey bar.*

INTRODUCTION

We are what we eat. Trite as it may be, it's true. We do it on average three times every day and it's the topic of many, many conversations. It's of particular importance for the hospitality industry as we are not just selling guestrooms, but experiences and memories. The hotel room is one contributing, and crucial factor for this; F&B is another.

When it comes to giving your guests an experience they will truly remember and share with their friends after the fact, what's proffered as eating should be considered a top priority. If your F&B is outstanding, guests may overlook one previous sleight or flaw they noticed. If you can wow visitors with your food selection, it can become yet another weapon in your marketing arsenal that will work independent of paid advertising.

So critical is food to a hotel's success that I've ardently followed all the latest trends in restaurants, grocery stores and all other related fields to see what hotels can apply to their own operations. From my perspective, the two biggest movements in contemporary food culture are the mainstream adoption of healthy eating habits and the emergence of new 'foodie' hotspots which emphasize pure indulgence. It's a divergence of sorts. People are frying and microwaving less while increasing their uptake of vegetables and fruits, and yet every week I hear about a new burger joint offering a specially crafted 2,000 calorie aberration or a boutique shop exclusively selling cookies, cupcakes or upscale donuts.

I touch on a few specific topics dealing with these trends. But another central focus is on the 'beverage' in F&B, which I interpret more-or-less as alcohol. These liquids have highly lucrative profit potential in addition to heightened positive sentiments through their uplifting effects. My thoughts on alcohol first run to wine due my own love for it as well as its ceremonious (and often obligatory) role for lunch and dinner. These articles, which begin the F&B section, take the form of a series under the name 'In Vino Veritas'.

There are always new trends and fads in the domain of F&B. This section covers but a few of what's happening. Learn what you can and don't get too hungry after reading this!

IN VINO VERITAS PART I:
MAKING YOUR WINE LIST WORK FOR YOU

Wine can be a big source of revenue for your F&B stream. It can also be intimidating. Aside from price, confusion and lack of knowledge are two barriers to purchase. Luckily, both can easily be avoided with a comprehensive menu redesign. This article is more of a 'Wine 101' for those properties without a well-defined wine program already in place. If this comes off as overly simplistic—which is one of the key points of my argument by the way—then chug ahead to subsequent pages where I discuss some more 'sophisticated' wine strategies.

To begin, let's use the example of the Yellow Tail wine brand as was wonderfully illustrated in the marketing book, "Blue Ocean Strategy". The parent company, Casella Wines, worked hard to diffuse any bewilderment surrounding wine purchases by making it very simple for those with limited experience to understand.

At their North American launch, they started with only one red and one white varietal, and didn't bog down the labeling with complex grape names, obscure tastes or vineyard source locations. All the bottle had was the official name, '[yellow tail]', and an illustration of a kangaroo—an animal wholly indicative of Australia and a clear marker for the brand. The flavors were always light, sweet and easy to get into. The bottle exudes fun.

I'm not writing this for the supreme echelon of eateries, but rather the in-between, family style joints. So, unless you operate a Michelin-star-winning, best-of-the-Zagat-guide, sommelier-employing restaurant, consider making your wine list more accommodating to those without a bachelor's degree in viticulture.

And by accommodating, what I'm really suggesting is a simplification. The last think you want is someone to stare slack-jawed at your wine list and mutter, "I don't know." The more options you give a person, the harder it is for them to make a choice, especially when they don't understand everything they're reading.

Most wine menus are sorted by red and white with subcategories for specific grapes. The broad delineators of red and white work, but the subcategories don't. Although it may come as a surprise for those inundated with F&B terminology, many people will not know the differences between a Sauvignon Blanc and a Pinot Grigio, or a Cabernet Sauvignon and a Pinot Noir. Chardonnay? Shiraz? Burgundy? Bordeaux? Who knows; who cares.

Start by making it fun. Instead of organizing by varietal, sort by dominant flavors. For whites, think 'sweet', 'dry', 'fruity' or 'tart'. For reds, consider 'light', 'strong', 'spicy' or 'bold'. Not only are these categories easier to understand, but they will inject the menu with excitement.

Next is brevity. A long list means more options. More options; more trouble. Work with your F&B Director to decide on a comprehensive menu that encompasses a full spectrum of tastes, but is also as lean as can be. See if you can fit it on one page in large type. How about half a page? What if you only had four whites and four reds? Would that make for an easy decision?

Third, don't clutter your wine list with too much information. Just as Yellow Tail never stressed the vineyard location, neither should you. Put the grape varietal and year of production in small type, then give an account of the dominant tastes, but keep these descriptors brief as well as alluring.

You will also want to emphasize local vintners if your location allows it. This is the one exception where I'd list the vineyard and winery. Out-of-towners and international arrivers will be curious to learn about the local produce. Take the time to educate them with perhaps a small blurb that highlights some unique aspects of the region.

Lastly, at the bottom or on a separate page, you can make it even easier by describing a selection of recommended wine pairings. Be sure to emphasize how each wine works to enhance and contrast the flavors of specific appetizers or mains. And naturally, use fun and moving descriptors to help nudge people in the right direction. Work with your F&B Director or in-house wine buyer to plan a new wine menu that stresses how fun and effortless wines can be.

IN VINO VERITAS PART II:
A CHECKLIST

The previous 'Wine 101' article covered some of the basics. This article, however, is dedicated to those outlets that a few categories higher in their presentation of wine as an important component of their F&B mix. As a caveat, this isn't intended for those five-star properties that cater to wine gurus. It isn't meant for those properties with wine lists scribed in gold leaf, leather-bound volumes which require three longshoremen to carry such printed tomes to the table. These 'destination wine outlets' still exist, as do their sommeliers with sterling silver tasse de vins dangling via tri-coleur ribbons around their necks.

Rather, this is devoted to the middle or upper-middle ground: restaurateurs who recognize the importance of wine to their outlet's revenue stream and who already appreciate the immense value that wine adds to their guests' mealtime enjoyment. With that, here's what I recommend:

- Be prepared to refresh your wine list regularly. Not only do vintage years change, but so too does the wine list that you will be selecting. Get used to it.
- Find two reliable suppliers or merchants and get to know them well. Rather than cruise the market, you are better off to create relationships with a few specialists. If you have a major operation, you may wish to expand the supplier list or even buy direct, but this is reserved for the big boys. You are a hotelier, stick to what you know, then let the wine merchants deal with their specialty.
- Think local first, then regional, then national. Every guest loves a local story, and is prepared to scrutinize a plethora of local vintages. Providing that you are not purveying turpentine, local vineyards offer you the opportunity to support your community and add novelty. As well, it's a two-way street; local vineyards you support will surely return the favor with a few well-placed referrals.

- Develop a mark-up strategy in line with your retail price points. Many restaurateurs use a sliding mark-up scale, reducing the percentage as the cost price increases. You should consider this, and as well, consider the retail price points. Sticker shock for many customers will set in at the $40 or $50 thresholds. Learn about your guests and manage your lists accordingly.

- Developing your own private label wine can be a double-edged sword. We worked with one outlet, whose own branded house wine (with a unique label that we designed) was so well priced and purchased that it outsold all of the regular selections. A house wine for catering can make sense as a practical option. You might want to resist selling it in the dining room so that it will not deter from the full selection that you offer.

- Don't serve anything you wouldn't drink yourself. There's no room for anything that doesn't meet your own standards. Okay, so we cannot have Chambertin every night, but surely, even the most basic Pinor Noir can be excellent.

- Follow Wine Spectator and other leading journals. Look for up and coming wineries. Encourage dialogue with your wine merchants. Be prepared to test wines and take a chance with your inventories.

- Bin end sales work. Everyone loves a bargain. Having one or two bottles that are marketed as 'limited quantity' encourage the customer to purchase.

- Have a clearly defined by-the-glass program. While somewhat excessive, I have seen fine restaurants offering a dozen different wines by the glass, some at prices well beyond the realm of logic. I am still somewhat sticker-shocked by the $15 per glass wines.

- Wine is all about fun. Fun comes from a knowledgeable wait staff who can talk freely about your wines and understand wine pairings. Since the wine order usually starts the meal, a good relationship between you and your customer can be created right from the start of the meal.

- I need not mention that wine contains alcohol. Your pourers have to recognize that patrons can get just as inebriated on a $15 Chateau Plonk as a $600 Latour; it's all a matter of budget. Safe Serve or Smart Serve programs must be adhered to, protecting your guests as well as your property.

IN VINO VERITAS PART III: MICROBREWERIES

'In Vino Veritas', a Latin expression that explicitly references wine. However, taken as a generalization, other alcoholic beverages are easily implied. Specifically, I want to address the growing microbrewery trend as a means of complementing and augmenting your wine list. And for those that aren't in the know, by microbrewery, I'm referring to a small, craft beer-making company that produces less than 15,000 barrels per year. There are even hobbyist nanobrewers who produce less than 100 barrels and do it because they like the process.

The concept of the micro or local brewery has existed for thousands of years, proliferating since the libation's invention in ancient Egypt and Mesopotamia right through to medieval times. However, the beverage was always considered more of a thirst quencher than a taste tester. Then came pasteurization, big national brands, imports and, ultimately, very limited options. Until recently, beer has never really been a mark of sophistication like wine. And to discover the alchemic and urbane subtleties of strange barley and hop combinations, you will have to travel to regions of Ireland, Belgium, Holland, Germany or the Czech Republic.

Much like how everything else has changed in our interconnected world, so too has the beer industry. The internet has played a big role in shattering the entry barriers for brewing. Keen brewers can instantly share recipes and techniques as well as find new ingredient sources and channels for distribution. Microbreweries are also a more realistic startup venture than wineries or vineyards. They require far less land, labor and production time. Plus, a microbrewery is hardly dependent on erratic weather conditions, operating indoors and year round. These factors aside, microbrews still only account for roughly 5% of total consumption in the US, but they are growing at a staggering rate relative to their mass-marketed counterparts.

Using American mainstays as an example, your restaurant's beer choices could include the Budweiser, Coors and Miller varieties, or you could proffer something more eclectic. This is no insult to these major brands' quality, but they are all so commonplace that they have become boring. There's no excitement, no mystery. True, some people may only be in the mood for a good old fashioned Bud Light. But would they be entirely opposed to a craft brew, especially if no major brands were on the menu?

Specialty drafts give you the chance to revitalize your menu with a little adventure and flair. It's no longer just a pale ale, but a bitter yet smooth malt with floral hop aromas and a bold, refreshing finish with hints of honey, coffee and almonds. Does this remind you of any other beverage descriptions? Oftentimes, the wine list is given the full attention of the F&B department while the beer list suffers from neglect.

There are pale ales, lagers, pilsners, honey browns, red ales, amber ales, blondes, light beers, wheat beers, dark beers, porters, stouts and plenty of other more obscure flavors. Much like the underlying function of your wine list, your beer choices should serve to augment your overall F&B experience. Just as there's a vintage to satisfy every person's tastes and to pair with each meal, craft beers are headed in the same direction. Having to explain such options will take up a larger chunk of a waiter's time and perhaps temporarily boggle a customer. Framing this positively, it's a chance for the waiter to establish rapport with a curious patron and thus increase the perceived service level. And just for trivia's sake, a beer sommelier is named a cicerone.

Microbrews are also an excellent way to support your local constituency. Your hotel might be located in or near a wine-producing region, but, as is more often the case, it is not. Breweries are essentially modified warehouses and can be situated practically anywhere.

Now I'm not suggesting that you turn your main restaurant or lobby bar into a brewpub. I'm merely proposing this as yet another unrealized point of differentiation. Fun and interesting beverage options can add to a guest's dining experience and therefore improve the quality of their stay. Plus, such craft beers are also a chance for additional beverage sales as people will be more inclined to have an extra pint of something new or foreign. Along these lines, you could also offer a flight of beers. Just food for thought, or should I say, beer for thought!

IN VINO VERITAS PART IV:
DESSERT WINES

I'm quite privileged to live in Toronto, which happens to be just over an hour's drive from Niagara-on-the-Lake, one of only a few well-known, wine-producing regions in Canada. Although not nearly as prestigious as other APAs in California or France, Niagara is recognized as a world leader when it comes to ice wines—a subcategory of dessert wines where the producers don't pick the grapes until after the first frost hits the vines.

When I last visited the winemaker Stratus in Niagara for a tasting, I was awed by their use of such sweet wines. No longer just an accompaniment to a chocolate mousse or crème brûlée, their ice wines were served with cheeses. The unbridled sweetness of a Riesling icewine matched with piquant cheddar. A fruity Vidal icewine paired with mellow Gouda. The complex red berry tastes of a Cabernet Franc icewine contrasted perfectly with a sharp, salty Blue Stilton. All exquisite.

What I learned: dessert wines aren't solely for dessert, nor are they solely for cheeses. What about pairing such sweet wines by the glass with appetizers? Think lobster bisque and Sauternes. On a recent trip to the Fairmont Le Manoir Richelieu in the Charlevoix region of Quebec, I sampled an apple cider ice wine with foie gras—a surprisingly playful combination.

Dessert wines have a rich history. There is a wide variety, and while Canada is known for its icewine, many other regions produce their own local gems: German Eiswein and Trockenbeerenauslese, Austrian Ausbruch, French Sauternes and Hungarian Tokaji Aszú to name a few. Sweet wines are often underappreciated. Incorporating them into your menu is an excellent opportunity for added F&B revenues.

The key to selling sweet wines outside of their predefined after-dinner utility is to offer them by the glass. For most of your customers, dessert or sweet wines aren't nearly as familiar as their red and white cousins. For others, they're just too sweet to consume at any significant quantity. Even though bottle sizes are often only 200ml or 375ml, it's still a hefty commitment, especially given that dessert wines edge on the expensive side. Offering sweet wine by the glass eliminates these obstacles. People will be more adventurous with a one-ounce portion—a suggested serving size that's adequate for a taste and keeps selling prices reasonable while still maintaining your margins.

Start by reviewing with your chef and F&B manager what sweet wines you currently stock and how a few common varietals might be matched with your selection of appetizers. Next, consider putting a cheese plate on the menu with suggested pairings. Better yet, how about a flight of dessert wines to give patrons a more formal introduction. Last, educate your staff so they can properly communicate how great these wines actually taste and how well they complement certain foods. Remember, dessert wines aren't just for dessert anymore!

IN VINO VERITAS PART V:
GO ON A TOUR!

Can you sell wine without ever having visited a winery or vineyard? Sure, it's done all the time. Plus, with the internet at your disposal, you can find out plenty more than is necessary to do the deed. But, will you sell wine better and more often if you've become personally acquainted with its production? I assure you: yes.

The more information you know about wine and the greater your personal connection to it, the more your passion for wine will be communicated to guests. And that passion will translate into revenue. What I'm talking about is putting a narrative behind the sales pitch. For instance, a guest points to the menu and asks, "Is this Merlot any good?" The waiter may reply with a simple affirmation, which isn't all that encouraging, or instead they could say, "Yes! Our manager toured that winery last summer and he specifically chose that bottle because it was exceptionally smooth and had a rich berry aftertaste you just don't find in other Merlots."

This not only adds credibility to the endorsement but also enriches the waiter's rapport with the patron. Think larger tips which translate into better team morale, but also consider that a congenial rapport will make a guest more lenient towards any mistakes. Not that you should be making any errors in the first place, but with a healthy rapport, a guest will be more open to pointing out the shortcoming and inclined to criticize without resentment. Lo and behold, this also trickles down the line into better TripAdvisor and Yelp reviews. In short, rapport building always works towards a better dining experience and attaching these little personal stories to items on your menu will certainly help.

Outside of viewing this from a guest's perspective, going on a wine tour is a great team-building exercise. It's your chance to get out of the office and have some fun. Seeing the grapes and wine firsthand as well as experiencing a variety of flavors all at once is a highly educational experience. And observational knowledge like this also seems to transcribe better than mere textbook regurgitation.

Furthermore, a tour is an opportunity to discover new wineries in your region and develop relationships with the vintners far and above what email tag will do for you—relationships that may pay off in terms of better deals and first pick on upcoming stock. To heighten the fun factor and to be as safe as possible, rent a bus so you can all stick together and not have to worry about designated drivers. Aside from the cost of the outing, the primary consideration is whether you are in the vicinity of a wine-producing region to make for an adequate day trip. Don't panic. You still have options.

For one, you'd be hard-pressed to find a major city that doesn't tout an annual wine tasting event, show or festival, typically held at a convention center. Better yet, court a vintner to send reps to your property for an in-house experience. Either way, it's all about attaining that direct knowledge to support recommendations to guests. As well, if they supply your kitchen, consider subbing the whole winery aspect with a local brewery, distillery, bakery or cheesemaker—anything that can help add that personal narrative to the menu.

IN VINO VERITAS PART VI: WHISKEYS

I know what you're thinking: another chapter not related to wine. Why are whiskeys relevant? In the same vein as micro-brewed or craft beers, they're now in vogue. Irish, scotch, bourbon or rye; single malt or blended; people are on the hunt for exotic breeds and aromatic flavors. A cursory glance of the web will tell you that distillery locations are as diverse and globetrotting as wine appellations. If you can feed the need, this may become a powerful revenue stream for your F&B department. Let's review some of the corollaries of investing in your whiskey selection.

1. *Rarity.* It doesn't take a lot of research to stock Johnny Walker Blue Label on the shelf—an expensive but nonetheless outstanding blended malt. As an alternative, how about offering Nikka from the Barrel, a blended whiskey . . . from Japan? Think about this in terms of the uniqueness of the drinking experience. If a whiskey brand is offered everywhere, it will not contribute to an experience that's anything out of the ordinary. Offer a rare elixir to make the occasion that much more exceptional.

2. *Rapport.* Whiskeys, like wine, require cajoling. If you expect people to throw down their doubloons on these brown liquors, you'd best keep your bartenders and waiters in the loop. Give them the knowledge to offer legitimate recommendations, which will in turn enable longer, healthier conversations to flourish, augmenting the overall guest experience.

3. *Markup.* Straightforward as it comes, whiskey by the glass can run up quite the bill. The more esoteric you get, the more opportunities you're giving customers to experience something apart from the staple (and comparatively inexpensive) brands like Wild Turkey or Canadian Club. If you've taken the time to assemble a formidable whiskey collection, people will take the time to explore that ensemble. Heck, they may get a little adventurous with their wallets, too.

4. *Prestige.* Unlike craft beers that may only be an additional talking point for guests and wait staff, brandishing the title of 'Scotch Bar' or 'Bourbon Tavern' has an elevated, patrician aura about it. Wine will typically be a secondary consideration for patrons to your restaurant—the cuisine almost always rests at number one— unless, of course, you're renowned for housing an exhaustive cellar (no small feat I might add). Inspired whiskey selections are for the true connoisseur. Such consumers will seek you out, appetizers and entrées optional. It's a niche market, but it's growing.

5. *Presentation.* Heavy markups may intimidate patrons away from a purchase. Whiskeys have a long shelf though, so it's not like you have to fret over spoilage. That leaves plenty of half to three-quarters filled bottles on the shelf, and when arranged together with the right lighting, it can amount to one damn impressive display. Imagine the typical bar, stocked with the usual suspects for rum, vodka, tequila and gin. Yawn. Now add 100 bottles of whiskey, all with artistic labels and distinctive glass designs. Wow.

6. *Pairings.* Everyone loves a good pairing. Just as revamping your wine menu is a chance to revitalize your gastronomic exhibition, the same goes for your liquors. Have fun with it. The peat-smoked zing of a fine Scotch matches exquisitely with some salty charcuterie while the dry bite of a Kentucky bourbon pairs nicely with a tapas-style spread of cool dips and olives. Again, rapport plays a part here, as educated wait staff will always be a cardinal element towards pairings and, ultimately, customer satisfaction.

7. *Glassware.* Top-flight products deserve something better than a half-dollar 'Libbey glass', with no disrespect of these excellent everyday tumblers. Consider martini bars. It's all about the details: an elongated bowl, a twist in the stem, an array of tinted glasses to offset the different colors of each concoction. Transfer this thought process to whiskey. Thick cut glass and crystal tumblers will extend your bar's aura of quality—even if it's only by a touch, but these tiny touches will contribute to a greater whole.

8. *Water.* Many whiskies are consumed with a drop of water to bring the flavor out. Others like ice. Still others use 'scotch rocks', which are stones shaped like ice cubes that are frozen, chilling the beverage without the dilution. Regardless of preference, this is not a tap water situation. Consider distilled water in bottled form to give assurance

to patrons. This aura of quality even extends to the shape of ice cubes your machine makes—another opportunity for a unique mark.

9. *Copy.* Give your patrons something to read while they indulge themselves—it's entertainment after all. Think tasting cards with brief blurbs on every spirit's history and what flavors to expect from each sip. Yet another tiny touch to append the overall guest experience. Consider integrating these factoids into the menu, but only if it doesn't amount to a cluttered read.

10. *Constituency.* Support your local producers, nuff said. Although this might not bear fruit for those outside of Kentucky or Scotland, do your research as you never know who has recently started roasting barley within a 100 kilometer radius. Yes, this is a chance to develop a relationship with a new supplier, and, yes, this is something to boast about. Guests at your hotel crave the local flair, so strive to deliver wherever possible.

IN VINO VERITAS PART VII:
AUSTRALIAN WINES

When autumn comes to the Northern Hemisphere, it's time to turn your oenophilic gaze on our southern neighborhoods where things are literally heating up. That's right; as our leaves shrivel and fall, and the snow cakes our once verdant yards, be contest in knowing that there's still plenty to look forward to. And chief amongst the southern producers is Australia; a country and a continent, as well as the world's seventh largest wine producer and, remarkably, now the fourth largest wine exporter.

The Aussie wine story is fairly peculiar as their ecosystem had no native grape stocks prior to the British infusion beginning en masse in the early 19th century. Even then, the continent's climate is widely erratic, capable of going from drought to flood and back all within a single decade—not the best for cementing cultivars and motivating financiers. (Nota bene: starting a vineyard capable of export quantities typically requires millions of dollars upfront.)

So it was that for the longest time, the semi-arid valleys and grasslands (Australia is also the flattest continent by the way) of Victoria, New South Wales, South Australia and Western Australia (four of the nation's now prominent wine-producing states) were reserved for shepherds, farmers and miners. That's not to say that winemaking was absent, but still an oddity.

Things started to change in the late 1950s. Primarily, science had bolstered the root stocks to better suit the unstable Aussie weather conditions and resist a certain sinister pest, and worldwide population booms warranted a greater supply. The industry reached a fever pitch in the mid-1990s as corporations swooped in with their economies of scale and marketing savvy to more formally debut Australian wines to the world market. The country hasn't looked back since, and indeed the grapevine business remains one of the country's largest growth sectors. (For a well-known example, look at the story behind Yellow Tail.)

As for the wines themselves, they may not hold the longstanding barreling traditions and prestige of vineyards in France and Italy, but that would be a naïve pretense to belittle the Australians' rich and complex flavors. Borrowing chiefly from the most popular Old World varietals—Chardonnay, Pinot Noir, Riesling, Sauvignon Blanc, Merlot and Cabernet Sauvignon—these wines are quintessentially New World. Brightly acidic with pungent sugars, the reds are rarely heavy and the whites never fail to dance on the palate. Given this archetypal taste profile, the nation's stable of wines is perfect for plugging the gaps on your menu where a flighty, fruity elixir is required.

My hunch is to start with the more established and bountiful producing regions including the Margaret River south of Perth, Hunter Valley and Mudgee four hours inland from Sydney and the Yarra River Valley outside of Melbourne. But none compare to the rolling hills surrounding Adelaide in South Australia (Barossa Valley, Coonawarra, Eden Plains, McLaren Vale and the Riverland), home to the Southern Hemisphere's largest wineries and most of the country's viticultural heritage.

Wines are a matter of 'taste and you shall receive'. Given its bourgeois and still largely experimental character, Australian labels are completely winemaker-dependent (aren't they all?). Use a buyer's guide or an expert wine merchant to select a few renowned bottles for initial sampling. As well, Aussie vintners generally keep an impressive cohort at any major tasting convention, so attendance to one of these events can earn you a powwow to learn more firsthand.

What's best is the price. Never outrageously marked up, the nation's bottles are generally very reasonable for the average patron and are ready-to-drink at a young age. Vintage is less of a concern, as their wines typically remain consistent year to year. With that in mind, Australian wines are fun and I'd highly recommend you stock one or two on the menu!

IN VINO VERITAS PART VIII: SOUTH AFRICAN WINES

Staying with our Southern Hemisphere theme, after Australia the penultimate exporter is another former crown colony, South Africa. And as with its Commonwealth counterpart, the nation's winemaking heritage goes hand-in-hand with European colonization.

For starters, sneak a glance at a world map, or recall the nation's location from memory; specifically, the region around the Cape of Good Hope at the southwestern corner of the nation. This area denotes the Cape Peninsula and, more broadly, the Western Cape, including the first Dutch colony, and later the first British colony, that would become the city of Cape Town. Special to the Cape Peninsula is the intersection of weather systems from the Atlantic Ocean and Indian Ocean currents with a more-than-generous contribution from the Antarctic that acts to drastically temper humidity.

All this, in addition to some very extraneous mountains, valleys and flatlands, amounts to hot, dry, sunlight-heavy summer seasons lasting from November to April, similar to the Mediterranean. However, certain appellations—'wards' as they are locally termed—experience sizably milder and wetter year-round conditions, especially those closest to the coast. This unique terroir has created many sundry microclimates, and thus, many diverse cultivars.

One part climate, another part topography and a third part colonization, to this day the Western Cape is where the vast majority of South Africa's viticultural activity transpires. The Dutch East India Company was the first to instigate this development, importing grapevines and harvesting the fruit for sailors to fend off scurvy during the passage from Europe to India and Southeast Asia. As you know, wherever there are fecund grapevines, there will soon be winemaking. Indeed, by 1659, a vineyard was established at Constantia just north of Cape Town.

Once the colony was folded into the British Empire, production sharply increased throughout the 19th century as a means to countervail the dominant French on the international market. With the bulk of South African wines exported to Great Britain, the nation's industry declined towards the end of the century following the dissolution of the preferential tariffs that precluded French vintages. For most of the 20th century, vintners suffered tremendously under Apartheid as worldwide boycotts thwarted overseas commerce and knowledge exchange.

But with the collapse of this racial segregation system in 1994, South Africa's winemaking quickly rebounded and is now the eighth largest worldwide producer and exporter. Adhering to the purview of the internal Wine of Origin administration, there are now roughly 60 active wards with most of the harvest controlled by several large cooperatives. Alongside this resurgence has come a renewed focus on international prospects as many vineyards shift towards the noble varietals of Cabernet Sauvignon, Chardonnay, Merlot, Pinot Noir, Sauvignon Blanc and Shiraz.

However, the reopening of trade routes has also allowed for a revival of South Africa's own cultivars and styles. Most pronounced are the fortified wines designed under the 'Cape Port' marker. Heavily influenced by Portuguese seafarers migrating through the Cape Colony, these spirits cover a wide range of varietals, both white and red, as well as winemaking techniques, comprising a narrow assortment of strict vintage classifications.

Three more atypical grape pedigrees nearing the top of South Africa's production list are Chenin Blanc, Colombard and Pinotage. Chenin Blanc, also called Steen, is originally from the Loire Valley in northwestern France and has been adapted mainly for dry dessert wines and sparkling whites as well as those in the Cape Port vein. Colombard, an offspring of Chenin Blanc, is a sweeter white used mainly for the Cape Port wines. Lastly, Pinotage, a deep red cross of Pinot Noir, was first crafted in the Western Cape and is now a required constituent in blends produced in the region.

My first morsel of advice is to consider these three varietals popular to South Africa, if only to offer the surface allure of something more exotic. Imagine your wine list already boasting a premier stable of the usual suspects; a label with an unfamiliar base ingredient may be enough to pique the more audacious patron and encourage extra sales.

As for dabbling in the Cape Port style wines, consider getting in touch with a Cape Wine Master, the highest formal qualification within the South African wine industry, to canvass their knowledge and stamp of authenticity. Due to their strengthened nature at or above 16%

alcohol content, the Cape Port vintages may be more suitable as aperitifs or dessert accompaniments. Save for their extensive local appeal, these fortified wines remain comparatively unknown most elsewhere. Hence, conspicuous labeling or their inclusion in pairing suggestions may be required to point customers in the right direction.

Whether you stock some of their more conventional fare or try your hand with fortified wines, South African bottles offer a good break from the ordinary. Just one more nation to consider for diversifying your wine list.

IN VINO VERITAS PART IX:
SOUTH AMERICAN WINES

I've chosen to approach the wines of South America as a singular unit; a move not borne out of any deficiency of viticultural narrative in each country or laziness on my part, but because of their common ancestor— Spain. The two primary candidates for discussion are Argentina and Chile given their top ten volumes of global production. As such, I will focus on these two nations. However, this does not preclude such other burgeoning and smaller growers like Bolivia, Brazil's Rio Grande do Sul, Paraguay, Peru (especially the spirit Pisco) and Uruguay.

Taken together, Argentina and Chile now make more wine by tonnage than the United States, respectively as the fifth and tenth largest worldwide producers. This was not always the case, however. Both nations were wracked by decades of turbulent governments and economic strife throughout the 20th century. Looking back even further, although colonization was the key spark for the import of grape stocks and grafts in the 16th century, Spanish overseers sought to restrict viticultural farming in the New World to avoid competition with vintners back home.

Nevertheless, wine culture prospered, giving us many unique tastes and stable appellations for which we can now fully reap the savory benefits. Of particular note, South America largely escaped the phylloxera blight that ruined vineyards throughout Europe in the 19th century. This devastation caused many French, Italian and Spanish winemakers to emigrate to Argentina and Chile, bringing with them their varietals and wisdom. But most of the production during this period was still devoted to table grapes and jug wine for local consumption.

It wasn't until the turn into the 21st century that South America really took to the world stage with a gallant desire to compete at the international level. For this, vineyards hired flying winemakers throughout the 1990s and 2000s to elevate the quality of wines to modern standards of export set for large buying countries like Great Britain, United States and more recently China, as well as a greater replanting and focus on the more pervasive commercial mainstays.

Nowadays, South American wines are widely considered New World in their taste spectrums, particularly the whites. But there are some peculiarities about them that can prop your wine list up with that extra slice of fascination. Namely, the early grafters didn't properly control their varietal lineage and as such some obvious mislabeling has occurred. No matter, the ampelographers are on the case.

Proceeding in alphabetical order with Argentina, what is most apparent about Argentine wines is that the vast majority of export quality production takes places in Mendoza and its neighboring province of San Juan in the Andean foothills directly west from the capital city, Buenos Aires. This high altitude, semi-arid cordillera environment, with its hot summers and sharp nighttime temperature drops, elicits softer flavors with bolder tannins in the reds. It's no wonder that Malbec is now the grape of choice, and you would be hard-pressed to find an appellation elsewhere in the world that does this varietal better.

Moreover, reds account for over 60% of wine exports with other key varietals including Cabernet Sauvignon, Syrah and the esteemed Spanish grape Tempranillo. Worth noting is the Italian Charbono strain, locally known as Bonarda, which was almost completely extricated from European fields by the phylloxera epidemic. Surviving in Argentina, it is now a flavorful runner up in popularity to the Malbec. Given their black skins, the Charbono is somewhat counterintuitive as the wine has a deep empurpled color yet a fruity, acidic profile.

An important postscript for the Argentine Malbec, they've been bred more towards the tart flavors of Cabernet Sauvignon and less like the conventional Malbec which belies a sugary plum and cherry taste. To bolster this dissimilarity, it's rather common to find Malbec as the major grape in a mix that includes Cabernet Sauvignon, Syrah and Petit Verdot which in turn creates a diverse array of wines to choose from.

On the white front, Argentine exports have more or less adopted the international cornerstones of Sauvignon Blanc, Chardonnay, Pinot Gris, Riesling, Semillon and Viognier while the jug wine varietal of Pedro Giménez continues to decline. From personal experience, if you plan to dabble with Argentine alcohol, stick with the reds and the most perfected of the lot, Malbec and Bonarda; the former for a solid expression of a familiar grape and the latter for something a tad more exotic and intrepid.

As for Chile, any agronomical discussion should include a brief overview of the country's svelte, latitude-crossing geographic borders along with the inescapable presence of the towering Andes. Together, these two have caused most of the premier Chilean flights to aggregate within the 800-mile stretch between the 32nd and 38th parallels centered on the capital, Santiago, where the climate most imitates that of the Mediterranean. The mild Pacific currents along with the rain shadow protection induced by the Andes and the coastal range provide vineyards with some of the most stable growing conditions in the world. Minimal weather fluctuations mean consistent vintages—a boon for rolling purchase orders.

Much like how Argentina has the Malbec, Chile has the Merlot, for which the country's harvest rivals the renowned incumbents in California and France. Chile also favors the Cabernet Sauvignon, although their produce leans toward a softer palate akin to a proper Cab-Merlot blend. Third in the reds, and contributing towards many of the country's taste discrepancies, is the Carménère grape, which, like the Charbono in Argentina, was largely destroyed by the phylloxera scourge only to live on in the New World.

Carménère, with its archetypal rubicund coloration and rich, mellow profile, has largely been incorrectly labeled as Merlot. Now that more professional vintners are active, this once popular French varietal is back in vogue nearly 150 years after its disappearance from Europe. The lost grape is recognized as a distinct lure for the country's wines, restored to its own pedigree separate from Merlot as well as thriving as a near-exclusive blending ingredient in Chilean mainstays.

These same 'mistaken identity' suits apply to many Sauvignon Blanc vineyards where the parent stocks have been found be of Sauvignonasse and Semillon descent, affording many Chilean whites with softer, floral notes instead of the quintessential fruitiness of other Sauvignon Blanc flights from the New World. Whatever the case, the top four picks of Cabernet Sauvignon, Carménère, Merlot and Sauvignon Blanc will definitely add some variety and perhaps a few interesting conversations to your wine list.

IN VINO VERITAS PART X: CHEESE TASTINGS

Cheese is often thought of as the lowly second-tier cousin to the eponymous grape-based libation, even though the two go hand-in-hand across the globe for fancy soirees of the wine and cheese variety. Take a closer look and you'll see that the craft and sophistication behind these semisolid dairy products goes just as deep as their alcoholic pairings. Swiss, ricotta, gorgonzola, parmesan, boccaccini, asiago, gouda, oka, goat, stilton, gruyere, camembert, mozzarella, havarti, halloumi, feta, you name it.

My appreciation for the depth of cheese in this manner was sparked a few summers ago when I sojourned to Cannes, France with my wife. While shacked up at a bucolic Relais & Chateaux property, Hotel Le Mas Candille, in the town of Mougins, we needed only to walk downstairs ten paces to reach the entrance of a Michelin Star rated restaurant, Le Candille, headed by celebrated chef Serge Gouloumès.

Most notable at first glance was the prefixed menu at 400 Euros per head. Not only are we talking about a truly empyrean bill (taking into account that this trip occurred before the recent recession and subsequent European currency reevaluation), but wine pairings were not included and tallied at an additional 200 Euros per head.

Jaw-droppingly expensive? Yes. A meal that I'll never forgot? Also yes. This was not a restaurant but a gastronomic adventure that took four hours from start to finish. No word of a lie, I never thought pigeon could be this tasty (not that I would had it before!). For dessert, we all enjoyed a marshmallow tasting as a precursor to our edible gold foil-wrapped sugar cane birdcages encasing marzipan canaries.

Aside from the utterly exquisite appetizers, mains and sweets, one striking feature was the cheese tray. Supplementary to the uncorking of our first glass of wine, a knowledgeable server wheeled over a cart adorned with 100 different types of cheese. That's right—100 delectable slices of dairy heaven ranging from aged cheddars and blues to obscure varieties of salted brie, all joined by a few select honeys, jams, jellies and home-baked crackers.

Two caveats. First, this is France, home to a centuries-old tradition of proud cheesemaking with each town's produce as unique as the next. Second, we were at a Michelin-lauded joint and I doubt the cheese cart would make a similar appearance at the nearest McDonalds. These two aside, what really struck me was the breadth of knowledge that the server effused after a couple of generic prompts. In fact, he was no simple waiter, but an in-house 'Affineur de Fromage'—an individual specifically responsible for the maturation and aging of cheeses. Think of him like a sommelier, but for cheese.

Reminiscing on this experience years later, I have now attended several recent wine tastings where each grape varietal was appropriately paired with a different cheese to complement and enhance the flavors of both. It's definitely a 'trendy' approach to flights, with wine vendors rapidly linking up with cheesemongers (those who sell cheeses) and catchy descriptors like 'artisanal', 'boutique', 'craftsman' and 'farmstead' creeping into waiters' cheese lexicons both near and far.

There are two more considerations that apply to the upper end of dairy delights. First, a horizontal cheese tasting is one where you cross-compare cheeses of the same type and region but made from different producers. And second, a vertical cheese tasting is one where you sample the cheese across a spectrum of different ages. While at Le Candille, I completed a 12-part vertical brie tasting, each cheese wild with classic creamy flavor and pungent differences in saltiness and sourness. Not only will I never forget this experience (and the hotel which gave it to me!), but it has forever heightened my intrinsic level of cheese appreciation.

Back on topic, knowing that premium cheeses are officially a burgeoning commodity, I beg the question: are your hotel guests ready? Would a cheese tasting on the menu actually sell? Or, would specially selected cheeses augment the perceived value of a flight that's already on the wine list? At the ultra-luxury end of things, would your restaurant benefit from the 'Affineur de Fromage' treatment alongside your sommelier? Perhaps, just as you offer wine by the glass, you can likewise recommend 'cheese by the slice' as an accompaniment. Just food for thought, or dare I say, cheese for thought.

IN VINO VERITAS PART XI: WHAT ABOUT CHINA?

Through my wine studies, one curiosity I've stumbled upon pertains to China. That is, the nation of over one billion people and rapidly proliferating wealth is starting to consume a lot of wine. Not only that, but China currently stands as the fifth biggest grape wine producer in the world (most for internal consumption), and yet they are still only in the infant stages of developing their own internal haughty viticulture and prize-worthy vintners. This is an article to more-or-less give you an update on where China stands in the winemaking scene and how their emergence will impact worldwide prices and distribution.

In terms of per capita statistics, China currently rests pretty far down the list at roughly 0.15 liters per capita per year. Although this ratio pales in comparison to countries where wine is life (France, Italy and Portugal as examples), when it comes to China you always have to consider the sheer scale of the country. France's population sits at 65 million, Italy at 60 million and Portugal at 10.5 million. China has 1.35 billion people; approximately ten times that of France, Italy and Portugal combined. If wine culture catches on in China, even by just a little bit, we are talking colossal increases of consumption.

And this is already happening. China has grown quite the voracious appetite for imports, chiefly from prestigious winemakers in France, Italy, Germany and the US. Think the big, eminent chateaus: Pétrus, Cheval Blanc, Mouton Rothschild and the classic Burgundies like Romanée-Conti and its cohort. Now these 'name' examples are just for France, but if you know these bottles then you know the caliber we are talking about.

The continued presence of a gigantic fine wine buyer and consumer like China suggests, through straightforward supply and demand, that worldwide prices are bound to increase, especially at the upper end of the market which is being yanked into the stratosphere. If you're scouting for evidence of this budding trend, look no further than Sotheby's with its Hong Kong location reaping huge rewards from this incredible rise in Chinese demand.

On an individual property basis, these sorts of macroeconomic analyses will probably have little impact in the short run, especially since this gross inflation affects Chinese domestic prices more so than wholesale elsewhere in the world. Just don't be surprised that the lurking aftershock of China's heightened consumption causes the entire market to float upwards as well. I say lurking because it will be a slow, years-long effect, but it will nevertheless impact your bottom line.

Perhaps now is the right time to explore the bevy of new growers and regions reaching maturity? These are factors which are simultaneously acting to buffer the supply side of things and, from their perspective, capitalize on the mounting worldwide demand. Moreover, given the abundance of flying winemakers and knowledge sharing via the internet, it is now easier for a grape producer or vintner to perfect their technique in a shorter time span. These wandering internal dialogues on the current state of wine quickly segued into a more encapsulating rumination about the Chinese consumer and what appeals to them.

With this nation's increasing affluence comes more outbound travel and more expendable cash for such luxury items as mid to top tier alcoholic beverages. What libations are popular with Chinese patrons? Are their actions abroad similar to how things are going at home? And more specifically, how can you better appeal to Chinese guests through a more engaging wine list?

Starting broad, there are many other alcoholic beverages that compete with wine for top esteem in mainland China—mainly beer (Tsingtao), baijiu, whiskey, brandy and rice liquors. Stocking just one of these mainstays might help to ease native Chinese guests by giving them a stronger sense of home when visiting a foreign land, thus formulating better impressions of your hotel. Then think of it the other way around. You are traveling in China, and with so many unfamiliar food choices, wouldn't it be somewhat calming to see a burger or a pizza on the menu once in awhile?

Current polls show that China's appetite for foreign wine currently only extends to reds. My first suggestion is therefore to ensure that your wine list has a robust selection of reds from wine-producing nations known to be at the top of their game (in the same vein as those abovementioned). This may seem prejudiced against white wines, but it's simply where the demand presently is. Plus, through my many red-versus-white arguments in the past, the general consensus is always that red pairs better with more meals, especially those with a meat or poultry main or a rich sauce.

From a purchaser's perspective, China's homegrown wineries are still too far in their adolescence for me to recommend a hearty investment for your cellars. Right now, a 'Chinese wine' on the menu is likely to be chosen more out of novelty than out of quality. But, as is the case with nearly every other industry, this booming nation is rife with fast learners and hard workers, so expect their producing regions to be making an increasingly significant impact on the world stage as the grapevines and vintners reach maturity over the next two decades.

It's important to also remember that like any other cosmopolitan jetsetter, Chinese travelers are looking to live the new and experience the unknown. Give them an authentic localized experience through your wine list and pairing choices, and you will undoubtedly see a strong appreciation for your F&B efforts. As well, offering one or two liquor options that are 'cross-pleasers'—those that appeal to Chinese consumers as well as those from another large demographic—may work better than dedicated attractors.

IN VINO VERITAS PART XII:
BOLD OL' BURGUNDY

If you are going to embark on a journey of wine discovery and education, knowing the basics about French wines is a must. There's no way around it. And one of the foremost appellation regions in France is Burgundy. Lying roughly in the middle latitudes of the eastern half of the nation and catching the tail end of the Rhone river in the northwestern Alps, Burgundy makes some of the best and most acclaimed wines in the world, with a proud viticulture dating back to the first Roman settlements of the area.

Before I started spending real money on bottles, my wine classifications were naively generalized by country name—France, Italy, Austria and so on. But once I graduated to the next level, I became keenly aware of the gross differences in winemaking and taste from appellation to appellation, beginning with the grape varietals that are grown. Burgundy terroir and wines are heavily controlled and, with only a few exceptions, their reds are made from Pinot Noir and whites from Chardonnay.

I love Burgundies. To me, they define Old World flavor. The reds are dry, savory and multilayered. The whites are spritely, tangy and rich with none of the domineering sugariness or fruitiness of New World crushes. In fact, both Pinot Noir and Chardonnay were bred and matured into their distinct contemporary lineages in this region.

My love of Burgundy peaked when I toured the Côte-d'Or department (as sub-regions are called in France) in style via air balloon, floating from vineyard to vineyard and sampling the world's finest drops alongside some mouthwatering cheeses and food. On a tangent, worth tasting are Burgundy's many Dijon mustards and its classical stew recipe, beef bourguignon, as well as its époisses cheese, an orange-colored salty, creamy curd dubbed the 'king of cheeses' that truly lives up to this name. This trip was pretty far from inexpensive I might add.

The Côte-d'Or department happens to be the epicenter for reputable winemaking in the region, all codified under the Grand Cru system as the stamp of supreme quality pertaining exclusively to Burgundy wines. If you're fortunate enough to get your hands on a Grand Cru (only about

1-2%, of total bottles from the Burgundy region) savor every drop as this mark of distinction is not handed out lightly; you are drinking one of best wines in the whole wide world. Secondary wines are classified as Premier Cru, followed by Burgundy AC.

The best of Burgundy is known as DRC, or Domain de Romanee-Conti. These wines are not just some of the finest in the world, but are so sought after that they hold records at auction houses that quite literally make them worth more by weight than pure gold. While the vineyard is considered a Mecca for oenophiles, the DRC complements of Grand Echazeaux, Echazeaux, Romanee-St.-Vivant, Richebourg and La Tache in private tasting rooms with a selection of vintage magnum bottles is a memory I'll never forget. And while there was a spittoon, I can guarantee you that not a single drop was wasted on the metal pail.

With this as a lead in, if you want your wine menu to connote the same esteem and sophistication as your cuisine, consider segregating your French listings by regional subsections. Think Burgundy, Bordeaux, Côte du Rhône and Loire Valley—wholly permissible because of the tight controls on grape varietal production within each region and the distinctive flavors that result. A Burgundy pinot noir tastes nothing like a Bordeaux cabernet sauvignon-merlot blend, and you'd be wise not to lump them as such.

Stocking one or two Grand Cru bottles, although quite expensive, is an important investment for celebratory cases where a group is commemorating a very special moment in someone's life. With only a dozen or so grand cru bottles in my cellar, I can remember every time they have been consumed. The last one? My 60th birthday a few months ago: Ruchottes-Chambertin 2000. And for those who are interested, it was drinking very well.

IN VINO VERITAS PART XIII:
TUSCAN TITANS

Now that I've touched upon my favorite wine regions in France (Burgundy), it's time to move on to Italy, and specifically Tuscany, probably the country's foremost producer. Located north of Rome proper along the Tyrrhenian Sea, this region of Italy (which I've visited on a couple occasions) is marked by its idyllic rolling hills of verdant greens abutting centuries-old towns of well-preserved brickwork, clay and religious artistry. This land is the home to three very popular tourist cities—Florence, Pisa and Siena.

It goes without saying that Tuscany (and all of the Mediterranean nations for that matter) has a longstanding viticultural footprint, dating back to before the Roman conquest of the Italian peninsula. During the Dark Ages, it was the pious monks who took the reins amidst the economic collapse of Western Europe. The current iterations by which we classify this nation's pedigrees today emerged during the early Renaissance when Northern Italian city-states awoke as European centers of commerce, bringing with them lots of fresh capital and a renewed demand for wine.

Nowadays, much like in France, Italy adheres to a scrupulous set of quality assurance protocols for its appellations. Look for the DOC or, even better, the DOCG label to ensure that you're getting a true Tuscan product. The emphasis here is that of quality over quantity, which means that, when combined with the semi-arid climate and the thin layer of top soil, Tuscany has a very low yield relative to other Italian regions. Not surprisingly, four-fifths of what's made are red varietals.

My experiences with Tuscan wines pertain mostly to that of Brunello, Chianti and Montepulciano. All three of which are made almost entirely from the Sangiovese grape, bestowing them with an opaque dark red-violet color and a fruity, full-bodied taste. This consistency in flavor means that Tuscan reds are great for pairings—a rich, tannin-heavy acidic drop matches perfect with any red meat, saucy pasta or other savory dish.

Aside from my own personal preferences and all the other varietals beyond the scope of a light article, I have only two quick suggestions so that I don't overstay my welcome. First, for the oenophilic neophyte, Italian grape, vineyard and appellation names can be quite intimidating, especially because of the language barrier. Look for ways to simplify or explain your Tuscan wine selection on the menu so as to reduce confusion and help with a sale. Better yet, lend a bit of knowledge to your servers so that they can extend their interactions with your patrons and heighten the rapport.

Second, Tuscan wines are amongst the most popular and sought after in the world. Ergo, getting your hands on quality product is easier said than done, or at the very least, will require a healthy investment upfront. Once you throw in the appropriate markups, you will be asking your customers for quite a lot of dough for each bottle, a number which might frighten more than a few people.

As such, consider how your Tuscan wines fit into the bigger picture of your wine list. Do they connote the top end of your selection, reserved for a select few? Or, if your restaurant caters to a more casual crowd, perhaps you could source from some of the more inexpensive labels that fit the quintessential Tuscan red taste profile but are not as well renowned for one reason or another. If you're lucky, you can even connect with a budding producer of 'Super Tuscan' wines, which breach the DOC rules because they blend international grapes like Cabernet Sauvignon and Merlot in with the Sangiovese for some truly enchanting results.

IS HEALTHY IN-ROOM DINING POSSIBLE?

When talking about the in-room dining experience—order-in menu, minibar and all—there appears to be a very powerful 'healthy food never sells' stigma amongst hoteliers. I don't believe this to be entirely true. Guests want healthier options, but the problem is that the quick-and-now tendencies of our genetic makeup can overpower any drive for dietary perfection, especially when it comes to hotel dining and away-from-home cuisine.

It's the same fundamental reason that proper weight loss dieting is so hard to sustain. We're hardwired for junk food; that is, any calorie vehicle that delivers an instantaneous fix to replenish a brain's sugar levels. And our brain craves sugar. Most people have enough basic nutrition knowledge to understand that fruit is a better source of sugar than a candy bar and that a salad is better than a greasy burger. Unfortunately, junk food is simply too readily accessible. No prep time, no fear of decay, just 'pop the top' and munch away.

Now more so than ever before, people are striving to eat healthy and seek out health-conscious establishments. It's a going trend, and if you can appease this emergent bracket of consumers with new features, then it could easily morph into an additional revenue stream. However, to implement any new facet of your operations in this regard is to first understand the chief obstacle of accessibility.

To do this, you must understand just how truly impatient the human brain is. When it gets tired and cranky, it will scrounge for sugar right away. You will need a heavy dose of willpower to stop it from compelling your body to grab the closest source available. If that happens to be grapes, then the brain gets healthy sugars, but if it's a can of soda, the brain gets junk. Either way, the brain gets its fix.

Most of the time, healthy foods are far less accessible than junk food, and this problem does not start and stop with the hospitality world. For starters, the shelf life of fruit is an iota of that for candy bars and potato chips (due to preservatives). Fruit rots, which means a hefty inventory replacement cost for hotels and households alike. This, plus fresh fruit and veggies can be significantly more expensive than the average piece of junk food.

You also have to consider another key aspect of accessibility: preparation. Cutting up an apple and mixing a salad are both laborious tasks when compared to opening a soda bottle and ripping open a bag of chips. All said, these are pretty good reasons to back up the 'healthy food never sells' mentality. Junk food is quick and healthy options don't last. Game over.

So, how does one make healthier options as accessible to hotel guests as their pre-packaged, processed counterparts without running a deficit? I would begin with awareness—how you phrase and how you highlight such options. It's not just a minibar or room service, but an 'in-room dining experience'. This more illustrious and pleasing terminology has to be displayed in large, bold text and situated where guests are guaranteed to notice. Strategically placed brochures in the front lobby, above the minibar and on the bedside table are a good start.

And of course, this can evolve into another point of differentiation for your marketing teams to use. Educating people on the options available to them is equally as important as the options themselves. Think about how your in-room dining menu is displayed on your website. Does your front desk staff discuss this service with guests upon arrival? Is it a feature conveyed in your promotional materials?

I'll mention one example that fits the bill. I arrive at a luxury hotel and there's a tray of fresh fruit, crackers and cheese waiting in my room. A handwritten welcome note on top adds personable warmth to an already pleasant touch. But the kicker is that beside the tray is the room service menu—hard not to notice, especially with the clear instructions that everything is available within 30 minutes, 24-hours a day. Given the gratuitous surcharges of the minibar items, this healthy menu comes off as fairly enticing.

Do you provide your guests with healthy snacks upon arrival? It doesn't have to be anything as exuberant as a full tray in each room, but perhaps some light refreshments by the front desk. That will make for a more social and enjoyable lobby atmosphere anyway. Or, given the on-the-go nature of business travelers, perhaps such guests could have the option of requesting a bowl of fruit to be placed in their rooms for an extra fee. Think quick, energizing food choices like bananas, grapes and oranges, all ready and in plain sight for the harried visitor. This could even be incorporated as a feature of your loyalty program.

Moving onto the menu itself presents even more opportunities to show off your healthier side. Salads are a no-brainer as are yogurt parfaits, smoothies and cleanly prepared seafood. Not only do you want to offer these, but you will want to consider giving a short explanation as to what your kitchen does to make them particularly nutritious and beneficial when compared to regular foods. Think in terms of organic, locally produced and bought fresh.

Additionally, there are subtle changes you can make to the classically-deemed unhealthy mainstays like pizza and burgers. For pizza, emphasize how your kitchen uses such nutritious preparations as whole wheat crust, high quality cheeses, less grease and an abundance of vegetables. For burgers, highlight organic, grass-fed beef (or another meat) and a gluten-free bun. Did you know that burgers can be made out of tofu, lentils, chickpeas, beets or a host of other sturdy vegetables? Consider one of the above to add some vegan flair.

The point is that there's always a way to spruce up your menu to appeal to a more health-conscious guest while not neglecting the junk food crowd. Additionally, many junk food addicts are yearning for a way to convert, but need the appropriate nudges to do so.

This discussion may even necessitate a total redesign of the in-room menu as well as a deeper appreciation for the presentation of that menu in order to attain full effectiveness. As nutritional awareness and healthy mindsets proliferate amongst consumers, this is definitely a topic to warrant consideration amongst your F&B management team.

SUCCESS TIPS FROM THE GOOGLE CAFETERIA

This may seem like old news by now, but perhaps we can still glean some fresh insights from what Google does behind the scenes. For over ten years now, the internet giant has maintained what employees and critic alike rave as a world-class in-house restaurant and café program. Their menu is healthy, organic, locally sourced and delicious, with a diverse range of foods to satisfy the diverse tastes of their workforce. For awhile there, the motto was, "I eat at Google!" from satisfied Google employees. From fresh ahi tuna and scallops to free-range eggs and eggplant ratatouille, this was and continues to be a massive expenditure. But it has paid off; the two most visible benefits being time saving and nutrition.

With a corporate cafeteria fare this good and considering that it's open at all hours and free, employees have much more incentive to stay close to work during their lunch hour. In other companies that house a cafeteria with 'institutional-grade cuisine', employees may feel obligated to travel up to thirty minutes roundtrip to get their lunchtime specialties. That's lost productivity considering that the company's restaurant is at most a two minute walk.

And the benefits of a proper diet should never be marginalized. Greasy, insulin-spiking foods have been shown time and time again to not only cause weight gain but also impede healthy brain tissue development. And a healthy brain is a productive brain. With the right nutritional support, you will encourage a more productive, less lethargic workforce.

Apart from these two obvious boosters are the social benefits. It's already part of many competitive strategies to provide a world-class cafeteria for top executives so that they can woo clients in-house. This tactic works. Dining with prospects in your corporate home, as opposed to eating out, provides a more intimate setting to build relationships and close deals.

But there's also the concept of 'cross-pollination' problem solving. The cafeteria brings people together from various departments. With that come differing opinions and areas of expertise. Perhaps something the spa director read in a recent health and wellness magazine would make for the crowning touch to an outstanding promotional offer for next season. If only the marketing director was eating at the same table to voice his woes, listen in on what his colleagues had to say and possibly discover a creative solution.

Bringing people together in a superior cafeteria setting can be highly motivational. It can also be inspiring. You won't be able to predict how this 'cross-pollination' might occur, but one thing is clear: the more minds, the more pollination. The better you encourage people to stay in for their lunch break, the better you will promote such imaginative decision making to naturally emerge.

Now at this point, don't stop and think to yourself, "Our cafeteria's fine." You should always be on the lookout for subtle ways to bolster your employee dining experience. Do you offer a variety of fresh fruits and tasty salads? Do you rotate through weekly exotic dishes or is it the same menu month after month? Consider some daily specials. Perhaps the shortcoming has more to do with ergonomics. How's the décor? Is it pleasing to the eye? Do you have enough space for a large number of employees to sit comfortably? The key is that you can't only think of offering a free cafeteria as a perk. It's a necessity—quality over plain proximity.

FOOD AS BRAGGING RIGHTS

I've emphasized in the past and I'll emphasize again now: your restaurant's menu cannot simply be satisfactory. Not anymore at least. It has to be outstanding to the point where guests will remember what they ate two, three or seven days later. You have to 'wow' guests with bold choices, unique combinations and fresh ingredients in order for your restaurant to count as a worthy selling point and word-of-mouth generator for your hotel.

Here's the issue. I liken the going trend in the cuisine world to that of an arms race. Take burgers for example. One diner updates their most indulgent choice to be a double patty oozing with four different types of cheese. A nearby competitor fires back by replacing the buns with grilled cheese sandwiches. Then, the original diner modifies their greasy double cheeseburger to include six strips of bacon and onion rings, all somehow organically sourced (like that would even make a difference at this point). This happens back and forth, back and forth, ad nausea.

Meanwhile, consumer expectations continue to climb as the bar for decadence increases, leaving all the standard fare behind. I used burgers as an example, but this could easily be substituted for pizza, pasta, salad, chicken or steak.

Whereas 10, 20 or 30 years ago, a steak dinner would surely please and astound hotel guests, now, unless there's something special going on, such a meal goes down with a shrug and a contented smile, but not likely a, "This was so utterly fantastic I have to tell all my friends about it" recommendation. The fact is that when you factor in such things as Yelp reviews, the Food Network (which constantly shows outlandishly dazzling gastronomy) and the general ADD nature of the times, a meal might be superb at the time, but will it be a talking point for weeks or months in the near future?

I'm not saying you have to reinvent how you cook meat. Rather, a little touch goes a long way. Take Jacobs & Co. Steakhouse in downtown Toronto for instance. Like all other high end steakhouses, every item on the menu is exquisite both in preparation and presentation. But, what sets this place apart, and what I will always remember about it, are its salts. When you want a sprinkle, instead of them sidling up with a shaker or grinder, they present your table with a minimum of three types of salt, all with palpably different colors, flavors and textures. This tiny, unique aspect goes a long way towards me remembering my time there, even though I haven't visited in years. It serves as the entry point for a host of other associated memories—the people, the ambiance, the food.

A good way to reframe your menu in this regard is to ask the question: Is my food 'brag worthy'? Will a person use your cuisine as a comeuppance when his or her friends start discussing the latest and greatest eateries?

I'm not suggesting that you completely change every menu item to push atop this supposed arms race (even though that's still a fun and exciting option!). Instead, look to infuse one or two dishes that are completely different than what's offered elsewhere. Or, incorporate an extra touch like the salt example above. And as always, go out and explore the wide world of restaurants, keeping an astute eye on what they do to make you remember your meal.

WHAT'S THE BUZZ ABOUT BURGERS?

In the last decade, we've witnessed incredible strides in nutritional food offerings in the supermarket and in restaurants. Going in the complete opposite direction is the burger. With ample amounts of meat, cheese and grease, burgers have never been synonymous with healthy snack foods.

Eating healthy is crucial, but so is indulgence. Instead of trying to fit a circle in the square peg, a new pedigree of burger joints aims to fit a humungous circle in an even bigger circular peg. These new restaurants treat the burger as the emblem of decadence, as if to say, "If you are going to cheat on your diet, cheat in style and cheat with us."

I was first clued into this during a visit to Los Angeles where a fellow Angelino ushered me to Umami Burger—'umami' being the little-known fifth attribute of basic taste (after sweet, sour, salty and bitter), describing savory flavor notes. Simply put, one of the best burgers I've ever had, and with such a unique combination of toppings. One should expect as much coming from the state birthplace of McDonald's, In-N-Out Burger, Carl's Jr., Taco Bell, Fatburger, Jack In A Box, A&W Restaurants and, you could argue, our modernized interpretation of fast food burgers around the world.

Upon returning to Toronto to extol my recent discovery, I realized the umami craze wasn't exclusive to SoCal. We now have two restaurants within a ten minute drive from my office jockeying for position as the most decadent and artery-clogging in the city—The Burger's Priest and Holy Chuck. To give you a mental picture, when I visited the latter, I had a double bacon cheeseburger with the buns replaced by grilled cheese sandwiches and topped off with a peanut butter and jelly milkshake. (I'm still working off the calories.)

The remarkable fact is that these outlets of gastronomic awe are attracting big crowds—crowds which leave a little bigger, but that's beside the point. These are not $6.99 burgers with fries. Full meals can land in the $20 range and the foie gras patty commands a staggering $35 with fries and a drink. Did I mention that the shoestring fries are outstanding? Clearly, it's not just the kids eating here.

Now turn the tables on your own menu. Reviewing your traditional hamburger and revamping this perennial favorite is neither complex nor costly. Think extremes—your F&B choices should either air towards incredibly healthy or wholly indulgent. And this doesn't even have to start and stop with burgers. Many of these changes are so easy that you could probably develop an action plan within 24 hours.

1. *You have a soup of the day, why not the burger of the day?* Imagine if your server said something like, "Today's soup is chicken vegetable, and today's burger is lamb with provolone and grilled onions." Surprising, alluring and all part of the experience.

2. *Create a completely separate burger menu.* Start with the basics: regular and cheeseburger then add a series of additional items. Depending upon suppliers, this could include lamb, chicken and turkey patties as well as vegetarian varieties made from lentils, chickpeas, beets or falafel.

3. *Be creative with the menu names.* Don't just call it a lamb burger with cheese, but something fun or fitted to a common theme, and then detail the ingredients.

4. *I am less of a fan of fries included with an order.* They too should be looked at as an opportunity for variation: regular, shoestring, curly, thick cut (wedges), sweet potato or Cajun spiced. Maybe even consider some variation to your onion rings.

5. *Have at least one outlandish burger item.* How about a triple patty with four different types of cheese and bacon? You may sell a few of these, but don't count on them as high turn items. They are chiefly on the list for discussion amongst your patrons and public relations value.

6. *The bun is also critical.* Cheap, factory-made bread is a thing of the past. Try pita, whole wheat and gluten-free. Kaiser buns and brioche are great for holding loads of toppings, preventing big patties from slipping and soaking up sauce.

7. *Burgers are fun to eat and they should be fun to sell, too.* Engage your wait staff with this special burger program. Involve them in the naming processes and topping selections. This could also include providing bibs and extra serviettes for those who order the 'monster' on our menu—creating a sense of anticipation.

8. *Burgers are a good fit with social media programs.* Have a property event where fans can taste your incredible new creations. Take photos. Post them on Twitter, Facebook and Pinterest. Create even more buzz with contests. Additional idea: put one or two burger creations on your social media only and see what happens.

Alas, you're not going to win any Weight Watchers® awards for these activities, but you will have fun, raise your profile and, hopefully, build revenues as well.

WHAT'S THE BUZZ ABOUT SLIDERS?

Over the past decade, we've witnessed burgers go from an ordinary menu item at any old greasy spoon or fast food location to a carte blanche for artisanal combinations of premium toppings and high quality patty ingredients. Sure, there are always the McDonalds of the world to fill out the bottom end, but now the glass ceiling has been shattered and the sky literally is the limit on where burgers can go. People are well aware of the artery-clogging implications of eating a slab of fried meat. Labeled as a comfort food, people aren't yearning for burgers seven days a week. But when they crave an indulgence, they go all out.

As it concerns your hotel, we are not so much discussing whether your restaurant should make an ultra-decadent burger as we are the concept of such an item appearing on your menu. It's something to get people talking and raise your brand awareness through word of mouth. It's a dish to draw in the locals and build your reputation with the community. After all, hoteliers are not in the rooms selling business. We are in the business of facilitating a memorable experience for our clients to enrich through lives.

What about sliders? For those unfamiliar, a slider is a mini-burger, digestible in anywhere from one to four bites. They've been around for a while now and are probably best known through White Castle, a North American fast food chain specializing in these yummy nibblers.

Recently, however, sliders have been embraced as a taster's menu item—a 'flight of burgers' if you will. For the price of one full-sized burger, you can get three or four sliders, each of a different meat type or topping combination.

At the core of this—in what could be called 'nichification'—is the simple notion that generic is boring. Not to say that people aren't in need of generic products, but that brands help form a part of a person's identity. And boring isn't a highly sought quality. While you might get away with decent revenues off of a neutered menu offering the run-of-the-mill gamut of pizzas, pasta, burgers, salads and mains, you will not be giving your patrons much to talk about. In other words, you will not be triggered a profound emotional response for your guests to better remember you for when they are next in town or looking for a bite. Sliders are but one tool in your arsenal to help 'spice things up' and give your hungry patrons an unexpected treat.

The broad question to ask your team is: what is your restaurant's niche? The more you specialize, the more you can perfect those items offered on the menu and the more extravagant you can get. Next, think of one or two ways where you can provide a cuisine option that will fulfill the outright indulgence quota. It doesn't necessarily have to be sliders or anything in the sandwich family, but hopefully these mini-burgers help get the ball rolling.

PERFECT HARMONY IN MONTAGE LAGUNA BEACH'S CUISINE

Montage Laguna Beach is a very special place. Located on an outcrop of rock overlooking the Pacific Ocean, the property commands an ideal setting as one of the country's premier destination resorts. Within the compound proper, the Studio Restaurant commands the absolute best of the best locations—on the furthest peninsula nearest the water and a near 360 degree panorama. Guests dine and watch the red sun dip into the Pacific every night through floor-to-ceiling windows. Outdoor seating (weather permitting, which, in Southern California, is pretty much a guarantee) or dining indoors, the setting is pure magic.

Speaking of magic, it is here that Chef Craig Strong holds fort. Together with Fabien Riviere, Restaurant General Manager, his team of sous chefs, kitchen support, seasoned wait staff and other team members deliver one of the finest dining experiences in the Greater Los Angeles area. The restaurant has also garnered numerous prominent accolades, all well deserved. I met with Chef Strong in his vegetable garden just outside of the restaurant. No ordinary garden, the plot consists of five raised stone planters, each some 20 feet long and two feet wide.

Chef Strong: These planters are 31" high, a height I am told is designed to fend off marauding bunny rabbits who inhabit the grounds and would certainly enjoy a fine, fresh meal.

Larry: Surely these few planters could not fill all of your needs.

Chef Strong: It's a start, of course, and a way for me to emphasize the fresh-to-table approach that we take with our menu. It also allows me to demonstrate to our guests the close relationship we have with our product. I can quite literally take guests out to the garden and clip herbs, edible flowers, even fava bean pods and leaves, and then cook with those ingredients. It doesn't hurt to have the raised beds. It makes it easier for everyone to see the plants and it saves my back!

Larry: Where do you source ingredients?

Chef Strong: We have close and personal relationships with several suppliers. For example, our fish comes from a purveyor who is so committed to product quality that he will give me the lowdown on what to buy each day.

Larry: Sort of like a spy for the menu?

Chef Strong: Not exactly. But if there are certain fish that he believes are the ones for me to select, it makes sense to follow this recommendation. In terms of produce, being in Laguna has distinct advantages. We are blessed in this regard. In season, our vegetables and fruit come from small producers who handpick what we need and drive it directly to our receiving doors. Our relationship is so close that I even have had the opportunity of discussing what the next plantings will be in advance of the season.

Larry: You're dealing with a very sophisticated clientele. Your diners have experienced some of the finest restaurants the world has to offer. Any thoughts?

Chef Strong: In a way that is more of a positive than you would like to think. Sophisticated diners insinuate an appreciation of the finer aspects of our cuisine and service. Our patrons live and breathe quality. For example, they know that a great steak is not measured by quantity, but by quality—smell certainly, but as well, mouth feel, taste and texture. It has to be styled perfectly too. They expect the best and we deliver.

Larry: They also won't have sticker shock when they see the prices.

Chef Strong: Value is not simply price-based. Our clientele understands. They know the value is inherent in the quality they are getting.

Larry: I was amazed to see young children dining with their parents. This is not an inexpensive dining option for five-year-olds.

Chef Strong: Well, we have a children's menu, of course. Moreover, our kitchen will satisfy the demands of any youngster with a respective simple dish. One of the pillars of all our Montage Laguna Beach restaurants is to allow our younger diners to build their own ice cream sundaes. We

	escort them to the kitchen and ask them to participate. Believe you me, it works.
Larry:	Your tasting menu is particularly impressive. What is the rationale behind the menu?
Chef Strong:	The menu is designed as a journey of taste bud discovery. Certainly, it changes over time, subject to availability of fresh products. We start with some incredible appetizers—a caviar taco, for example. Then, we move to oyster vichyssoise with smoked salmon and dill; a tuna tarter with a spaghetti squash salad; a Dungeness crab and ricotta cavatelli, fine herbs with a lemon glaze; herb pasta sheets covered with shaved black truffles; Hudson Valley duck breast and confit with wheat berries, apple and onion marmalade, raspberries and calvados sauce; kobe beef with fava beans, maitake mushrooms, potato puree, bergamot bordelaise, and Guanaja chocolate sphere with sea salt caramel and Guinness foam.
Larry:	You forgot to mention the wine pairings.
Chef Strong:	Wine is an amazing complement to a meal. There is no doubt that the wines selected as matches for our tasting menu represent a wide range of tastes. Each wine in its own right is spectacular. When combined with our tasting menu, they form the perfect balance.
Larry:	Anything you want to add?
Chef Strong:	You cannot pin the success of any operation on any individual. Think of the Studio Restaurant as a musical presentation. With Fabien as our conductor, our patrons are guided through the various segments of the symphony, leaving satisfied that we provided more than a meal but a lasting experience.

MEETING THE DEMAND FOR
HEALTHY MEETINGS

We are what we eat—a pithy statement but nevertheless thoroughly and completely true. Cancer, obesity, type II diabetes, acute and chronic sicknesses, joint pain, muscular strength, balance and raw brainpower comprise a short list of bodily functions influenced by what goes down our esophagus. If I've come off a bit 'hellfire and brimstone', it's only because I care for your health as well as that of your guests.

Eating well will make you smarter, and in the short-term—say, an intensive day-long meeting—stave off fatigue and increase productivity. It's taken us decades, centuries even, to accumulate the dietary acumen and scientific data to point with certainty towards what foods promote wellness and which do not.

On the heels of this buildup of nutritional knowledge comes a widening public desire for healthier food options as well as many savvy organizations to help steer us in the right direction. Thrive! Meetings & Events is one such firm and I sat down with their president, Tracy Stuckrath, to discuss what hotels can do to get caught up on this all-so-imperative trend.

How important is food quality to meetings these days? Are a majority of people aware of how food can affect productivity?

It's vital. Food quality is becoming more important to meetings each day as sessions and articles on 'brain food' are appearing in industry conferences and publications every year. But, the implementation is not yet at the forefront of catering menus nor do a majority of people understand how food can affect their productivity.

The increasing focus on growing and eating locally, childhood obesity, gluten and allergen-friendly cuisine and sourcing sustainably are slowly catching on, but it has not made it to hotel banquet menus yet. Some reasons for this include:

- Lack of nutritional education in those creating the foods (hotel chefs) and selecting the menus (planners)

- Sourcing options for large volume properties (some local farmers can't produce enough)
- Fear of changing what we've always done (our guests love the cookies for dessert and breaks; 'no one eats well on the road'; in season foods in some areas are limited)
- Budgetary constraints of the events (eating locally and in season can potentially be more expensive depending on the time and location)
- Corporate policies don't allow for local sourcing because of national food service contracts

How often do you partner with hotels for their meeting programs? What do you feel can be improved in this partnership?

Some hoteliers understand the benefits of offering healthy eating options for their guests—for example, Fairmont Hotels and Wynn Hotels—but most still don't and the majority have not translated such healthier options into the banquet menus. Last year's groundbreaking partnership between Tulane University School of Medicine and Johnson & Wales University uniting doctors and chefs in improving the nation's health through the instruction of culinary medicine is a great example of how hotel chefs can improve their relationships and partnerships.

Frequent visitor programs are also a great way to attend to guests' needs. By collecting personal preferences of guests—allergens, dietary preferences and exercise habits—hoteliers can ensure the needs of their guests are met. But, this takes training for front and back of house. Collecting the information is one thing, but making your staff aware of and understanding of the customer service opportunities is a whole other aspect. Hotels need to understand the risks and opportunities when providing healthier options.

For those guests who are 'resistant' to change, how would you convince them to alter their eating habits?

It's a hard thing to do. Just as with any program, change of habit or process, a person needs to be ready to make the change. We can't force them to eat a specific way, but we can help them make small modifications that, combined, end up being large changes. I went 'cold turkey' when I found out about my food allergy, but not everyone can do it. My suggestion is to start with a food journal. Write down what you eat on a daily basis for two weeks. Understanding where, when and what you're eating before you make any change is a huge step.

Is reeducation an overt exercise or do you simply let the food do the talking so to speak? Do you feel that any overt education on healthy eating augments the meeting experience?

Education is key, but so is taste and comfort. Just like Mikey's brothers in the 1970s Life Cereal commercials, food that is supposed to be good for you still has a bad rap in some circles. So, for food 'to do the talking', flavor has to be a prerequisite in making something healthier and meeting special dietary needs. Just because it's healthier or gluten-free doesn't mean it needs to taste bad. Those options should meet the same quality and taste standards as everything else a hotel is serving.

Education also needs to include how to easily make healthier choices for ourselves at home and on the road, but also how to implement those changes to meeting menus. Some people think because they are on the road, it gives them the opportunity to eat poorly 'just because you can'. But that mindset is changing. A growing number of people who need or want to eat healthy on the road because they do at home, find it hard to do because of menu options at restaurants or what they are served at a meeting. Additionally, if they eat well at home, eating poorly on the road will wreak havoc on their bodies through lethargy or loss of concentration.

An extremely important aspect of education is food safety. All staff must know the ingredients in the foods they're serving, how it's prepared and how it's served. For instance, is the calamari with cornmeal crust fried in the same fryer as the chicken fingers with white flour (gluten/ wheat allergies)? Is the chef using a separate sauté pan for the sausage and cheese-free omelets (dairy allergy or vegetarian)? Did you put the pastries on the shelf above the fruit and eggs of the vertical buffet (crumbs from the pastries can fall on the fruit, making the fruit and eggs inedible for celiac and wheat allergic guests)?

Thinking broadly, are more hotels catching on to the idea of healthy food for meetings? Where have they yet to capitalize?

Some hotels are catching on. Fairmont Hotels instituted its 'Lifestyle Cuisine Plus Menus' in 2011 in response to requests the chain was receiving from its President's Club members and guests. As well, there are a handful of hotels across the country that understand the need, but broadly, there is still a vast disconnect, especially when it comes to catering menus. A few ways to capitalize include:

- Reviewing menus to find ways to use less processed options and add more fresh, local ingredients
- Training staff to know and understand the ingredients in what is being served as well as how to safely serve guests
- Assessing current menus to find items which already meet dietary needs and creating versions of the same item so they can meet special needs

GOING LOCAL, TAKEN TO A
WHOLE NEW LEVEL

Le Manoir Richelieu, a historic property under the Fairmont banner, sits in the heart of the UNESCO-recognized Charlevoix region of Quebec. Known for its impeccable farms more closely resembling rural France than North America, the area was Canada's first summer resort colony for wealthy patrons beginning in the late 18th century. The property originally opened in 1899 but, following a fire, it was completely rebuilt by June 1929 under the guidance of architect John Archibald.

The most recent renovation and expansion was finished in 1999 to the bill of $140 million. Le Manoir Richelieu now stands as a majestic French castle atop a cliff overlooking the scenic Saint Lawrence River with a full 18-hole golf course that is frequently cited as one of Canada's best. It caters to anyone looking for an incredible getaway or a unique meeting venue.

Thus, reaching the level of executive chef at such a property is no easy feat with plenty of other candidates vying for the job. Here, Executive Chef Patrick Turcot took up the challenge of delivering a menu that not only embraces the bounty of local produce, but also goes beyond the call to generate pure excitement and a lasting impression.

Before my tasting meal, I met with Chef Turcot in his office, a dual functioning administration center and private dining room for experimentation. My mission was to learn more about the region of Charlevoix through its hybrid culinary style of both haute Parisian fare and bucolic Quebec traditions adapted over the centuries of short growing seasons and relative isolation from the rest of North America.

We stated with fois gras-stuffed macaroni (from the General Manager's private farm) paired with apple cider ice wine from the nearby L'Isle-aux-Coudres. As Chef Turcot explained, "The true hero of the culinary arts is the local farmer. The quality of our ingredients has the greatest impact on the final dishes we deliver. In many ways, I think of my job as that of a symphony conductor, harnessing every aspect of our cuisine, tweaking every note, and then delivering a combination of flavors, textures and colors that excite the palate as well as the eye."

The menu of Le Charlevoix, the property's primary dining room, proudly diarizes the produce that is harvested within 50 km (30 miles) of the resort. I noted the names of 16 different farms that provide vegetables, fruits, milk, cheese, poultry, duck, veal, beef, game, beer, cider, chocolate and baked goods. In addition, local fishermen are cited for a wide range of products, including lobster. Rarely do you see a menu that heralds the source with this much precision.

The menu, which changes regularly based upon local availability, included a four and five-course tasting menu, a vegetarian option, seven appetizers, three soups and 11 main courses of five different fish and six different meats. As well, there were separate menus for both the cheeses and the desserts.

The theme for my appetizer course was lobster. A serving of lobster parmentier (French shepherd's pie) to start with lobster bisque and green tea flavored mushrooms. Then came the entrée of fois gras-stuffed deer fillet, crosnes (artichokes) and duck gravy—all fantastic.

Chef Turcot sees his role as more of an educator and experimenter. While I was there, I witnessed him working with several apprentice chefs. This is especially evident when Fairmont Le Manoir Richelieu hosts "Gala des Grands Chefs" every year. It's an opportunity for local chefs to share ideas and demonstrate their unique recipes. Chef Turcot and his team are more than happy to host, absorb and integrate these ideas, making a constantly evolving menu.

CATERING 'THOUGHTFUL FOODS' TO INCREASE MEETINGS PRODUCTIVITY AND RETURN VISITS

I first met Chef Murray Hall at a late summer conference and he enthralled me with stories of just how much the quality of foods can affect the productivity of meetings and conferences. Since that time, I've kept a keen eye on my own diet and how certain foods affect both mood and energy levels. Needless to say, Chef Hall is right, and during our recent chat, he offered some very valuable takeaways both for hotels and for your own dietary goals, which, believe it or not, are one and the same.

His Background with Food

According to Chef Hall, his life has always been imbued with a strong passion for the culinary arts. Growing up in the 1980s in the small mountain town of Salmon Arm, British Columbia, Canada (current population roughly 17,000), access to mass produced and heavily processed goods was always a challenge. This meant that the concept of 'local food' was already common nomenclature, long before it became trendy circa mid-2000s.

Chef Hall's passion emerged from his mother. He reminisces on the days he would go strawberry or cherry picking then head home to make fresh pies and jam preserves. It was this near-constant hands-on experience that fostered his early love for cuisine.

Chef Hall attended the culinary school at Caribou College in Kamloops, British Columbia then completed his apprenticeship at the Banff Springs Hotel in neighboring Alberta. Taking advantage of opportunities within the Marriott organization, he worked in Bermuda and Hawaii before settling in Toronto with the Dolce Hotels and Resorts brand. This move was enticed, in part, by the appeal of helping start a newer brand from the ground up. He currently works as the head chef at the BMO Institute of Learning which subcontracts its culinary preparations to the Dolce organization.

Seeking a Brand Differentiator

With just over 20 properties mostly in the United States, Dolce Hotels and Resorts had to create unique points of differentiation to make its brand identifiable amongst a glut of bigger names. A company-wide symposium was held four years ago during the height of the recession to discuss ways to do just this. Meeting productivity quickly became a hot topic.

Known for its unique corporate retreat and conference settings, Dolce specializes in providing the best atmosphere for effective meeting time usage. Chef Hall attended the symposium and sat on a council of all the organization's top chefs. Stemming from their talks emerged the concept of the continuous coffee break and that of 'Thoughtful Foods', a branded cornerstone of the Dolce culinary experience denoting their health-minded focus.

As for the coffee break system, some people need a rest at 10am, some at 10:30am, others at 11am. By having an area where snacks were constantly replenished, they could better meet the varying needs of their guests. This way, fatigued business guests can get the much-needed boost whenever their bodies call for it and not simply when the clock allows.

Nutrition Hubs

The continuous coffee break idea evolved into a true point of difference through a strict focus on healthy snacks. By serving foods that were more nutritious for breakfast, lunch and all breaks in between, their guests wouldn't suffer from any post-meal bodily shutdowns. Through its exaggerated form colloquially known as a 'food coma', the best illustration of this being the exhausted feeling you get an hour after a intense bolus of red meat or sushi for lunch. Thus, the Nutrition Hub was introduced as a continuous provider of both deluxe coffee and highly nutritious 'Thoughtful Foods'.

And the science isn't too difficult to understand either. When the body absorbs a large amount of food, it sends more blood to the stomach, liver, intestine and other digestive organs—especially true for fatty cuisines. With a limited supply of blood, this takes away from the overall blood supply to the muscles, slowing you down, and the brain, which burns sugar and oxygen faster than anything else in the body. The end result is fatigue and a propensity towards inactivity—a sensation that is further exacerbated as a three, four or five day conference wears on.

However, if the body receives a consistent input of whole grains, fruits and vegetables, this lethargy never sets in. Healthy foodstuffs are easier on your digestive organs, drawing less blood away from the surrounding tissues. Moreover, because they contain a wider spectrum of nutrients, they will induce the perception of satiety faster—that is, portion control.

One other important science tidbit to be aware of is the glycemic index. This measurement relates to how much a given food will raise blood sugar levels. High glycemic foodstuffs are what you want to avoid and pertain mostly to refined sugars like ice cream, candy, cookies, soda pop and low-grade starches. Such foods will cause a massive insulin spike—the hormone that controls blood sugar levels by converting sugar into fat. The end result of eating a high glycemic food is that, after the initial sugar rush, you crash as the insulin takes hold.

Overall, healthy cuisine throughout a conference affords business guests increased productivity as they are able to push past the midday lull in stride. With the evidence in plain sight, it's no wonder that Dolce chose this as a central focus to distinguish its brand. Guests may remember Dolce for not only being more contentious and considerate with their food choices, but also for the increased levels of activity afforded to them by the availability of healthier alternatives.

Meet the Guests Halfway

Chef Hall remarks that the conceit of eliminating meat and high glycemic carbs from the menu is great in principle, but tenuous in reality. You have to ease guests into the wellness-minded options so that you don't completely alienate them. Some people are open to new ideas and trying new foods. Others just want their meat, potatoes and a diet cola.

Either way, people have cravings you can't ignore, especially when their mental energy is being taxed from constant meetings. Eventually, a 50-50 balance was found between nutrition and indulgence, with nuanced actions taken to make these indulgences as hearty as possible. It's all about nudges—small changes that make a big difference.

At Dolce properties, nothing comes prepackaged. Everything is made in-house, fresh and gluten-free. Periodic signage is used to educate guests on the benefits of wholesome ingredients and encourage them to try something slightly foreign. High glycemic grains are replaced with ones that are high in fiber and protein. Seeds, nuts and leafy greens are added to the menu wherever possible. Whenever shellfish is needed, the sourced animals are farm-raised to ensure cleanliness and a lack of toxicity or heavy metals. As well, the menu is constantly changing on a five-day cycle to make the Nutrition Hubs more active and exciting.

These are just a few of the changes implemented, but the psychology of portion control was also an important consideration. If you leave out bags of potato chips, a person is likely to eat the entire allotment. But if you present the chips (which in this case happen to be baked kettle chips made in-house, of course) in a giant bowl for people to serve themselves, the tendency is for a person to put less on their plate. On certain days in the cycle, Chef Hall's team will dehydrate fruit chips as the afternoon treat and supply them in a large bowl. This portion control attitude pervades all aspects of the operation.

Some More Specifics

Menu design was also critical to dispelling opposition and complaints. Chef Hall opened by demonstrating this through some very delicious examples.

The first was a chocolate chip cookie. Instead of buying in bulk, Chef Hall's version is made with quinoa flour and organic dark chocolate. You get your sugar hit through a bona fide source—that being the dark chocolate which contains fewer refined sugars—then you get your carb from the quinoa, which is known to be a low glycemic, high protein grain.

Next is Chef Hall's turkey chili. For starters, turkey is a better meat to use than beef because it is lower in total fat content. And from there, he substitutes the red kidney beans with pinto or azuki varieties—ones with more nutrient content.

As you'd expect, a crucial aspect of the Nutrition Hub is its coffee. At its core is a machine that can make any espresso or cappuccino drink in under 20 seconds, all top of the line. From there, one of the best ways to improve is to control what sugar additives people use. A tasty sugar and honey substitute is agave nectar, extracted from cacti in Mexico and the Southwest US. It's low on the glycemic index and doesn't have the strong aftertaste associated with other sugar alternatives like maple syrup. Another sought-after replacement that Chef Hall uses is stevia.

Cost Comparison

From a management perspective, yes, the costs of going healthy are higher. Food has to be bought fresh and you can't rely on goods kept in cold storage for a year. But it's worth it. High quality food is something that guests truly remember and the evidence is in the quality scorecards. Before Dolce initiated this program, the cuisine was ranked as a 7/10 or 8/10—not bad enough to deter loyalty, but not good enough to stand out either.

And in this business, as you know, mediocrity is death. Dolce had to make a distinction and by upgrading their food offerings in this manner—a process which is three years in the making—word is getting around. We are what we eat, and many corporations are returning to Dolce properties not because of location or exceptional amenities but because of the cuisine.

Chef Hall was also quick to point out that this shift is far more about healthier alternatives than about going organic. Organically-grown foodstuffs are more expensive, but don't necessarily taste any better or offer a significantly greater share of nutrients. A grape is still a grape and most people cannot tell the difference in taste between organic and regularly-grown.

Chef Hall would love to go wholly organic as there are still some prevailing health benefits, but the main problem is allocation costs. In a restaurant, you're allowed to markup organic dishes by a few dollars, but this doesn't apply to catering. As such, Chef Hall has a very rigid budget to shuffle and, for now, organics just aren't in the cards. One sticking point on this issue is lettuce—commercial hydroponics (that is, controlled-environment agriculture) just doesn't get it right and he insists on buying natural. The difference here, as Chef Hall notes, is immediately palpable.

Health and 'Thoughtful Foods' as Mainstream

The concept of healthy eating isn't new and indeed several other prominent hotel chains have already implemented their own wholesome menus. Central to Dolce's approach will be staying on the cusp of this trend by continually augmenting their cuisine and offering vibrant new dishes. Dolce helps their chefs by hosting regular symposiums for the council to exchange recipes and educate one another on the latest vegetarian and raw cooking techniques. On a micro level, Chef Hall is constantly searching for new local produce sources to reduce food mileage—heightening taste by increasing freshness.

In general, the principle that eating healthy reduces daytime fatigue is gaining mainstream appreciation, but it still has a long way to go—leaving plenty of room for Dolce to grow its meetings business and with 'Thoughtful Foods' as a prime vessel to this end. Chef Hall likens all this to a 'slow-moving ship' and the best way to go is to meet people halfway through smart, balanced food alternatives.

On a personal note, I love what Chef Hall and his ilk are doing. Our culture is so obsessed with what's cheap and flavorsome that we often forget what our body really needs. Offering wholesome alternatives may be the opportunity we need to rekindle the idea that the best food in the city is at the hotel. We need culinary leaders like Chef Murray Hall to regain this reputation and help people live a healthier lifestyle in the process.

NO CARBS, NOW WHAT?

Carbohydrates: bread, pasta, rice, risotto, corn, cereal, crackers, potatoes. They've nourished us for millennia, allowing civilizations to swell to unnaturally large numbers. Now, a nutritional trend reaching mainstream appeal stands to redact their gloriously supportive reputation. Followers of the latest chic diets widely classify carbs as 'the enemy', demonizing them for their starchy fat-promoting content, their ability to raise blood pressure and their respectively low nutrient-to-sugar ratio.

If you've ever dabbled in contemporary literature on the subject, then you know that there's a lot the average person doesn't know in terms of how various foodstuffs affect such everyday and far-reaching worries as colds, weight loss, allergies, heart health, cancer prevention, mood stability and skin repair. With preventable pathologies like obesity, diabetes and arthrosclerosis on the rise (at least in Western cultures), now is the time to fight back with the meal choices we make. Food thought leaders purport that 'cutting the carbs' may be the panacea we so desperately seek, and many are firm believers.

To me, it appears as though we are on the precipices of a modern day 'food revolution', with many of the agrarian influences of the past century—which at the time were necessary for our sustained population growth and the deterrence of famine—now evidenced as unswervingly hazardous to our wellbeing. Three books I've read which have been fairly epiphanous include "The China Study" (2005), "Anticancer" (2009) and "Wheat Belly" (2011). Mind you, carbs aren't universally panned, but they are increasingly getting the brunt of the scorn, especially what we know deem as 'refined' or heavily processed carbohydrates.

Celiac disease and gluten intolerance sufferers as well as those making a lifestyle choice (the Paleo Diet for example) are now a fairly prevalent bunch—certainly a non-negligible audience and one who's more choosy about where they dine. If you want to build an empathetic image for your restaurant and also attract this growing cluster of patrons, your menu may need a few adjustments, particularly in the 'carbless' and low sugar department. However, while ostracizing carbs from your restaurant's menu may be met with applause and appreciation from your wheat-allergic and weight-watching consumers, there's a grave corollary that's being overlooked.

Meal appreciation does not necessarily equal satisfaction. That is, people may appreciate or respect the fact that you've embraced this popular trend, or others like vegetarianism, but does that equate to venerable word of mouth and return visits? Aside from flavor, presentation and customer service, a significant portion of food satisfaction comes from satiety, a cuisine trait largely dependent on the bulk. And nothing delivers bulk better than carbs. If a meal doesn't fill you up, you are less emotionally inclined to give it a stellar review or, ultimately, a recommendation.

Another problem with going 'sans carb' with your cuisine is that carbohydrates are traditionally the lowest-cost-highest-profit food purchase. There's a reason why you can supersize your fries and drink but not your burger. Sure, to achieve satiety and a higher degree of emotional satisfaction you could load up a patron's plate with extra meat or veggies, but then where's the profit? Ergo, the big problem I pose today is: how are you going to leave your guests happily satiated without the carbs and without sacrificing your revenue margins?

What's Gluten? Why Care?

Before we delve any further, some clarification is in order. Dovetailing the 'no carb' movements is a hearty campaign for 'gluten free' menus led by those with serious allergies. Gluten isn't a carb; it's a protein naturally found in grass-borne grains (wheat, barley, rye and so on). It's what allows dough to rise into a puffy, delectable shape (alongside yeast), and it's also employed as a stabilizing reagent for other colloids like ice cream. Furthermore, extra doses of gluten are often mixed back into dough or other base grains for additional chewiness upon baking.

Given this molecule's origins, it's not hard to imagine why these two trends are practically interchangeable. When we talk about 'carbless' cooking, gluten-free is very often also implied. However, unlike simply replacing the carbohydrates in any given dish as part of a lifestyle choice, upholding gluten-free meal preparation is vital for those with allergies or sensitivities to this protein.

So, why care about gluten? With acute side effects including bloating, cramping, fatigue and diarrhea, the gluten-intolerant folk are ardent in both their search for sympathetic establishments and their avoidance of noncompliant operators. Given that estimates place the spectrum of gluten sensitivities, wheat allergies and celiac disease sufferers as affecting upwards of 1% of the US population, this is relatively small, but nonetheless important demographic.

Being inclusive by appeasing this minority becomes all the more crucial when we're talking group business and catering. If your menu excludes these one-percenters outright, be prepared for parties to silently take their sustenance needs elsewhere in order to accommodate one or more gluten sensitive members.

Personal Experiences

My inspiration for writing this article initially stemmed from my own trials and errors in the land of no carbs. As someone who has become very active in watching my diet over the past few years, refined sugars and carbohydrates were the first to go. Barring exceptions (which are still quite frequent because my wife is a tremendous baker!), this means no rice, noodles, bread, flour, pasta, pastries, potatoes, corn, couscous and everything derived from said products (beer, crackers, cookies, chips and so on). Tough life, huh?

I'll say this—and I'm sure many who have gone along a similar path will concur—cutting the carbs is hard. Menus become minefields with plenty of untouchables and waiter-eye-rolling ingredient substitutions. For the first few transitional weeks, I was getting sugar headaches, carb cravings, lethargy spells and rumbling stomach pangs, all of which altered my emotional state and not necessarily for the better. Although these irritable feelings dissipated, for a dieting neophyte they are still quite irksome.

Results don't lie though. Without upping my exercise regimens, in the months that followed this experiment, I'd dropped ten pounds, lost a few inches across the waist and my annual physical churned out healthier blood pressure readings as well as a slightly lower heart rate. Additionally, once I was over the initial hump, there were no more cravings and no more fatigue.

Throughout this grand endeavor, I went on a research binge for carb alternatives to supplement my diet with high nutrient stomach-fillers and perhaps alleviate some of the harsher side effects during the gradual purge. My goal was to find cheap substitutes that wouldn't elicit the same insulin spiking effects as the more pedestrian carbohydrates (that is, digested sugars trigger insulin release which in turn causes fat production and weight gain).

Broad Solutions to Consider

Without too much boasting, my findings are enough to fill a 300-page book. Overall, it's not a one-size-fits-all solution, but there are some very worthy 'carbless' candidates for you and your F&B team to consider. What follows is more a general discussion of ways to keep your patrons full in a no carb world with some broad tips to apply. I don't want to delve into individual recipes and ingredients; I'll leave that up to the ingenuity of your chefs.

Definitely not on this list were fish, meat, poultry or anything else from the animal kingdom. From a purely volume perspective, attempting to deliver the same satiety (and emotional fulfillment) that a meal with carbohydrates gives by including larger portions of your main is just not practical. It costs too much. Just look at the pricing models for steakhouses to see how they compensate for gargantuan mains—not everyone can get away with these chunky charges!

True, this is only a suggestion. If you feel as though offering a bulkier slice of your main dish will help keep the consumers coming back, then by all means go for it. Just know that your margins might suffer, which may cause fiscal problems later on down the road. The lone, ubiquitous exception to this conclusion was eggs. They are relatively inexpensive and universally applicable to your cooking needs.

One of the most salient restaurateur answers worth addressing is to include both a regular and a gluten-free menu. While this might alleviate some concerns (and it's certainly a stepping stone solution I recommend), it's becoming increasingly transparent that special cooking methods must be adopted in order to properly isolate gluten contaminants, similar to what already exists for kosher, halal and vegan preparations. Hence, an all-or-nothing response in the kitchen is what's truly needed; either you are holistically gluten free or you're not.

Next to consider are seeds. Seeds (chia, amaranth, quinoa, flax and so on) are technically in the carbohydrate family, but they have a much higher nutrient-to-sugar ratio as well as more protein. This not only makes them better for you gram-to-gram, but because of their complex spectrum of fibers, they are harder for your digestive system to breakdown into simple sugars, meaning that they don't produce as heavy an insulin spike as other more basic carbs (that is, they're lower on the glycemic index).

Legumes present another vegetarian opportunity to placate the body's hunger and calorie needs. They're cheap, they come in dozens of colorful varieties and many pedigrees have prodigious antioxidant levels. I'm sure any professional chef knows how to properly prepare a bean medley salad or baked beans. Just be sure to account for potential allergies (peanuts are a legume by the way, not a nut).

While on the topic of nuts, they too are extremely filling and loaded with good calories. Think cashew stir fries and infusing almonds or pine nuts in mixed steamed veggies. Crushed nuts can also be effortlessly blended into seed-based salads and they can be used as a batter substitute for coating fish or meats. Opportunities abound, but so do allergies; proceed with caution.

Then, of course, there is the vegetable realm for you to explore. Many types of cabbage (I'm fond of red) are volumetrically filling as well as monetarily feasible. Green salads don't have to have a base of arugula, radicchio or spinach; consider rainbow chard, watercress or kale. As well, look to the big blue ocean for solutions, namely seaweed. Although not technically a vegetable in the strictest sense, seaweed and kelp are nonetheless packed with vitamins, minerals and other forms of nutritional goodness.

For more background information, I highly recommend you take a cursory look at such in vogue cuisine approaches like the Paleo Diet or the Slow Carb Diet as well as older iterations like the South Beach Diet, Dr. Atkins's nutritional protocols and the Grapefruit Diet. Also, veganism, vegetarianism and raw foodism offer three great sources for inspiration as well as recipes that exclude animal products or, in the case of a raw diet, cooking itself.

The Bread Basket

Another touch point worth discussing is the bread basket—that loaf of fresh dough (with butter and olive oil) to whet the palate while picking your appetizers or mains. In many restaurants, this basket is a subtle but essential part of the overall dining experience as well as the first chance after your guests take their seats to boost the satiety-satisfaction dynamic. Yes, bread is perhaps the cheapest foodstuff you could offer a patron at this early juncture, but you should start to think of some slightly more expensive alternatives so that your carb-abstaining guests aren't completely alienated when you plunk down that sliced baguette.

Again, it's not a one-size-fits-all solution. Olives drizzled in oil, herbs and spice? Not everyone is a fan of this Mediterranean fruit's salty bite. Then how about cherry tomatoes sprinkled with oil? I know many people who don't like uncooked tomatoes—something about the skin texture. A bowl of mixed nuts perhaps? Allergies. Three or four different cheeses? Dairy qualms, and it's not vegan. A tray of fresh fruit? Good luck keeping your margins with that.

All these objections can make the process of choosing a 'bread successor' quite nauseating. Just know that you will never fully appeal to everyone (much like other aspects of your hotel!). However, good hearted amuse bouche gestures like this won't fall on deaf ears. Frankly, I would go the less conservative route and use this as a chance to give your guests something to talk about. Edge towards the wild. Surprise visitors with a simple yet elegant food solution which is impossible for them not to remember. Perhaps the bread successor may be a one-bite portion of an appetizer the executive chef is considering adding to the menu. You serve it, then you return and ask your patrons what they thought—rapport at its finest.

Ingredient Quality

One last consideration is the quality of your ingredients. From a physiological perspective, a sated person results from both volume (stomach expanding to meet incoming bolus of food) as well as nutrient concentration. When certain nutrients interact with the intestinal lining, they cause the release of gastronomic hormones which signal the feeling of satiety. Carbs have a propensity to be low in nutrient and vitamin concentration, so you end up eating more than you have to because it takes longer for the corresponding hormones to be activated. Fruits and veggies are quite the opposite, meaning that they will give you the sensation of being full with less overall food consumed.

High quality, organic foodstuffs tend to have greater quantities of nutrients and vitamins relative to the same items grown under less meticulous conditions. For example, you will feel more stuffed from an omelet made from three organic free range eggs than one whipped up using three regular store-bought eggs of equal mass. Whether one can decipher an actual taste discrepancy between non-organic and organic foods is in the eye of beholder. What this means for you is that if you ensure that you source from the best (which might often be a local producer to concurrently fill the 'fresh to table' trend), you are thereby increasing the nutrient concentration in your cuisine and more adequately satiating your patrons on less overall food.

TECHNOLOGY

A unique conversion, the Hotel Berlin, Berlin specializes in its technological-laden and flexible configurations for meetings and conferences.

INTRODUCTION: CAMERA AS A
TECH BOON FOR HOTELIERS

Technology is such a vast and encompassing term that I thought it best to start with something small or at least a device that is getting smaller every year—the camera. You may remember the days when a digital SLR (single lens reflex) camera was a serious investment. A four-megabyte image was considered hefty. Memory storage cards were typically 32 to 64 gigabytes, puny by today's standards. An iPhone can now beat these dated standards.

Growing up in an era of 35mm SLR film camera gear, the experience of buying one of the new digital boxes was beyond anything I could imagine. The camera I eventually selected was the Olympus OM-D, one of many new compact SLRs offered today. The basic model with zoom lens came in at about $1,500, which considering the feature set is a pretty good deal. Here is what impressed me, and importantly, why you should consider acquiring one of these pieces of new technology for use at your property:

- *Compact size with a high-quality image.* The days of having to be big to be effective are over. My latest camera weighs less than half that of a full-size SLR, and in many ways offers superior performance.
- *So easy to use, even a GM can do it!* No kidding, I was able to master perfect images within minutes with barely a read of the intimidating instruction manual.
- *Basic controls are a cinch.* The lighting controls and low-light capabilities allow for great images without a flash. You can shoot guestroom features and staff photos with natural light—even in low-light situations—and still have exceptional results.
- *The wide angle of the standard lens is adequate for most situations.* I spent an additional $1,000 for a Lumix ultra-wide lens (14 mm equivalent) for room shots, but it is not essential. Imagine the whole room from the doorway, with no image curvature.
- *The auto-stabilization eliminates the need for a tripod.* This is key. Tripods take a long time to set up properly. Plus, they are cumbersome.

- *Color balance eliminates the need for Photoshop correction of most images.* There are further in-camera options for special effects that work miracles. The point here is that having to Photoshop every image before it can be posted online eats up time and chews away at available funds. Having the camera automatically take care of pesky issues for you frees up your 'on location' time for more important matters like shot direction or capturing those rare candid moments.

Does having a camera of this quality eliminate the need to hire a professional to undertake your next website? Hardly, as there is more to shooting a perfect photo than just the camera technology. All professionals must have 'the eye'—the mental skill of lining up an aesthetically pleasing shot from various angles. The French coined the term 'mise en scène' to describe the beauty behind this principle.

The bottom line is that having a camera like this and shooting documentation of people, staff, events and your property is a cost-effective way to enhance social media as well as the odd business-urgent picture. But it doesn't eliminate the need for people. And this is the running theme I wish to emphasize in this section: consider new technologies, as there are tons reaching the market every year, but think of them more as adjunctive solutions and not substitutions for tried-and-true guest service carried out by your front line team who directly interact with guests.

WIFI IS FREE, OF COURSE?

Obstinacy is easy to point out, but hard to change. I am finding that even today many hoteliers are unwavering when it comes to changing their position on the offer of free wireless internet connectivity at their properties. As a staunch proponent for offering free WiFi to guests, I've amassed quite the argument to support this claim. Hopefully this will not fall on deaf ears.

We're entering the second decade of the new millennium. The world is moving fast. The internet is near inescapable and many of us can't live without it. Free web service is no longer a luxury item or value-added service. It's an essential service. Ask yourself: Do you charge a surplus for heating, air conditioning and water usage? Why then would you do so for access to the internet?

One clarification before going any further. What's in demand is free wireless access, not the wired, antiquated kind. After all, smartphones and tablets can only access the web this way. Wireless connectivity also allows you to work from anywhere without having to negotiate pesky Ethernet wires.

Now, imagine yourself visiting a friend's house. You want to do a fact check on your smartphone. You could simply use up your 3G data plan, but instead, you ask the host for their WiFi password. How ridiculous would it sound if the friend replies, "Sure, that'll be ten dollars."

As a hotel marketer, one common rebranding technique I've used is to accentuate the ease of transition from the real home to the guest's room. Phrases like 'feel right at home', 'let us cater to your every need' and 'we're the perfect hosts' exemplify this sentiment. How is charging extra for an essential service homely? You wouldn't expect it at a friend's house, so why expect it at a hotel or resort?

With more and more people 'hooked' to the web, the consumer expectation favors free WiFi. Starbucks, McDonalds and many other restaurant and retail giants already offer this complimentary service, and their clientele aren't spending nearly as much as they would on a hotel room. Don't start the guest-hotel relationship on the wrong foot; this is an easy expectation to meet.

When discussing this with consumers, what polarizes them the most are the actual dollar figures behind this surcharge. Some hotels have the audacity to charge $20 per day for internet connectivity—a fee more in line with 1999 than today. It's insulting and an instant turnoff. Moreover, with the prevalence of smartphones, guests may choose to run solely off their 3G networks and accrue charges there rather than appease a hotel's exorbitant internet fees; done out of spite, of course.

Another clarification. Many hotels have settled on a pseudo-tiered system. They will offer a basic connection free of charge then require a sizeable payment in the range of $15 to $20 for the 'high speed' edition. Having experienced several renditions like this, I am attest to the utterly atrocious bandwidth that this type of free service entails. Even something as simple as downloading emails is numbing—purchasing the upgraded version is all but a must in order for the internet to work with any sense of normalcy. This scheme is flawed and not likely to garner endorsement for your hotel.

Not only do these excessive fees instill a negative disposition towards your property, but it prompts your guests to wander offsite to, say, the closest Starbucks or McDonalds. There are already quite a few apps that help smartphone users locate nearby such internet hubs. Now you have an F&B problem. But look on the bright side. Free WiFi is a tool to keep guests at your hotel and spending money. By making them pay, you're encouraging them to leave their rooms, decreasing potential mini-bar revenue, and to avoid the lobby bar. Do yourself a favor and don't let internet obstinacy become a detriment to your F&B sales.

Free WiFi is not a make-or-break feature, however. True, some discerning consumers might not choose your hotel specifically for this reason, but they are in the minority. In most cases, the lack of free WiFi will be a small, and entirely avoidable, grievance which may contribute to a guest leaving your property not wholly satisfied. The mediocre online reviews and lackluster word of mouth that follow are also part of the package.

Lack of free WiFi will boost the feeling of resentment, but will not tip the barrel. My question to you: Why risk it? When you do offer this complimentary service, it will imbue your guests with the sense that you empathize with the plight of the modern traveler—one little feature to amplify positive feelings. Compared to refurnishing rooms or upgrading facilities, free WiFi is a very cheap endorsement to buy. And from a social media perspective, when the internet is served on a silver platter, it's an open invitation for guests to sing your praises online.

One more note on loyalty programs. Many include free in-room internet access as a feature to help sell memberships. But why would someone new join a loyalty program if your hotel hasn't made a good impression with their essential services? Is heating and air conditioning a part of your loyalty program, too? Guests will not sign on to your loyalty program just to negate inflated daily connectivity fees. They will buy in because they're impressed by your core service offerings and amenities, which should already include free WiFi.

Enough of reasons, let's look to solutions. Even with all the aforementioned advantages and disadvantages, many hoteliers are reluctant to change due to legacy contracts. Don't let this be your excuse for transferring additional fees onto your customers. Guests don't care about legacy contracts. If this is the only thing holding you back, bury the internet surcharge into the nightly rate, much like you already do with the room's utilities. Or, read through the original agreement and you are bound to find a buyout option. Pay it and move on. This one-time fee, in addition to the installation charge for wireless hubs and repeaters, is nothing compared to the long-run revenue losses from unhappy guests.

Even though I believe outright that free WiFi is the best solution, here are three intermediate solutions to stave off the inevitable:

- *Package Deal:* Offer free access as part of a larger amenity bundle which might also include free meals or spa discounts. Get creative. Think of it as a 'lifestyle package', showcasing an array of features that make your brand exceptional.
- *Tiered Plan:* Make WiFi free only for premium rooms or suites. The waived fee becomes an added perk, helping validate the more expensive purchase and giving regular guests another incentive to upgrade.
- *Enhanced Web Portals:* In addition to being a web gateway, these systems can integrate amenities such as laundry, dry cleaning and room service. Portal companies are known to handle the WiFi network installation and upkeep costs, satisfying guests with free access in exchange for popup and banner advertisements.

The real solution, however, is a fundamental change in hotelier mindset. Any obstinacy towards free WiFi is indicative of a hotelier unwilling to adapt to the times. Complimentary internet service is a perfunctory task much the same way that your property has to be listed on Facebook, the major OTAs and perhaps Twitter. It's not written in stone that you must maintain an online presence, but it will surely hamper your business to not conform. Treat free WiFi the same way.

I can't stress how truly important this paradigm shift is, particularly when considering the next generation of travelers and any future technologies that evolve in the coming decades. As sad as it may seem, the baby boomers (myself included) no longer have complete command of the North American market. To many current teens and young adults, a lack of free internet is an assault against part of their core beliefs and certainly not a loyalty builder. You have to lay the seeds with the tech-savvy generations to ensure long-term survival. Free WiFi is part of the bigger picture. Keeping an open mind to the rapidly shifting consumer mindsets is now as important as ever.

FREE WIFI: LEARN FROM THE AIRPORTS!

I read a lot of online hotel reviews for properties all over. My goal is to try to figure out what simple things can be done to improve the reviews. Is it fair that people are dishing out one-out-of-five stars reviews and the sole reason given is a lack of free WiFi? No, but that's just the way it is. Free WiFi is an easy excuse for online ridicule, but it's also an easy problem to fix. And in terms of remedying the problem, hotels can learn quite a lot from how airport lounges and waiting areas are coping with the same situation.

The most widely adopted of these is the advertisement-supported free internet service model. Make people watch a 30-second ad clip in exchange for 30 minutes of free internet then make them watch another ad for every subsequent half hour chunk. It's reasonable and many people only need about half an hour to do their web routine—email, social media, news websites and so on. This tactic can also involve some lucrative profit-sharing between the hotel and the ad provider.

Probably the biggest complaint against this system is that the generic ad-supported internet is too slow. The airport's answer to this is a tiered system. Basic internet is free, but in order to get reasonable bandwidth, you have to pay. Of course, the real thing is disguised as a 'premium' service, but they're not fooling anyone. This system can get annoying for the consumer because the slow service is often too slow to begin with. And with the 3G data plans on smartphones able to function better than the slow service, there's little incentive to pay additional fees for faster bite rates, unless you need it for video downloads or file transfers.

Again I have to resort to the conceit of expectations versus value-added extras. Just like how humans are dependent on water, our livelihoods are reliant on the internet. Free WiFi is an expectation and you have to consider it as such. Anything else and you will be scorned, whether you are trying to cover the cost through a tiered plan or as a loyalty reward. The ad-supported system works, but only if it's fast enough to work properly. Plus, if your free WiFi is fast enough, then perhaps it will give people an additional reason to hang around the lobby, enjoy a drink or two and encourage a more social atmosphere.

WHOIS IS A CRUCIAL INTERNET TERM FOR HOTEL OWNERS AND OPERATORS

Imagine losing your website and your email. Imagine having to pay a ransom to a mysterious hijacker to recover your prized URL. Both scenarios are almost unthinkable and yet they still can happen if you're not careful. You simply need to look up the WHOIS for your respective property's website. WHOIS is the quick search designation for who owns a particular site.

To start, go to any WHOIS engine such as Network Solutions or Go Daddy. Enter your URL and see what the results are. The data shown will provide you with your expiration date (also your renewal date), the administrative and technical contacts, and importantly the hosts' email information. Screen capture this information and print.

Most of you now will want to simply pass the details on to your IT department and let them worry about it. But before you do, as an owner or senior level manager, you should make yourself aware of some basic web information so you can at least appreciate any ensuing problems. Start by asking yourself three questions:

- Who owns your website's URL, your official brand.com?
- How would you personally access the back-end directories for this URL in the event that you had to make a change to, for example, a new web provider?
- What can you do to ensure that your URL does not expire?

Let's examine each of these issues. First, I would pass the ownership of your URL to the lawyers. It is intellectual property and has value in the many millions of clustered alphanumeric sequences available in cyberspace. However, legal ownership has zero bearing on the registration of your URL on the internet. There are only two individuals or companies that are recorded for any address: the administrative contact and the technical contact.

The administrative contact is the individual who is able to make ownership changes to the domain—that is, moving it to another administrator—or technical changes, such as the host server (also called the DNS or domain name server). The technical contact only has the ability to control the secondary functions like DNS. The administrator can swap the technical contact but not the other way around. This all makes total sense, and on a day-to-day basis, this information is typically never relevant. Problems arise, however, when a change is required. And here is where the ugly truth boils to the surface.

For most hotels, the first move onto cyberspace was seen as something of an afterthought—one likely made well over a decade ago. Accordingly, the GM typically delegated the initial web work to a sales or marketing assistant, the IT manager (often a contractor) or a local web developer. No questions were asked of who the administrator or technical contact would be. Domain prospecting and hijacking were definitely not common knowledge.

Now, in present day, suppose you decide you want to modify the website and the new web provider happens to have a different site hosting platform. And yet you can't! Why? Because the administrator is listed as that junior marketing assistant who parted with your company four years ago. Worse still, the email he or she assigned to the administrative contact was her long-since-abandoned Hotmail account. A change can be made, but it's complex, frustrating and time consuming.

Another potential nightmare: You find out that your site has ceased to operate and the URL is not functioning, or worse, has been assigned to another individual demanding a king's ransom for its immediate return. How did this happen? The URL expired; the registry contacted the administrator at that long-abandoned Hotmail account. After the notice period, a cyber-squatter picked up the address. You would have gladly paid the $20 per year renewal fee, but now you have to pay $5,000 to an attorney representing the person who prospected your technically-defunct URL.

So what do you do? First, do not delegate. Do this yourself. You can't leave ownership issues to anyone but the owners.

Second, look at your renewal date. If it is less than 10 years out, renew it for another 10 years. The cost will be at most a few hundred bucks. But in doing so, you will eliminate at least one risk for the near future. If you do not know how to renew this, ask your web company or IT manager.

Third, examine the administrative contact name and email. Are they familiar to you? The decision as to who to designate the administrative contact is critical. Ideally, it should be someone very senior in your staff. The email address should be one associated with your property or management firm, not a private Gmail or Hotmail account, allowing you access to make changes if that person leaves your team.

Fourth, examine the technical contact name and email. This can be the same as the administrative contact. Ideally, however, it should be an individual with an email that is not a part of the same address as your own website. If the site goes down and you need to change IP addresses, this task will be difficult if you don't have the technical access. Remember, the administrator can change the technical contact at any time.

Following these simple steps will avoid issues that can impede commerce on your website and cause havoc throughout the property. Why not do it today? Check your WHOIS information and save yourself a potentially tremendous headache.

ENTER KIMPTON'S NEW LOBBY TABLETS

I'm a big proponent of tablets, both for heightening interactions with guests and for back-end uses. That's why I was especially excited to get in touch with some of the top people at Ascension Software to talk about their latest creation. Using part ORION system and part third-party XML feeds, they have launched a new iPad application designed for kiosk stations in hotel lobbies, and this app is already being put to the test at all Kimpton hotels. Discussing this software are Joe Adkisson, President, and Rich Sipe, VP of Mobile Technology.

Ascension's first move was to mature ORION from a hardware-based platform to a web-based, pseudo-CMS dedicated to guest services running on the guests' own web-enabled device or smartphone. Rather than thinking of it as a content management system (CMS), consider it more as a content aggregation system (CAS). The software works to combine the various clusters of data across various back-end systems. Furthermore, it gives guests a pathway to point their requests directly at hotel operators, bypassing and alleviating the front desk. It is this concept that forms the backbone of Ascension Software's new iPad app.

From the get-go, Ascension had some lofty criteria, set forth by Kimpton, to meet. The app had to merge fun and function. That is, Kimpton didn't want to build just another advanced picture show application for tablets. What Ascension asserts as paramount to their task is that an engaged guest is a returning guest. By building an interactive app that could make lobbies more social, this would in turn get guests to engage with the Kimpton brand and increase loyalty.

Besides fun and function, the solution also had to be fast and cheap. For this, the iPad was a clear winner. The iPad is a light and reasonably inexpensive piece of hardware. Presently, Apple leads in sales, they have the most apps and their tablets have the best screen. Additionally, more people are familiar with how the iPad works relative to other tablets.

The next concern was the physical install, of which micro-location and theft were potential obstacles. Putting the iPads in a secure, fully enclosed mount swiftly eliminated any issues of theft. And instead of placing the iPads on the front desk countertops—which would lead to front desk staff awkwardly competing for attention with the tablets—the kiosk stands were consigned to an underutilized section of the lobby floor to better distribute traffic flow. Furthermore, because the iPad has only one wired requirement (power), the kiosk can be placed virtually anywhere within reach of WiFi. All said, the physical prerequisites for a tablet station are affordable enough for even a strapped-for-cash independent hotel.

Along the same lines as theft are the worries over information security and guest privacy. With this in mind, ORION does not force-push situational data onto social media and it auto-logouts after a short period of time, reverting to the homepage. As well, the software adamantly prevents monetary transactions so that 'walk away' people need not worry about leaving sensitive information out in the open.

Fleshing out the 'function' side of things, Kimpton approached Ascension about building an integrated tablet app primarily to augment and enhance their existing concierge services. Although a human presence is always preferable, an iPad kiosk adds additional value to its guests. For this, Joe and Rich walked me through exactly what their software can do.

Expanding on the ORION system meant that not only would the iPad app boast some exciting front-end features, but it would still hold its own behind the scenes. The system requires no hardware onsite and all data can be aggregated through the cloud for a seamless display to guests and lobby visitors. Additionally, ORION is highly time-sensitive. For instance, hotels wouldn't want people to be reminded of Christmas events come January. Normally this requires a manual switch-off, but ORION does this automatically, greatly reducing the operational heavy lifting (and thus, barriers to usage) that have caused many other systems to falter.

Back to the idea of a digital concierge, one of the key objectives for Kimpton was to promote their award-winning restaurants. To start, Ascension's iPad app pulls information straight off of the XML-encoded regular website so that it can highlight a celebrity chef and keep up-to-date with menu changes. More importantly, however, the app is integrated with OpenTable to provide a clear call to action for interested customers to book through the iPad.

Next up is the software's boarding pass feature. What Ascension found was twofold. First, the task of printing off boarding passes for guests was a cause for scorn in numerous online reviews. People hate waiting for this simple task to be completed. Tying into this, the boarding pass process was hogging the time of front desk staff and business center computers. Thus, incorporating this functionality into the app became a crucial way to speed up operations.

All tied through a clear homepage, there's also a five-day weather forecast; each individual hotel's social network feed parsed in a proprietary Ascension aggregator; a media gallery of the hotel; an activities section to shed some light on what's happening around the hotel; and local tips which act as a more direct concierge substitute using information pulled and parsed from Google Maps and third-party providers. Another brand-bolstering feature is the 'Find a Kimpton Hotel' button which directs the viewer to a map of the continent with pinpoints to represent other Kimpton locations, giving customers that extra nudge to stay within the brand. Rounding out the 'fun' side is the Photo Booth, where guests can photograph themselves and apply a range of color filters before emailing or posting the image onto Facebook—a nifty little tool to stave off momentary boredom in young guests.

This article might seem a little heavy-handed in support of what Ascension has accomplished. But my hope is that the multitude of tasks and diverse functionality of this iPad app will convince you of how effective these devices can be for augmenting your guest services and in heightening customer loyalty. Ascension has found some straightforward and some very creative solutions to nearly any objections you might have for installing lobby tablets. They're cheap, and a robust, interactive application is a great starting point for engaging guests. That's something I couldn't agree with more: engaged guests are returning guests.

OPTIMIZE YOUR REVENUE THROUGH A RESERVATIONS CENTER ENHANCEMENT

Awhile ago, I had a chance to sit down and discuss some of the benefits of outsourced inbound central reservation offices (CRO) with John Smallwood, chief executive officer of Travel Outlook. Consider the operations of your own reservations center: Who answers reservation requests during lunch breaks, on weekends, or after hours? Does a call to reservations go to voice mail? In peak hours, do inbound reservations requests roll over to the front desk, where telephone calls interrupt guest service activity? Or, does a reservations call ever go on hold, pushing guests determined to stay with you to their favorite OTA to make their bookings, or heaven forbid, to a competitor? And, what does a poor reservations call say about your guest service level?

These scenarios are real. Their impact on revenue generation is substantial. Since the 2008-2009 economic downturn, most hoteliers have resisted adding staff to all departments, including reservations, looking at alternate ways to meet business needs.

A chain property can always rely on their corporate team to fill a personnel gap. For independents, selecting an outsourced CRO to augment the reservations team can meet these needs without building your internal staff. This is where companies like Travel Outlook come in. Rather than just serving as makeshift filler, these new systems seamlessly integrate and fulfill their role on par or even better than your current reservation team. This is what I gleaned when I approached John for an interview.

What are the key differences between your inbound call center and those of your competition?

For starters, our competitive advantage stems from extensive training and hiring the best agents available, often in the cities where we have client hotels. We pride ourselves on the training and performance of our agents. We closely track our performance in the two most critical areas: time on hold and call conversion. For most clients, our conversion of qualified reservation calls to revenue typically exceeds 70%.

We accomplish these results because of our intense focus on our agents' background and training. We've found that it is much easier to train a hotel professional to function in a call center environment than it is to teach a call center agent what they must know about hotels. Because of this, we concentrate our hiring efforts on finding the best and brightest hotel professionals to answer calls. In fact, many of our current agents worked as reservationists in our client hotels, enabling the hotel to reduce overhead while also retaining knowledgeable, experienced staff to answer incoming reservation requests.

We train our agents on our clients' individual Property Management Systems (PMS). Because we're able to book reservations right into a client's PMS, this saves our clients GDS commissions and other pass-though fees. Travel Outlook is entirely virtual, meaning that we're not restricted to hiring agents in one particular location, so we can often hire an agent who resides in the same regional market as our clientele. This is invaluable when a guest asks a simple question like, "Can you recommend something interesting for us to do after dinner?"

How does the cost structure work for hotels?

Typically, we charge only on consumed rooms for reservations we book, similar to how a travel agent is paid via a commission rate. There are no per-minute charges and no per-transaction fees for our service; hotels only pay us a percentage of actual room revenue received from the guest after the guest has paid and departed. We don't charge for service calls or cancellations, and we don't charge for the initial set up or training costs. For some clients though, we implement a hybrid approach, combining a reduced per-minute charge with a smaller commission rate.

Our value proposition is simple. We expect that our skilled, professional team will generate more than enough revenue to pay for our services and also add revenue to the hotel's top line, allowing the hotel to focus on serving the guest. The end result: higher net operating income.

What are the benefits of using an inbound call center to handle reservations?

It's not economically feasible for a hotel to hire enough in-house reservations agents to answer every single call that rings in, to not put any callers on hold and to spend the time needed to sell each caller using a defined multi-step sales process unique to the hotel. By recruiting a CRO to augment in-house reservations, it's guaranteed that the hotel's voice channel ADR will increase, in addition to these other benefits:

- *Increase occupancy*
- *Heighten consistency*
- *Improve social marketing ratings.* (By allowing the front desk team to concentrate on in-house clients and not bogging them down with reservation calls, this can help to maintain and positively impact online review site rankings like TripAdvisor.)
- *Brand equity*
- *Professional reporting*
- *Staying in step with technology*

What qualities do you look for in hiring new telephone operators?

Prior hotel experience particularly in customer service (for example, front desk or reservations) is a key determinant for us when looking at potential new hires. We also look at computer skills, forward-leaning sales experience and positive outlook to a commission-based structure.

What about quality control?

The system is 100% transparent. We record every reservations call onto our cloud storage facility. Each month we provide full reporting, documenting parameters such as call conversion, ADR, hold time, call denials and call volume. Clients can and regularly do request recordings for a specific interaction.

We also have a small team of shift supervisors assigned around the clock. In addition to managing the agent interaction, call dynamics and assisting with caller requests, supervisors are also responsible for doing live call monitoring through their shift. This provides an opportunity for the agents to receive live feedback on their performance and, if needed, the ability for a supervisor to cut into the call personally and resolve any issues that have been communicated.

WHAT DO GUESTS EXPECT FROM THEIR MOBILE EXPERIENCE?

Meeting consumer expectations is everything. It's the basis for good reviews, word-of-mouth recommendations and return visits. The problem is that expectations are changing so rapidly that it's becoming increasingly difficult for hoteliers to understand what exactly guests want, let alone actually meet those requirements.

To help address this issue, I sought out Marcus Robinson, the CEO of Monscierge, which is a company specializing in integrated software solutions for mobile devices. I've keenly tracked their Guest Experience Management (GEM) reports released twice a year which perfectly articulates the company's dedication to helping hoteliers see the bigger picture.

Each quarter, Monscierge publishes a GEM report on the latest hospitality trends. How did those emerge? How do you conduct your research?

After interviewing over 1000 hotel properties from around the world and countless guests, sifting through endless amounts of industry data, and never ceasing to try and enhance the guest experience, we discovered we had begun to amass a ton of very useful information. We made the decision that it would benefit everyone if we shared this information as we collected it.

An academic process underpins everything we do. We spend more time on research than almost any other part of the process. It leads our strategy and allows us to measure our successes. Each team is responsible for a different type of research that goes along with their normal responsibilities. Our GEM reports are a combination of the findings from various teams, depending on the topic. Our methods include direct questions to hotel operators, touches logged on our lobby devices and researching industry trends.

You talk a lot about evolving guest expectations. Can you elaborate on this?

It isn't exclusively guest expectations that are evolving; it's the entire world. The mobile revolution is causing somewhat of a digital renaissance. The sad fact is: guests are already ahead of the industry curve and are now demanding change in the hospitality space. Rather than being seen as innovators and leaders in this space, guests see brands as dated, and in fact, lagging behind the rest of the world. There are a few forward thinking brands that are now waking up to this trend, and they are willing to commit the resources to become competitive in this space.

Apart from the obvious, how has technology impacted guest expectations? Are consumers becoming increasingly fickle?

Free quality internet access has gone from a luxury to a mainstay. The rising tide of social media reviews gives potential guests access to all kinds of hotel information before they travel; they can easily compare prices and amenities. Smartphones have made this information readily available at any time and place. Guests are becoming used to brands utilizing location-based marketing, mobile discounts and special perks for checking in.

Guests have options and they use technology to evaluate those options. Increasingly, mobile is becoming the platform guests choose to make their decisions. I don't think they have become fickle; I think they have always wanted quality combined with value. As it becomes easier and easier for guests to make informed decisions, we will see them choose options that are more tailored to their own preferences.

What are some present day expectations that might not be wholly transparent?

Most new expectations are fairly apparent, or they should be. But guests now want more of a local experience, immersing themselves in the local environment with shopping, dining and entertainment. With so much information to choose from and an overabundance of reviews, the problem guests now face is how to refine their choice from this information overload.

What services that are now considered value-added will soon become expectations?

We've seen the transition of signage and self-service options from value-added amenities to integral guest experience components. This was confirmed by the AAA recently when their diamond rating system for North America was revised to include digital signage as part of its rating evaluations. The new guidelines incorporate member expectations regarding hotel fees, recognize emerging shifts in design trends, and reflect a more personalized approach to enhancing guest comfort and satisfaction.

The hotel industry is oftentimes described as technologically lethargic. What can managers do to get up to speed and stay ahead?

The biggest technology trend at the moment is mobile. By now, most hotel managers should have a mobile plan in place for guests. Quickly behind that should be a plan for a staff app that enables them to interact with guests and each other. OTAs have taken the lead in search and bookings in the past. It seems that the resultant revenue hit has many hotel operators keeping their eyes peeled for the next industry-changer.

Mobile apps are a hot topic these days. What do you think are the most important features a hotel can offer on this platform to reinforce a brand?

The most important thing a brand can do is 'connect' with their guests. This can take on many forms, but we see the future of travel as an experience that begins at home and continues through the guest's stay all the way until they return home. The brands that are able to stay connected with their guests through this entire journey will be the most successful. Brands should be asking themselves, "Do we have the platform in place to do this now?" If the answer is a 'no', they need to realize that there are brands putting this in place now, and these competitors will be at a clear advantage moving into the next three to five years.

As smartphone and tablet ownership continues to soar, consumers are interacting with brands across multiple platforms or touch points. It's important for marketers to adjust their strategy accordingly and consider this range of touch points as a whole, while tailoring the brand engagement with guests in ways that suit the experiences they expect on each platform.

Research carried out by the Internet Advertising Bureau found that while consumers are using multiple devices to get online, the types of online activity vary amongst platforms. Each device has its own niche. It's important for hotels to have a holistic strategy for different types of mobile devices whilst being able to present a consistent experience across the entire customer journey from research, booking, reconnaissance and right through to review.

With the prevalence of third-party review sites and social media, trust (or lack thereof) is becoming a major issue. How can hotels work to deliver trusted, expert opinions?

Hotels have been providing guests with trusted recommendations well before the internet was even conceived. Distrust comes when expectations are not met. Hotels that monitor their online reputations see what their guests are seeing. Managers can then work to maintain a consistent standard in both reputation and experience.

What is the greatest untapped opportunity that cutting-edge technology offers for the tourism industry?

Advances in location-based technology have made it possible for travelers to view the spot where they are standing as it looked at different points in history. This can go hand-in-hand with the local experiences today's guests are seeking.

What aspects do you see as most important for the future of travel? Where is there the most potential to grow?

The future of travel is about choices. There's a lot of talk about replacing the 'personal touch' with all of the self-service options out there right now. We feel that technology is meant to enhance guest interactions, not replace it. There's an increasing trend to remove physical barriers between staff and guests. Large format touchscreens provide the perfect focal point for staff to come out from behind their desk and stand side-by-side with guests.

Are there people who will always want a personal greeting? Yes. Are there people who would rather not speak to anyone and go straight to their rooms? Yes. The truth is: we all want a bit of both when it suits our mood. This is about meeting each guest where they want to be met at that particular moment as well as giving operators a new and effective tool to enhance their own efficiency and their guests' enjoyment.

AN INTRODUCTION TO STATISTICAL MODELING FOR HOTELS

Do statistics and hospitality mix? For an industry that prides itself on the emotional experience, such left brain enterprises like statistical analysis seem all too illusory. Yet, such data-driven mathematics can yield tremendous results, first and foremost by narrowing your target market to maximize the efficacy of your marketing engine. I've employed Virtual DBS, a company that specializes in these sorts of deductive analyses, to lend their voice to the discussion, both in terms of a thorough explanation of what they do as well as outlining some of the key benefits of statistical modeling. For this, I sought John Dodd, Executive Vice President.

What is the purpose of analytical modeling? Can you describe the basics of it?

The purpose of analytical modeling is typically twofold:

- *Better Understand Customers or Responders.* By statistically profiling a group of customers, respondents and other segments using demographic information appended from third-party compiled data sets, we provide a highly illustrated but mathematically precise explanation of the most prominent characteristics of the customers and prospects with whom our clients communicate. This can enable more relevant copywriting, more efficient media purchasing, more targeted direct marketing and more persuasive creative.
- *Boost Response Performance.* Using modeled mailing lists, email lists or telemarketing lists scored with predictive modeling algorithms, our clients achieve a statistically significant lift in response performance over established baseline in their direct marketing efforts. This returns a higher volume of new customers from smaller target populations, essentially saving money and making money at the same time.

What are you looking for in an ideal consumer?

Typically, the best consumer is one who spends a great deal of money over a long period of time, with high purchase frequency and the most recent purchase having occurred just yesterday (that is, very high Recency-Frequency-Monetary-Tenure, or RFMT). However, every modeling initiative is customized for the specific business rules of each client. As such, the characteristics of an 'ideal' consumer vary widely according to the requirements of our clients. In many cases, the consumer isn't even a consumer—it's a business (B2B modeling).

How do you go about pinpointing these 'cream of the crop' customers?

Typically, we start by segmenting our clients' customers into four roughly equivalent quartiles (25% 'buckets') or tiers—Platinum, Gold, Silver and Bronze-based on their specific buying behaviors using RFMT. We profile and index the Platinum, Gold, Silver, and Bronze groups against a statistically relevant prospect universe across a host of demographic (B2C) or firmagraphic (B2B) elements, and then develop a predictive scoring algorithm that ranks prospects based on their degree of resemblance to the platinum customers.

Can you describe the 'inside/outside' technique?

Because Virtual DBS maintains a multi-source, comprehensive marketing database of virtually every consumer and every business in the US—including several hundred demographic, lifestyle and behavioral attributes—we have the distinct luxury of employing all of these 'outside' data elements in conjunction with the proprietary 'inside' elements supplied by our clients (product details, transaction values, purchase dates, customer tenure, etc.). This 'inside/outside' data approach brings the maximum breadth of intelligence into our modeling efforts, thus bringing maximum predictive power into our propensity scores.

How do your analyses interpret social media platforms?

We consider our statistical methodologies to be 'data agnostic' in the sense that we can use any and all customer data in our models, provided

321

that the data sets are relevant. Hence, if our clients' customer or responder data sets include social media characteristics, we can certainly include those attributes in the model.

Where is the industry headed?

While the database marketing and analytics industry continues to morph as new media channels are unveiled (including social media), the mathematics underpinning sound predictive modeling are based on tried-and-true objective statistical principles that have proven to be virtual inviolable for many decades (and, in some cases, even centuries).

PRIVACY WHEN THEY WANT IT, SERVICE WHEN THEY NEED IT

When was the last time you had to 'hunt down' a server in a retail store, a restaurant or other service environment? Yesterday, last week, last month? Consider a guest while on vacation or after a day of meetings. Suppose this guest decides to relax near the pool or perhaps at the hotel's secluded patio space. This tactic may ensure privacy, but it also means no servers will be in sight. Normally, if he or she wanted a drink or some chow, they would either have to wait for a staff member to amble by or get up and wave one down.

Now consider the reverse scenario. A guest plucks down in the restaurant or lounge and the patrolling wait staff checks in every five minutes. I mean, they just will not leave the guest alone! Frankly, it's getting annoying.

One of the trickiest aspects to mastering guest service is finding the golden mean between neglect and obtrusiveness. We all know it's not physically or fiscally possible to keep staff members on watch in every nook and cranny of your property, but now, however, there appears to be a thrifty solution in the works that is wholly entwined with the rise of mobile technology.

One company spearheading this innovation is ServiceGem. In a nutshell, ServiceGem functions as a 'virtual' staff paging system that guests can access via their cell phones. Here's how ServiceGem works from a guest's perspective.

Via signage, ServiceGem emulates an airplane overhead call button which tells the flight attendant that, firstly, you need assistance, and secondly, the precise location where you are. There will be a display sign at your patio location listing a telephone number, text number and QR code. Plugging any of the three into your cell phone informs a server of your exact location on the property so they can come and promptly take your order.

Another lucrative advantage of this mobile-centric service solution and its real-time reporting package is its ability to heighten team accountability and allow operators to staff more efficiently. Installing a mobile request system for even one or two out-of-the-way hotspots can increase your staff coverage and thus heighten perceived service levels and guest satisfaction.

As a hotelier, the fine line between helpful levels of service and annoying guests has always been conundrum. This nifty trick appears to be a viable solution and a natural extension of the 'on demand' mobile service revolution that has already permeated many other industries.

BUILDING MOBILE APPS TO BOOST MEETINGS

It's no secret that mobile software-apps—are emerging with many new and interesting functions to change nearly everything about our daily lives. It's widely known that the convergence of hotels, social marketing and real-time guest interactions is already well underway via mobile and tablet devices. All pursuits in this field tend to obey the general paradigm that their usage will in turn enhance a guest's perception of a hotel. Apps built for improving meetings work the same way.

If there's a piece of software that can increase an event attendee's ability to enjoy an upcoming, current or past conference, this ignites a virtuous cycle of positive outcomes. In the aftermath of a successful meeting, the planners would subsequently receive higher recognition for their efforts, increasing their ability to propagate future business ventures. Likewise, the meeting or conference center (often a hotel) would indirectly share in this praise, contributing to a myriad of desirable metrics further down the road—more business bookings, heightened occupancies and, ultimately, increased revenues.

Many of your sales teams are already utilizing electronic group-RFP search engines such as Cvent. This program enhances your property's ability to secure new business. But what about enhancing the experience for your conference delegates once they are on property? That's the basis for Cvent's new meeting and event mobile app division entitled CrowdCompass. This is a totally new field. I had an opportunity to talk to the Director of Sales, Matthew Donegan-Ryan, and got a firsthand demonstration. CrowdCompass aims to be a holistic and interactive mobile platform with many takeaway lessons for hoteliers to better understand how technology will impact this side of the industry and how smartphone integration can augment guest satisfaction.

CrowdCompass's main function is for onsite coordination—showing when and where various sessions are taking place (in addition to a reminder system built around this). It's a self-service product principally targeted at event planners who are then given the power to edit content within the app in much the same way as a website's CMS. But the developer has added two other crucial features which give this software more depth to both organizers and attendees.

First, CrowdCompass is designed to help phase out 'static' promotional materials for upcoming conferences—printed guides, brochures, pamphlets, web graphics and so on—by allowing organizers to update event schedules and supplemental information as they become available. By using the app, an attendee will always be up-to-date with what is happening (or what will be happening) at a convention as well as offer an access point for any attached PDFs, powerpoints or other documents meant to complement a given seminar. Moreover, the app can be strategically released at the same time as an event's announcement even with some of the blanks not filled in (time slots, speakers, sponsors, award galas, food vendors and so on), making it a preliminary sales tool for planners, organizers and hotels.

Second, CrowdCompass is social. The app allows for a high degree of sharing by integrating with social media (at the organizer's discretion) as well as possessing functionality across multiple devices (mobile and tablet with compatibility for both iOS and Android). This is important as it gives more power to attendees and enhances their appreciation of a conference.

For example, a business guest wants to attend two sessions at the same time. No decision agony required. He chooses one, and afterwards, he can use the app to discuss his selection as well as read about what was covered in sessions he missed from other attendees. This, in addition to the app's ability to store seminar documents for download and further study. In this way, CrowdCompass becomes a 'digital hub' for all conference activity.

Using Apps to Enhance Meetings Business

I'm of the 'old guard' insofar as I believe that sometimes our phones can sometimes get in the way of person-to-person interactions, especially at large-scale meetings where a multitude of introductions and handshakes are perfunctory. But statistics don't lie. The billion-plus smartphone owners (myself included) are on their devices constantly and over 90% of business users prefer to receive information on an app than through a reflexively-designed website or via paper. You have to meet consumers at the channels they want to use, and in this sense, apps are the way to go.

Let me remind you that CrowdCompass is intended for licensing to meeting planners and organizers, but that doesn't mean that hotels should remain neutral or abstain from encouraging or endorsing mobile integration for conference attendees. Think of all the ancillary benefits you can afford your guests via cooperation with an app controller (in this case, a meeting planner). By helping feed pertinent details, from basic shuttle information to more elaborate information on local attractions and nightlife, it all boils down to providing the best possible experience for your business guests. Even if a conference does not take place on your property, an app that improves the event experience for attendees consequently reflects well on partnered hotels. For this virtue alone, you would best consider meeting apps like CrowdCompass as yet another ancillary method to augment guest satisfaction.

THE LATEST MOBILE TRENDS WITH GUESTDRIVEN

Nowadays, it's safe to say that 'going mobile' is de rigueur. More than that, it's a necessity, not only for fostering brand awareness amongst Gen-Xers and Millennials, but for attaining newly heightened levels of RevPAR. GuestDriven's primary software platform functions as a mobile concierge for guests to purchase services and amenities straight off their smartphone or tablet. To get further insight into the inner workings of mobile integration, I reached out to Zachary Amzallag, GuestDriven's Sales Manager, for answers.

You talk a lot about guest behavior and social media prior to booking. What is the exact relationship between these two? How is it changing?
Well, they are really two sides of the same coin. Now that travelers have choices and the means to compare all options conveniently, they do. So, whereas a hotel used to be able to get away with a few bad customer experiences in the past, today, one bad review on TripAdvisor, Yelp, Google or Hotels.com can mean the difference between thousands of dollars of lost revenue on one end, and a favorable CondéNast editorial PR boost on the other.

What services can you integrate into the software?
It all depends on how far the hotel in question wants to go. For instance:
- Curated City-Guide with content on par with BlackBook, Time Out or Zagat.
- All hotel amenities and services with four level order escalation via email, SMS or phone.
- Full blown geo-location capabilities, itinerary, location triggered in app messaging.

Has there been any backlash to the potentially 'invasive' nature of the GuestDriven software?

When a new guest books a room at one of our clients' hotels, they are invited to personalize their stay by signing up via that hotel's GD Pre-Arrival. The hotel then gets a clout-like score on the guest to see if they're likely to be the hotel's next reviewer on TripAdvisor. Conversely, when the guest opts in, they get to personalize their stay with recommendations based on their actual collected likes and tastes. Full social media integration 'gamifies' the process, making it sticky and fun. It's like a Klout for hotel travelers.

Hotels now know the social influence, wallet spend, likes and dislikes of a traveler before they check-in. And since it is a voluntary opt-in offer, there has been no more backlash to this then, say, using your Facebook or Twitter account to login to Klout or Rotten Tomatoes for movie reviews.

Where do you see mobile apps having the most influence on the hospitality industry?

First and foremost, when you establish a direct relationship with a guest, you run the chance of eliminating the role of the OTA the next time they return for business or pleasure. And since returning guests spend 30% more than first time guests, you've just cut out a hefty commission pay-out and increased RevPAR by 30%.

On the flip side, Priceline, HotelTonight, Airbnb and countless others are capitalizing on the convenience of mobile technology at the expense of hotels. Neilson affirms that 79% of smartphone and tablet users in the US have used their device for purchases. $60M in hotel booking was done via smartphones and tablets last year alone. If hotels are not capitalizing on mobile booking and striving to create meaningful relationships with their guests, they can be 100% certain someone else is.

COMPELLING LESSONS FROM THE NEW GUESTDRIVEN SYSTEM

Using web and mobile technology to enhance a guest's onsite experience as well as enrich a guest's relationship with a hotel is becoming a very salient method towards both heightened loyalty and loftier occupancy numbers. Everyone knows this. The question is how, or more precisely, what additive features and design elements are actually effective in this pursuit.

Since MConcierge rebranded itself as GuestDriven, they have launched an interactive product called the Pre-Arrival system. Their VP of Sales & Marketing, June Tang, was kind enough to demonstrate its various features. Hoteliers take note as there are many facets of this software pedigree that can bolster your business prospects.

(1) Initial Booking—{x}—(2) Arrival—{x}—(3) Departure—{x}—(4) Planning Next Trip

This flow, and in particular each {x}, shows where social media and other online B2C communication channels can hope to improve loyalty and brand 'word of mouse' (the buzz phrase to describe digital word of mouth). It's a simple pathway, but well worth highlighting because it's all too easy to forget that the 'moments between moments', as highlighted by the {x} markers, are where relationships are formed.

Don't wait until a customer reaches your property to start the rapport building. Pounce on the opportunity the second they book with you or engage you on one of your electronic channels, then expand that connection digitally until the point of their arrival when you can shift into the more appropriate person-to-person level of communication. This 'intermission' space is where new platforms, GuestDriven included, thrive. Let's see what features this new breed of software brings to the table to help B2C relationships proliferate.

1. **Pre-Arrival.** You can never underestimate the importance of simplicity and fluidity of design. Just look at Apple's products and their sales numbers. GuestDriven's front end display interface for

prospective and incoming guests, branded as their Pre-Arrival system, fits this in-demand paradigm. Borders, textures and shading can match a client property's theme to subliminally get the feel of the brand across, all while colorful photography of onsite features, amenities and regional attractions fills in the center. Having a picture-centric design helps with interactivity and memory retention as well as increasing online exposure through an augmented chance of social media sharing.

2. **Data Capture.** As straightforward as they come, oftentimes we overlook how important it is to really know your customers and continually record their preferences to refine their experiences. In the beginning (and by that I mean 20 years ago), this meant relying almost entirely on past guest histories whilst new guests were technically blank slates. Now, with social media footprints and big data, it is possible to know all your customers quite well before you ever even have the opportunity of meeting them.

3. **Open CMS with Big Data Aggregation.** Every hospitality consultant that is up to speed on the tech game knows the vast importance of a CMS. The beauty of these back-end editors is that day-to-day operations are taken out of the hands of professional programmers and left for actual hoteliers to manage. This reduces costs, increases the speed of updates as well as allowing for more frequent updates. The GuestDriven system goes a step further insofar as it aggregates guests' online footprints amalgamated from such sites as Facebook, Twitter and LinkedIn into social scores, guest types, guest personas and spending power. From there, you can build custom email or social media campaigns, selecting from such fine-tuning instruments like the channels you want to push, whether a person is close to the property or not, or when he or she is active during the day, in addition to all those mentioned previously.

4. **Direct Communication.** Stemming from the flexible CMS interface, each guest becomes something akin to an open file where every subsequent interaction is marked. For instance, as deduced from guests' Facebook interests and hobbies, managers can coordinate and direct efforts with other managers to better customize onsite experiences. Equally practical is a system's ability to allow for and document direct contact with guests. The example June showed me for GuestDriven was an incoming

traveler who was inferred from his digital profile to be a food critic and blogger outside of the nine-to-five weekday jaunt. To develop the relationship and build word of mouse through this individual, we wrote the foodie a quick email asking whether he would like to dine with the F&B director one evening. Simple, 'beyond the call' touches like this can really go a long way to building a hotel's fan base.

5. **Wish List.** Getting back to the front-end, there's a few more elements that add to the interactivity recipe for boosting a guest's experience. Taking a design cue from Amazon and nearly every online retail store out there, this feature allows guests to add certain attractions to a personal bulletin as a reminder for when they are on property. This also translates into more data capture on the back-end, allowing for concierges, social media managers and any other team member using the system to engage such guests in a consequent dialogue about their wish lists as well as help them plan day excursions and the like.

6. **City Guide.** Built in and around the wish list feature is the software's commitment to deliver picture-laden profiles of neighborhood attractions, restaurants, museums, cultural events, nightlife and anything else that's pertinent. To develop and curate this catalog—in terms of what is displayed at the top, on the first page and in accordance with the property's own recommendations—requires heavy research as well as constant communication between the onsite staff and the software's account managers in order to accurately portray the attractions that best convey the brand. Up until very recently, such 'city guides' have often been classified as features exclusive to luxury properties. But, with a flexible interface as well as proper coordination between various departments, this is now fully accessible to economy and boutique hotels. As well, advanced systems are becoming quite adept at coalescing past guest research as well as data capture specific to each user in order to exhibit individualized guides that predict what a certain guest would find most interesting.

7. **Gamification.** A buzz word for good reason, to 'gamify' a system is, of course, something far easier said than done, but there are some definite positives if you can incorporate one or two features that work towards this archetype. Nowadays, games and traditional

information-centric websites are merging, all underscoring the principle that interactivity heightens emotional involvement and everything thereafter, which includes brand awareness, social media sharing, onsite spending and return visits. GuestDriven's approach to this is through a front-end scoring system. Guests can increase their score via social shares about the hotel (tweets, Facebook likes, etc.) and once certain benchmarks are reached, they qualify for rewards such as onsite perks or vouchers at the hotel. The key with gamification is to start small and not to overcomplicate then grow the degree of interactivity as needed.

8. **Call To Action.** What good is an uber-advanced interactive portal system if there's no impetus for guests to access it? It's crucial to hype such an interface through your first line of communication with incoming guests: email reservation confirmations, websites, social media, electronic promotions or even personal recommendations. The bottom line is that you have to get your hotel's portal for guest out there in order for them to actually use it! So, covering your bases and blanketing your existing digital marketing channels is definitely a solid start.

WHAT'S MOST IMPORTANT IN A TRAVEL TABLET APP?

Daniel Brody is the President of iHorse Technologies, a company specializing in technology solutions for business, and he's been working in conjunction with the tablet ebook/app company PadWorx Digital Media Inc. The app he demonstrated, called 'There's NOTHING Like Australia!' was a prototype for a new breed of interactive tourism apps, in this instance showcasing the great nation and continent of Australia. It was bold; it was intriguing; it wasn't quite like anything I had seen before—videos, immerse sounds and sliders, all generated from a core gaming engine.

I arranged this interview to expand on the 'There's NOTHING Like Australia!' app you showed me. How does the software work?

Built on a proprietary engine that allows for customized features and pan-platform distribution, the 'There's NOTHING Like Australia!' app provides each reader with a unique opportunity to see 13 of the best locations in Australia through the eyes of various travelers. Interactive, first-person journals relate the ideal journeys of everyday tourists, providing readers with a fun and insightful ground-eye view of Australia. Also distinctive, innovative full-bleed video is incorporated directly into each storytelling experience.

The app also boasts a guide section that beautifully presents over 100 of the best places to visit. Readers can learn about museums, spas, outback wilderness excursions and much more. And with its 'Itinerary' feature, any of the 100 places can be selected to build up a potential trip as unique as each reader.

What do you find is different or unique for apps built specifically for the hospitality industry? What do these consumers want?

In true left-brain right-brain fashion, consumers want to simultaneously know and feel. They want to know the important facts that will help them decide the where, the when and the how to travel. As well, they want this information presented quickly and cleanly within the app.

At the same time, consumers appreciate an app that gives them a flavor of what they will feel when they arrive. For the 'There's NOTHING Like Australia!' app, we gave consumers the best of both worlds by providing both narrative and informational content. Presented as 'Experience' and 'Discover', users can feel what it is like to travel to 13 locations within Australia by reading a series of interactive, text and image journals. All this is complemented by video, sound and animation effects to fully immerse a reader.

How important is interactivity for tablet apps?

Interactivity is the defining feature of all apps. But there are degrees of interactivity and the bar is continuously being raised. Users not only want to decide what content they consume and in what order, but they also want ever more interaction in how they consume content. Personalization, socialization, customization and 'gamification' are quickly becoming expected features of all apps, even in the travel and hospitality industry.

What do you feel will be most important for hospitality tablet apps in the near future?

Obviously, information comes first. Above all else, users want to make informed decisions about how to spend their time and money. Apps that cater to this need will be more sought after than those that don't. Building on this, users want interaction and information rich apps that anticipate the types of questions they have about specific products as well as stream specific user profiles towards desired content as quickly as possible. Hospitality apps must leverage social networks—particularly the experiences of other users—to dovetail the brand message, but this must be done in a useful and meaningful way. Hotel apps will need to be truly mobile, presenting travelers with relevant information in real-time based on their individual preferences and GPS location.

CONCLUSION

To summarize the most recent technological developments can be a laughable venture as by the time any 'summary' is published, it will be subverted by the next batch of software and hardware products introduced to consumers. We are simply moving too fast. Luckily, the hospitality industry has some leeway in that our business affairs are not wholly dependent on keeping pace with the newest and greatest. We are a people business, and no technology will eradicate the need for face-to-face interactions. But there are a few trends that you must subscribe to if you want to sustain successful operations.

First and foremost is the empowerment of managers and team members to use curate a property's digital communications and brand image without a programmer intermediary. This is occurring via social media integration and real-time updates. All apps or new software products which are incorporated into a hotel's operations must consider how they are linked to the hotel's social networks. This feature is vital for driving online interactions to generate more word of mouse and heighten SEO. Team members therefore play a central role in all novel software integrations as they are the ones that update the social networks with quotidian news items and they are ones who liaise consumers face to face. Moreover, given the alacrity at which we are moving, all these pursuits must be done quickly, and the only way to accomplish this is by allowing your team to function on their own.

Another cardinal feature to think about along these lines is interactivity. How do guests—past, present and future—interact with a given product? It has been shown that such interactivity is a surefire way to increase brand perceptions and recognition, so what technology is on your slate to stay in touch with this trend? Another buzz term to remember when mulling over ways to heighten interactivity is 'gamification'. That is, how can a piece of software be used in a manner akin to a game to help entice consumers to like your brand? This plays upon the psychological drive for instant gratification, of which games can deliver in full. Consider this when you must try your hand at a tech upgrade.

The fact remains that there's a plethora of new software products vying for your highly limited free cash. You can't try them all; you can't even try a few. It simply costs too much—both in time and in money—to invest in new technology without an immediate projection of positive ROI figures. As such, what I recommend, and as I've highlighted in the previous section, is to stay up-to-date with the trades and consider all options before prudently tendering from one or two tech firms to meet your needs.

SOCIAL MEDIA

Recently opened, the Fairmont Grand Kyiv reflects traditional hotel opulence to reinforce its dedication to luxury, but with everything you would expect from a fully modern property.

INTRODUCTION

I've long held mixed feelings about social media and its effects on all industries. There's no denying that it has changed the way we conduct business, and not necessarily for the better. But rather than denying social media's preeminence and persisting in judging it wholly through a negative light, it would be far more prudent to accept the evolving digital-dominant landscape and adjust your operations accordingly.

In previous writings, I focused more on the 'how to' of the now social media giants like Facebook, Twitter, LinkedIn and YouTube. This information is readily available online, either through writing I've collaborated on or through the countless other resources on the World Wide Web, all free and all helpful in various ways. Instead of continuing along these lines, this next section devotes more time to discussing the imperative for monitoring your online presence and using electronic channels as a means of augmenting customer relations.

Monitoring and rapid response to consumer questions and opinions has become a part of the new definition of proper online brand management. Having a page on Facebook or a Twitter account is now standard; what matters is how much you value contributions from your fans. Thus, these popular social networks for businesses have been relationship management channels, and not necessarily sales channels, as well as important vessels for garnering candid feedback.

There will always be new entrants to the social media game, but it appears as though things have stabilized to some degree. People only have so much time in the day to devote to leisurely pursuits on their favorite websites. As such, I find myself more fascinated by the broad trends and what we can infer from activity on the more popular networks rather than nitpicking the outcomes of the latest Facebook feature update or a hip new software to hit the marketplace.

Although I am still skeptical about social media's long-term effects on how we communicate, you must nevertheless follow the adage of 'meeting consumers where they are'. This isn't just a phenomenon of the Millennials anymore; baby boomers, Gen Xers and, as pointed out, citizens of such rapidly proliferating nations like China are all plugging in and getting online. People of all generations are presently using social media for anything and everything, so rather than being the proverbial ostrich stuck on dry land, be like a llama in a river, swimming with the current downstream towards future success.

MANAGING REAL-TIME REVIEWS

Mobile domination is afoot! Smartphones now have the numbers and the 'smarts'. Rethink your website, rethink your social media and rethink your external sales channels. As always, with new technologies come new dilemmas, and the topic for today is real-time guest reviews. Rather explicit by its namesake, real-time reviews are those live tweets, Facebook status updates and foursquare comments, or the ten-minutes-after-the-fact TripAdvisor reviews. They could be posted via laptop, but given their immediacy, the delivery vessel is most likely mobile—smartphones and tablets.

To address why real-time reviews matter is to address why immediacy matters. What's the rush? Why does it matter that I expedite my online follow-up to remarks about my hotel which run the gamut from the good and the bad to the tragically ugly? Damage control for one. But, more importantly, one that's less obvious is heightened loyalty—a pillar for any successful business.

Let me explain through an 'old-fashioned' example—email. An acquaintance messages you with a matter requiring some semblance of urgency on your part. You rebound within a few minutes (not that you wouldn't otherwise) asking for more details. Henceforth, a precedent has been set in terms of the appropriate breadth of time between correspondences. How then would you feel towards this acquaintance if your initial, hastened reply was left unanswered for two whole weeks? Barring extenuating circumstances, it doesn't appear as though you're very high on his or her priority list and, frankly, it's quite rude.

Apply this communications scenario to real-time reviews. A conciliatory reply to a scathing Twitter comment two days after the fact is like throwing a bucket of water into a fire after it has already consumed the forest. It's too little, too late. The world is moving fast and you have to keep pace. Survival of the fastest.

This alacrity can impede your marketing and loyalty-building efforts, but lo and behold, the opposite is exceedingly true. Suppose a recently departed guest rejoices at length about your F&B service on your hotel's Facebook fan page. Then, your team sends a personalized and sincere hank You' note within ten minutes. "Wow, that was fast! They must really care what I think and value my patronage," thinks the surprised and enthused user.

If the hotel's praise came an hour later, it probably wouldn't evoke this same level of amazement. It's a sliding scale, like ripe fruit on the countertop that spoils slowly but surely. In short, timeliness is everything. (Nota bene: the 'Thank You' note can be expounded into something far more impactful than a mere show of gratitude; consider calls to action like targeted recommendations and upcoming promotions.)

Additionally, it's important to consider that because this subcategory of reviews occurs in real-time, there's a distinct probability that the person in question is still onsite. Your response can steer the remainder of a guest's trip, for better or for worse. A patron raves about a lunchtime entrée? Thank them and suggest a dessert. Someone complains about certain aspects of the guestroom? Have a staff member give them a call, post haste.

The Latest Tidbits in Social Media Trending

One other nugget of tangential information worth mentioning at this point is the visual media revolution. With faster internet connections, 3G/4G networks and smartphones, pictures and videos are as easy to share as text-based data. Yes, I'm talking Instagram and Pinterest, which now command over 100 million avid users. I say 'avid' as habitués of these two picture-sharing channels do a lot of sharing. As a picture is really worth a thousand words, third-party visual media contributors will play a hefty role in propagating hotel reviews.

But that's neither here nor there. These are two more contributors to the real-time development and networks to supervise. Commend users for their candid photography of your property and reach out to those who gripe, same as you would with any other channel.

For us, this can only mean one thing: more points for brand exposure. As well, more opportunities for real-time reviews. With that in mind, I've outlined four general steps that you should take to address this growing concern.

Step One: Monitoring

By now, you know that real-time reviews are important; what's the first step? Easy: monitoring. With hundreds of millions of tweets a day, a dozen global-reaching social media outlets and still countless other online travel review sites, the concept of watching each one separately 24 hours a day is apoplectic. The understated beauty of social media monitoring platforms is in their capability to aggregate what's relevant to your property onto a single screen. This function alone merits investigation and possibly money down.

A further benefit is how these types of software can streamline your respective personnel. With all your networks drawn through one portal, task assignment is far less confusing and shared responsibilities can be actualized with full accountability. Plus, if a senior manager needs to take the reins, they need only remember one password and not a couple dozen. Efficiency gains you time, and in a time-sensitive era like this, saving those seconds really adds up.

Regardless of whether you heed my endorsement of these aggregating systems, constant monitoring in any way, shape or form is paramount. How else will you be able to promptly reply to your critics?

Step Two: Planning

Apply social media monitoring to real-time reviews and you'll swiftly ascertain that monitoring is but one element necessary for effective management. The key ingredient—the meat to all other potatoes and sides—will be the responses and actions you execute. And in order to perform with perfection, you must plan as best you can.

Do you have a structure in place so that designated staff members are empowered to answer and act without needing approval on every piece of minutia? Have you trained and retrained your team on the appropriate lexicon to use for each outlet? Do you have a series of standard responses outlined for common situations such as displays of gratitude, basic information queries or managers' contacts? Have you amended your crisis communication protocol to include best practices for online complaints and derisions? Do you have to judge every instance on a case-by-case basis, or is it possible to define several concrete criteria for automation? Are you putting your best online foot forward?

While you shuffle your resources, my recommendation is to keep the lines of communication at a minimum. Social media managers—the day-to-day administrators—should report straight to a director, be it PR, HR, S&M or any other acronymic department where you slot this tech specialty. You don't want time to slow you down, so ensure that your organizational hierarchy favors empowerment and flexibility.

Step Three: Interact

You will be evaluated by your online presence. Just as real-time reviews are out in the open, so too are your responses. Leisure shoppers scrutinize how managers react to negative appraisals on TripAdvisor. Savvy Facebook users inspect hotel pages to browse recent happenings and hotelier receptiveness. Aside from a soapbox for promotions, this site is actually a rather handy resource for travel information. Even Google plays a part in all this. The corporation's SEO algorithms increasingly rely on social mentions and activity, especially those hailing from their own backyard (such as Google Plus).

As we're dealing with real-time sensitivity, a cardinal tenet to follow is to be proactive with your interactions. This starts with your response rapidity. Under every Facebook comment or TripAdvisor business reply is a date or timestamp, so managers' accountability is thoroughly public information. Moreover, quick replies intuit greater compassion on the part of the hotel. Like a bizarre Dutch auction, the longer you wait, the less impact your follow-up will inter.

The word 'proactive' connotes much more than sitting vigilantly by a social media monitoring platform, mouse-trigger finger itching. Take the initiative and query guests via email survey or even a Twitter message. By being the first party to extend the olive branch, it will, again, demonstrate that you value consumer patronage, which in turn builds long-term loyalty. Maybe you get an answer, maybe you don't, but at least you tried. And if past decades working with direct mail firms and email newsletters are any indication, this number is always above zero, so your efforts will not go unnoticed.

Facilitate Interactions Through a Flawless Mobile Interface

Peripheral to real-time interactions, but nevertheless prodigiously significant, is the fluidity of your mobile site—composed of a series of trending issues all under the catchy monikers of 'Internet 3.0' or the mobile revolution. Alas, I'm likely already preaching to the choir on this one. You know that mobile applicability is the future, and yet it's still not mission critical to deliver absolute perfection.

As a proponent tour de force for mobile-friendly websites, Google, through its Mobile Ads Blog, has delivered some very grave statistics. It's a clear win-win for mobile: two-thirds (67%) of consumers say they are more likely to purchase if a site is mobile-friendly while another two-thirds (61%) say they're more likely to leave a site in favor of a competitor's if it's not mobile-friendly. Additionally, Google, in collaboration with Ipsos Research, reports that four out of five US smartphone users recruited their mobile devices to aid in shopping research where another 35% of this camp also completed the translation through the phone.

Going mobile implies capture—the ability for you to motivate consumers towards a purchase. With an impending increase of mobile-only internet users over the next decade, the only evident way to heighten revenue from these channels is to be scrupulously mobile-friendly. Enough with the implicating metrics already, let's get down to methodology.

The foundation for all this hubbub is an HTML-5, mobile-ready website—flawless, fast-loading and fulfilling. It's this third one that's the real sticking point. Consumers are on the prowl for a more customized experience and mobile is no different in this regard than web browser cookies on your laptop. Think of your mobile site as an interactive travel guide for curious guests, all personalized for their goals and tastes. That's the penultimate vision. Add to that straightforward connections to your social media networks, favored online review pages and your own internal feedback channels, and you have a recipe for real-time success.

Step Four: Measure

It's a no-brainer that you will need accountability, both to manage your social media champions and to ensure that your efforts leave a positive impression. It's a given that your online reputation management team must hold the belief that they can make a difference for your organization; this passion alone will undoubtedly maximize success. Of particular importance for real-time monitoring is the ability for your frontline staff to properly divide individual tasks and write coherent replies both swiftly and with an actionable corollary for other managers to improve at least one aspect of hotel operations.

Working wonders in this regard is to formally integrate social media with every department. Make it a company-wide effort by introducing your social media managers to your chefs, your engineers and your housekeepers so that they can comfortably parlay directly with one another to speed along guest requests. Ensure that managers across all departments comprehend the value of an earnest and endearing online presence and what it can mean for long-term sales forecasts. Do this and triaging online criticism will automatically become a consummate priority.

Which brings us back to the aggregate software; the same instruments you employ to accelerate daily communications are tantamount for accruing quarter-over-quarter and year-over-year data. When investigating your software purchasing options, it is crucial that your choice includes these respective analytical features. Astutely managed online reputations will pay dividends in full, but implicating metrics of any significance will only reveal themselves with the passage of time. Be patient, then reward your social media managers will factual affirmations of their progress.

A Pertinent Caveat

I feel it worth mentioning that although most critics have the best intentions when they make their opinions known to the world—both for you, the hotelier, to improve as well as the future customer at large—there are a scant few who have more diabolical agendas. People will 'phish' or 'troll' by posting bad reviews and objections due to personal grudges or to procure free compensation. These should be fairly easy to spot as their content will likely be ridiculously warped or outright slanderous will little supporting evidence.

Don't worry. The average consumer is well aware of these tactics and can often sense internet trolling just as well as you can. My advice: stand behind your product and don't succumb to their games. Keep an optimistic tone and be forever accommodating in your responses. Others will see this and respect you for it. As well, just because a comment is outrageous in narrative does not exclude the fact that it was posted in the first place. Something somewhere and somehow had to motivate this person to spend his or her fleeting minutes to rail against your hotel in particular. Behind this flaming curtain are one or two morsels for you to learn more; the rub is in the transliteration.

The Bottom Line

Managing real-time reviews abides by the same ebb and flow as any other online foray, only quicker. The speed of a response is respected almost as much as the content of a response.

To judge the sweeping importance of this issue, put on your future-vision goggles and imagine where the proliferation of mobile technologies will take us in 15 or 20 years. Will people use their phones to buy their weekly allotment of groceries? How about as a TV controller? Will phones ever bridge the 3D domain? The sky's the limit, and given real-time reviews' correlation with mobile utility, you best act now and become accustomed to acting very, very fast.

HAVE LOCATION-BASED SOCIAL MEDIA SERVICES STALLED?

In my first book, I wrote about how hoteliers could use Foursquare, a network experiencing exponential growth at the time. As a rising star, it was critical that hoteliers know the playing field and be ready to anticipate marketing tactics for this new channel.

A lot has happened in the online realm since then, and yet it doesn't seem as though location-based social media services have flourished into the omnipotent customer influencers as previously purported. Yelp has reached critical mass. Then there are other emergent geo-social networks like MyTown, Loopt, Hotlist, Geomium, Socialight and many others either active or now defunct.

There's movement, but the hype engine has stalled. However, just because location-based services aren't getting a boatload of press coverage to tout their business successes does not mean that web companies aren't hard at work to refine functionality and develop a more alluring end user experience. Nowadays it seems as though every smartphone app is attempting to incorporate some form of location-based service.

One bright light: Facebook. It has "Places" with its own check-in system. This friend-connecting behemoth has made good use of the Gowalla team's wisdom—a Foursquare competitor which saw key members join the Facebook banner in January 2012. One experiment in June 2012 was Facebook's Friendshake, which allowed users to find other online friends close by using the GPS technology in smartphones. This attempt was met with scorn over its privacy-invading potential and was quickly squashed, although it might reappear in another form.

Elsewhere, in a rather bold move in July 2012, Foursquare launched their Promoted Updates services, enabling corporations to advertise to nearby customers. Like its social media brethren, Foursquare is seeking a means to monetize. It's a double-edged sword—money lets them pay more programmers to build more application features and enrich the user experience, but advertising-laden pages may alter consumer perceptions and detract from the end user experience.

The bottom line: location-based services are a work in progress, but should hotels care?

It depends entirely on your existing consumer base, and for the most part I can't bestow a positive endorsement for this geo-social media niche. Their significance is marginal, not mainstream. Yes, location-based services are a way to reach out to new customers, but on a minute-by-minute comparison, your time would be better spent elsewhere.

Going by the numbers, as of January 2013, Foursquare (the largest geo-social network independent of any internet flagship like Facebook, Google or Yahoo) currently lists over 20 million active users—big by anyone's standards, except for Twitter and Facebook which both have over 500 million. If you are scrounging for the time to manage your social media campaigns, this simple number comparison should tell you how best to allocate your resources.

Second, you have to factor in the stigma associated with location-based services. Friendshake was deemed a 'stalker app'. It was toxic, highlighting people's innate aversion to making their present locations public knowledge without consent at every occasion. If geo-social networking is viewed as one more step towards decreasing personal privacy, is this something you want to wholly embrace?

Next, ask yourself whether your current clientele are the types who might use location-based services. Has Facebook Places caught on amongst the baby boomers or is it more an outlet for harried, money-strapped GenXers and Millennials? Is Foursquare still primarily a tool for urbanites seeking local tips and restaurants? Your use of these avant garde technologies has to be congruent with your target audience.

For instance, I don't foresee geo-social networks aligning with business trips. That is, would a surge of activity on Foursquare sway a corporate traveler to stay at one hotel versus another? Pre-established loyalty programs and company deals are two far weightier decision factors. Then again, fortune favors the bold and the creative. Perhaps Foursquare or Facebook Places could be harnessed as fun tools to revitalize a conference venue, directing businesspeople to various meetings and breakout rooms via the check-in system depending on whoever is already there.

Location-based services can, however, be adequately leveraged for your F&B portfolio, as has already been demonstrated by international chains and by independent restaurants. Offer a coupon with check-in at one of your outlets. Use said coupon to highlight one or two exceptional menu items. All together though, location-based services haven't reached the critical mass where they're imperative marketing tools for hotels. Stay in the loop, however, and I'm sure good things are coming.

SOCIAL MEDIA MARKETING IN CHINA FOR HOTELS

The world's most populous country and the second largest economy as of this writing, China is exceedingly difficult to ignore. To many Westerners, the nation is still largely a mystery and widely misunderstood behind antiquated perceptions of their government, censorship laws, outsourcing and many others. For hoteliers, all this can perplex to the point of noninvolvement.

Lest you forget that where there are people, there are eager travelers, and this bastion of humanity is no exception. Outbound tourism from China has already risen significantly in the past 20 years since they reopened their borders to the capitalist world. Given the causal relationship between prosperity and travel as well as the nation's stable economic forecasts, this trend is bound to continue. However, a broad rallying cry does not preclude the hard work and tact you will need to penetrate China's curtain, never mind the startup costs of adapting to the nation's internal social networks and hiring Mandarin-fluent personnel.

At first glance, it may seem as though China is a segment best left for the big boys, the major chains with enough disposable cash to set up dedicated teams for this task and go through the obligatory trial-and-error learning curve. However, it doesn't take a marketing guru to see that reaching over a billion people can be very lucrative, and for this platitude alone, independent operators and management firms should consider methods of heightening brand awareness in the heart of Asia.

Plant the Seed

With a teeming population that is increasingly affluent and a booming technology industry, it makes sense that China has the most social media users on the planet with over 300 million citizens accessing the internet for this purpose. The nation is also considered to have the most active 'netizen' base per capita with a nationwide average of 46 minutes per day spent online and over 95% of metropolitan Chinese people who traverse the online sphere also involved in social networks. Moreover, it's indicated that this isn't a millennial phenomenon; adults within the prime, cash-laden demo of 55 to 64 are equally if not more active online than US users between the ages of 25 and 34.

Even with these astoundingly favorable stats, it still begs the question: Why bother? For one, staying away is a lost opportunity to grow your business in this emerging and diversifying market. But will your efforts and resources actualize a numerically positive ROI anytime in the near future?

The answer to this will, of course, hinge on the product you offer, its unique appeal to Asian travelers and your marketing strategy. What I advocate is a long-run seed-planting mission. China will continue to grow and so will both its netizen activity and the influence of social media over purchasing behaviors. You can play a role in educating this keen population about your hotel and why they should visit you, whether for business or for leisure. If you hit the ground running with a solid team devoted to increasing your brand awareness in this market, then results will be forthcoming. But first, you have to know the terrain.

A Note on Censorship

As you probably already know, the government polices the internet in China very scrupulously. There's no Facebook, Twitter or YouTube so that external influences can be better managed through their own internal equivalents where individual posts, searches or blogs can all be censored, banned or deleted with ease. If you're not comfortable with this ethical quandary, then this country might not be your cup of oolong tea.

If, however, you are open to a moral outlook that doesn't completely kowtow to the Western ideals of transparent free speech, then there are still some fairly standard rules and asterisks to get comfortable with. First, watch your language. Promote your property and steer clear of all political mumbo-jumbo, especially in and around the country's 'blackout' dates where certain internet activities are suspended. This caution also extends to SEO, metatags and any jargon you hope to use to promote your property.

Nor are the Chinese blind to these censorship activities; skepticism towards news agencies and formal institutions is a common trait (although this should not be confused with a lack of patriotism).

As such, citizens increasingly trust personal recommendations and peer-to-peer channels overtop of government-sanctioned advertising portals—all the more reason to put your stock in the country's social media.

An Overview of China's Social Media

Don't be intimidated by the unfamiliar names; the nation's spectrum of social networks fills the same diverse niches that apply elsewhere around the globe. As such, we will keep this discussion to the basic and currently most-in-vogue sites. Read through this introduction to get a sense of what their social media landscape is like.

A caveat: like the metrics accrued for Facebook, Twitter and their ilk, we rely on the number of registered users, which doesn't necessary correlate with the exact number of actual users because some people may have multiple or now defunct accounts. Also note that people may own accounts for different networks, so the total registered user stat for one site may have sizeable overlap with another.

1. *Tencent QQ and Qzone.* The national company Tencent has been an incumbent in the online realm since the late 1990s when they developed an ICQ-like instant messaging program commonly referred to as QQ. Working in much the same way as Windows Live Messenger (which, for reference, currently has over 300 million users worldwide) and relying heavily on banner ads for revenue, QQ also has an international portal called IMQQ for a combined total of just under 800 million registered accounts, with daily usage frequently exceeding 100 million.

    This platform is valued first and foremost for its simplicity of utility, but also because peer-to-peer communication is a good means to circumnavigate government censorship actions and manipulations, making it very important for younger generations. Aside from the core instant messaging function, QQ allows users to play games, access blogs and use a virtual currency amongst others.

    It's also a vehicle for Tencent to cross-promote its other platforms, free and paid, which can all be accessed via a person's QQ account, thus helping maintain Tencent's status as the largest social media community in China in terms of total registered users. One other such service is Qzone, which lets individuals write personal diaries and share visual or audio media, with many features overlapping those of Facebook or MySpace. Qzone is especially popular amongst teens and young adults with over 150 million users who update their profiles at least once a month.

2. *Wechat.* Another Tencent creation, and also known as Weixin, this is a mobile voice and text app with over 100 million users. It's also one of the fastest growing channels, trickling out from an educated base in first-tier cites and spreading throughout the country as smartphones continue to proliferate. Wechat also incorporates location-based, dating and media-sharing services with Instagram filtering abilities.

3. *Sina Weibo.* Sina is one of Tencent's largest competitors within the Chinese social media landscape, especially when it comes to mobile. Their Twitter-like Weibo network controls nearly 60% of the micro-blogging realm with a total account base of over 360 million as well as millions of new posts per day largely drawn from educated people in first-tier cities. The other 40% of this space is primarily filled by Tencent's and Baidu's Weibo products as well as Fanfou. (It should be noted for Baidu, a vast web services corporation, their Weibo network is but a small portion of their business when compared to their search engine and pay-per-click streams.)

   The common uses amongst all three micro-blogs are to read and share breaking news, product information or gossip as well as images and videos. Much like Twitter, this platform has public messaging, retweets, favorites, URL shortening and hashtags. It also features verified accounts for celebrities, pundits, companies and media organizations to talk directly with fans. Accessed by more than 20% of China's netizens, Sina Weibo is a big driver of consumer activity as well as social discourse. Its functionality has recently been expanded to include a location-based service along with international versions in other languages including English.

4. *Renren.* Regarded as the most direct analogue to Facebook, Renren started in much the same way with a fervent base of university students followed by rapid expansion to other demographics, especially those with a college-level education, for a present total of

over 145 million registered users. This platform not only provides a very similar blue-on-white layout as its American counterpart, but also houses most of the same features including personal profiles, wall posts, commenting and media sharing. Renren is the leader in this social media category with direct competition from Kaixin001 which operates in a very similar manner.

5. *Douban.* Significantly smaller and appealing to a more niche audience, Douban's open forum network has over 60 million registered users. Primarily designed for connecting fans of music, movies and books, this specialized service also allows unregistered netizens to access most pages with 80 million active users per month. Along with the likes of Diandian and P1.cn, these blogging sites can be thought of as the Chinese equivalents to Tumblr.

6. *Youku and Tudou.* These two websites function as video-hosting services like YouTube and Hulu. Following a merger by these two companies earlier this year, their combined worldwide traffic is ranked just behind that of the Google-owned counterpart. Both sites allow users to upload such content as music videos, personal videoblogs, candid amateur movies and professional clips from films and television. As well, there are fewer restrictions on content length and copyright infringements than for YouTube, although monitors screen every video for censored topics and phrases.

Recommendations

This range of networks presents many opportunities both for direct advertising and brand awareness creation. It has been widely noted that for Chinese consumers, social media has a much greater influence than it does elsewhere. This alone might be enough to convince you to get involved.

However, as these networks reach maturity through second-tier and rural areas in China, the authority that social media has on purchasing decisions will likely follow the same model as their Western equivalents—fad then fact of life. In the end, it comes down to personal recommends and creating an experience that allows an individual to identify with the brand, before, during and after services rendered. Hence, all the same general rules apply—use quality content along with timely posts and interactivity to develop fans.

Developing a social media strategy for China, like that in any other territory, boils down to targeted awareness promotions, monitoring and understanding your demographics. Even though it's primarily a 'young person's game' and aligning yourself with the next generation should be a foremost objective, it's also crucial to realize just how active the older and more established members are in the online sphere. People of all ages love to discuss recent purchases and share personal reviews as well as use social media for product research.

If you plan on venturing into this lucrative market, definitely budget for higher average costs. First, maintaining a profile page on many of these popular networks requires a monthly fee. Second, not only must you have a team fluent enough to converse in real-time with potential customers and maybe even those whose opinions may not suit your goals, but in order to gain that peer-to-peer traction, you will likely have to parlay with key opinion leaders (KOL).

Think of these people as critics or cyber-celebrities with paid-for services or gift-giving eliciting sponsored micro-blog messages or recommendations on their public pages. They operate as pundits for specific ranges of products as well as for self-promotion. KOLs also interact extensively with other KOLs, and given the influence that such bloggers have on data-gathering customers, this means that a few well-placed subsidies can go a long way to disseminate your message and get that initial burst of followers.

The Bottom Line

I researched and wrote this piece to give you a flavor of what social media is like in China. Whether you choose to involve your hotel or not is entirely up to you. If you feel as though this might be a beneficial move, there are two vital considerations.

First, you must ensure that your existing social media department is operating competently and that all your present campaigns are producing noticeable and actionable results. There's no point to extending your reach if it will not be executed with efficacy. Get your house in order before you expand your cost structure.

Next, how does your property actually appeal to Chinese travelers? Along these same lines, ask whether your hotel is fit to handle guests from this market? Do you have the appropriate translations for your menus and pamphlets as well as Mandarin-speaking staff? Do you offer a semblance of home with some traditional Chinese dishes on the menu and perhaps a few customary services? An honest and thorough appraisal of the answers to these questions will act as the kernel to your marketing approach as well as a justification of your intentions.

MASTER SOCIAL MEDIA IN CHINA
TO MASTER IT AT HOME

The growth of China's economy is equal parts fascinating and staggering. Living in North America where capitalism, consumerism and urbanization have long been ingrained into our societal framework, it's almost unfathomable to comprehend the inner logistics required to apply these systems to a country of 1.4 billion at the breakneck speed which China is currently achieving. As well, the news that reaches our eyes and ears covering this furious growth is undoubtedly warped from what's actually happening on the ground. All we can bank on with certainty is that with increasing GDP comes more monetarily empowered citizens and subsequently more globetrotting travelers.

I still yearn for more information coming directly from people based in China who are witnessing the country's maturation firsthand. Lucky for me, I was approached by the people at Web Presence In China to help show me the way. My chats with their Director of Online Strategy, Ernie Diaz, who lives and works in Beijing, were particularly enlightening, and he has some bold words which all hoteliers should note even if their long-term strategies don't necessarily involve this millennia-old nation.

For starters, what Ernie advises is to take whatever preconceptions you have about Chinese consumers, burn them, and then chuck the ashes out the window. For a country this big, a one-size-fits-all model is bunk and negligent; they are a widely diverse people both demographically and psychographically. Within this context, China has a burgeoning middle class that's ready and willing to consume goods at Western proportions and with Western variability, but this is a relatively small number of the total population. There are still hundreds of millions of citizens who are very slowly graduating from the impoverished proletariat social order, remnants of the Maoist Cultural Revolution days.

The growing pains of this clash between old communism and new capitalism are strongest felt in the China50, a loose term to describe the 50 some odd Tier 2 metropolises with populations greater than two million. These are cities where expansion is off the charts with bulging trade, immigration and manufacturing, but without the pomp and ceremony of shiny new 100-story skyscrapers or mind-bending Olympic facilities. As the government pushes to transition China from an export-centric to a high per-capita-annum consumerist nation, the China50 is where the bulk of this new bourgeoisie will be found, and despite being in the minority, they still comprise over a hundred million potent consumers.

Little Emperors

When assessing this emerging urban middle class, you have to first consider the demographic effects of the One-Child Policy initiated in 1979. This has to be one of the most controversial population control tactics of the modern era, with antagonists claiming extreme rates of female infanticide, gender imbalance and forced abortions while proponents assert that this measure has helped curb famine, epidemics, rampant slums and overwhelmed public services. Viewed through a raw financial lens, one of the most salient outcomes is a narrowing and concentrating of wealth amongst the only-sibling offspring.

Enter the Little Emperor Generation. With the future of a family dependent on an only child, all the love, attention, pride, shame, wisdom and money gets funneled into this one individual. Keep in mind that the One-Child Policy has been difficult to enforce, especially in more rural settings, but census figures nevertheless indicate compliance at approaching half the total population. Hence, compounded over 30 years and millions of families, this regulatory measure has in effect created China's new middle class.

Moreover, as we enter the second generation of its application, children are now the benefactors of wealth trickling down through four law-abiding grandparents and two only sibling parents. In many cases, this has had the opposite effect; a single child scrounging to support his or her parents on top of the four grandparents, cleverly labeled as the '4-2-1 Problem'. However often this harmful consequence is occurring, the overall trend is that of wealth concentration within a smaller, younger population.

Bestowed with preternatural quantities of affection and surplus cash might give you the immediate perception that Little Emperors are a bunch of spoiled prima donnas, but this is another stereotype you must turn to ash. Alongside their unremitted parental love comes a heavy burden of responsibility as well as unceasing disciplinary oversight. They are their families' only hope for a brighter tomorrow, and this isn't something best left to chance. In this regard, Chinese parents are no different than that of anywhere else in the world. They simply want, and demand, the best for their kids.

The first logical step to success is higher education. But with limited schooling availability in rural and semi-rural areas, the best option is a send off to the city—a China50 city. As such, Little Emperors for the most part are astute, well educated and, in tandem with having the fiscal backing to enjoy a posh lifestyle, they are savvy, discerning consumers. Moreover, city life in China has influences unknown to the countryside, namely the allure of the internet and the lurking presence of the nation's top trading partner, the United States. The urban middle class increasingly lives and breathes via websites and social networks. As well, English is the most commonly enrolled second language amongst students, but note that this is of the textbook variety and not necessarily conversational.

Travel Starts on the Internet

Even with whatever online information censorship protocols have been administered by the Chinese government, the World Wide Web has nonetheless opened China's citizens' eyes to a planet of new adventures and possibilities. Travel is one of the highest aspirations for the Little Emperor Generation, and they are thinking both domestically and internationally. Remarkable gains in outbound vacations are already being seen for those countries closer to home like South Korea, Japan and Thailand.

Of note for certain members of the hospitality industry is the spread of Hollywood movies, made more readily available through television, internet streaming and the exponential growth of domestic multiplexes. Films are just as powerful for Chinese citizens as they are for us; they make us think, they make us dream. This, in conjunction with flourishing travel discussions on social media and the heightened spending power of young urbanites, means a greater desire to traverse the globe, especially Western regions so often highlighted by popular movies (think Los Angeles, New York City, London and Paris).

In line with current trends elsewhere in leisure travel hotspots, Chinese tourists increasingly want what other globetrotters seek: a local authentic experience. Related to this, Ernie and I discussed at length the dissolution of the clichéd Asian sightseer group—those packed buses carting native Mandarin speakers around to all the area's stock tourist locales with nothing that's truly local in between. Younger Chinese travelers revile these sorts of dull, standardized methods of seeing a foreign land, much like contemporary tourists from everywhere else in the world.

Modern vacationers from China are now researching, discovering and planning their own escapades, independent of those established through Western partnerships with the Chinese Travel Service (CTS), the government's tourism and travel authority. Solo leisure travel is on the rise in favor of group tours; a feat largely accomplished by harnessing the power of word of mouth recommendations through social media as well as stylish travel blog websites and online review sites (TripAdvisor is popular there too).

To give you a better picture of what's happening over there, understand that social media and consumer-driven websites have a greater inherent value to their users in China for two main reasons. First, due to the censorship issue, there's an inclination to take messages from 'official' sources with a grain of salt. This starts with government communications but extends out to any brand employing marketing tactics which might be considered deceptive. Second, even though the merits of ecommerce are well understood, speedy broadband infrastructure has yet to be systematically installed throughout China, meaning that websites with colorful high-res photography and flash take too long to load. Such lag causes the consumer's mind to wonder, as coined by the term 'cognitive drift'. Hence, low-tech channels such as text-based social media rule the day.

As a caveat, it's important to mention at this point that, even though my prose to some extent expresses the present scenario in absolute terms, you should be aware that everything is in fact a gradual progression. China is a nation of vast history and cultural diversity, with the emergence of Little Emperors (soon to become Big Emperors as they mature into the later stages of adulthood) and internet-born travel as well as the decline of generic tour groups all occurring at once and over a lengthy timescale. Needless to say, there are many other contributing factors.

Taking Action

Speaking on general trends and population dynamics is all well and good, but how do we leverage this information into action? Yes, China has millions of wealthy citizens and millions more soon to reach middle class status, with many of them craving more global travel. But how do we tell them about our brands? How do we get them to visit our hotels?

There is always the de facto approach of establishing ties with the CTS middle men, and engineering a Mandarin-based website and top-down marketing campaign for use within mainland China. You have to keep in mind the inherent resistance to these methods—distrust of official brand messages and lag time when trying to load image-rich websites. Ernie suggested something a bit more 'grassroots'. Rather than try to appeal to consumers through conventional means, why not focus your energies more towards social media activity and building a presence on popular travel blog sites? A prominent example to explore is www.mafengwo.com.

The internet has been transformative in the way we do business and China is no different in this regard. The consumer drives the conversation and if you want to build awareness and develop a following in this market, you have to get on social media. With this as the overarching goal, there is a fairly scientific approach you can take.

That strategy involves hiring someone fluent in Mandarin to act as your Chinese liaison on their social networks. This can be a person recruited in your region to operate onsite under the direct tutelage of your social media manager and PR team. Or, you can outsource the posting of materials and question responses to an individual or company within China, leaving you with the task of feeding them answers, pictures, videos and any other information which might help a Chinese traveler plan their upcoming trip.

Either way, you need to give people direct value in what you post and be timely in your useful, transparent follow-ups. Even if you are more inclined towards outsourcing, this will be a wholly multimedia-driven endeavor. As well, don't expect to cultivate an email list for your newsletter; keep it within the domain of social media. Tell natural stories that are authentic to your hotel, city or area and, slowly but surely, the fans will come knocking.

In fact, what the collective of gurus have been preaching as effective, organic social media programs for hotels everywhere else in the world also apply to China—even more so here given Chinese citizens' stalwart reliance on low-tech, consumer-driven channels. Also, best not to assume there's any inherent social networking differences apart from the language barrier and the new social networks you will have to become familiar with, such as Sina Weibo, Tencent QQ, Renren and Youku. Because of this ground-up, word of mouth approach, if you can learn to market to travelers in China, then you will be a veteran at handling travelers from anywhere else.

Furthermore, this person you recruit need not be a full-time employee straight off the bat. Consider testing the waters with an intern or a short-term contract so that you can learn the ins and outs of each major social media player as well as understand what level of communication is required. This might be especially important if your property is not situated in a territory that's top of mind for Chinese tourists. You will have to work harder to get in on the travel conversations, but you will also have the advantage of being able to talk about your hotel as the ambassador for the region by informing Mandarin speakers about all there is to do around you.

Ernie and I ended our chat with a mutual understanding that perhaps the first step is not the hiring of additional staff or the outsourcing of online efforts, but that it all starts with the executive committee. Affluent Chinese travelers are out there and they number in the millions, but they will only show interest in you if you show a genuine interest in them first. In other words, it takes courage at the top to get the ball rolling.

HOTELS AND KLOUT DON'T MIX

Hotels, take heed. There's a new web-born trend snaking its way into the methods by which we determine who gets complimentary perks and who does not. I'm talking about Klout scores and I believe you will find them to be rather dangerous.

For those unfamiliar, Klout is a social media analytics tool that measures a person's online social influence. The Klout score algorithm is primarily derived from an individual's Twitter profile, taking into account the number of tweets per day, retweets, replies to your posts, hashtags, lists, followers and followings.

The San Francisco-based company has already received some hefty criticism on the integrity of its formula. But this hasn't stopped brands from cashing in on this new metric by appeasing high Klout score Twitter users with freebies and other comped goods, all in an attempt to better promote their products. It's the classic celebrity endorsement model turned on its head.

The best example I could find of this in the hospitality world is the Klout Klub at the Palms Casino Resort in Las Vegas. Their hope—at least what I presume—is to gain market share by offering instant room upgrades for those with high enough Klout scores in return for online acclaim and diffusion of the brand name throughout the Twittersphere. An interesting business idea, to say the least!

This strategy conforms to the Gladwellian framework of persuading the 'mavens' into action on your behalf. Target a few specific and very influential people for the same, or even better, result of targeting the whole. It's a bold idea, but I believe that it will fail, and here's why.

Twitter endorsements for hotels are fickle.

I've come to have a serious love-hate relationship with Twitter, and Klout only serves to exacerbate my points of disdain. So please, allow me to demystify the relationship between Twitter, or all social media for that matter, and actual revenue generation.

The Palms Casino Resort, Las Vegas

I'm not writing this as a derision of the resort itself, but rather, using it as an example to show how a forward-thinking strategy can elicit unexpected and possibly dire consequences. For those who have a high enough score to enter the pearly gates of the resort's Klout Klub: good for you. Take the free room upgrade, tweet about it and reap the rewards. But for us regular folk, it's cause for chagrin.

Most of us have lives outside of the Twittersphere and will never have the time to achieve a Klout score necessary for their definition of VIP status. I can't help but feel the primal urges of both jealousy and anger towards the resort and those who have been rewarded due to this single metric; a metric that doesn't appear to be based on any solid framework of talent and labor.

Why would I consider a property where I'm required to pay for a 'better' room (versus a free upgrade) just because I'm not on Twitter for 12 hours a day? But that's just me. I'm sure the other 99% of people below the Klout score cutoff would never feel envy towards a hotel that merits social media addiction (please note my sarcasm here). Perhaps, as a baby boomer, I'm not part of this property's key demographic. But even still, this type of electronic favoritism will probably not deliver a solid incentive for mass appeal. In trying to build relationships via those with high Klout, they are disenfranchising everyone else.

On the one hand, I wholeheartedly encourage hotels to be active on Twitter and treat the software as an 'online concierge' for their past, present and future guests. Social media can be an excellent tool to keep customers informed and to promote various aspects of your brand. Yet on the other hand, segregating the way you treat guests based on Klout scores is a form of prejudice that is bound to exclude more than it includes.

In One Ear, Out the Other

The Klout algorithm has a critical flaw in that it presupposes more followers and more tweets per day directly equate to more real-time influence. It's a fully modern interpretation of 'in one ear, out the other' and the marketing maxim of 'less is more'.

First, when it comes to the quantity of followers, did you know that you can buy an extra 1,000 for $20, or even less? True, these 'fans' won't be replying or retweeting, but they still contribute to the final tally for Klout scores. This practice is highly unethical, but it's only a matter of time before people feel the need to game the system as a means to stay ahead.

Second, and much more importantly, is the lurking negative effect of tweeting too often per day. Few, if any, genuinely care about your day-to-day activities like laundry, walking the dog and a rabid gym schedule. Nor is it imperative that you retweet or quote verbatim this week's world-shaking news event. At a certain point it all becomes white noise and mundane. When you gain a reputation for tweeting too often per day, people may end up skimming your posts instead of reading them.

It's a subconscious spam filter. Take someone who tweets 45 times per day and the few quality messages related a given hotel are near instantaneously pushed down into the nether regions of cyberspace by newer tweets. Moreover, because the algorithm is heavily dependent on frequency, it forces those with a high Klout score to keep pumping the system full of this balderdash—by any means necessary—to perpetuate their current rank. This can serve to further a skimming mentality by followers.

Therefore, I pose the question: are tweets about your hotel more likely to be read when coming from someone who posts 45 times a day or 3 times a day? I've said it before and I'll say it again, quality trumps quantity, even in the Twittersphere.

You will get your day in the sun by courting a 'Twitterati' to frolic in the supreme experience of your hotel. But once they leave, it's like they were never there. And their followers have moved on, too. You've had your 15 seconds of fame. What if, however, someone who only tweets once or twice a day lauds your property? Because it's one of only a few tweets posted that day, it will attract the eye much more readily. But people who don't tweet often probably have low Klout scores so their opinions don't really matter, right?

Customer Loyalty Is Something You Earn

There's nothing wrong with using Klout scores as a metric to find guests and the social 'mavens' with the most influence. It's what you do with those metrics that matter. One of the main arguments in favor of harnessing Klout scores is that it's a good way to tap into new networks and find new customers. While I don't argue the fact that this tactic can increase your brand awareness, I contend that it is far easier to retain existing customers than it is to find new ones.

Applying this principle unveils yet another logical fallacy in Klout scores. If you have to go out of your way with free perks in order for Twitter pundits to celebrate your name, then there's something seriously wrong with your regular operations. Shouldn't your standard guest experience be enough to deserve acclaim, or at least a positive mention?

Your guest services should be exemplary, whether you're hosting a person with 70,000 Twitter followers or a Cro-Magnon who has yet to join Facebook. The superfluous bonuses you offer to Twitterati might broaden your awareness with a dirge of exciting tweets and get you a few new customers in the process, but if you can't deliver a consistently excellent experience for the everyman then you are in trouble.

And the tweets you get from these pundits will set the bar fairly high. Suppose these new customers try out your product and it doesn't live up to what they have been sold because they aren't getting the Klout VIP package. Failing to meet expectations can do you more harm than surpassing expectations can do you good. Are you going to upgrade every person who is come off a Twitter recommendation in order to meet their expectations? No, you'd probably go broke.

At the other end of the spectrum, suppose a consumer is fully aware that a hotel endorsement on Twitter has been derived from an individual's high Klout status. Is this consumer to then assume that he or she won't be entitled to the same experience? Should he or she therefore come to take all such endorsements on Twitter for that property with a grain of salt? Either way, it's a vicious path to set down on.

The real litmus test would be when you stop handing out perks. Do your Twitter pundits still praise your name? Do they bother to spend for a room upgrade they previously had for free? Do they even stay with you, or do they decide to try the place down the street?

It's your job to get new consumers through the door, and employing mercenaries with lofty Klout scores to accomplish may work. Just keep in mind the lightning pace at which Twitter moves. Once your Twitterati check out, so too are the tweets about your hotel. More importantly, for any new recruits you do in fact gain by these methods, you will have to work especially hard to convert them into devoted supporters. And you will not be able to buy your way out of every situation. You will have to earn their loyalty by delivering a quality experience.

Online Life Versus Real Life

The big debate amongst people who analyze social media is whether it can actually influence people in real life to spend money. I argue that this relationship is nearly inconsequential. I would much rather have a well-connected individual praise a hotel to their friends in person, or in their own blog, than post dozens of encouraging tweets. Word of mouth is the obvious trump card, but relevant to this specific quandary: is there any significant association amongst Klout scores, word of mouth and monetary influence? Yes, but the nature of the relationship must be treated on a case-by-case basis.

As a hotel marketer, I wouldn't only consider a person's Klout score, but I would take it in conjunction with their occupation. Look for industry pundits whose followers are already cued in to look for hotel recommendations—travel writers, hotel senior managers, prominent chefs, tourism bloggers, sommeliers, meeting planners and public speakers to name a few. These are individuals who will not only tweet about a property, but will talk about it with others in person.

Moreover, their career paths (that is, what they do outside of the Twittersphere) have all bestowed them with a reputation for expert insights on the hospitality world. When I want a quick laugh, I'll follow a comedian. When I want to learn about new places to travel, I'll follow someone working in tourism. Klout isn't all bad, but it should definitely not be treated as the sole point of delineation.

Researching this topic before scribing this passage, I came across a story of a person failing a job interview because his Klout score was too low. Sweeping disappointment set in. Yet I look at it the other way. Why would you want to work for a company that puts this much weight in something as trivial as a Klout score? The interviewee should count himself lucky he isn't working there because god only knows what other maligned values are at work.

BRAND KARMA, NEW TECHNOLOGY FOR A MATURE SOCIAL MEDIA AGE

Brand Karma is one of the hottest social media monitoring tools to emerge in the face of too many online networks to keep track of and too much information. Experiencing exponential growth in 2012, Brand Karma works by sifting through and analyzing the thousands of online reviews and posts. I approached Jamie Pagel, the Senior Vice President, to find out more about what makes Brand Karma tick with the hope that you will learn a bit more about what's required for contemporary social media aggregation software.

What functions does Brand Karma incorporate?

- *Hotel Review Sources:* The most influential online travel agency and review sites
- *Social Media Monitoring:* Thousands of travel-related newsletters and influential blogs, Twitter, Facebook, YouTube, Flickr
- *Semantic Analysis:* English, French, Chinese (simplified and traditional), Japanese, Spanish, German and Italian
- *Global Reach:* 500,000+ hotel rooms under contract
- *Reputation Management:* Real-time monitoring of all social media from review sites, OTAs, Twitter and Facebook, pulled to a convenient 'inbox' for quick review with translations, workflow processes and the ability to post a management response

How does Brand Karma compare with other programs that monitor social media?

Monitoring is only the first step in using social media to drive revenue to your brand or hotel. A good platform has the ability to synthesize all the information obtained through the monitoring process, analyze it and deliver actionable information to the various stakeholders at the hotel and above-property.

Brand Karma is the only tool to accurately simulate the research process a consumer goes through before making a travel purchase decision. Brand Karma contextualizes social media postings in multiple ways: By Topic, Trended Over Time, By Demographic, Against Brand and Local Competitors. Brand Karma's biggest differentiator, apart from its technological developments, is the consulting and service-oriented side of the business. We're holistic. The other monitoring companies don't synergize all aspects of online exposure and help brands through all stages of the journey. We work to connect the dots directly back to revenue.

What do you see as the future for Brand Karma and social media monitoring?

Streamlining our product offering to even more closely match the way our clients want to use the information. It's an ongoing battle. We've learned which parts of our offering bring the highest value to different types of clients and we're looking to make it easier and more cost effective for users to get the information they need to do their job more effectively.

BLACKBOOK INNOVATION FOR ONLINE REPUTATION AND SOCIAL MEDIA MANAGEMENT

Social media is, well, social media. You can't avoid it and everyone's talking about it. My biggest headache is that there's just too much of it! Stepping up to the plate are the social media monitoring companies with sophisticated software to help refine and summarize the endlessness of online data. However, this is a relatively new field, and as a result innovation and evolution are unremitting qualities. Circos Brand Karma is one such company that is on the vanguard. With the launch of their Blackbook Reports analytics tool, I chatted with Senior Vice President, Jamie Pagel, to expand on some of the latest industry trends and what his product can do.

Start with the elevator pitch. What's Blackbook and how will it help?

Brand Karma was one of the first in the social media monitoring and analytics for hotels space. Along the way we have learned that there are lots of different needs within the travel industry, and many stakeholders want to understand the performance data and online reputation for hotels and markets. The Blackbook is designed to package the most important and current information about a particular hotel or a particular city, and then get it into the hands of a GM, owner, travel agent or tourism board so they can understand it at first glance.

Apart from the obvious concerns for attracting customers, why should a hotel care about its online reputation in relation to the competition?

In regards to the competition, social media is the way to see how you are doing relative to your comp set and relative to the market in the public eye. That is a big part of Blackbook because the traditional types of guest surveys are not going to give you that scope.

As it relates to sales and marketing, our goal with social media is to get our clients to position and communicate the benefits of their hotel in the same way customers are talking about them in an online review or a social media posting. By doing so, the social media feedback and the voice of the customer become congruent with what the hotel puts in its brochures and on its website. This consistency can have a dramatically positive impact on the hotel's search rankings and ultimately drive more traffic.

Finally, as it relates to revenue management, there are opportunities to raise your rates when you know you're at the top of your market. If you are first or second on TripAdvisor in your market, people will recognize in their research that you are the best. As such, you should be able to demand the top rate without much resistance.

The two editions of this new service—the Market Blackbook and the Hotel Blackbook—differ substantially. Can you describe their basic divergences and how a hotel manager might use both for self-analysis and improvement?

The Hotel Blackbook is a deep dive on a specific property and its individual performance. Anyone can buy this report for a particular hotel or even buy a report for a competing hotel and a hotel in a different market to gain further insights. We analyze data that is publically accessible to everyone on the internet; we just save you a ton of time by summarizing the vast amount of social media content into a concise, legible report.

The Market Blackbook, on the other hand, is designed to look broadly at a particular market and the top 20 hotels that compete in that market. You will not find the same depth of information about each specific hotel, but you will find a pretty useful snapshot with ranking information, trends and hot topics for each property. We also include macro insights about the market where we summarize the overall trends, what has changed and who is on the rise.

Where does Blackbook source its usage data and how does it interpret what's most important?

Via public-facing APIs, our data sources include the big review sites, OTAs, social networks and blog sites, information procured as either rich media (photo and video content) or social postings (status updates, tweets, etc.). Because we have data on virtually every hotel worldwide, we determine a hotel's market share-of-voice by looking at the number of postings or comments a particular hotel receives over a definite time period, benchmarked against every other hotel in the regional market.

Based on your experience, where are the most vital areas that hotels devote their resources when it comes to online reputation management and social media presence?

We have a framework we use to talk to our clients called the 'Four Ms': Monitor, Measure, Manage and Monetize. Each stage builds up in value to the hotel.

We believe that all hotels should, at the very least, participate in the Monitoring stage; listening to their customers using social media.

Then, there are opportunities through either the Blackbook or a social media measurement tool to benchmark and Measure how you're doing versus the competition or year-over-year. It's not just listening to the data but digging into it to understand what insights can be gleaned.

Management gets to engagement and the decision to join the conversation, including things like setting up a Facebook page, responding to reviews on TripAdvisor and really starting to make it a two-way dialogue with customers.

Finally, once you've engaged the customers in a meaningful way, you've entered the Monetization phase. That's where we really start to see the value come out, with hotels able to turn social media into a channel for bookings, increased brand value and all the things that folks in the C-suite care about.

There are some hotels that manage but do not monitor, and that's fine. We believe that this is a dangerous game, however, because you may miss out on a critical post or something that can dramatically impact your online reputation.

What's the next step for the online world? Are there any areas hotels aren't taking advantage of?

User-generated content is really increasing as a factor of mobility. Consumers no longer have to wait until they are home or in their office to write a review about a hotel. Between 35% and 40% of all Facebook activity is now conducted from a mobile device. Also, Pinterest and Instagram are a testament to the increased demand of visual content— they are certainly well-established but not yet as big as Facebook or Twitter. These sites have a lot of potential, especially for visually attractive hotels or luxury hotels.

A REVIEW OF REVIEWPRO AND SOCIAL MEDIA MONITORING BENEFITS

The breakneck pace of social media can be a headache in terms of reputation management, but it doesn't have to be. Having to check and follow up on Facebook, Twitter, LinkedIn, YouTube, TripAdvisor, Orbitz and a host of other sites is a quagmire of time consumption. As the presence of these social platforms continues to expand, getting all the information in one place and updated in real-time is a necessity for time management and corresponding response efforts.

Enter ReviewPro, one of several social media management and online review analytics products available to do precisely this. Rather than give a simple overview of what the software does and its benefits, I used my time with ReviewPro's Josiah Mackenzie, Director of Business Development, to effectively answer the question: will using this software actually improve your hotel business over checking popular social media websites and OTAs individually?

What's important to remember here is that there is now some very compelling research that shows just how influential online consumer activity is on future purchases. Josiah was quick to point out that 92% of internet users read reviews, of which 35% change their choice of hotel after browsing social media reviews. As well, he cites Expedia's statistic that a 1-point increase in a review score equates upwards of a 9% increase in ADR on that site. Additionally, it was found that 79% of TripAdvisor users are reassured when hotel management executes a proper, public follow up to a negative review.

A key feature to look for in social media monitoring software is the capacity for internal communication. Anyone can manage social media via notifications received from each network then assign responsibility for follow up through email. But this manual process is slow. By aggregating all your social media platforms along with your coordinated response efforts and deadlines for follow up in one place, it streamlines this workflow process, saving you time. And to heighten accountability, ReviewPro generates individual usage reports as well as executive summaries for senior managers.

One of the biggest concerns with any new technology is adoption rate. Having the proper tools to monitor usage is a heavy 'top down' method of enforcing accountability. Two more ways that the software increases employee engagement are through an attractive, implicit user interface and via automated reports that refine content to focus on each user's specific duties.

Josiah notes that platforms like ReviewPro inherently support the notion of hiring a social media manager. However, this is certainly not mandatory, and the decision to hire or outsource this is more a function of property requirements than the software's capabilities. ReviewPro operates through the cloud; being onsite isn't essential. I emphasize that ReviewPro and other products of this nature fully support the notion of using social media to broadly understand guests' perceptions of your brand and service levels. Any large-scale interpretations of the data are within the realm of the GM more so than a social media manager.

On the other hand, ReviewPro, under the curtain, is a highly complex piece of software, and when taken in conjunction with all the other social media networks, OTAs, analytics websites and matching access codes, having to disperse these tasks would be inefficient and confusing. Who has time to memorize all the ins and outs of every platform then act upon them? It's best to have an executive sponsor of this program—a social media manager—someone appointed to know the logistical back-end and all corresponding networks then filter the information for other actionable persons.

The second major benefit, and in all probability the 'meat' of the software's functionality, derives from its analytics tools. As the basal level is ReviewPro's newsfeed, color-coding reviews based on degrees of satisfaction as well as updating the system with social media mentions collected from public APIs and brand pages. From all this data, ReviewPro creates analytics and can compare your overall rating against up to 10 members of your predefined competitive set. Central to these analytics is the Global Review Index™, an all-encompassing benchmark of guest satisfaction based on numerous social media and OTAs. Lastly, what I found exceptional was their proprietary semantic analysis that mines guest reviews and examines word use instead of only rating numbers to reveal customer sentiment.

And where the semantic analysis becomes most beneficial is in its ability to accurately interpret customer expectations in relation to their overall satisfaction levels. This is best illustrated through examples. Suppose that the semantics tool notes a high frequency of the words 'room' and 'small' as well as phrases like 'rooms are small' and similar permutations. Is this indicative of rooms that are, in reality, tiny and perhaps claustrophobic? Or, does this mean that the room size is misrepresented in promotional materials?

What we're discussing here is expectation management. If your brochures and website only show PhotoShopped markups of your best suites, then what will prospective consumers anticipate with their purchases? More importantly, what will a guest feel upon arrival at his or her actual room? By identifying this discrepancy, your marketing team now has a more concrete direction upon which to act. This case presents two options to increase overall satisfaction: change expectations about room size by altering promotional materials, or, to a lesser extent, modify the in-room furnishings so there's more perceived space.

Josiah cites a real-life case study pertaining to an island resort. The property was advertised as a beach locale, but in reality it was situated ten minutes by car from the nearest sandy knolls. Standard rating aggregates only picked up on a mediocre average. The semantics analysis, however, highlighted the error in full, making it blatantly obvious that past guests were angry at being deceived. With a shift change in marketing strategy to address the property's true beachfront status, subsequent reviews have shown definite improvements. By altering the expectation, the resort improved satisfaction.

Using the semantics tools in conjunction with the competitive set analytics helps put the benefits of this software through a monetary lens. That is, as a first time visitor to New York City, what should you expect for a room costing $250? I use NYC as the example city because of its potentially outrageous ADRs when compared to the rest of the world averages. A semantics aggregate can help you decipher what's critically important to a traveler. Moreover, knowing where your competitive set stands can give a strong indication of the average expectation at this broad price point.

Where this becomes especially lucrative is in its potential for reevaluating your ADR, not just what services you offer. Having a numerical affirmation that you are performing better than your competitive set can give you the confidence to raise rates without significantly affecting occupancy. I would proceed with caution when making an inference this wide, but nevertheless, when you're tracking significantly better than your competitors, marginal price increases may be in the cards.

ONLINE TRAVEL AGENCIES

Philadelphia's Hotel Palomar epitomizes the modern trend towards ergonomic space and functionality, helping it surpass its numerous citywide competitors.

INTRODUCTION

I've never tried to hide my hatred towards online travel agencies (OTAs). Like all viable businesses, they (rightfully) put their own interests ahead of others, and as is the case here, to the detriment of others. What happened is that hotels have been over-reliant on the OTAs as a distribution channel. This has had the immediate effect of eroding hotels' margins—funds which would normally go towards the consummate process of continual upgrades in addition to marketing efforts that reinforce the brand.

But there's a more profound outcome at play here, one which isn't readily apparent on a balance sheet. Because the OTAs display all hotels as a list of possibilities on one page with an emphasis on price, they are subtly dissuading consumers from being loyalty to one particular brand or major chain. After all, with so many properties to choose from, why does it matter whether you choose a Hilton, Marriott or Starwood? There's only one scale for all hotels, whether they be two star or five star, and I see this as a precipitous problem for us all. When every product is displayed in the same format, then everything garners the same perception, which in turn makes all the products out to be of interchangeable quality. It is a gradual decline into commoditization—a trait more appropriate for the global trading of rare materials than guestrooms. Hotels are anything but interchangeable and it is each property's uniqueness which should be emphasized.

Another key topic covered in the following articles pertains to the effects of travel review sites—closely related and covering similar territory but not the same as the OTAs. These websites are double-edged swords. I love and commend their intrinsically democratic nature, but on the other hand, many users do not know how to properly judge a hotel. These wannabe critics misappropriate certain features and give extraordinary weight to items which are otherwise rudimentary and germane in their current expression.

On the one hand, we must adapt our practices to meet the ever-evolving behavior of our consumers. But on the other hand, there are forces at work here which are downright bad for business. Even though I tend to take a 'hellfire and brimstone' approach to these issues, there is always light at the end of the tunnel, and a hotelier who is able to shrewdly navigate these tumultuous times will ultimately prevail. The pitfalls of the OTAs and travel review sites are felt industry-wide and thus the correct response may not be readily apparent or within your power to alter. I implore you to read the following passages and keep an open mind when attempting to think of solutions to this problem.

USING TRIPADVISOR TO MAKE
A TRAVEL DECISION

By now, I expect that you have a member of your staff dedicated to reviewing and responding to comments posted to your TripAdvisor listing or other online review site (I use TripAdvisor as it is the most prominent within this class). These responses are designed to do a number of things from complimenting a reviewer to acknowledging a fault and addressing the underlying issues. The practice of making these responses is pretty much ingrained in every property's social media program. But what about these responses? How do they help your TripAdvisor rating, and importantly, how do they help convert website visitors into property bookers?

Take a previous scheduled vacation of mine for instance. I was planning a trip to a European city that I had never visited previously. With no leads or referrals (a rarity), I attempted to select a hotel solely from the commentary and manager's responses available on TripAdvisor. This is an exercise you should try yourself. Here were my findings:

1. It may seem obvious, but TripAdvisor listings are sorted by location on the basis of each property's respective star ranking. The better rankings top the list. In cities where there are hundreds of properties listed, eye fatigue makes it very difficult for anyone to sort through more than 20 to 30 hotels at a time. Clearly, the higher up you are, the better.

2. Hotels are also sorted by categories: Best Value, Family, Luxury, Business and Romance. Check to see where you rank in each of these criteria. Again, the same ranking issue applies; the prospective purchaser will tire after the first two dozen entries. Note that you do not assign these categories; they are based on reader response. This means that while you may think of your property as a business destination, it might not be ranked as such by the TripAdvisor crowd.

3. When it gets into the meat of your TripAdvisor ratings, rest assured they will be read thoroughly. This includes your responses, so read and write carefully. Do you use the same language or boilerplate

answer for every single one? Do your responses show that you really listened? Many that I found shrilled through the ear with such a sanitized tone that they reeked of lawyer's counsel instead of appreciative resident manager. When you respond, make it genuine and treat each answer with a personalized commendation.

4. Photos are an important part of the TripAdvisor experience. The photos taken by guests are characteristically awful. Those provided by the property can be much more practical. Make sure you have a selection that covers the guestroom and the bathrooms. Less important are scenic vistas, exteriors and common spaces. Whatever you do, set priorities for your selections.

5. TripAdvisor business listings are mandatory. This program gives you at least some added control over your presence on this website. The price of this utility is based on a number of factors with plenty of potential to heighten your exposure.

6. TripAdvisor is not enough. Sadly, I left TripAdvisor more confused about my hotel selection then when I began my search. I was less than impressed by some of the reviews: the text often addressed issues that were 'micro' rather than 'macro'. Do you follow a recommendation just because the front desk receptionist smiled at the guest or because there was a fruit basket upon arrival? I would rather hear about what's truly impactful such as the unique features of the property and guestroom comfort, both of which appear to be diluted by the minutia of critic wannabes. If I am to be considered as a potential consumer, then perhaps the manager's response feature is a good place to subtly reiterate any general information that would interest people like me.

I believe that TripAdvisor has at least some degree of usefulness; for checking up on a hotel that is on promotional special or included in a package. But as a primary search vehicle, frankly, there is too much variability to base a final decision solely on this site. Other sources such as well-wrought, professional reviews, real (traditional!) travel agents and travel publications seem to offer the additional depth and knowledge that give a traveler like myself the detail necessary to make monetary decisions. And, of course, never discount word of mouth.

If you are to judge TripAdvisor from my experience, then there are a few key teachings to write home about. For me, even with its prowess, it isn't the end all of hotel reviews, but one avenue for discourse with a propensity for minor grievances rather than sweeping issues. Hence, it's a good place to learn about where you are lacking and what needs polishing. Also, my own desires for hotel reviews might serve to reinforce any upcoming plans to incorporate guest reviews and live-feed testimonials into your property's home page.

Consider TripAdvisor as just one platform amongst all your other social media feeding you both future customers as well as suggestions from past visitors. As always, the key is in how you respond and what corrective actions you take.

HOTELIERS ARE GUILTY UNTIL PROVEN INNOCENT

This is an actual case, one that I believe underscores a fundamental flaw in our current social media environment.

A relatively new property has an on-going dispute with a neighbor. The dispute has nothing to do with the operation of the property, but rather the concern that the property will cause a reduction in property value due to noise, increased traffic and parking challenges. The neighbor is vocal about his concerns and expresses them to the municipal government, sighting possible bylaw improprieties. The local government rejects the neighbor's appeal.

Not satisfied with the outcome of the official complaint process, this individual resorts to social media as a means of extracting his revenge against the hotel. The approach involves writing extremely negative reviews, which are duly posted. The hotel manager reads these reviews and is puzzled by their context. In particular, the general manager notes the following:

- The review includes information that was revealed in confidence to the local neighborhood association and was unknown by anyone else, including the staff.
- The same reviewer posted very positive reviews of key competitive properties on the exact same day as the negative review.
- The day of posting is the same day that the municipality rejected the individual's bylaw complaint.

Round One

The general manager appeals to the website to have the review removed, the basis being that it wasn't genuine. The predictable response (company name removed): "Removing reviews is not something we take lightly, and it is only done when it violates our Terms of Service or Content Guidelines. We understand that you may be frustrated with our decision to keep the review intact, but unfortunately this is our position. We would again remind you that you can contact the reviewer directly or publicly comment on the review. Many reviewers respond favorably to business owners who are willing to engage in a constructive conversation."

Round Two

Not content with this automatic response, quite literally received within minutes of the complaint submission, the general manager provided a complete detailing of his analysis. The response took a couple of days, but read as follows (company name removed): "Thanks for taking the time to write us again. Removing reviews is not something we take lightly, and it is only done when it violates our Terms of Service or Content Guidelines. We understand that you may be frustrated with our decision to keep the review intact, but unfortunately our position remains the same.

"While we share your concern about the possibility of a defamatory review on our site, we don't adjudicate disputes between businesses and their reviewers. Congress acknowledged this predicament by passing legislation that provides statutory immunity to online service providers for the content of third-party posts. See 47 U.S.C. §230. The case law is clear on this point in support of online service providers because of concerns that they would otherwise be forced to remove third party posts every time someone raised issue with their contents. See Carafano v. Metrosplash. com. Inc., 339 F. 3d 1119 (9th Cir. 2003); Zeran v. America Online, Inc., 129 F.3d 327 (4th Cir. 1997); Barrett v. Rosenthal, 40 Cal. 4th 33 (Cal. 2006).

"That said, we will revisit your request if you provide to us a final judicial determination that the contents of a review are defamatory and will, at our discretion, remove such a review and take appropriate action with respect to the user responsible for the review. We encourage you again to contact the reviewer directly using the private messaging function on our site in order to constructively address your concerns. We do not recommend that you engage in anything other than a well-meaning dialog with the reviewer in order to sort out any misunderstandings."

Next Steps?

Needless to say, the general manager is not happy. Does a 'final judicial determination' mean that the property has to institute a local proceeding to deem this comment as defamatory, when that is clearly obvious to anyone reading it? Is defamatory conduct by a reviewer considered protected under the constitution as free speech? But what about the rights of the hotel? With rating averages calculated instantly and negative reviews having a clear impact on bookings, how can a hotel effectively respond?

My Recommendation

Hoteliers need to band together. An honest, but unfavorable review is acceptable, and should be considered a teaching tool to improve operations. However, reviews that are clearly suspect should be withheld from publication. The pendulum has swung too far to the favor of the reviewing agencies, who now wield too much unregulated power.

Moreover, consider just how laborious it is to go about seeking the removal of an online review. By the time this actually happens—if it actually happens—thousands of dollars of revenue might already be lost. Part of regulating the power of these reviewing agencies must come in the form of more open communication channels between the website and hotels. If managers have to spend so much time mitigating online defamation, then when will they have time to fix real issues?

WHO WATCHES THE WATCHMEN?

Catchy title, huh? Too good to be mine, of course. I'm quoting Alan Moore's 1980s magnum opus comic-book-turned-movie "Watchmen" set in a dystopic, Cold War-dominated Manhattan where an era of superhero watchdogs has come and gone, and the world teeters on the edge of nuclear destruction. Scrawled in graffiti across dingy, crime-laden back alleys is the phrase 'Who Watches the Watchmen?', thematically exploring the debate of police oversight and double-checks—nigh, triple-checks—on the institutions we are told to blindly trust.

A current news item for which I have my reservations has been the lawsuit against price fixing in the hotel industry. Both sides have facts to back up their claims, and every hotel manager no doubt has an opinion on the matter one way or another. Personally, I don't see the plaintiffs getting too far on this one, both in terms of injunctions against the OTAs or even in compensatory damages. However, I believe it to be part of a budding mindset amongst hoteliers.

We're scared and rushed for time. Sometimes too rushed to be scared. The landscape of hotel reservations and coordinating guest services is increasing an electronic endeavor. Events, trends, websites, systems, reviews, apps; all have to be monitored on a daily basis. Most internet-based booking services are geared towards offering the cheapest prices while neglecting brand features. Any person can now derail your reputation through a series of well-placed online remarks. In short, too much of the industry's locomotion is falling out of our grasp.

I see the price fixing class action lawsuit of 2012 as a manifestation of this percolating frame of mind. We recognize the need to fight back in order to retain our control and our liberty to conduct business fairly. We just don't know how to fight back. Not yet at least. OTA rate parity is itself a vast issue, not including any of the suspected price fixing. Instead of debating whether that lawsuit will bear fruit, I instead want to push on another hot button: third-party review websites. To clarify, there's extensive overlap between online booking agencies and travel review sites, as is the case for Expedia, Orbitz, Kayak, Hotwire, Travelocity and many others. For now, let's stick solely to the latter.

To illustrate this, I'll start with the neighbor dilemma, something a colleague experienced firsthand. A relatively new property had a tiff with a neighbor—nothing to do with actual operations, but rather the concern of reduced property values due to noise, traffic and parking challenges. The neighbor expressed his concerns to the municipal government, which rejected him outright. Not satisfied with the official outcome, the neighbor turned to social media for revenge with a series of scathing reviews. It was immediately apparent that the reviews were fictitious because they contained confidential information and were on posted within 24 hours of the municipal government's decision.

These things happen, and they wouldn't be that big an issue if the review website was more compliant to urgent requests. When the general manager appealed to have the defamatory comments removed, he was stonewalled with boilerplate replies and denial of responsibility. And so the reviews sat there in full view for two weeks while the review website 'diligently' processed his plea. A micro example, yes, but who knows how many potential customers were turned away during that time.

Then there's the cases illustrated by the New York Times article from Sunday, August 26, 2012 entitled, "The Best Reviews Money Can Buy." Although more a portrait of online book reviews, the message is clear and easily transferrable for hotels. Consumer reviews are valued for their verisimilitude. But what happens to this illusion of truth when, as the editorial cites, it's estimated that as much as one third of online reviews are dishonest? On a similar note, for a nominal fee you can buy Twitter followers and Facebook fans, or bribe your way into five-star bliss on TripAdvisor. This said, what measures are and should be in place to effectively differentiate between those bona fide opinions and those solicited?

Initial thoughts run to government oversight. The Federal Trade Commission has guidelines stipulating that companies or products publicly declare all paid-for endorsements, but their jurisdiction ends with the 50 states. Policing the internet? Good luck. Just ask SOPA and PIPA about that one. Likewise, every third-party review site stands behind its own policies. They take fabricated appraisals seriously. However, these are mere words on a page and don't speak to actual policing efficacy.

Whenever user activity edges on nefarious, as in the neighbor dilemma, it's still an arduous process of seeking corrective action from the website administrators whose hands stay clean throughout the ordeal. As for preventing a slanderer from posting in the first place, each site has its own system of checks and balances, but if users keep their profanities and trolling language under wraps, it's all but a guarantee their venomous remarks will make it on the page. Either way, hotels remain at the mercy of the travel review sites with little to no power to reprimand them for any apparent negligence or damages.

Enough of the potential for anonymous harm; let's focus on the damage created by too many positives. And there's a fleet of oil tankers full of positives. In fact, according to the 2008 study at the University of Illinois cited by the New York Times article, as much as 60% of all product reviews on Amazon are five stars and 20% are four stars. That's a serious skew and hotels aren't excluded. Perform a casual browse through TripAdvisor and the story reads the same. Positivity in online evaluations has become a marketing tool much like everything else. But putting all claims of fraudulence aside, if every review is a raving approval, then how's a consumer to gauge what is actually superior?

With so much capacity for maligned falsehoods and solicited affirmations, it calls into doubt not only a hotel's credibility on such a website, but the system itself. The illusion of truth is faltering. People no longer trust what they read online, or, at the very least, assess reviews with a jaded eye. Third-party travel review websites were designed as external customer advocates and hotel watchdogs, but who is watching over them?

Many argue that the intrinsic nature of free market economics acts as the foremost regulator—the genuine reviews will inevitably drown out the fictitious ones. The cascade of events goes like this. Someone pays for a slate of highly positive reviews. A bona fide consumer reads these reviews and bases a purchase on them. Then, aggravated by the discrepancy between the reviews and the reality, this consumer pens a corrective discourse for others to know the truth.

Although I'd love for laissez faire to rule the day, the numbers don't add up. In this case, the authentic review is one amongst perhaps dozens. How would a second user accurately distinguish real from fake, especially if there are more solicited appraisals still in the queue? Should he or she simply ignore every review that's a five star ovation? By the numbers, such a consumer would then be disregarding over half of what's out there!

Another solution is already being put to good use by message boards across the World Wide Web, and its rollout would seem unavoidable for travel review websites. Remove anonymity by forcing users to post through their Facebook accounts or with verified credit card information. A step in the right direction, albeit Facebook accounts can still be forged and revealing names on credit cards may be seen as a breach of confidentiality. Most travel review sites tied into an OTA have similar systems in place where users can only post a review once a purchase has been made, but even this has some gaping loopholes. Purchase orders can be faked and oftentimes the review doesn't have to be for the hotel last booked.

Despite these potential solutions on the horizon, again, they are mere words and actions need to be taken to restore credibility and make the system fair for all. Now, not tomorrow, now. Because, at the present, we're the patsies. It's the hotels that inevitably suffer from waning consumer trust and diluted brand recognition while the real culprits walk away scot-free.

I can't understate the volatility of these present conditions. In times of crisis, even when the consequences are elusive, the only way to effectively promote a change for the better is to band together. Instead of presenting a class action lawsuit for price fixing, perhaps one should have been filed against online travel review websites on the grounds of negligence and vicarious liability. I welcome the lawyers to chime in . . . particularly one willing to work on contingency!

A RATINGS EVOLUTION BEYOND TRIPADVISOR

If you will indulge me, I wish to bloviate on a particular issue that concerns a current client of mine and their organizational needs in the online space. This client owns two franchise properties located within a few miles of each other, one a Hilton Garden Inn (HGI), the other a Hilton Resort. Ergo, this unique situation lets us draw some interesting comparisons.

From a product standpoint, each of these properties is consistent with their own brand standards. The HGI has adequate furnishings, functional bathrooms and minimal extras. The public areas are not lavishly excessive (admittedly with a spectacular courtyard and poolside), and the restaurant and bar services are mostly self-serve. As a contrast, the Resort is utterly magnificent. Newly minted, the property has all of the amenities that one would expect from a luxury resort.

As you would expect from a superb operator, both properties also deliver exceptional guest service. Within their respective classes, they quite easily exceed the averages. Contextually, there is a higher level of service in the Resort with valet, concierge services and a greater front desk presence, not to mention a full-service restaurant and bar.

There is no question that even the most uninformed traveler would easily be able to differentiate the two products as distinct middle and upper echelon experiences. Clearly, both from a product and service standpoint, there are two distinct experiences offered to the guest, both excellent but certainly not interchangeable.

Enter TripAdvisor, which makes no distinction between the two properties, as both receive near identical and near perfect scores in their gross aggregate. If one was to make a travel decision solely based on TripAdvisor scores, the price difference would lead one to choose the HGI over the Resort; the former being priced lower to reflect its middle-tier selection of furnishings, amenities and services. (I wave my finger at TripAdvisor as it is the preeminent online review site used for travel research. But the argument I am about to put forward may as well apply to the rest of the websites which facilitate this modality.)

Another obvious question I find myself stymied by is if a guest pays more for a room, does he or she have higher expectations? Thus, if the property does not meet these superior requirements, the ratings given by guests in turn suffer. Yet, TripAdvisor does not have any shiningly thorough way to differentiate between properties with limited service and those offering a complete range of services; all properties are assessed on the same scale.

When selecting among products or regions that have a solid degree of familiarity, it's quite simple for the traveler to make a decision from the TripAdvisor ratings coupled with a reasonable knowledge of the brands inscribed. Yet, the proliferation of manifold brands makes it increasingly difficult for the customer to know what each brand has to offer. How do you know definitively if the product is limited service, economy, midrange or luxury? Is the generalized categorization from the last sentence even appropriate for today's highly stratified marketplace?

I'm led to believe that our industry has in many ways surpassed the value afforded by TripAdvisor. Just about every property has finagled their ratings capabilities to the maximum. As properties have honed their skills and focused solutions on flawless guest services, the rating differences on TripAdvisor have narrowed substantially. Every property (that's worth staying it!) is a 4.5, 4.6, 4.7 or 4.8; the spread is no longer statistically significant.

This is not to say that TripAdvisor lacks all significance or utility. Its inherent bipartisan universality makes it an important tool for what it was originally designed to achieve: red-tagging properties that do not deliver quality services or value while providing general managers with immediate, qualitative and actionable guest feedback.

But I believe that there is a need for TripAdvisor and all other online hotel review sites to expand their horizons. More specifically, there needs to be more distinctions based upon the types of properties: full service versus limited service; higher price versus lower price. Just as you wouldn't compare a slasher horror film to a John Grisham courtroom drama adaptation, it's not fair to hold budget hotels to the same ubiquitous rating scale as a boutique luxury abode.

In the interim, we just rely on a consumer's intuition, both to know what they want and to take TripAdvisor's point system with a grain of salt. After all, online rating sites are but one component of the purchasing decisions; I only wish there was third-party information to point viewers in the right direction prior to passing judgment. I'm aware that there are quite a few hubs that dog-ear specific strata of hotels, but these have thus far failed to reach the prevalence of the major online review sites or the OTAs which also host such functionality.

REVISITING ROOM KEY

When Room Key was first launched in January 2012, I admit I was skeptical. My primary detraction was that the website, even with the horsepower of six major chains, lacked the wherewithal to complete the consumer purchasing journey—from flight to hotel and finally to car rental. This, in addition to the egregious head start that the OTAs already have, makes for a formidable case against Room Key's long-term viability. But numbers don't lie and the latest digits have me doing a double-take.

Using their patented normalization analytics process, the research firm Compete Inc. stated that Room Key obtained more than 4 million unique visitors during July 2012 with over 6 million total visits through the month. Tallying these stats points to a growth rate hovering near 20% per-month. Their results indicate that roughly 90% of this proliferating traffic came from the founding brands' sites (Choice, Hilton, Hyatt, InterContinental, Marriott and Wyndham) while less than 2% came from paid or natural searches. Additionally, it's reported that Room Key has a similar click-through rate back to partner sites when shoppers come from external search pages.

Compete Inc. accounts for these lopsided percentages by classifying Room Key as an evolving meta-search engine whereby a pop-up window redirects users to the booking website upon leaving a founding brand's internal pages. It's an exit traffic strategy, accruing users already accessing a partner's brand.com (hence 'meta').

According to Google Analytics, the September 2012 figures estimated that Room Key received more than 14 million travelers per month. Adding more powder to the keg was the announcement that this meta-search tool was to add three new partners—La Quinta Inns & Suites, Leading Hotels of the World and Millennium Hotels & Resorts—rounding out the site's breadth of economy, midscale and luxury offerings.

Furthermore, as of May 2012, Room Key finished its integration with Travelocity's Res99 network, adding to their inventory on the site. No doubt this action greatly expanded consumer choices. But, as Compete Inc. observed, it had also countervailed the flow back into the founding brands' websites with Res99 amassing over 11% of the total booking-driven transfers for June 2012; a percentage that was increasing month-over-month and potentially deflecting users to an OTA to complete their reservations.

Despite all the positive growth markers aggregated by Compete Inc., the real skull-scratcher was that, whether assisted by Res99's incorporation or not, the founding partners' ratio of bookings lost to the OTAs independent of Room Key visitation increased to nearly 24% for July 2012. All in all, Room Key was making progress, but dangers still lingered in the shadows.

To me, this heightened meta-search traffic appears to be of the 'preaching to the choir' lot. The exit strategy model is a closed loop, feeding off guests who are previously exposed and already loyal. Room Key works a powerful adjunctive for visitors to the partners' brand.com pages, but ancillary nonetheless. That 2% natural and paid search metric means that there aren't many new consumers reaching the website and thus it's not significantly advantageous towards augmenting voice share. People appear to still be making their final reservations through their preferred OTAs, but due to Room Key's accurate property information and comprehensive design, it's becoming the perfect cross-reference tool.

By this interpretation, Compete Inc.'s statistics were a tad underwhelming, but not entirely doom and gloom. With increased traffic comes an increased opportunity to deliver a simplified and pleasurable travel booking experience. Exposure is the first step. However, consumers need to be incentivized to fully switch from an OTA to Room Key. Part of that motivation will come from persevering with the expansion plans and adding more hotels onto the website. Room Key is a distribution channel that consumers are indeed using and your property should be included.

On the other hand, I believe a more efficacious answer is in overtly advertised loyalty programs. Make it known that booking through Room Key, other similarly sponsored reservation engines or directly through a brand.com site (and not through a third-party, high commission OTA) is the only way for a traveler to earn their respective program's loyalty points or rewards. This is a strong policy and it has clear demarcations. I'm sure there are other solid hypotheses as to how to make Room Key truly effective beyond mere through-traffic into a workable competitor for the OTAs. My take in the short-term is by emphasizing loyalty.

LIBRARY HOTEL COLLECTION:
THE SECRET TO TRIPADVISOR SUCCESS

A late 2012 issue of Condé Nast Traveler extolled the success of the Library Hotel Collection's four properties. Perennially, the organization's boutique-style hotels rank in the Top 10 of the 437 TripAdvisor listings in New York City proper. How is it that these small (not one property exceeds 103 rooms) and less-than-brand-new properties continually deliver such stellar results?

I'm lucky to have worked with Adele Gutman, the chain's affable VP of Sales, Marketing and Revenue. In her own words, the answer is simple, "We cherish our guests and we let them know by our actions that they are appreciated. We respect their needs and care for them as we would a member of our family."

Easier said than done. I was determined to learn for myself, so I joined Adele on an inspection of all four properties. Here are my observations:

- *No 'Innkeeper Syndrome' here.* These hotels treat their guests to a number of supposed 'extras'. This means free WiFi in guestrooms, the lobby and all public spaces. It also includes: free breakfast, free in-room bottled water, free all-day coffee and snacks, free evening wine and cheese, and free newspapers. That's a lot of 'free'! In an era of endless add-ons and drip pricing, the impression left with guests is probably one of awe or, frankly, incredibility.

- *Flawless housekeeping.* I viewed six guestrooms and could not find an error or item out of place. The bathrooms were small and nothing new, but literally sparkled. The hallway carpets had no stains or scuff marks on doorframes, nor was there anything misplaced in the lobbies or restaurants.

- *Small, efficient 'people-sized' facilities.* These are not large properties. Check-in feels more like walking into a private home than a hotel. The restaurants and lounges have a clubby feel to encourage guest interaction, yet it is not overbearing.

- *The lounge acts like a living room.* The private quarters are small. There is room service only during the day, not 24-hours—a definite faux pas for many in the business. However, they try to make the clubrooms and other common spaces such as rooftops so inviting that it encourages guests to spend time in the lounge. This gives the staff an opportunity to interact with the guests and build the relationship. It also expands the guests' enjoyment of the full space in the hotel. The guestroom size itself becomes less important when the common spaces feel like your own living room. And it works.

- *Distinctive with memorable elements.* Each property is unique; from endless collections of books and the use of the Dewey Decimal System to the number of rooms and an ode to the movie Casablanca in its namesake property. These little subtle details act as the adjectives and adverbs to the nouns and verbs of the hotel experience; they add texture, color and true character.
- *Everyone cares.* I met over two dozen people, perhaps more, and everyone appeared concerned for their guests' wellbeing. Their actions were not stilted or fake, as they exhibited genuine service orientation. It's a system of consummate perfection that includes managers continually reviewing and offering constructive coaching for their team members. They were always looking for ways to heighten the air of luxury, and to treat guests like princes and princesses.

It is refreshing to note that getting back to basics works. The Library Hotel Collection does not set a goal of over-wowing their guests with excesses and grandeur. Rather, they wow them with kindness and use the tools available to everyone in the hotel business: common sense with a shrewd guest focus. This may be difficult to duplicate in a 300-room or a 600-room property, but the lessons learned here are nonetheless universally applicable. Treat the guest as you would a friend visiting your own home or better, and you will be amazed at the results.

A NEW APPROACH TO ONLINE DISTRIBUTION AND INTEGRATION

Arising from discussions about Room Key, the OTAs and where online hospitality channels are headed, I had a conversation with Moe Ibrahim, the CEO of the reservation and experiential website Journeyful. It's a fascinating take on online distribution systems.

The platform is designed to be cheaper than a hotel's existing booking engine so that every channel becomes a direct channel. If a hotel generates a booking from its website using Journeyful's white-labeled booking engine, it's a small commission. If the booking comes wholly through journeyful.com, it's the same small commission. Ditto for travel agents that book through the platform's wholesale booking system and for mobile.

The company's goal is to consolidate all of a hotel's bookings on one platform at a very modest transaction fee. I undertook this interview as a part of the long search for methods of disrupting the OTAs' stranglehold on hotels. Perhaps the concepts built within Journeyful can help properties realize that the OTAs aren't the only way to sell rooms.

What's your take on the OTAs and their influence on the industry?

Since 2005, I have been investing in and turning around troubled hotels in Asia. Initially, the OTAs had been our allies in profit, bringing in bookings from markets that our hotels hadn't been able to access; namely, leisure travelers from countries in which we had no sales presence. Given this awareness penetration, we agreed to pay their hefty commissions, typically between 20% and 25% of the gross booking value. As this was incremental revenue to our hotels, our interests were aligned.

However, over time, a greater percentage of our rooms were being booked through these OTAs. It became clear that the OTAs were no longer supplementing our occupancy, but rather, competing openly against our own marketing efforts in our primary feeder markets, quickly cannibalizing our direct business. The OTAs were and continue doing this by:

- *Google AdWords and Paid Search.* Using this tactic, an OTA runs a guerrilla Google AdWords and paid search campaign, buying variations of a hotel name as keywords. This means that customers looking for that specific property are directed to the OTA website, often lured by misleading taglines like '50% to 75% off'. Some OTAs are doing this despite the fact that there's no contract with the hotel—they are aggressively targeting consumers and feeding off of the hotel's marketing efforts.
- *Artificial Strike-Through Pricing.* When pulling up hotel rates on an OTA, the strike-through pricing is often fictitious. It gives the illusion that great savings (once again 50-75% off) are available on the OTA. Comparing the 'discounted' rate on the OTA website with that on the official website will show it's the same rate. OTAs will show prices before taxes and service fees, again confusing the consumer.
- *Share-Shifting.* Suppose a user searches for a specific property on an OTA and there's no listed inventory. Often, the OTAs will quickly avert the customer's attention to the immediate competition.

On the grand scale, the OTAs have brainwashed hotels to abandon one of the most basic tenets of yield management: demand is largely price inelastic. This means that lowering your room rate will not increase demand over the long-term. It often creates a temporary demand bump for your property, but as your competitors also lower prices, occupancy will redistribute across the competitor set and everyone suffers from reduced margins.

As more and more guests demand discounted pricing, and more and more bookings are directed through third parties where commissions can be as high as 40%, hotels are being squeezed on all fronts. Moreover, the latest features being introduced by these OTAs are frequently designed to divert guests completely towards those hotels paying them the highest commissions. It's no longer about quality for the consumer; it's now about maximizing profit for the OTA.

As a result, the hotel industry is becoming less profitable for hotel owners. Ultimately, this hurts the customer as less profitable reservations means less money will be invested in service and maintenance. Hotels are losing, travel agents are disappearing and consumers will lose. The only winners are the OTAs.

We first opened our dialogue by discussing the merits of Room Key. In your opinion, where does the website stand right now?

Room Key is an OTA. If it looks like an OTA and gets compensated like an OTA, it's an OTA. Moreover, its practices of recommending different hotel options for a consumer during a search and using third parties to quickly populate the site with inventory inherently conflicts with the philosophy of generating direct business for a hotel. Theoretically, it's a good thought; an OTA owned by the travel industry—but this is not Room Key in its current form.

How do OTAs tap into consumer behavior patterns?

Let's first examine the OTA model. This model is designed to influence consumers based purely on price. In fact, OTAs take great strides to commoditize hotels. They often don't even mention the hotel, just the price—share-shifting at its purest.

Next, examine consumer behavior. It is estimated that a leisure consumer averages nearly 23 site visits per hotel purchase, visiting an average of 8 to 9 sites roughly 2 to 3 times each. This infers a definite lack of trust. For a hotel, it's not just about the leisure consumer. Hotels get business from travel agencies and corporate groups. What happens to those contracts the moment a hotel uploads a flash sale rate on an OTA? Technology and online distribution are moving so fast that it's all too easy for hotels to use these tools the wrong way.

What are some other ways that the internet is affecting traveler behavior?

More and more, bookings are happening last minute. Guests are putting up anonymous bad reviews on sites like TripAdvisor with the expectation that the hotel will contact them and give them a free stay. The internet is a powerful tool that has the potential to create real value for travelers and hotels alike. Unfortunately, today, there's a tremendous amount of confusion amongst travelers.

SHALL WE TINGO?

Before I get into my observations and conclusions regarding the latest online travel agency, Tingo, let me take you to a parallel retail experience. Suppose you decide to buy the latest LCD or Plasma television. You go to the local big box electronics retailer and make your selection amongst a myriad of brands, many of which are at best vaguely familiar. They all look great in the showroom. But, how do you know if you got the best price?

Retail Price Protection

The retailer generally offers some sort of guarantee that its price will be equal to or better than that advertised for a competitive retailer. Moreover, they will give you the difference if you bring an ad to them displaying a better discount. These guarantees often include protection against their own price reduction for up to 90 days in the future.

Few buyers are as doggedly meticulous as to follow every price change in the marketplace. Plus, the time taken to go back to the store in order to save a few dollars is really not worth it. Thus, the systems generally afford retailers a limited downside liability by offering such a lucrative price guarantee.

The Tingo Model

Tingo is designed to work in the same capacity. Buy a hotel room from them, and if the price of the room goes down in the future, they will automatically protect your investment by cancelling and reissuing the reservation at the lower price. There is no additional work required on the part of the buyer. Tingo does this on its own without even notifying you until they have secured the price reduction. For the hotel room purchaser, this is the equivalent of buying a price protection plan for your stay.

Revenue Management Issues

While all of this may seem ideal for the guest, I am wondering why any hotel would want to opt in. Here's the deal in a simplistic example. You have ten rooms and sell eight at an average of $100 each through Tingo. You want to sell the last two, so you drop your price to $90. You may not sell these remaining two rooms to new customers, as Tingo will automatically convert two of its rooms from $100 to $90. Depending on how you manage your inventory, all of your sold inventory would now be at the lower rate.

Every price reduction you take now has the added cost of giving this benefit to everyone who has already booked with you through Tingo. To avoid this from happening, revenue managers can only look at increasing prices as you get closer to the arrival date, rather than enjoying the flexibility of making decisions to alter prices up or down based on market conditions. In effect, Tingo would seriously raise the costs of any last minute price reductions, as all previous sales would be subject to discounts.

Why Would Any Hotelier Do This?

The concept of giving something extra is a good one. Savvy hoteliers do this not by reducing price, but rather, by giving upgrades upon check-in or through value-added features. Customers who are repeat guests, VIPs, members of hotel loyalty programs and certain credit card holders also receive additional bonuses.

But offering a price guarantee, at least to me, runs smack in the face of yield management strategies. This is one more cog in the wheel of turning hotels into commodities. Customers are already having problems differentiating one hotel chain from another. For the consumer, Tingo now takes the time of a purchase out of mind. It's no longer about following rates or adhering to a given set of brands, but just locking in a reservation and hoping for it to drop.

The Bottom Line

Unless you are pretty certain that your rates, once established, will only go up and never be decreased as dates approach, you may want to give

Tingo a try. But, like my stance with the other OTAs, steps taken to benefit the consumer often harm the hotel.

Certainly, upon reading this, I hope that you would check to see how your property is represented and if customers booking through Tingo are indeed offered a genuine price guarantee. If you are unhappy with what you see, speak to your revenue manager and have him or her manage your inventory appropriately.

A CALL FOR A COMMISSION FREE DAY

All properties rely (to varying degrees) on OTAs for leisure bookings. It's inescapable. And for most, it's a love-hate relationship; everyone appreciates the room generation, seemingly on demand. But this volume comes at a price, as for an independent property, the commission rate can be as much as 30%. Commissions at that level make us all yearn for the good old days of traditional travel agents and their standardized 10% rates. How do you stop? How do you wean your business off this seemingly endless gravy train of near-instant reservations generated through an impressive global electronic distribution network?

Don't get me wrong, the OTAs are brilliant marketers. They rely extensively on broadcast advertising, having the critical mass and clout to generate high levels of awareness. They also have a better reservations system than most hotels. They also book airfare, making it easier for a consumer to complete their vacation planning in a one-stop-shop manner. But being brilliant marketers does not mean they are the hotelier's salvation.

Rather, my feeling is that the OTAs are the quintessential Trojan horse for the hotel industry. It starts when we let them in and give them our remnant inventory. First we're happy to have the business, filling dead spots in the calendar and smoothing out occupancy valleys. Then slowly, they win customers over to only book through them, minimizing hotel loyalty programs and ensuring their permanent survival through detailed contracts that protect against possible channel conflicts.

Living in Ancient Troy

In ancient Troy, the Trojan Horse allowed the Greek army access to the city, and once inside, well, it wasn't pretty. Now think of your property as Troy. You probably started with a few reservations on just one or two OTAs, but with the advent of a revenue management system, this was rapidly expanded to cover the entire spectrum. Computer programs now assist your revenue manager in allocating inventory and maximizing coverage. This only accelerates the success of OTAs' full penetration of your annual occupancy plan.

Run the numbers. Extend your OTA share to double or even triple its current level with no increase in occupancy, swapping rooms with those generated through your brand.com channels. Once you've done that, take a look at your bottom line. How do you feel about the resultant figures? Many hoteliers I have spoken to are aghast when they analyze this scenario.

Time to Fight Back

I have read many of these OTA contracts. Well written and professional, they have but one (in keeping with the classics theme) Achilles Heel. There is nothing written that mandates you to give them inventory if you do not want to. Inventory supply is voluntary. The best defense is to give them zero inventory—nothing, nada, zilch. Many will say this is too harsh and too hasty. After all, you have owners to satisfy and rooms to fill.

What I am proposing is an OTA-free day. It works like a meat-free day. For one 24-hour stretch, you abstain from consuming any animal protein, thereby affording your body a brief period where it can expunge most of the meat-induced carcinogens from the body. If a hotel can pick one day, one day where it allows zero check-ins except through our own direct sources (brand website, telephone direct, central reservations and so on), then it will be able to see if it really needs the OTAs, or whether it can live without them. Now apply this to the industry as a whole with every hotel in a region choosing not to partake in the OTAs' business model for one 24-hour period. What do you think the results would be?

As a rallying cry for all, we would need a date the entire industry could agree on. Sure, there would be hotels that say, "Wow, what an opportunity for my property." But, if we all banded together, then we would get a feel for whether we could survive without a steadfast dependence on the OTAs. And the success measurement would be its impact on the bottom line, not simply occupancy levels.

If this approach worked, we could extend the OTA-free period to a full week. Then, as the commission costs in the plan became reduced, funds would be put back into building revenue through promoting the property directly. This idea is purely hypothetical and rather grandiose, but I propose as one possible way to unchain ourselves from the enslavement of the OTAs. The question is: are you ready to fight back?

EXAMPLES OF EXCELLENCE

The Adobe Grand Villas in Sonoma, Arizona has each room modeled after various aspects of the Wild West, guaranteeing a fun and memorable experience.

INTRODUCTION

This last section of articles is the most straightforward. Through work and through travel, I've come to know a fair number of hospitality leaders—hoteliers who are more than just competent and can offer valuable insights for those willing to learn. Whenever I visit a property, I make a habit of interviewing the general manager, or other senior ranking director, and reporting on the successes of what they do so that all may share in their acquired knowledge. Over time, these dialogues and hotel reviews add up, and they have been summarized here for your reading pleasure.

My hope for you is to learn from the best as well as the rest, and then form your own conclusions. Study the following passages and I guarantee you will find answers and tips applicable to your own situation, whether on the surface or hidden within the responses provided by my interviewees. Oftentimes, a hotelier may perform a successful action so effortlessly that they are no longer conscious of what they are doing exactly. As such, you really have to read between the lines. No person or property is the same, so take pieces from each article then form your own judgment about what makes for a great hotelier and a great hotel.

IN SEARCH OF HOTEL EXCELLENCE: HOTEL BERLIN, BERLIN

A trip to Berlin saw me stay at Hotel Berlin, Berlin (no this is not a typographical error, the property's name is 'Hotel Berlin, Berlin' located in Berlin). And while I have been to Germany many times before, this was my first outing to the capital city.

As a relatively frequent traveler to Europe (typically three to four times per year), my travels have generally taken me to London, Paris or, when on holidays, to more Mediterranean destinations. Berlin, somehow, never appeared on my radar. Before discussing the property, let me give you a brief overview of the city.

If you are a baby boomer, perhaps your thoughts of Berlin are of President Kennedy and the Berlin Airlift. Or, if you're younger your memory might move to the scenes of the wall being dismantled. Both of these images are wildly outdated. Berlin is alive, rejuvenated and clearly bucking the malaise that many other Mediterranean and North American cities felt during the ripples of recession economics. The architecture is a mixture of refurbished and ultramodern. The Tiergarten in the center of the city rivals Manhattan's Central Park and the traffic is nowhere near as bad as London, Paris or other capital cities.

My daughter studied fine art in London and had previously captivated me with the stories of the contemporary art movement taking over Berlin. The East Berlin suburbs apparently have very cheap rent for artists who typically need big open spaces. When visiting, I browsed numerous private art galleries while the museums and public spaces were equally impressive. On a Sunday afternoon, it seemed as if the entire world was out on their bicycles or walking with kids in strollers. The shops were crowded with buyers, not just gawkers. The food was excellent; the wines unique and, of course, the beer exceeded all expectation. As you can tell, I'm quite enthusiastic about my trip.

Hotel Berlin, Berlin is located in the western side of the downtown core, just south of Tiergarten and a block away from Potsdamer Platz, a bustling commercial street. This location makes it well suited for both leisure and business. During my four-night stay which encompassed a weekend, the guest mix was about equal. It was indeed refreshing to see conventional visitors intermingled with backpackers, tour groups and FITs, all seemingly content with their stay.

The property's 700 rooms are laid out in a five-story hollow square pattern with a center corridor spine breaking the square in two. Meeting rooms on the main floor are creatively identified through geographic city names, clustered into areas defined as continents. Breakout rooms are identified with island names and located throughout the property. This unique approach creates a positive atmosphere amongst business customers and helps sort out what would otherwise be pandemonium.

Our meeting was in the Washington Room. One minor and unusual complaint: the rooms had so much sunlight that it partially drowned out the visuals on my PowerPoint presentation. Compare that to most environments we see in hotels these days where meeting rooms tend to be so drab and caked in artificial fluorescence that the audience is half asleep before the presentation even begins. No worries here—the whole world is going tablet anyway! Last of all, free WiFi with excellent bandwidth throughout the property keeps everyone in touch with their office and loved ones.

I had a luxury suite which had several features that were both quite unique and impressive. Setting this aside, I had an opportunity to inspect some of the core-style guestrooms. The smallest room, which might be considered a 'petit', was a model of efficiency and offered property management the ability to deliver a competitive market price point. As the rooms increased in size, so too did the bed size, number of chairs and added furnishings. All rooms utilized modern graphics on their walls, themed with other property elements, to create a high degree of both consistency and memorability.

Food and beverage revolved around the restaurant named Julius. Daily buffet breakfasts are included with your stay and were in keeping with the tradition of providing a multitude of items to allow for different selections daily. The restaurant seems to expand somewhat caterpillar-like, as additional linear sections are added on as necessary to meet seating requirements. We enjoyed one light lunch in the restaurant, which was efficient, tasty and well-prepared. Our welcome night dinner was sensational, with various white wines demonstrating the efficacy and craftsmanship of local winemakers.

I asked the property's managing director, Cornelia Kausch, to describe some of the challenges she's facing with the business and her approach to maintaining the property's success. "Like our namesake city, Hotel Berlin, Berlin reflects the new values of responsive accommodations. Be efficient, with a look to our past, but also with a keen eye to the technologically-enhanced future. Our growth will come from the management of our channel mix and further development of our own brand.com business as we continue to evolve the characteristics that differentiate us."

When asked about specific business drivers, Ms. Kausch responded, "Our FIT business will continue to be driven by the buoyant local tourism marketplace. Our MICE programs respect the need for productive, cost-efficient meetings, which are well-served by our location, layout, critical mass, venue style, value-driven price points and commitment to this sector."

After my brief stay in Hotel Berlin, Berlin, I am convinced that Ms Kausch and her team are on the right track to deliver on her business goals. And for those that haven't been, I'd definitely recommend that you check out Germany's capital city!

(Since the publication of this article, Cornelia Kausch has taken the role as Country Manager for Pandox AB, responsible for the company's four properties in Germany including Hotel Berlin, Berlin.)

IN SEARCH OF HOTEL EXCELLENCE: WICKANINNISH INN

In late June, I took my summer vacation by flying out to the west coast of Vancouver Island, Canada, staying at the renowned Wickaninnish Inn just outside of the remote, surfing Mecca of Tofino and right on the rocks overlooking the mighty Pacific. But what caught my eye first were its ratings. Travel + Leisure readers voted the Wickaninnish Inn as their top-rated Canadian resort in 2012, and the Inn has consistently ranked as their top Canadian resort, or near the top, since it opened its doors in 1996. Additionally, Condé Nast Traveler ranked the Inn on their Gold List as Best for Leisure Facilities in 2012. What makes this place so perfect?

Becoming an official member of Relais & Châteaux only 15 months after its opening, the Wickaninnish Inn has a strong family origin. Construction began in the summer of 1995 with 46 deluxe guestrooms and The Pointe Restaurant, and the site has a chronology of expansions, including the Ancient Cedars Spa, the Lookout Library, the Driftwood Café, a fitness room and the Beach Building which includes 30 additional rooms. As of now, the Inn totals 63 deluxe guestrooms and 12 suites.

At the end of my vacation, I reached out to the Inn's Managing Director, Charles McDiarmid, to glean some more information about what makes for a spectacular stay. Mr. McDiarmid, whose father launched the Wickaninnish Inn, previously worked at the Four Seasons Vancouver and his experience there has been critical for bringing the Inn from great to exceptional.

McDiarmid's time at the Four Seasons greatly influenced his training protocols. Two key lessons were, first, the importance of properly motivating and encouraging staff members and, second, creating those magical moments for each and every guest. Even though it's a Canadian property, McDiarmid is adamant about hiring internationally, employing people from 14 countries across six continents. In fact, his HR Director makes a point to visit Asia and Europe once a year to maintain relationships with leading hospitality schools.

All this coalesces into extraordinary guest services. This is critical when considering the resort's isolation and the need to truly make visitors feel comfortable and at home. Global hiring certainly helps, as it means they can accommodate guests in an array of languages.

The average length of a guest's stay at the Inn is about average for luxury properties—2.3 days for fall/winter and 2.9 for spring/summer; perhaps somewhat lighter than expected for a resort. Based on my own experiences, I would chalk this up to two main factors: a variable climate that is not receptive to 'lying by the pool' resort behavior, and the isolation of the property. Given those attributes, the length of stay is still higher than expected, most likely due to the superb accommodations and F&B offerings.

My room was indeed luxurious, but not over-the-top lavish. Sitting at my panorama ocean view (recommended room type) window was a pair of binoculars and an accompanying bird guide, perfect for exploring the surrounding old-growth temperate rainforest and nearby national park. The weather on Vancouver Island is so variable that instead of an umbrella, the hotel supplies a full attire of rain gear with boots of all sizes ready at check-in.

In fact, the strong occupancy numbers for the fall/winter season are primarily due to avid storm watchers. Due to the ocean-oriented climate, it rarely snows in Tofino (unlike the rest of Canada!). People come specifically to the Inn to view the ten-meter waves crashing onto the beach and cliff rocks, which can be done from the sandy beach itself, from the restaurant or from each guestroom's window-side fireplace along with a glass of red wine.

This brings us to the F&B side of things, which, considering how remote the Inn is, operates under the assumption that guests will eat most meals in-house at The Pointe Restaurant or the Driftwood Café. As such, there is excellent selection on the menu and items cycle frequently. There's a tremendous focus on local cuisine and the chef is constantly searching for artisanal suppliers on Vancouver Island. Not only is the wine list exhausting, but equal thought was given to the scotch menu—260 whisky options in total. It's even common for people to drive up from Victoria for the day (a 4.5 hour drive each way) just for the food!

I can't emphasize enough how picturesque the views were from my guestroom. It was truly like waking up in paradise. No wonder so many people migrate to this part of the world in search of spiritual solace. But, mind you, that solace doesn't come cheap. The Wickaninnish Inn is not overly revenue-managed and follows a traditional rate structure preset according to the season. I arrived in late June to the tune of just over $500 per night (food and beverage extra).

At such a profound ADR, this case study ushers in the subject of what people really expect for such a price. Is it just sensational surroundings and exceptional F&B, or is there something more, something extra? What level of guest services do people expect at this caliber of resort? What are people's sticking points?

Obviously, with top accolades year-after-year, as well as stellar online scores, the Wickaninnish Inn is doing a lot more right than wrong. If you have the time and want to experience one of the Canada's (if not the world's) most unique properties, I definitely recommend you go check out the Wick!

IN SEARCH OF HOTEL EXCELLENCE: AVARI TOWERS, KARACHI, PAKISTAN

When you think of Karachi, what image or emotion first comes to mind? For me, being in Toronto and inundated with the oftentimes hellfire and brimstone of American news media, this Pakistani metropolis doesn't particularly evoke positive sentiment. I'm fairly geographically educated (I'm in the hotel business after all!) so I know that Karachi is a bustling port at the crossroads of Asia, Arabia and East Africa, and is a financial powerhouse now home to over 20 million people of numerous cultural and religious backgrounds.

Pakistan itself is a country to watch. It's the sixth most populous country in the world and a burgeoning manufacturing center, falling right behind India in terms of socioeconomic progress. Although the government has been hit with a few military coups in the past, it nonetheless follows a democratic constitutional system that elects more women to parliament than any other Muslim-majority country.

But Karachi is also consistently ranked as one of the most dangerous cities in the world, suffering from trafficking, burglaries, rioting, extortion and ethnic clashes. Furthermore, many people in North America now only envision Pakistan as the country that harbored Osama Bin Laden and the immediate neighbor to the tragic warzone that is Afghanistan. It isn't a stretch to say that Karachi doesn't rank very high on Westerners' bucket lists.

Despite this inherent stigma, it would be juvenile to assume that Karachi offers no lessons for the world abroad. And indeed, that's exactly the case when discussing the Avari Towers and their commitment to good old-fashioned service with the General Manager, Gordon James Gorman. The Avari Towers, the flagship property for the Avari Hotel group, is a five-star hotel and rated the best accommodation in Karachi on TripAdvisor. Despite room rates far exceeding local competitors, the Avari Towers consistently outperforms even the major international brands in the city. It's been family owned and operated since its inception, and Gorman attributes much of the hotel's success to the earnest dedication to service from the chairman, Mr. Byram Avari.

Normally, the title 'In Search of Hotel Excellence' is reserved for properties to which I have visited and had a chance to parlay with a senior director. But Gorman is an avid reader of mine, and with over 40 years in the hotel business under his belt—five of which at the Avari Towers—he is proud to exclaim that he's saved the best for last. After a dozen energetic emails detailing the Avari Towers' unique service offerings, it's undeniable that something special is happening here—an oasis of luxury amidst so much apparent turmoil.

What Gorman emphasizes is personal, physical service through many creative forms. As you would have it, his recipe for success is to treat all guests with the same level of service and gratitude that he would expect from his closest friends. This commitment begins with a phone call to guests once they are in transit from the airport to the hotel in a designated limousine. Gorman frequently meets guests upon arrival in the lobby, welcome drink and key card at the ready.

Just take a minute and let that image simmer; arriving in Pakistan, escorted directly to your hotel and greeted without delay by the GM, a boisterous Scotsman no less. Talk about first impressions—very reassuring. I stress that face-to-face communication is the only way to build genuine rapport and this is a clear-cut example.

Along these lines, not only are staff members trained to be friendly and attentive—carrying the company's mission statement on a laminated card in their breast pockets at all times—but also, they are habitually more appreciative of a warm handshake than a tip. In fact, tipping at the Avari Towers' adheres to a rather unorthodox and altruistic custom. Their in-house Tips For Life Foundation ensures that whenever gratuities are given to staff members from the guests, the money is shared with street kids and orphans.

This high caliber of introductions is carried forward to when guests first reach their rooms. Here, they are welcomed with an Avari Apple (grown onsite) and served with a crisp napkin, fruit knife, fork and handwritten card. If guests want more refreshments, they need only call room service or head over to the fruit bar at the breakfast buffet, as you would expect from a five-star locale.

But there are many other subtle and exceptional touches apart from the entrance. For instance, if you find yourself in the dining room, don't be surprised if an adolescent staff member approaches you and asks if you want your shoes cleaned. Free of charge, you will be given a pair of comfy slippers for the five-minute duration that your shoes are polished and scented.

Gorman was also very excited to discuss the hotel's new Sock and Shawl Butler Service. The day you're scheduled to depart, a butler will visit your room with a letter from Gorman and a silver tray. On that tray is an Irish linen handkerchief carefully wrapped around a flower along with a selection of at least ten different colors of socks and ten different colors of soft Pashmina shawls for your choosing—keeping your feet snug and your neck warm. The silk shawls are purchased from boutique shops in Karachi and Lahore (the country's second largest city with 11 million people), while Gorman himself selects the vibrant cotton socks during his regular trips to Bangkok and Edinburgh.

"During my five years of managing this fine hotel, I've yet to meet a guest who didn't smile when presented with a brand new pair of socks or a luxurious, soft Pashmina shawl," remarks Gorman. "Many of our regular guests often hoist their suited trouser legs to compare sock colors or shawls in the restaurant during breakfast. It's a very communal experience, and one of the highly personalized services that delights international travelers to Pakistan; a small token of our sincere gratitude for their support."

And I'm very thankful to Gorman for bringing this to my attention. Giving physical gifts is an excellent method to develop healthy (and memorable) relationships with guests. In the end, the Avari Towers is yet another terrific illustration that upgrading your guest services doesn't necessarily have to be a purely technology-centric enterprise. There's a reason why this hotel is a shining star with a very loyal following in a city that may be troublesome to visit. Gorman, his staff and their unique expression of service no doubt play a key role. Just a reminder that you must always be creative in your approach. Constantly look for ways to add the personal, face-to-face touch.

IN SEARCH OF HOTEL EXCELLENCE: HOTEL PALOMAR PHILADELPHIA

Have you ever been to Philadelphia? Rightfully described as the 'Birthplace of America' for its prominent role in US history, this city often flies under the radar when flung into a category that includes other East Coast cities like New York, Boston, Washington and Miami. This said, sojourning to Philadelphia is a must; art, museums, history, sports, architecture, cheesesteaks, the city has it all. Convincing, huh?

A past business trip there afforded me the chance to stay at the Hotel Palomar in the central, chichi Rittenhouse Square neighborhood. Renovating the 1929 Art Deco husk of the former home of the American Institute of Architects, this 230-room hotel is now fully LEED-certified and totally ultramodern. Arising from all this splendor was my meeting with Wendell Bush, the affable Chief Experience Officer (General Manager), discussing, of course, his management philosophy.

As background, the Hotel Palomar is part of the 50+ properties that make up the Kimpton Hotel & Restaurant Group. Founded in 1981, the core idea behind every Kimpton asset is the oft-zealous attitude of 'hospitality with personality'. Bill Kimpton, the founder, strives to embrace guests' desire for one-of-a-kind experiences, life-enriching amenities and fun-meets-function touches. Given the success of the chain, it is well worth noting their unique formula, as this Philly property is a clear beneficiary.

Further, Hotel Palomar will be joined later this month by a Hotel Monaco, another iteration of the Kimpton brand in the historical district nearby. Thus, it is interesting to see how both downtown properties will function in light of the fact that their own parent firm is enabling mild brand cannibalism.

Wendell Bush did not follow the traditional educational or experience path to General Manager, but he has hospitality in his blood. His family operated a restaurant in the Southern United States and he grew up understanding the value of service. He instinctively understands the relationship between a hotel and the guest is human interaction. In my stay on property, it was not unusual to find him in the lobby, bar or restaurant talking to guests, asking about their stay. Augmenting this, the

Hotel Palomar's modest lobby space was typically a crowded scene. With complimentary wine every weekday evening and an eclectic vibe, there were plenty of opportunities for Wendell to take up his welcoming post opposite the threshold.

Wendell used the word 'fun' when describing how he wanted guests to remember his property. More specifically, he remarked, "Everything that our team does to interact with the guest is designed to instill upon them a positive spirit. We want their stay, or dining, with us to be one of the happier moments in their busy day. We know how stressful work is and we don't want to add to this side of the equation. To us having fun brings service to a whole new level: participatory, involving and intelligent."

The frontline staff are all young, typically in their 20s and early 30s. Wendell noted that the management team's success is based less on years of experience and more on commitment to learning, taking the initiative and enthusiasm for the world of hospitality. He cited examples of staffers who observed front desk operations for less than a day, and then unbeknownst to him, were checking in groups the next day (unsupervised!) when another staffer called in sick. And yes, the work performed by these individuals was flawless.

For those unfamiliar, Philadelphia is renowned as a center for the arts, academia and world-class museums. The recent opening of the Barnes Foundation catapults the city to a level of sophistication reminiscent of the capitals of Europe. This augers well for the Hotel Palomar, as its architectural heritage and artistic décor blend seamlessly. Capitalizing on this, the property has adapted Kimpton's 'Live Like a Local' program with quarterly concerts by local musicians. "All of our activities contribute to property differentiation. The luxury hotel market is fickle. There are many other good properties in Philadelphia. We see these edges as critical to protecting our top of mind awareness," said Wendell.

Later, I asked Wendell whether he was concerned about the opening of Kimpton's Hotel Monaco just over a mile due east of his address. Rather than seeing this as a competitor, Wendell was sanguine, "We've loaned them some of our best managers so we know they're going to do well. Look out Philadelphia: now there will be two properties preaching the Kimpton logic of marketing the fun side of hospitality!" The lesson from this: always evaluate how you can make your hotel experience exciting for your guests.

A CASE IN COOPERATION WITH SEAWORLD ORLANDO AND THE RENAISSANCE HOTEL

Florida knows tourism. Aside from international trade, farming (think oranges!), the space industry, services and a myriad of universities and tech firms, tourism continually reels in well over 70 million wayfarers and $50 billion year after year. Boasting itself as the top tourism destination in the world is an easy claim for this seaside state.

With this precedent, attending a Visit Florida symposium is 'kind of' a big deal, if you catch my drift. This is especially true when it's symbolically held in Orlando, a million-plus city built from the ground up by the idealism of American resort travel and the ever-ostentatious Walt Disney. The event itself was a who's who of the industry and thoroughly inspirational.

Staying at the Renaissance Orlando at SeaWorld, I was treated to a topnotch and totally inclusive experience as the hotel and its gargantuan convention halls are directly adjacent to one of Orlando's premier theme parks, SeaWorld Orlando. Upon leaving, I was able to swap a few words with Tim Swan, the Director of Sales at SeaWorld, as well as corral Peter Psihas, Director of Sales and Marketing for the Renaissance, to discuss the hotel's partnership with the amusement park, especially with regard to groups business.

Tell me a little bit about SeaWorld and the Renaissance Hotel (situation, growth, leisure/groups mix, etc.)

[TIM] SeaWorld is on the verge of celebrating 50 years as a brand, and our evolution in Orlando makes it seem like we've only just begun. The reasons for that are many. First, what was once SeaWorld Orlando now includes Aquatica, SeaWorld's Waterpark and Discovery Cove. These additions ensure our parks remain 'must see attractions' for visitors. Second, our uniqueness in Orlando has broad appeal to both tourists and residents alike. Our mission to 'celebrate, connect and care for the world we share through the power of entertainment' resonates with everyone, especially in today's world where people seem to be gravitating towards a more caring approach to conservation. And third, tied into the other two, is our evolution from a single theme park attraction to a collection of three world class parks, and seven official hotels, collectively referred to as SeaWorld Parks & Resorts Orlando.

[PETER] We have 781 spacious guestrooms (450 sq. ft.), including 65 newly remodeled suites. Our hotel has strong appeal in both the group and leisure markets, typically seeing a balanced mix of each over the course of the year. We have outstanding facilities for both segments, but our convention facilities feature 76 meeting rooms located on two levels and two very peaceful, secluded outdoor lawn spaces to accommodate all types of events.

Describe the extent of your partnerships with other hospitality businesses and some of the specific programs you've developed.

[TIM] We have maintained very solid working relationships with our partner hotels for many years. But our relationship with the Renaissance, as well as the other official hotels of SeaWorld, has evolved significantly in the past couple years. For one, we extended a collection of benefits to all guests who stay at our official hotels. These benefits include things like complimentary transportation to the parks 365 days a year, access to an exclusive 'behind the scenes' tour and free Quick Queue, our front-of-the-line program at SeaWorld.

[PETER] We partner first and foremost with SeaWorld. Aside from the aforementioned Quick Queue, our packages also include behind-the-scenes tours at SeaWorld, both exclusive and complimentary. One other noteworthy partnership item is that we 'allow' SeaWorld Vacations to sell us on SeaWorldGetaways.com. This is an unusual practice for a Marriott property but because we have such a deep partnership with the park, we're able to make this happen. SeaWorld Vacations is easily one of our highest producing wholesalers and a solid contributor to our success.

Apart from a Shamu 'floatie' in the bathtub (which I took home!), what are the other ways that you profile SeaWorld in neighboring property?

[TIM] When you stay at any of our official hotels, their connection to SeaWorld is wholly transparent. We have a 'SeaWorld Vacation Planning Center' in the lobby of each property. The hotels have a custom video that plays in the rooms to highlight the guest benefits available and to introduce guests to all of the experiences available in our parks. We also provide access to products that others can only get upon arrival in the park, making their visit that much more convenient.

[PETER] The SeaWorld Vacation Planning Center is where we introduce SeaWorld, but we have more subtle ties as well. These include: the lobby waterfall, virtual aquarium loop that runs behind the front desk, Mist (our lobby sushi bar), the Wyland mural and corresponding blue color tones throughout the hotel. We also have characters, such as Shamu, stop by at brunch time on the weekends; this is really great for the kids.

How do you lever your partnership for the development of your group convention business and leisure planning?

[TIM] As an official hotel of SeaWorld, the Renaissance Orlando at SeaWorld is promoted on our website, offering consumers the very best values available for an Orlando vacation. Together, we offer consumers the area's most convenient location, with easy access to all of Orlando's favorite pastimes. The exclusive benefits available to guests also make their experiences with our parks seamless and offer savings as well. And for no extra charge, we provide vacationers with memories they'll cherish for a lifetime! On the group side, we work very closely with the team at the Renaissance Orlando at SeaWorld to provide groups with special ticket offers, easy access to the parks for events, and special programs for any 'free time' organizers can muster around their group itinerary.

[PETER] We have a few unique items that help us book group business. One is we offer discounted tickets that allow group guests access to the park either for the entire day or for portions of the afternoon. The proximity makes these options very attractive to group guests. We also encourage our groups to consider offsite events at SeaWorld's ballroom, Ports of Call or other more distinctive venues inside the park whenever possible or practical.

How closely do you work together on issues where there are special group needs, such as our recent Visit Florida event?

[TIM] We work very closely with the sales team to ensure our proximity is an asset to their efforts to secure group business. We pride ourselves on flexibility and will do whatever we can to provide groups with a great experience. Sometimes that involves events, other times it is animal appearances at the hotel or even just ticket options. Whatever it takes; at SeaWorld Parks & Resorts Orlando, we're in this together!

[PETER] We have a great working relationship. If anything comes up with a group, SeaWorld is always open to assisting us. The partnership is what sets us apart from our competition and really defines the guest experience here at the Renaissance. It is a great example of the Renaissance brand marriage to the neighborhood.

WINDTOWER LODGE:
A CASE STUDY IN ADAPTATION

Windtower Lodge & Suites is an interesting case study on how a hotel can adapt to uncertain market conditions. The 102-room property was built nearly 20 years ago in the town of Canmore, Alberta, Canada, not far from the world-renowned ski area and national parklands of Banff and just over an hour's drive west of Calgary.

In case you are unaware, Alberta has experienced a massive oil boom, bestowing the Canadian province with a surge of wealth and labor. In the early 90s, the town was 3,000 people strong. Now, it has a base population of 10,000, not counting all the weekenders driving up from Calgary who live in chic new condominium developments. The main street has retained the feel of a tradition Western town, but it's dotted with a plethora of high-end restaurants and bars.

Knowing only the basics of the scenario, you would think that the Windtower would be exceptionally prosperous—winters filled with skiers and summers brimming with eco-travelers. But the Banff tourism industry isn't keeping pace with the province's growth. The core issue: Japanese and American tourists who supported the area in the past have flat-lined, and not only for the ski season but for golf in the summer as well.

No longer are hotels within Banff-proper selling out all the time. And as a 'feeder town' to the nearby national park, many of the newer hotels in Canmore were built on the speculation that the industry would continue to grow. This was especially true for properties grazing the Trans-Canada Highway like the Windtower (the highway that winds from Calgary through Canmore and onto Banff). So now Canmore is experiencing increased competition in a town where demand is basically stagnant.

What is a hotel that caters to skiers to do when all the skiers are gone? You can't rely on local business—there are plenty of new housing and apartment units for rent. You can't rely on F&B—the town has an abundance of culinary favorites. And you can't rely on Calgarians as they are much more likely to travel to the city on a day trip then drive home at night, or proceed straight to Banff and skip Canmore completely.

The Windtower's solution: selling long-term stays and month-to-month rooms. Beginning over five years ago, the executive team strategically implemented a conversion from short-term FIT and group business, focusing on delivering a quality residence for long-term transient stays. Probably the first thought that comes to mind when you think 'long-term stays' is retirement homes. But this isn't the case. Retirement home living requires too many government mandates for it to be feasible as part of a mixed operation. True, Windtower does get the odd retired couple here and there, but these are typically those who are in-between selling their house and finding a proper assisted-living facility.

The Windtower targets seasonal workers in summer and sports groups in winter. During the warmer months, Alberta is a hotbed of primary industry. Although oil and gas have been the stereotypical big draws for the province, that's mostly happening further north around Fort McMurray (roughly a 9 hour drive north). The Banff region continually hires crewmen for mining, building construction, highway maintenance and environmental cleaning agents in the national park. They all need temporary homes in the area and Windtower has been fitted as an ideal residence for extended stays.

Of the 102 guest rooms, just over half of them have been redesigned for long-term stays; the most significant feature being the kitchen added to every room. The executive team negotiated deals with crew company chaperones to place workers at Windtower who need residences while working on an industry job for the summer months. All said, Windtower's occupancy on month-to-month units now represents 50% of the total summer business.

The sports groups typically come in the winter months. As you would imagine, they are there to train on the Olympic-level ski facilities and perfect their skills for months at a time—downhill, cross-country, slalom and heli-skiing are all within an hour's reach from Canmore. In order to accommodate this worldwide demand, Windtower consulted several leading sports organizations to build a second, athlete-caliber gymnasium. The teams that stay there even have their logos festooned throughout to increase the homely appearance.

Windtower includes a daily breakfast as a part of the rate, but for lunch and dinner, the team's personal chef is allowed to use the hotel's kitchen to prepare special dietary meals and the hotel's restaurant so they can dine together as a team. This risky venture started off slow, but now they have more sports associations wanting to stay with them than there are rooms.

The F&B strategy reflects this as well. Instead of maintaining an evening restaurant with a non-ideal dining location to compete in a crowded market, Windtower only offers a complimentary breakfast. Lunch and supper are out, except for special occasions, specifically UFC Fight Nights. For the past six years, they have gotten every pay-per-view UFC offering and opened up the restaurant for locals with chicken wings and beer. Not only do they sell out, but this has become a great engine for raising local awareness and generating additional referrals. It's a small touch with big results, and the local bars are only now catching on.

In the end, converting to a month-to-month system has differentiated Windtower in the face of stiff competition. But it has also had the additional benefit of greatly reducing costs. With the rooms only requiring cleaning once a week, a hotel geared for extended stays only requires about one third the number of maintenance staff. This is especially important considering the rapidly inflating labor costs in this booming province.

Furthermore, with this new business model, Windtower's sales do not experience the typical peaks and valleys of conventional FIT-oriented rural properties. As such, the executive team hasn't needed a full sales force to push his product. Instead, they rely on the tried and true word of mouth, limited (highly targeted) Google Adwords in conjunction with a solid website for a foundation, as well as targeting sports associations and crew companies. The model works.

But this isn't to say that Windtower has completely abandoned short-term clientele. They still generate huge numbers of walk-ins looking to experience the pristine winter slopes or take advantage of the hiking trails, golf or mountain biking opportunities in the summer. Canmore is nonetheless a tourism town and Windtower will forever be entwined to this business.

With its capacity for long-term residences, Windtower has the flexibility to retrofit its rooms purely for the short-term market if the economic climate improves. However, there's now too much competition in the immediate vicinity and the executive team has smartly positioned the hotel away from its neighbors and any caustic price wars that might happen in the near future. All said, it's a great example of a hotel successfully adapting to unsympathetic marketplace conditions.

IN SEARCH OF HOTEL EXCELLENCE: ST. REGIS BAL HARBOUR

I had heard about the new St. Regis in Bal Harbour on the northern tip of Miami Beach (opened January 2012) long before I vacationed there. After all, a capital expenditure of nearly one billion dollars is not easy to hide in today's hospitality investment circles. This is enough to make anyone curious, especially a marketing consultant such as myself. Did this new landmark hotel meet and surpass all the pre-launch hype? While on property, I dined with the General Manager, Marco Selva, to discuss just this in addition to a thorough site inspection.

The St. Regis Bal Harbour sits on land formerly occupied by the Americana resort, and subsequently reflagged as the Sheraton Bal Harbour. The five-acre beachfront block sits directly opposite the Bal Harbour Shops, considered to be the finest open-air mall in the world by those who have no real need to look at prices. The property's 243 rooms and suites are flanked on each side by private residences, a logical way to generate the necessary upfront capital to make such a grand venture possible. Each of these wings has separate motor entry ramps and service quarters, thereby minimizing congestion. Ingeniously, the hotel's ballroom-level entrance is one floor below the lobby; it works rather brilliantly when you see it in action.

Stepping out of one's vehicle and into the St. Regis lobby is a truly awe-inspiring experience. The hotel owes a lot to designer Yabu Pushelberg's keen sense of broken sightlines, powerfully oversized furnishings and world-class contemporary artwork. (The artwork alone is worthy of a visit and would not look out of place in the MOMA.) Proceeding to reception enamors with a heightened sense of anticipation of good things to come—a key takeaway. In essence, this 'sense of arrival'—critical to escalating a guest's positive first impression—provides a bold statement of lush décor and extravagance.

Assembling the team to execute the service needs of this property was no small matter. In speaking with Mr. Selva, he indicated that his greatest desire was to seek a staff component with a profound luxury hotel background. "I wanted to meet each team member personally, to see the commitment to service in their eyes. For only then would I know if they were serious about the task we were initiating here in Bal Harbour." My stay confirmed Mr. Selva's goal. Each staff member I spoke with was not only performing his or her job, but was also executing individual touches to make me feel comfortable. There was not one situation where I felt that a staff member was merely going through the motions and not committed to their craft.

Mr. Selva plotted an interesting strategy for their primary dining room, J&G Grill. He noted, "Our property's restaurant had to make a critical welcoming statement to the local community, more of a regular dining spot than just for special occasions. We did this by doing away with the traditional formalities such white tablecloth setting, opting for contemporary, stylish, place mats instead. We also adapted price points for food items and entry-level wines to be consistent with local restaurants."

St. Regis Bal Harbour's geographic origin markets are indeed interesting and speak to the general economic shifts for that whole chunk of Florida. The primary feeder market is New York. But key secondary markets include Brazil (Sao Paulo, Rio de Janeiro), Russia, Eastern Canada (Toronto, Montreal) and other South American clusters. On my short stay, I witnessed many guests returning from shopping trips at the mall, laden with a myriad of designer bags. It is clear that this sartorial proximity is a big draw.

Mr. Selva agreed and added, "In recognition of this important element to our mix, we have created a unique promotion in concert with Neiman Marcus. We call it our 'Curated Closet' program. A stylist pre-shops for our customers, stocking the closets of their suites with items they may wish to consider for purchase. Guests (men or women) can then select without any hurry in the comfort of their own rooms, conveniently adding those items they wish to take home onto their guest folio."

This is a very innovative idea. I often hark that a creative use of your location and immediate situation will make for an excellent point of differentiation. In Florida, every hotel is on the beach. Advertising on this alone might not prove effective. Here, the St. Regis Bal Harbour has the ocean, but it's also across the street from outstanding shopping, and through such marketing techniques as the Curated Closet, it's quite apparent that this property is taking full advantage of their closeness.

A new property, the St. Regis Bal Harbour is clearly off to a fast start. Occupancies and ADR are well above target and among the highest in Bal Harbour or all of Miami Beach for that matter. This prompted me to ask about the competitive set. "Our guests are not really comparing us with other local properties. Rather, we compete with the finest resorts in the world," said Mr. Selva. "However, that doesn't mean that our customer base ignores price considerations. While we are premium-priced, we strive to constantly deliver value in terms of quality, amenities, location, service and extras by providing the absolute best in everything that we do."

In summary, the St. Regis Bal Harbour is an example of hospitality at its finest. For those who can afford it, this hotel is proof that America has not lost the ability to deliver a top-drawer combination of products and services. For those owners or GM's who are considering renovations or new builds, a weekend trip to this property should definitely be on their radar.

AN INSIDE LOOK AT ARIA IN LAS VEGAS

Las Vegas, Nevada makes for a superb case study in hospitality. Even though in my mind every resort and hotel around the world has something extraordinary to hark back to, the properties in this desert city are truly unique amongst the global cadre. It's a town where better can only mean bigger—more glitz, more glamour, more shops, more thrills, newer technology, a setting where any building under a 1,000 rooms is laughable and every hotel casino needs a high disciplined army to keep the engines chugging.

Adding to this 99-ring circus is the fact that any new development requires hundreds of millions invested before a single shovel jabs into hard, parched earth. And money down of this quantity doesn't exactly mix well with a worldwide recession and housing market collapse for which Las Vegas was an epicenter.

Yet, there was a mirage in this desert of failed construction projects that hit Nevada in and around 2007-2010, and I'm not referring to the casino The Mirage, a very successful property, I might add. Rather, it's one of the latest sister properties under the MGM Resorts International banner—ARIA at CityCenter. While staying there for the first time, the Executive Director of Guest Services, Shannon McCallum, was kind enough to sit down and answer a few questions about her perspective on ARIA's operations.

When CityCenter opened in 2009, what was the initial strategy to differentiate this complex from other properties in Las Vegas?

With ARIA as its centerpiece, CityCenter was designed as a complete resort destination with sophisticated hotels, unique restaurant offerings, dynamic entertainment, exciting nightlife, spectacular architecture and an unprecedented public art collection. ARIA, specifically, has refined and redefined the Las Vegas Strip combining the AAA Five Diamond hotel experience with a remarkable collection of dining and entertainment venues and an unparalleled luxury retail destination at the adjacent Shops at Crystals.

Crystals is home to more high-end flagship boutiques than any other shopping center in the country including the largest Louis Vuitton in North America as well as unique-to-market retailers including Stella McCartney, Donna Karan, Nanette Lepore, Tom Ford, Lanvin, Mikimoto and Versace.

Our other distinct Las Vegas hotel experience, the all-suite Vdara appeals to guests who love the energy and excitement of Las Vegas but choose to enjoy it within a non-gaming, smoke-free environment. Ideally located between Bellagio and ARIA, Vdara guests have access to all of the city's finest amenities. And of course, our location is home to Mandarin Oriental, a brand recognized as one of the preeminent hospitality brands.

The opening happened to come amidst the nadir of the recent economic downturn. How did you adapt the initial plan to weather the storm?

When the CityCenter vision was formed, it could have been considered 'the best of times' but by the time it opened, it was essentially 'the worst of times'. There were many uncertain days leading up to the opening of CityCenter. Among the many developments underway in Las Vegas at the time, ours was the only one that made it to the finish line—and, we opened on schedule!

However, opening on time and with a limited budget brought difficult decisions. For example, we had to evaluate and adjust our hiring start dates and training timelines. We didn't have as much time to get our team ready as other hotels may have had in the past, but the decision to open on time and within the adjusted budget was a much better option than not opening at all.

MGM Resorts International is by far one of the biggest players in the Las Vegas hospitality space. What level of cooperation exists between CityCenter and other mutually owned properties?

All of our Las Vegas sister properties work closely together on a variety of levels. This includes ARIA, Vdara, Bellagio, MGM Grand, Mandalay Bay, The Mirage, Monte Carlo, New York-New York, Luxor and Excalibur. Our teams share best practices with each other, from operating techniques to employee communications. While we each have our own hotels to operate, we want to ensure all of our brands are successful; collaboration and communication are critical.

Having such a diverse collection of resorts also benefits the guests in many ways. Two years ago, we launched M Life, our loyalty program that allows guests to earn and redeem rewards across all MGM Resorts properties nationwide. Additionally, we benefit from MGM Resorts' corporate infrastructure, which provides us access to advanced technology infrastructure and marketing expertise as well as other corporate support.

Focusing on ARIA, what do you feel is at the core of the Aria experience?

Service and attention are at the core of the ARIA experience. We are home to two AAA Five Diamond Awards—one for ARIA and one for ARIA Sky Suites. We were recently awarded the prestigious Forbes Five-Star for Sky Suites as well. Achieving and maintaining this caliber of service is critical and our team goes out of its way to provide every guest with a memorable experience at every turn. These accolades are a true testament to the team members who provide impeccable service and attention to detail.

What do you do to develop your relationships with past, present and future guests to heighten loyalty?

In order to enhance our relationships with guests, we reach out prior to their stay to provide information and offer assistance with dinner reservations, entertainment options and special room needs. Our goal is to get to know our guests and make their experience as individualized as possible. If we find out that our guests are celebrating a special occasion, we take steps to ensure they are recognized. Anticipating the needs of our guests, whether they are new or returning, is very important.

Additionally, our employees are empowered to make decisions in the moment to ensure they are able to react and respond to guests needs. Our M Life loyalty program is also a big driver of guest loyalty. Guests are encouraged to stay within the MGM Resorts family and enjoy benefits as a result of their time with us.

CityCenter is one of the most modern complexes on The Strip. What features does ARIA incorporate that embrace new technologies as well as new methods of interaction between staff and guests?

ARIA is indeed one of the most technologically advanced hotels on The Strip. Unrivaled in-room technology allows our guests to control the air temperature, lights, curtains, television and many other features from a tablet at their bedside or from the television screen. The system has a personalized arrival statement upon the guest's first entry that turns on the lights and opens up the drapes to provide spectacular views of the mountains or The Strip. Upon departure, our guests can conveniently check out with ease via a simple text message, email or their in-room TV. Additionally, our RFID Chip room keys will not demagnetize when they come in contact with a phone or other electronic device. All of these features add to the ease of the guest experience at ARIA.

INTERVIEW WITH HEATHER MCCRORY, REGIONAL VICE PRESIDENT FOR FAIRMONT

For those unfamiliar with the iconic Fairmont Royal York in downtown Toronto, its room count fluctuates between 1,365 and 1,472 depending on suite allocations, along with bustling F&B and a cohort of 1,200 employees. Managing dual responsibilities as the VP of Central Canada for Fairmont Hotels and Resorts as well as the Royal York's GM, Heather McCrory has championed a multi-million dollar renovation amidst a treble of stiff competition from new luxury entrants including Four Seasons, Ritz-Carlton, Shangri-la and Trump.

Managing all this points to a leader with a definitive type-A personality. But I didn't meet Heather in her cozy office just to pay homage. I wanted to know what it takes to reach the top of the industry while still maintaining your sanity!

You have been called a 'Hotel Superwoman' for your abilities. How do you manage the seemingly impossible task of being GM of Canada's largest hotel, let alone your other responsibilities?

There is a certain degree of sacrifice that one has to make. But the secret lies in balance; delegating to my executive team and focusing on leadership development within our vast organization. By ensuring dedication to mission-oriented goals and reminding everyone that our relationship with the guest is paramount, our priorities will shine through.

That's easy to say, of course, but what of the complexities of meeting the demands of owners and delivering the brand's values to the guests?

Wow, all at once? The common thread is delivering special moments to our guests. When we all focus on this core objective, there is clarity to our actions.

And the same route to accomplishing this objective?

There is no question that there are financial targets we have to meet. We are fortunate that the strong business climate in Toronto has translated into excellent RevPAR growth. Looking back, it's funny how despite all the new high-end competition, our ADR continues to climb and our 2012 occupancy percentage hovered at 75%, a record high. Further, the gear up towards the PanAm Games in the summer of 2015 has provided a 'line in the sand' in terms of capital project delivery and a further impetus to accelerate our renovation activities.

Tell me more.

We have a commitment to a very substantial renovation totaling—a critical upgrade of our guestroom stock and an enticing enhancement of our Fairmont Gold product. In effect, we have created a 'hotel within a hotel', with some 103 luxury rooms differentiated through larger room size, separate elevators and check-in, enhanced services including complimentary food and beverage components: breakfast, open honor bar and evening hors d'oeuvres. In doing so, the Royal York not only matched other downtown product, but with our F&B leverage, delivered value that exceeded that of our new competitors.

What business impact have you seen from these new luxury properties?

It certainly has been a busy time for Toronto. Those who have not been here in the past decade might not even recognize the downtown, which at times seems to be a sea of construction cranes. All of this is good news for the Royal York, as the city centre once again reinvigorates the waterfront—literally, our front yard! But to answer you more specifically, the addition of this new luxury room stock has created a new super-premium pricing tier. For too long the Toronto hotel market has had to deal with price compression: a narrow spread between the higher and middle priced products. These new entries, as well as the enhanced Four Seasons in the Yorkville area, have created a whole new pricing echelon. This means that we can demonstrate excellent customer value for our core product while effectively positioning the new Fairmont Gold within this strengthened high end segment.

Tiered pricing?

Tiered products actually. We define completely separate competitive sets for each of our Core and Gold products, managing both with individualized STR reports and revenue management programs. And we have the added advantage of being able to upsell between products, a particularly apt tool in the convention segment.

When you ask someone where they're staying in Toronto, they typically say the Royal York, not the Fairmont Royal York. What of the brand?

There is no question that the Royal York is an icon. We're Canada's classic downtown hotel while the Banff Springs, also a Fairmont property, is Canada's iconic resort. It's no wonder that our name gets abbreviated. The genesis of the Fairmont chain was to create an international presence for the old Canadian Pacific Hotels brand: a name that clearly has little relevance outside of Canada. Thus, the DNA of the Fairmont chain incorporates the core elements of what we believe in: engaging service, unrivalled presence and being authentically local. We are equally proud of both our Fairmont brand and our Royal York traditions.

Let's finish with the issue of personal and work life balance.

It's true that my husband often drives to our cottage north of the city while I am finishing the day's work. Balance means that members of my team take all of their vacations. It also means ensuring that everyone on staff knows their responsibilities in their role as a team member to both the guest as well as the owners. Balance is at the very core of how we successfully operate and how we will continue to grow in the future.

INTERVIEW WITH CHRISTOPH GANSTER, GENERAL MANAGER OF FAIRMONT GRAND HOTEL KYIV

A conference date in Kiev, Ukraine, (locally spelled 'Kyiv') afforded me the opportunity to stay at one of the newer properties under the Fairmont banner—the Grand Hotel Kiev. For those of you who have not yet visited this Eastern European city, it should definitely be on your radar. In the years since the dissolution of the Soviet Union, Ukraine has forged a unique identity built on a proud culture, deep heritage and firm economic growth.

Kiev, the nation's capital of 2.8 million people, is dominated by iconic domed Orthodox churches and Soviet empire-style low-rises. The city rests on the banks of the Dnieper River, with a high embankment separating the old town where the Fairmont is located, and the upper town which bustles with modern businesses. The short distance between the two is easily traversed by a funicular with the equivalent of a 15-cent (US) charge.

The hotel itself lives up to the adjective in its name; traditional in appearance both inside and out, yet its behind-the-scenes infrastructure has been built from the ground up. All told, this downtown property comprises 258 rooms including 56 suites, a remarkable ballroom with additional meeting facilities and an utterly spectacular center atrium. During my stay, construction just across the street on a new expressway entrance continued unabated. Despite my windows facing the fracas, the Fairmont is so well insulated that I could not hear anything.

Christoph Ganster was selected as the first GM for the hotel's opening in 2012, having previously served as GM for Fairmont's Cairo property. I met him in the hotel's Strand Restaurant for breakfast, which gave us a chance to discuss his home base.

What is it like launching a new property in Kiev and what lessons are there for others who might be considering a similar venture?

We are particularly fortunate as I was able to advertise for key staff positions within the Fairmont network, and in doing so, was able to bring key team members in to get the business underway quickly. Yet, this process was restricted by government limitations on the number of foreign nationals that I could hire. At the same time, I was looking for managers with a working knowledge of Ukrainian or Russian languages. That was a challenge.

Moreover, the local hospitality service culture is not yet at the Fairmont five-star level. This meant that the local talent pool, while strong and enthusiastic, required a considerable degree of initial, as well as on-going, training. The good news was that our owners had provided us with an excellent physical product. Thus, our focus was to take advantage of this magnificent structure, devoting our primary energies to imbuing a culture dedicated to service excellence.

Has the product changed since opening just over a year ago?

The rooms' product has not, although at this time, we probably would have preferred more rooms and fewer suites. One significant change was our use of the atrium. This is the signature public space in the hotel, located on the second floor in a central courtyard and decorated with a wonderful gold-leaf-and-glass dome. Originally designed solely as a second F&B outlet, we quickly assessed that a significant revenue opportunity was being wasted versus the nominal return from duplicate F&B facilities.

Thus, our implementation of this room as a second, more intimate ballroom has proven to be a runaway success. The space is remarkably flexible: important meetings, weddings, social functions and, yes, even some F&B. As an extraordinary example, a romantic guest booked the entire room. That's right, just for two! We set up a table in the center of the atrium, amorously surrounded by hundreds of candles. The rate for the room rental for the evening exceeded the typical gross revenue of the outlet operating as a restaurant outlet.

What has been the reception to the hotel since its opening?

In the luxury segment, Kiev is already serviced by the Intercontinental (which happens to have the same owner as the Fairmont), as well as the Hyatt Regency. We wanted something better; something that would differentiate the property from both these existing products. We knew our physical product was of the highest standard. Thus, our focus was to deliver a superior service standard as well.

What learning has there been from this experience?

Time. There is just not enough. Your management team should be onsite (or nearby) at least nine months prior to opening. This provides you with the time to get staff training underway and to perfect your systems. Even now, more than a year after launch, we are still 'writing the book' on our opening.

(Since the publication of this article, Christopher G. Ganster has moved on to be General Manager at the Raffles Praslin, Seychelles, also part of Fairmont Raffles Hotels International.)

IN SEARCH OF HOTEL EXCELLENCE: ABIGAIL'S HOTEL

By all accounts, Abigail's Hotel would not be on the radar of most travelers. After all, the property is not affiliated with a major chain or a representation firm such as Leading Hotels of the World, Preferred Hotels & Resorts or Relais & Chateaux. Yet, with Abigail's ranking as the top property in Victoria, British Columbia on TripAdvisor, I decided that a further inspection was warranted.

Victoria is the capital of British Columbia—Canada's westernmost province—with a population of 330,000. Located off the mainland on Vancouver Island, Victoria is considered a haven for Canadian retirees and my quick survey of the tourist scene confirmed this. The downtown waterfront district is dominated by Fairmont's majestic Empress Hotel, with other major chain properties located snugly around the rejuvenated port area.

Abigail's Hotel is about five minutes by car (ten minutes walking) from the center of town. I was encouraged to walk, but not knowing our way, felt more comfortable driving—a trip we did several times each day as parking was just a few dollars a day and free in the evening.

The heritage property houses 23 rooms and was built in 1930, having been converted from an apartment building in the 80s. Comprising two separate buildings wrapped around a small motor court, the property's Tudor style façade is quaint and inviting. My room comprised a well-decorated, modest-sized bedroom with fireplace and a somewhat triangular-shaped bathroom. Well equipped, comfortable for sure, but certainly not fully up to the modern standards one would expect in a luxury property.

The well-appointed common rooms comprised a reception room flanked on either side by a living room to the right and a breakfast room to the left. Walk straight ahead and you are in a small but very pleasant courtyard. With no elevator, this property would not meet any accessibility requirements. Regardless, it was an exceptional experience.

Hitting All the Right Notes for TripAdvisor

What I just described in the past few paragraphs would have you scratching your head as to how Abigail's has achieved its top TripAdvisor rating. It certainly isn't the physical attributes or amenities of the property that delivered these accolades.

What drives the excellent rating is the service: personalized and professional. With a small but dedicated staff, Abigail's has found the expert balance between helping and being overly obtrusive. Breakfasts are made to order by a chef and supported by efficient and happy waitstaff. A complimentary happy hour provided excellent snacks in the pre-dinner hour. Free wireless was also on tap. Throughout the stay, it was impossible to find fault. This level of service would be difficult, if not impossible, to achieve in a property of 200-plus rooms without enormous (and not affordable) staffing levels. This supports my hypotheses on achieving high TripAdvisor ratings.

- Service is more important than physical structure.
- Guests do not like to pay for extras and your ratings may suffer as you add costs. The final bill at Abigail's had two lines: room and tax.
- Positive staff attitude trumps any fancy new room features. This is something to keep in mind as you seek to add items: the guest benefit might not be there!
- Creating a relationship between staff and guests is paramount.

REMINISCING ON SEDONA AT THE ADOBE GRAND VILLAS

Towering red rock mesas glimmering under a beating desert sun, a silence only pierced by the squawks of far-off falcons and the scrunch of tumbleweed, crystal-clear air that soothes any sinus and over six hundred kilometers of mountainous trails. The location? Sedona, Arizona, a short drive north of Phoenix and the perfect vacation hotspot.

From an accommodations standpoint, Enchantment is perhaps the most recognized destination spa, situated a few miles out of the hustle and bustle of this resort conclave. But search TripAdvisor and a 16-room property, the Adobe Grand Villas, stands proud atop the pile. My visit with Michael Merilli, General Manager and Executive Chef (a rare and interesting combination), provided some insight behind this online triumph.

First to mind, the property redefines décor. The doubters and cost accountants might deem it kitsch, but, alas, it works. Each 825 sq. ft. room is completely different in its look, feel and theme. Our suite was called 'Wagon Wheel' and included a covered wagon as a bed, saloon doors to the bathroom, old hand water pumps as faucets and more western doodads than a movie set. Walking into the suite, beyond a decorated vault-weight door, your sense of sight is overwhelmed by the smell of fresh bread baking in an in-room bread maker. The layout and large floor pad allows these items to form a cohesive environment without the guest stumbling for space.

As Michael explains, "We want our guests to feel at home. Home means the smell of fresh bread, free snacks, free bottled water and a western-style breakfast. The cost of a bread maker is a small one-time capital investment; the ingredients for a high quality loaf are still less than a dollar. Given all this, the value created for our guests is incredible." Effusive comments in the guest book left in our suite reinforced this methodology. They were long and detailed with thoughts ranging from constructive to outright appreciation, surprisingly with many from younger guests.

Discussing the online travel agencies, Michael added, "It is clearly a love-hate relationship. We allocate one room to the channel and when sold we consider adding another room. The advantage that we have is that each of our guestrooms is unique. As all 16 rooms are identically priced, we can assign any room décor to the OTA buyer. Our repeat customers (approaching 60% of total sales) know what room they want, either to repeat a past experience or select a new one. To get exactly what's sought, they can only make that selection by booking through our site or by calling us. Long term, our goal is to sever ourselves from the OTAs completely and the best strategy for this is loyalty, word of mouth and public relations."

Specifically in regard to TripAdvisor, Michael noted, "When we started, our scores were clearly less than perfect. But we learned from our mistakes. Each rating provided us with timely feedback from our guests. We used this information to perfect our service and help manage our staffing. The key is that you have to act immediately upon a posting. Now, our minimum standard is five out of five stars. When it comes to providing exceptional service, you can never let your guard down."

On the future, Michael was optimistic, "We've experienced some of the worst of times for the resort business. Buffered somewhat by the perennial business in the Sedona area, our growth rate was stalled and occupancies limited to the mid-60s. As a small player in the market, but among the rate leaders, our unique product offering and the number one rating puts us in a great position. It's a matter of constantly evolving our product to meet vacillating guest needs."

A TALE OF NORTHERN CALIFORNIA AT THE TIMBER COVE INN

I've known the people at Timber Cove Inn for quite some time now. Maybe it's the gentle Pacific breeze or the tranquil seclusion of sparsely populated Northern California, but the senior managers and staff at this coastal resort property are some of the nicest you will ever meet. They also have a lot of wisdom to share when it comes to marketing a hotel that is somewhat 'off the beaten track' and a two and a half hour drive from the nearest international airport (San Francisco). It's my pleasure to interview the General Manager at Timber Cove Inn, Keith Hill.

Tell me a little bit about the history of Timber Cove Inn.

The area surrounding the hotel was originally inhabited by Russian traders over 200 years ago. The coastline of the Timber Cove region is so stunning and inspirational that pioneering photographer Ansel Adams spent a great deal of time in the area capturing timeless images.

The Inn itself was designed and built by Richard Clements, opening its doors in 1963. Mr. Clements' design was inspired by the great Frank Lloyd Wright, perhaps the most respected architect in U.S. history, which is evident immediately upon arriving at the property. The near exclusive use of redwood and stone to construct the framework of the Inn and the manner in which it was contoured to the rocky bluffs of the Pacific both represent a truly unique configuration that brings along with it unforgettable character and tremendous sense of place.

The Inn is conveniently situated adjacent to the famed Coastal Highway 1, offering dramatic views of the Pacific regardless of which direction you are traveling towards the Inn. Over its history, Timber Cove Inn has offered reasonably priced accommodations in a world-class setting, granting us one of the more diverse and extensive guest demographics you will find. The location and feel of the property naturally lends itself to romantic couples who want to disconnect from the distractions of their daily routine and recharge their batteries in one of the most peaceful environments you can imagine.

Sonoma County is best known as a premier wine destination. Yet your location is still another hour off the beaten path (i.e. Santa Rosa). How do you attract oenophiles?

The truth is that we must be creative, proactive and maintain excellent partnerships to provide this kind of experience. We are surrounded by a wealth of accomplished wineries and the best terroir for chardonnay and pinot noir this side of Burgundy, but most of these wineries do not have tasting rooms. Thus, Timber Cove Inn is in a fortunate position to present itself as the sampling destination for the best of what the region has to offer, including the celebrated new Fort Ross-Seaview AVA.

We accomplish this first and foremost with a wine list that almost exclusively features Sonoma AVA wines. Wine flights are offered daily and we can pair wines from the region with our tasting menus or anything else you choose to enjoy. Now that we are approaching the start of our second year together as a unified management team, we are working towards putting together a series of locally-driven food and wine events. We can also arrange private tours of several nearby wineries with enough notice. Finally, there are two tasting rooms—Fort Ross Vineyard & Winery and Annapolis Winery—within reasonable driving distance from the Inn for those seeking a more traditional wine country experience.

Again, Jenner, California is not on the main road. F&B has to be a critical component in your guest promotion plan.

First and foremost, with few other dining alternatives available near the hotel, it is very important that we diversify the dining experience from meal to meal and day to day. It is also critical to provide variety within each menu, which is not an easy task to accomplish in a remote destination. We offer lunch picnic baskets to enjoy on the grounds or on nearby hiking trails. We maintain exceptional selections in both Alexander's Restaurant and the Sequoia Lounge, which provide varied menus both from a compositional and price point perspective. Everything we do in F&B embodies our conscious effort to keep the dining experience fresh for guests staying with us for multiple nights.

In addition to maintaining variety, it is our responsibility to provide cuisine and services that rival the stunning views and world-class wines our region provides, and the bar is set very high. We view our F&B program as a creative outlet to provide an attractive amenity for our guests rather than just 'three square meals'. The Fort Ross Vineyard mushroom foraging experience in winter is an example of this. A renowned mycologist leads a group of hotel guests through the redwood forest foraging for mushrooms, followed by an educational rendezvous in one of the most beautiful tasting rooms you will ever see to celebrate your 'treasure' while sipping great wine. All the while a four-course wild mushroom-themed dinner is prepped and paired with some of the best wines that Fort Ross Vineyard has to offer—the perfect way to end a day of adventure. What's not to love about that?

What approach do you take to business and weddings?

Social groups such as weddings, anniversaries and birthday celebrations naturally flock to Timber Cove Inn due to the intimate feel of the hotel and photogenic location. Due to our size, it is also not uncommon for social groups to 'buy out' the hotel for exclusive access to the entire property. Corporate business groups represent a bit more of a challenge for us because of the lack of consistent cellular service in the area and on property. While we do offer wireless internet coverage property-wide, most corporate groups are unwilling to give up cellular connectivity for any significant length of time. A cellular signal repeater has been identified as a necessary addition to the Inn in order to capture this business, and thankfully our supportive ownership group agrees.

How do you maintain staff levels and promote guest training?

This is one of the most lucrative places to work on the entire Northern California coastline and we are the largest employer for quite some distance in any direction. We also offer benefits for full-time employees so the Inn represents a very attractive employment opportunity worth driving for, and some of our staff commute from an hour away.

Having said that, employee housing is necessary to attract talent outside of the immediate area, so we rent nearby housing for this purpose. In small hotels with a limited number of managers such as

Timber Cove Inn, peer accountability is critical for consistent delivery of great service, making group training so very important. We have budgeted for several examples of group training in 2013, both in the areas of sales and guest service.

IN SEARCH OF HOTEL EXCELLENCE: FAIRMONT LE CHATEAU FRONTENAC

When you have a property that's more than just a hotel, but an icon for a city (and perhaps a country!), calling the role of General Manager complex is an understatement. Such is the situation that Robert Mercure finds himself in as one of the leaders of Fairmont Le Chateau Frontenac in Quebec City, Canada.

Approaching 120 years old, the property sits on federal government land adjacent to an archeological site of Chateau St. Louis, the original seat of the French government in North America. It was from this location that the 1600s colonial governor oversaw operations that stretched from Louisiana to the Great Lakes. That building burnt to the ground in 1834 and it took some 60 years until the original portion of the Chateau Frontenac was built in its place. The present property, inaugurated in 1893, has been expanded numerous times and now comprises some 618 rooms on 18 floors. The property dominates the old walled city of Quebec (itself a UNESCO heritage site), with a copper roof, multiple turrets and sloped peaks. To say that this hotel's exterior appearance is totally unique is an understatement—it's on practically every postcard of Quebec City that's bought!

Inside, the property is anything but cookie cutter. The massive lobby looks more castle than hotel, with every surface symbolically carved or emblazoned. Each subsequent addition required careful architectural consideration. The result is a labyrinth of corridors, all heavily decorated and festooned. Just study the map on the elevator landing and you will quickly appreciate that housekeeping efficiency was never the architects' priority.

To prevent total bedlam, the hotel is simplified into ten room rate booking categories, with significant variations in each category. My room was considered a mini-suite—windows on three sides and tucked into the dormers of a multi-roof peaks.

Sure, there are numerous chain properties available as alternatives. Yet, when in Quebec City, I can't imagine staying anywhere else. Bragging rights come from sleeping in the location where Churchill, King and Roosevelt attended the Quebec Conferences of 1943 and planned the D-Day invasion, or, in more modern times, where Reagan and Mulroney discussed the early forms of NAFTA. The hotel oozes history from every pore.

My conversation with Mr. Mercure focused on the property and some of the unique challenges at work. He acknowledged that the property's room stock needs upgrading to keep pace with standards. With the last major remodel in the early 90s, it's showing some age. Many of the TripAdvisor comments accurately reflect the high degree of variation in current room quality and age.

Whereas summer peak traffic fills the property from May through September, and the world famous Bonhomme Carnaval provides a two-week respite each wintery February, the group segment is a critical component to off-season success. Even here, the property has a need to increase the available space for meetings.

To address these issues, Mr. Mercure was eager to discuss the major expansion plan coinciding with their 120th anniversary. The focus of this renovation, the tenth or eleventh in its history, has seen complete guest room revitalization and an expansion of meeting space, creating some of the most unique venues in North America or perhaps the world.

Speaking of the modifications to the guestrooms, Mr. Mercure was quite excited, "It is true that our guestroom stock was in dire need of enhancement. But this was no run-of-the-mill hotel renovation. Almost every room has unique elements. We never knew what we would find when we removed walls or tried to change plumbing fixtures. Each room, in effect, was its own mini-archaeological exploration, albeit only from the past 120 years."

Food and beverage was also a key element of this redesign. While my meal with Mr. Mercure was in the illustrious Le Champlain dining room, the ambiance was nonetheless indicative of old world and the menu still rather traditional. Mr. Mercure and his executive chef had plenty of ideas for a full menu overhaul—something for which they admit should have been done years earlier. Food menus are in need of constant revitalization, more so than even the décor or refurbishments.

The three pillars of Fairmont management are expressed as: Unrivalled Presence, Authentically Local and Engaging Service. Mr. Mercure has a fourth axiom: Protecting History. From all the postcards, you would think that this property is a cash cow, regardless of who's in charge. Clearly, this is not the case. Not only must he keep pace with the heightened expectations of the modern consumer, but he also must appease the preservationists at large. With great historic presence also comes great expense and Mr. Mercure is hard at work to balance this delicate equation.

APPEAL TO A GUEST'S HEART WITH ONSITE DOGS

While staying at the Fairmont's Le Château Frontenac in Quebec City, one employee showed such warmth, poise and professionalism that I had to take notice and write about it. I'm talking, of course, about Santol, their canine ambassador.

The Mira Foundation originally trained Santol as a guide dog before he was singled out for his affectionate and charming personality. The Château Frontenac then entered a mutually beneficial partnership: Santol was to act as the hotel's canine ambassador while continuing with The Mira Foundation in a fundraising capacity. Visitors to the hotel are encouraged to pet and socialize with Santol, who is a beautiful cross between a Labrador and a Bernese Mountain Dog, and one of the friendliest animals I've ever met. The simple act of having a dog onsite instantly helped me feel at home, brightening the mood for all passersby.

When I got home I was more than compelled to tell friends about this experience. With a quick Google search, I discovered that canine ambassadors are a feature at select Fairmont locations throughout the world. Extrapolating my post-hotel fervor to the thousands of guests who might have had similar dog interactions, this equates to a lot of people talking about Fairmont, whether this was intended or a mere by-product.

I also contemplated this program's social media implications. People love to take pictures of dogs and post them on Facebook, Twitter or Instagram. As it pertains to Santol, how many photos do you think have been posted with the caption 'taken at the Château Frontenac'? Whether the Fairmont brand name is explicitly mentioned or not, this is nevertheless an excellent example of word-of-mouse marketing. People like to 'like' cute animal pictures after all.

With so many hotels in the world it's hard to stand out, but Fairmont has shown that simple is still impressive. Times may change, but an adorable dog will win people over every time. This goes to show that sometimes, instead of innovation, you simply need to appeal to a guest's heart.

SUCCESS ON A GRAND SCALE AT MONTAGE LAGUNA BEACH

The moniker 'Best Resort in America' is not taken lightly. There are many contenders for this title and among them is Montage Laguna Beach. It's an awe-inspiring property located less than an hour south of LAX, in an enclave worlds away from the hustle of Hollywood and the surrounding suburban sprawl. Celebrating its tenth anniversary this year, the property holds the much-coveted Forbes Five Star rating for hotel, restaurant and spa as well as the five-diamond rating from AAA. Both are well-deserved accolades for this oasis of hospitality excellence.

Within the 30-acre compound, Montage Laguna Beach comprises 248 rooms, including 60 suites, 3 villas, a full-featured spa, three restaurants, two pools, private residences, an extensive meeting/conference/event area and probably enough marble, brass, fine carpet and exotic hardwood to tailor a small cruise liner. Carved into the side of a cliff, every room faces the ocean. While this often means walking long, somewhat confusing corridors to get to your room, the journey is worth the effort.

Some 700 team members share the responsibility of upholding the impeccable guest service standards. On my most recent stay, I could not find a single service fault among my innumerous staff interactions. While no property is absolutely perfect every time, this hotel comes pretty darn close! It is with this backdrop that I spoke with Todd Orlich, Montage Laguna Beach's General Manager, while enjoying a delightful breakfast at The Loft, one of the property's many excellent dining options.

Larry: This is one incredible hotel. It's alive with excitement. Every guest seems to be completely enchanted. Please tell us the secret to this success.

Todd: The Montage story, while only ten years young, continues to unfold. It is a story that starts with our CEO and Founder, Alan Fuerstman, and reflects a deep commitment to searching for the absolute best team to be a part of the Montage experience. Our desire for finding the right staff is all-encompassing. It starts from the moment an individual completes their application form, through the hiring process, through the early stages of their position here and continues as their Montage career unfolds.

Larry: So that means you, as General Manager, personally interview everyone for all staff positions?

Todd: No one slips through the system. And yes, my signature appears on every authorization to hire in this organization. Getting the right team is so essential to our guest service mantra that the hiring of every line staff member, from housekeeper to wait staff to culinary, deserves executive overview. Let me take you through the process.

Once the application is completed, a member of our management team will conduct a detailed telephone interview. Those candidates who successfully complete this first step are brought in to meet in person with a member of our human resources team. Individuals asked to continue to the third phase of the process are invited back to spend a day with current Montage Associates working in the department in which the applicant has expressed interest.

The most impressive individuals then interview with the department head who would oversee the applicant if hired. The fifth and final step in the hiring process is a panel interview with members of our senior staff, which includes me. Panel interviews take place every Friday from 2pm to 4pm to ensure these meetings can be effectively coordinated with the senior staff.

An individual's hiring is only the first step in their journey to being a successful member of our team. The first few weeks, depending on the position, include intense training and hands-on supervision. Our Associates' careers with us consist of ongoing educational and developmental opportunities starting with MORES, a two-day orientation process that lays a foundation of everything they will need to know. We strive for a cohesive, guest-focused team driving towards a common goal of service delivery.

Larry: This approach seems to favor group tasks over individual performance.

Todd: Guest service is a symphony of small, individual, one-on-one success stories. Take us for example. We just arrived in The Loft for breakfast and were greeted by the hostess who showed us to our table. From the moment a guest is seated, we rely on the kitchen and waitstaff, line and pastry chefs, along with the bus staff to deliver impeccable service that leaves each of our guests completely satisfied with a memorable dining experience.

Our collective success extends beyond The Loft hostess or pastry chef, however, and also includes the IT, purchasing, and accounting departments. These individuals ensure that each guest's bill is accurate, processed in a timely manner and effective in utilizing metrics recordings that supplement our ongoing efforts to refine and perfect our menu.

Any mistake or slip up along the way and the 'wow' on the guest's face is gone. Remember, our guests are well-traveled. They have stayed at some of the finest resorts on earth. They know quality. They have very high expectations and standards—standards that we have to exceed each and every day. It's more a collection of individual efforts working in cohesive harmony than a group task.

Larry: We talked about 'Mores' and the recognition that an individual's habits and manners form a critical component to the team members.

Todd: It actually is a little deeper than that. We have named our orientation training 'Mores' and also conduct an annual Mores examination which everyone takes—including me! Every associate must achieve a 90%+ score. There are additional bonus questions so associates can actually receive a better-than-perfect score of 110%. (At this point, Todd asked our waiter what he got on his last Mores test. A proud response of 104%, then with a sigh, down from 107% the last time he was tested.)

Larry: Montage opened the Beverly Hills property about five years ago and more recently the property in Deer Valley (Utah). I also understand another property slated to open just over a year from now. Are the same steps being taken in all properties?

Todd: Each of our hotels and resorts follow the same success formula: the finest location within the area; the best construction with particular attention to fine details; a respect for the local community; and the application of our values and Mores.

With each new property launch, we take a group of managers from the already established Montage properties to lead the way. For Beverly

Hills, our second property, about 25 managers including myself, moved to the new property to ensure that the 'Montage culture' would be encoded into the DNA of the new property. Deer Valley was easier on the existing properties with only a dozen or so coming from each of Beverly Hills and Laguna. As we launch other hotels, the strain on the three other Montage properties will be lessened.

Larry: How does technology play a role in the Montage program?
Todd: We could not be where we are today without the systemic application of systems to guide us and improve efficiencies. We have an extensive IT team that continuously evaluates everything from guest TVs and internet to POS terminals and forecasting programs. This resort is ten years old, and as such, some of the technology is not as 'state of the art' as a property that just opened. Life expectancies for technology are short; our plans identify needs and respond accordingly. One element that will not be replaced, however, is the need for direct personal communication between the guest and our staff.

Guest service is not about just filling the need, but more importantly, filling it in a way that makes the guest feel great about the experience. It's delivering those magical memories that make our guests want to return again and again.

CONCLUSION

The Hotel Abigail in Victoria is a stellar example of differentiating a property through the combination of unique décor and furnishings as well as outstanding guest services.

FORTES FORTUNA ADIUVAT

I wish I had paid more attention to my middle school Latin or my junior year ancient history classes. It seems as if every powerful and pithy quotation has its roots in an archaic language or owing to some idolized field master. In this case, I reference the ever-venerated Roman general and dictator, Gaius Julius Caesar, notorious for conquering France, England and then all of the Roman Empire.

'Fortes Fortuna Adiuvat', transliterates into English as 'Fortune Favors the Bold'. Caesar was a firm believer in this, willing to bet decade-long military campaigns and hundreds of thousands of lives on his wit and audacious tactical advances. He even paid tribute to the Roman goddess of luck, Fortuna. Aside from a minor miscalculation involving the betrayal of some close friends around the Ides of March, Caesar was already primed for the annals of history.

This idealistic tenet holds true today, even if you aren't a rampaging warmonger like Caesar and are a much more earnest hotel manager. Fortune does indeed favor those hoteliers who take bold steps.

Boldness in hotel management and marketing comes in many different, and largely creative, forms. As the industry warps under the tugging forces of electronica and generational divides, never forget that courage will forever be needed to stand apart and make an impact. Here are several examples of 'Bold Marketing Strategies' to help get you in the mood and remind you of what the hotel industry is truly capable of.

Holiday Inn: For the first to have computerized reservations and the first to take bookings online. Holiday Inn was also the first international brand to open a hotel in China. Holiday Inn has so many firsts! A simple trip to their website shows just how far this industry has come.

Westin Hotels: For the advertising campaign "Do You Know Who She/He/We Are Sleeping With?" This was an intrepid selling line that captured the imagination of television viewers across North America. Does anyone still remember when hotels advertised on all the national networks with campaigns that focused on their core values?

Howard Johnson: For their 'Kids Eat and Stay Free' program. The cost of a cot in the room and a simple children's menu captured the imagination of family travelers. There is some dispute as to whether other chains had precedence, but HoJo is the one that made it the staple of their business.

Sheraton Hotels: For creating the 'Four Points by Sheraton', the first promoted budget-priced variation that haloed the original brand. At last, a knock-off brand segmentation project that worked wonders! By creating a lower-priced product, but still including the recognized Sheraton brand name, this product attracted budget-savvy customers who eagerly relied on Sheraton for an extension of their quality assurance.

Kimpton Hotels: For their 'Lonely Goldfish' promotional program. There are so many great initiatives taken by this boutique chain that it's hard to choose which one deserves the most praise! Alas, I had to pick one. From a public relations standpoint, the goldfish program delivers some of the best return on investment I've ever witnessed. How much do a goldfish and water bowl cost after all?

Four Seasons Hotels & Resorts: For, amongst many other daring maneuvers, removing the shampoo and amenity pouches then replacing them with mini-bottles. Four Seasons is a leader in so many ways that it's hard to single out the greatest impact they have had on our industry. I chose the mini-shampoo bottles, as I'm old enough to remember how ludicrous it was to use shampoo foil pouches in the shower.

Hyatt for 'Passport Gold' and **Hilton** for 'Hhonor's; the first true hotel loyalty awards programs. These two were the precursors and progenitors for a myriad of consumer incentive programs. Now, pretty much every property, chain or independent, has the opportunity to participate, and a lot of times, we better partake if we hope to keep their customer loyalty base.

This is just my list. Which bold and broad actions would you like to nominate? The hotel industry is unique and yet it has so many similarities with other fields where daring, courage, creativity and imagination are revered. Like Caesar, you must be bold and take risks if you are to jump ahead of the competition. Not all of those ventures will be profit blockbusters but you can't hit a home run if you don't step up to the plate.

ARE YOU AN OSTRICH OR A LLAMA REDUX

The undercurrent of the first book "Are You an Ostrich or a Llama?" hinged on its title; that there are two broad types of managers, those that learn and those that don't bother listening. And I mean truly listening—people who constantly reevaluate their own performance as well as that of their entire team. In real life, ostriches might not have their heads in the sand, but that's the going metaphor so do your best to not become one.

I find it rather funny that the people reading this book are those already primed to learning, so give yourself a pat on the back for making it this far. Hopefully by now you've adopted a llama-esque approach to the hospitality industry and any management practices for that matter. In many cases, an issue can be solved with a clever mix of compassion, empathy and willingness to learn and share new knowledge.

Through my experience, one of the key traits I've found for good managers and leaders is that they are always learning and contemplating new opinions, systems of belief and methods to best conduct their business. I say contemplate because this is very different than incorporate. The best leaders are never the proverbial 'weather vane' directors who always shift strategies and approaches in whichever way the wind blows. Often, the best leaders are slow to react as they take their time to properly consider all options before acting. But when they do finally make a decision, they commit to it wholeheartedly and with a confidence that motivates the entire team to follow.

This is my hope for you: to be great leaders in the field of hospitality. It is not an easy task and it will take years of practical experience. Reading this book is a step in the right direction and I hope my guidance has given you a step in the right direction.

GLOSSARY OF TERMS

ADR: Average Daily Rate; a calculation of the total room revenue for a day divided by the number of rooms sold, generally excluding ancillary revenue, such as F&B, parking, etc.

B2B: Business To Business.

B2C: Business To Consumer.

Comp: Room given on a complementary basis. As a verb, "He was comped."

CMS: Content Management System; the 'back-end' of a modern website, allowing for revisions without directly involving a programmer.

CRO: Central Reservations Office; an incoming call center for which prospective customers phone in to book a hotel room. The telephone number listed for a hotel, either on the website or in a print directory, will most likely redirect to the property's or chain's CRO.

CVB: Convention and Visitor Bureau; a government-run organization dedicated to raising the tourism profile and awareness for a given city, municipality, region, state, province or country.

DofM: Director of Marketing; can also be referred to as the Director of Sales and Marketing (DofSM).

ES: Extended Stay; a guest who utilizes a room for a period longer than 14 days, typically renting the accommodation on a monthly basis.

F&B: Food and Beverage; referring not only to the outlets, but as well, catering and room service.

FIT: Frequent Independent Traveler; as in leisure guests who are not part of a specific group, wholesaler or tour operator package.

GDS: Guest Distribution System; a computerized system generally utilized by airlines and hotels, and managed by traditional travel agents.

GM: General Manager. In some properties there are some variations, with a two-tiered senior management including a Managing Director and a Hotel Manager (other variations exist).

IT: Information Technology.

MOD: Manager On Duty; when the general manager is not in house, his/her replacement becomes the MOD.

OCC: Percentage Occupancy; the ratio of rooms in use to total rooms in house; often comped out of service rooms are not considered as in use.

OTA: Online Travel Agency; agencies operating primarily through the Internet.

PMS: Property Management System; the software used to internally manage and integrate rooms, revenues, ancillary services, etc.

POS: Point of Sale; being the data accumulated through cash registers/computers located throughout the property.

RevPAR: Revenue Per Available Room; calculated by taking the total revenue of the property and dividing it by the number of rooms times 365, or the number of days in the revenue period.

RevPOR: Revenue Per Occupied Room; calculated by taking the total revenue of a property and dividing it by the number of rooms occupied; generally more useful in analysis of properties with a high degree of ancillary revenue, such as a spa, food & beverage and a golf course.

RM: Revenue Manager; responsible for analyzing competitive rates and advising the general manager on setting room rates to maximize yield on occupancy.

SEO: Search Engine Optimization; the process of enhancing how a property is found when using search terms within Internet search engines.

SEM: Search Engine Marketing; a term to denote all paid searches which are not generated organically within a search engine.

Share of Screen: How much a single image, product, advertisement or idea dominates a user's electronic viewing screen. The more space it commands, the more likely it will be that a user notices it.

VIP: Very Important Person. A person who is 'VIP'd' typically receives a special welcome amenity, upgrades and personalized reception from a key member of staff.

Word of Mouse: Word of mouth which transpired through any digital means. It earned its name because of the computer mouse necessary to make these interactions possible (excluding more recent touch devices like smartphones and tablets).

ACKNOWLEDGEMENTS

I'd like to extend a special thanks to everyone at LMA Communications Inc. who has worked (and survived!) with me over the years. Without your dedication to serving our clients, this book, and its predecessor, would not have been possible. Specifically, I'd like to thank my son and editor, Adam Mogelonsky, and the book cover's graphic designer, Ryan Tong.

Next, my deepest thanks and admiration go out to all those I interviewed in order to make this book whole. In alphabetical order by last name, this includes Victor Aburto, Zachary Amzallag, Laurence Bernstein, Daniel Brody, Joseph Cooke, John Dodd, Darren Edwards, Christoph Ganster, Keith Hill, Moe Ibrahim, Jason King, Jamie Pagel, Shannon McCallum, Heather McCrory, Todd Orlich, Peter Psihas, Marcus Robinson, John Smallwood, Craig Strong, Tracy Stuckrath and Tim Swan.

I would also like to thank those individuals whose names do not appear as an interviewee, but who nevertheless provided valuable insights and information to help scribe this book's chapters. In alphabetical order by last name, this includes Joe Adkisson, Reggie Aggarwal, Wendell Bush, Alyssa Bushey, Ernie Diaz, Matthew Donegan-Ryan, Alan Fuerstman, Fred Gluckman, Gordon James Gorman, Adele Gutman, Cornelia Kausch, Murray Hall, David Jennings, Josiah Mackenzie, Charles McDiarmid, Robert Mercure, Michael Merilli, Fabien Riviere, Marco Selva, Rich Sipe, June Tang and Patrick Turcot.

Lastly, I'll like to especially thank my wife of 32 years, Maureen, who has put up with me all of this time as well as my family, friends and clients who I've had the pleasure of knowing over the years. Life is a winding road and our time together has been a critical influence for me to write on the topic of hospitality.

ABOUT THE EDUCATIONAL PROGRAM

In tandem with writing in hospitality journals and the publishing of this book, Larry Mogelonsky has also created an online educational program for hoteliers. Entitled "Llama Digital", this interactive training tool allows managers and staff members to access articles through a web portal, and then respond to questions based on the material they just read. Users can be students currently enrolled in hospitality schools or those active in the business who are looking to sharpen their expertise.

The articles in the online program are derived from this book in addition to Larry's previous book, "Are You an Ostrich or a Llama?" The questions are designed for a more detailed analysis of the issues through the form of written responses so that, in conjunction with learning better managerial skills, hoteliers will also improve their writing proficiency. Furthermore, the system is built to promote a strong student-instructor dynamic whereby all questions can be graded with feedback provided so hoteliers can receive constructive criticism. All of this happens online, so users can interact from any place where there is internet access.

To learn more about the Llama Digital educational program and how it can enhance your learning in the hospitality field, go to www.lmadigital.ca.

ABOUT THE AUTHOR

Larry is the founder and chief executive officer of LMA Communications Inc., a Toronto-based advertising and consulting agency that focuses on the hospitality industry. He earned an Honors Bachelor of Civil Engineering degree from Concordia University in Montreal, Quebec and a Masters of Business Administration from McMaster University in Hamilton, Ontario. He is also a Professional Engineer, accredited in the Province of Ontario.

He commenced his marketing career with Procter & Gamble, working in their advertising department as a brand manager on many well-known product lines. Next, he moved to the service side of the business, spending several years at Bozell Palmer Bonner (at the time Bozell was one of the world's 'top ten' advertising agencies), shifting laterally as managing director of their retail/promotions division, Promotion Solutions Group. During his tenure at the agency, he created a hospitality and tourism team, which served Four Season Hotels & Resorts, Howard Johnson, and American Airlines.

It was the era of giant agency mergers and Larry took the decision to hang his own shingle, founding LMA in January of 1991. As one of its first assignments, LMA was promptly charged with the role of strategic planning for Preferred Hotels and Resorts Worldwide. LMA conducted worldwide surveys and wrote the strategic program that is still in place today. In addition to Preferred, LMA increased its hospitality presence with hotel clients across North America, Asia and Europe.

Today, LMA works with hoteliers across the world, helping them solve marketing challenges and grow their businesses. Larry also serves as a mentor for LMA's young and diverse team members. His knowledge of hotel marketing has been demonstrated through the accumulation of many awards—over sixty-five at last count—at HSMAI (Hospitality Sales and Marketing Association Institute), more than any other Canadian agency. This includes the only win of the coveted Platinum level award outside of the United States. LMA was also awarded 'Worldwide e-Marketing Agency of the Year' by TravelClick.

Currently, Larry continues to write on various topics in the hospitality industry. He is one of the most frequently published writers in the field of hospitality marketing, with weekly contributions in five of the world's top industry publications. He is an associate of G7 Hospitality, Cayuga Hospitality Advisors and Laguna Strategic Advisors. This book is the follow-up to his first entitled, "Are You an Ostrich or a Llama?" published in 2012. Larry is actively involved in several voluntary charitable board roles. He has also lectured at the Cornell University School of Hotel Administration, Ryerson University, Hotel Association of Canada and for Hotel Valuation Services.

Larry lives in Toronto with Maureen, his wife of over 30 years, and a 120-pound Bouvier des Flandres named Caesar. His wife and two children, Sam and Adam, are all active in the field.

You can follow all of Larry's hospitality writing on his blog at: www.larrymogelonsky.com where you can subscribe via RSS feed, or via his weekly e-newsletter. Alternately, just email him at larry@larrymogelonsky.com.

CPSIA information can be obtained at www.ICGtesting.com
Printed in the USA
LVOW06*2308130913

352396LV00002B/2/P